An Evacuee's Story

A North Yorkshire Family in Wartime

John T Wright

Published by and Copyright © John T Wright, 2007
Harbury, Warwickshire
England

Acknowledgements:

The author extends his sincere thanks to all of those that have given so generously of their memories and time, which have proven invaluable in compiling this book. Whilst space prevents my listing all of these individuals, I wish to acknowledge the particular contributions made by Catherine Brown (Kitty) of Pickering; Monica Tingle of Hartburn, Stockton-on-Tees; Eric Ward of Orpington; Stan Ward of Brotton; Alan Clark of York; Maud Eskriett of Haxby; Brian Mann of Haxby; Angela Hewin of Harbury; Irene Reynolds (Aunt Renee) and my cousins Jimmy Nolan and Keith Reynolds. Especial thanks go to my long-suffering wife, Enid.

ISBN 978-0-9556768-0-2

Available from www.lulu.com and good book sellers.

I wish to dedicate this memoir to my wife and family, not forgetting my cousin Jimmy; who was more like a brother to me at that time.

CONTENTS

Mother holding George, Renee behind the author. Middlesbrough 1939.

Preface

" Our deeds still travel with us from afar
and what we have been makes us what we are."

George Eliot 1819-1880.

As I entered the winter of my life I found myself reflecting on what had happened to my family and myself in what seemed an age ago. The 'winged chariot' of time now hurries by too fast, but in my young days the seasons were long and seemed to last forever. In order to call back the old days I would need to penetrate the fog of the years and get inside the mind of the boy that I once was. I would have to reassemble and set down my dim, swirling thoughts and vague half memories in some sort of chronological order. It seemed to me that it would be a great pity if my family's wartime experiences should be lost and gone forever.

The passage of time tends to threaten the accuracy of half-remembered places, people, happenings and feelings. Family stories passed down through the years can be inaccurate with the true facts elusive and difficult to verify. Although there was now snow on the roof, I thought that I should make the effort while there was still a bit of fire in the grate. I would have to 'tease out' the tangles in the interwoven threads that made up the tapestry of my childhood. Life is never a closed book; words can be powerful weapons that can help bring to life the thoughts and feelings of days long gone. To be a youngster living through a global war is an incomparable experience; a time of great emotional upheaval and change, and I felt it deserved to be recorded and preserved.

I have been fortunate enough in recent years to make contact with various people from my past; some of whom I had not seen or heard of for more than sixty years. Their willingness to help and their recollections of those distant times have been invaluable and I found that a few words from them would often trigger long forgotten memories of people, places and events. Looking back can stir up mixed emotions - some painful and some pleasant. The pleasant and poignant memories linger in our minds and seem eager to come out, but the sad and painful ones are often pushed to the back so that they can no longer hurt us. They crouch in the deep recesses of our minds like long-taloned demons awaiting their chance to leap out and lacerate us again. Certain passages of this memoir proved very painful to recall, but pain is part of growing up; we all learn from it. By bringing the painful memories into the open can make them easier to cope with.

I have sought to recapture some of the events of yesteryear and my own and others responses to them. The question that arises is: 'How permanent are the experiences and associations of childhood?' How much bearing do they have on our later lives? To my mind past events have undoubtedly had a lasting and potent effect. What happens to you in the first ten years of your life can never be eradicated. We carry the past with us. It is in our blood and our bones. Things that happen in life are connected and our experiences as youngsters tend to have a 'knock-on' effect like the ripples on a pond that spread outwards when a stone is thrown into it. I truly believe that the war played a major part in the formation of my own, and most of my close family's, characters and personalities; they made us what we are and I think the same applies to all of those who lived through the war years. So as not to hurt or upset relatives and descendants, I have changed the names of certain people.

I have tried to place our family experiences against the fluctuating fortunes of the war - which makes victims of us all. We, like lots of other ordinary families, lived through events that were to change the world forever. Our daily lives were lived out within the turmoil of a world conflict; our small commonplace acts were carried out against a backdrop of world-shattering events and it is the little things that make the story whole. They were traumatic times that many young ones will scarcely be able to comprehend but I hope that this journey into the past, which I have thoroughly enjoyed, will be of some interest. In writing it, the past held me tight in its grip: so much so, that it made me feel young again and everything else seemed to fade into the background. I felt that I had to get it written down before life's fast moving currents pulled me under.

Some readers, of course, will have lived through those same traumatic times; some may view these long gone events as just 'water under the bridge' and of no great significance; while others may say we should not live in the past; that we must let it go. I believe that many of the younger generations would like to know how it was; I feel that they should know of those dark years when the world went mad in order to shape a better future. A history should not only honour the dead, it should help to make the present more understandable so that we do not make the same mistakes again. I hope that my memoir will serve as a tribute to those who died too soon. Like the Book of Common Prayer, I can now honestly say, "I have considered the days of old and the years that are past".

1. Beginnings

"Come on sweetheart, up you go!" said Mam as - with George balanced in the crook of her left arm - she helped me up the wooden steps. Never having been on a steam train before, we were thrilled and excited at the thought of the great adventure to come. As I reached the sill of the carriage I kept a tight grip on my wooden Tommy gun that had a spring and a ratchet that made a loud rat-a-tat noise when I turned the handle. This much-treasured toy, made by Dad five months earlier, had been a present for my fourth birthday and I really loved it. My brother, George, who was two, clung on to his ragged teddy bear as the authorities had stated that we were only allowed to take one toy each. Mam gripped the vertical handle beside the door and pulled herself up into the maroon and cream railway carriage.

She had another six toddlers to look after apart from us and, after getting us seated, Mam heaved the heavy brass-handled door shut. Pulling down the long leather strap she closed the window, fitting the hole in it over the brass peg to keep it shut. The long, plush, upholstered seats of the 3rd class carriage faced each other and had a slightly fusty smell. Mam hoisted our meagre items of luggage onto the netting of the brass-railed rack, checking at the same time that she looked respectable in the long rectangular mirrors screwed to the walls. Shortly afterwards, a railway guard appeared wearing a shiny, black-nebbed cap, a brass buttoned waistcoat and trousers of the same thick, heavy, black material. After slamming shut any doors that remained open, he blew loudly and shrilly on his whistle, waved a green flag above his head and clambered into the guard's van. The great beast seemed to snort as the mighty pistons squirted out clouds of steam and the glinting, well-oiled, steel rods began to force the huge, shiny-metal wheels into motion. Very slowly we began to move and the great black train groaned, chuffed and wheezed as it ponderously heaved its fully laden carriages out of the station and we were off, blissfully unaware that we were never to see our house and our pet tortoise again!

1

Gradually the train settled into a clanking 'diddly-dee; diddly-da' rhythm as it picked up speed and we gazed out at the ugly squalor of our sprawling industrial town. The old, smoke-blackened buildings were far from pretty and, on the outskirts of Middlesbrough, ramshackle allotments lined the tracks. We were travelling on the North Eastern Railway line - designed by the renowned railway engineer George Stephenson - which had been one of the first in this country - opening in 1836. Just over one hundred years old, this part of it was certainly showing its age.

A month earlier, on the third of September 1939 to be precise, war had been declared and, thankfully, none of our family had the slightest inkling of its dire consequences for us. On that sunny Sunday morning Mam had turned the knob on our Ecko wireless set in its brown Bakelite casing, and it took five minutes for the humming, glowing, glass valves to warm up sufficiently for it to operate. Bakelite was the only material that could be moulded at the time the set was made and it was called a 'wireless' due it to being powered by a heavy, electric accumulator - a kind of transparent, wet cell battery made of thick-glass in which a row of vertical lead plates submerged in sulphuric acid could be seen. It had to be recharged (for a small fee) every two weeks or so.

Two days earlier the Government had closed down all the regional broadcasting stations to ensure that everybody would have to listen to the new BBC Home Service. Dad was not with us as he had rejoined the army the previous year. Whilst on leave, being good with his hands, he had made a rectangular, wooden box with a secure handle, which Mam used to carry the accumulator to Rogers' electrical shop on nearby Newport Road whenever it needed charging. The wireless and the accumulator were rented from there and a heavy, fully charged accumulator was brought home in its place.

At 11.15 a.m. on that fine morning, the two of us had sat by the wireless with our Mam and her teenaged sister, Renee, who was at our house more often than she was at her own and she was a great help to Mam as she often looked after us and we loved being with her. We were dressed in our Sunday best clothes having just come back from the Sunday service at St. Cuthbert's Church where, in his sermon, the vicar had reminded the large congregation to listen to their wireless if they had one. In a solemn tone of voice, he had told them that, "BBC broadcasts are being made at fifteen-minute intervals and an announcement of national importance will be made soon. Let us pray that the news will not be too bad. Hope springs eternal in the human breast. God bless you all!"

Mother held us very close as she sat with her attention riveted on the set and we eventually heard the thin, reedy, tired-sounding voice of our seventy years old Prime Minister, Mr Neville Chamberlain. Mam had once said to Renee, "Some folk call him 'the undertaker' because of his grim and severe appearance and his old fashioned, black tailcoat and out-of-date wing collar don't help matters. Since last year's meeting with Hitler in Munich he has lost all credibility, but I'm sure he thought that he was doing his best for the country at the time." He gravely ended his announcement to the nation with the words, "Consequently, this country is at war with Germany!"

We were too young to understand what it was all about and as Mam switched off the wireless she looked bewildered and stunned. The fact that war had finally arrived must have been a frightening and terribly uncertain prospect and there was no means of stopping or questioning it. The colour drained from her face and there were tears brimming in her eyes as George and I sat there bewildered not daring to break the silence or move a muscle. Even at that tender age, by some mysterious process, I had sensed the extreme gravity of the situation and was aware that something really bad had happened. It seems that at that moment right across the nation there was a communal holding of breath. Who knew what the future held? Everyone had been aware of the impending danger, but they had prayed that it wouldn't come to this. For Mam there was a feeling of numb disbelief and it became a matter of adjusting the brain to accept what the heart already knew!

Our mother, Evelyn Wright, was thirty years old and Dad, who was five years older than her, was serving with a Royal Artillery Regiment on his second spell in the forces. Fourteen years earlier, as a young man, he had enlisted into the East Yorkshire Regiment and had seen spells of service in India, Egypt and China. Whilst in India he had taken a course at the British Military

Hospital in Lucknow where he qualified as a Nursing Orderly and in 1932, after seven years of service, he returned to Civvy Street.

Dad as a young man serving in the Army.

In the latter years of the worldwide trade recession, he was fortunate enough to obtain employment as a steelworker in a Middlesbrough foundry. He thought that, having seen much of the world and having 'done his bit', his Army career was over, but it was not to be. His aunt lived on Booth Street, just a few doors from the Bradford family home, and it had been on one of his visits to her that he met Granny Bradford's eldest daughter for the first time. She was a shy, quiet and warm-hearted young woman with an open child-like innocence and he loved the way she moved and the soft cadence of her voice. When she smiled her whole face lit up and Dad was entranced and couldn't keep his eyes off her. She was small and slim with a good figure and shapely legs and she always tried to look smart and fashionable. On their first date she had worn a cloche-hat; artificial pearls; a waistless and bustless, knee-length frock and low-heeled, buttoned, strap-over shoes. With regard to fashion, Middlesbrough was a provincial backwater, which always seemed to be about ten years behind the latest London styles.

They were rather shy and tentative with each other at first, both being afraid of rejection, but Dad persevered and set about romancing and winning her. Fortunately for George, and me, Mam had returned his affection and they started to meet on a regular basis and were soon a courting couple talking dreamily of their future together. They were soon completely at ease in each other's company. Often two into one *will* go and they became as one (or 'an item' as they would say these days). There was a joy and spontaneity in each other's presence and Dad was totally smitten as each set the other's heart a-flutter as they fell into that deep and intense love to which I owe my life. They became inseparable and were completely devoted to each other. Hating to be apart, they stored up the others touch and smell until they were together again.

Early in 1934 they had walked hand in hand up the approach road of the newly built Tees (Newport) Bridge to join the cheering crowds that lined the route beneath colourful streamers and buntings. Large shields, bearing the Royal crest, had been fixed on to every lamppost and the bandsmen of the 1st Battalion of the Durham Light Infantry kept the flag-waving onlookers entertained. When the royal party, accompanied by a retinue of civic dignitaries, arrived in a cavalcade of gleaming, black cars, they had watched as the Duke and Duchess of York completed the official opening. Mam thought that the Duchess looked stunning in her pale-coloured, fur coat with its thick, fox fur collar, her white strap-over shoes and her white gloves. On July 7th of that same year, Mam and Dad were married in St. Cuthbert's Church - the year that the driving licence, which cost five shillings (25p), became compulsory.

My brother George and I, were born during Dad's six 'civilian years', in my case, almost exactly nine months after the wedding. New blood from old blood! To Mam we were both little miracles - sublime gifts from heaven - and to her childbirth was a powerful and mystical event. I was brought into the world by the local midwife in the front bedroom of a small rented house at number four Stanley Street. Our redbrick house was the second of a long row of two-up, two-down, mid-Victorian, terraced houses that faced each other across a grimy side street that ran off Cannon Street where Jack Knaggs little general dealer's shop stood on the corner. Later that year the Silver Jubilee of King George V was celebrated and the coppers collected from the local residents helped to pay for the parties that took place in our gaily-decorated streets.

It was an area in which the teeming masses of unskilled labourers, dockworkers and the unemployed lived out their poverty-stricken existences. Two, towering, cylindrical gasholders, that stood within a high-walled compound, dwarfed the houses and we lived and played in their shadow. When fully inflated, the gas tanks loomed up through the smoke while, at other times, they shrank so low that the superstructures surrounding them were silhouetted against the sky. The locals took these monolithic landmarks for granted, scarcely noticing that they were there within an encircling, skeletal framework of vertical iron columns, catwalks and metal steps. As the gas was pumped in the gasholders soared up again blotting out the light and making the workmen on the top looked like midgets as they were silhouetted against the sky.

This part of Cannon Street and the streets running off it had an unsavoury reputation and its name was derived from the cannons of the 'The Yorkshire Volunteers' that had been kept there in the early 19th century. It was a very rough area where the police, swinging their wooden truncheons, patrolled in pairs, rather than singly as they did in the quieter and more respectable parts of the town. Our area was known as 'Foxheads' and it was probably named after a firm of iron makers called Fox, Head & Co. that had once had iron-rolling mills nearby. The doors of one row of houses had doorknockers in the shape of a fox's head and similar motifs could be seen at the ends of the stone lintels of all the doors and windows. It was a lively and turbulent neighbourhood to say the least and disputes were usually settled by means of the fists of the tough, hard drinking men and women. In that rough and ready cauldron of teeming humanity it was not uncommon for drunken women to fight in the open street; the 'scraps' usually taking place outside the pubs from which they had just been thrown out. As a crowd gathered they would punch, pull each other's hair and scratch until they were arrested and carted off in the police 'Black Maria'. They were then left to sleep off the effects of the drink in the police cells beneath the Town Hall.

In the year between my birth and George's, Mam had given birth to a stillborn baby boy. They say that into every life a little rain must fall and that summer it came down in buckets. Mam said tearfully, "The heavens must be weeping for him," as she carried his tiny body down the steep and narrow stairs in a battered, tear-stained shoebox. There is no loss more heart rending to a mother than that of her child and a few days later he was placed in the coffin of another person thus allowing him to be decently buried in consecrated ground. At that time, children who had not been baptised into the church were not allowed a Christian burial; it seems they were cruelly destined to spend eternity in limbo. Very close to tears, Mam said, "His little soul has gone back to heaven whence it came. He will be loved and cared for by the angels. He is now a new star in the Milky Way, and if you look very carefully on clear nights you might be able to pick him out."

At times she was very worried that I might soon join him as I was a weak and sickly child prone to picking up all of the illnesses common to the infants of our crowded and socially deprived neighbourhood. Every day I was given Virol spread on bread or toast in the belief that it would build me up. This bone-marrow preparation, said to be the ideal fat food for children and invalids, came in a small, white stoneware jar that cost 1/6d (7.5p).

The year after George came into the world Dad, being an army reservist, was re-enlisted into the Army but this time with the Royal Artillery. He had to do his basic training again at the Woolwich Arsenal in South London. In 1938 he was posted to the barracks at Hartlepool on the coast a few miles north of the river Tees, where he managed to find a small terraced house to rent and we moved into it. Mam's fifteen-year-old sister, Renee, came with us and was a great help as she enjoyed looking after George and me. When war was imminent Dad sent us back to Middlesbrough. Before long he was posted to an 'ack-ack' (anti-aircraft) site near Blyth in Northumberland on one of the great gun emplacements tucked away in the high sand dunes just to the south of the busy harbour where submarines were based.

In order to protect the harbour Blyth Battery, also known as Fort Coulson, had been built during the First World War. Next to it was a searchlight and an engine room, but it had been decommissioned when the Great War ended and parts of it had been used as beach amenities, with the engine room being used as a toilet block. It was reactivated in the early months of the war and Dad, being thirty-four years of age, was looked on as an 'old man' by the young conscripts. His earlier military service and experience of army life was - on the whole - much respected by them. A series of these anti-aircraft batteries formed part of the North Eastern coastal defences and they were located in large, camouflaged, concrete bunkers and emplacements with their guns pointing seaward. The huge, long-barrelled guns ran on steel rails, which enabled them to be rotated through an arc of 180 degrees.

Our 'new' home was in another small terraced house on Cannon Street, a little closer to the Newport Bridge. It stood in a low-lying area that tended to flood whenever we had heavy rain and behind it was a narrow, cobble-stoned, back lane from which sacks of coal were tipped through a wooden hatch in the wall at the end of our yard. There were no gardens in our part of town, the dreary street was our playground, and in it crowds of small, noisy, raggedly clad, undernourished children shouted and clamoured every day. Fishmongers would come round trundling two-wheeled handcarts shouting "Caller Herren!" (meaning, 'fresh herring') as gusts of wind blew gritty particles and filthy bits of paper around in the grey back alleys. The houses extended in row after grimy, monotonous row all looking much the same with their chimneys belching out smoke for the greater part of the year. It was autumn but there were no rosy apples ripening anywhere near our treeless streets. Every week the window ledges and the round-edged, front doorsteps that led directly on to the flagstones had to be scoured with a donkey stone. In our noisy, crowded, vibrant, close-knit community, women were much respected if they scrubbed and polished until they were ready to drop.

Like all the other unbeautiful, unpretentious houses we had no bathroom, even though the planners had called them 'dwellings for artisans'. Victorian, wall-mounted, swan-necked, gas brackets were fitted only in the two downstairs rooms and these provided hissing, dim, eye-straining light from flimsy, white, asbestos mantles that broke easily. They were about the size and shape of the head of an old-fashioned clay smoking pipe and burned smelly coal gas. To light our way to bed Mam used candles or, if she could afford the fuel, a paraffin lamp with a glass shade that was inclined to flare, smoke and need constant adjustment. In the tiny kitchen a gleaming, black-leaded, cast-iron, coal-fired range provided warmth and was used every day for baking and cooking. A large, black, iron kettle always seemed to be simmering and steaming on the hob.

At the end of the high-walled, cemented yard was a brick-built coalhouse and water closet that we called the 'lavvy'. Our cast-iron mangle (known as the 'wringer'), with its heavy wooden rollers stood here and Mam would turn the large handle on its side to squeeze out the excess water which drained into a fluted, zinc-coated tub. Whenever she washed Dad's shirts she had to cut the buttons off before putting them through it, and, after drying and ironing them, she had to sew them on again. Our long, galvanised, 'tin' bath hung on a nail in the outside wall.

The house, rented from a local solicitor, was situated some 400 yards to the east of the Newport Bridge - one of the many bridges built by the local firm of Dorman Long & Co. Ltd. It spanned the tidal river Tees, once noted for its fine salmon but now badly contaminated by the effluents that had poured into it from the many industries along its banks over the years. The river formed the boundary between North Yorkshire and County Durham and the bridge was unique in having a 270 feet (82.30m.) long stretch of roadway that could be lifted vertically to a height of 120 feet (36.5 m.) above the river by means of a system of huge steel and concrete weights and counterweights. This allowed high-masted ships to pass below it as huge pink-eyed rats with naked tales ran along its wooden pilings. The local people were proud of this technical marvel that was the first of its type in this country. It was the largest and heaviest bascule bridge in the world and it was raised and lowered on average eight hundred times a month or - putting it another way - twenty seven times a day. Hundreds of workers crossed it to reach the growing number of industrial sites on the northern bank, thus reducing the long journey round to the next, far older, roadbridge upstream at Stockton-on-Tees.

Previously a small ferryboat had plied the river at this point and the only alternative had been to use our other well-known landmark - the Transporter Bridge - that stood about a mile down river and had been opened in 1910. It was another of Dorman Long's engineering triumphs. The steel superstructure, with a winding house perched on top of it, towered high above the widening river and its girders were held together by millions of rivets. An iron stairway with over two hundred steps climbed to a metal walkway across the top and you had to have a good head for heights to cross the river at that dizzying height. Far below a small gated gondola, that carried just eight vehicles across at a time, hung on steel cables. This traversed the river suspended from a trolley system that ran on rails, but, from the walkway the cars looked like tiny toys.

Middlesbrough with its population of some one hundred and forty thousand inhabitants was bordered to the south by the Cleveland Hills, on which there was a square, Napoleonic, stone tower. It stood on the highest point at Eston Nab at the seaward end of the long, elevated range known as the Eston Hills and its position ensured that when the beacon was lit it could be seen for many miles across the Tees Valley and up and down the coast. Many people 'escaped' from the dirt, smoke and noise of their day-to-day lives by going out to these areas on a weekend - if they had the means to do so. Some joined local rambling or cyclist's touring clubs to visit the lovely countryside, while others caught the train out of town and hiked for miles in the fresh air.

The people of Teesside often had to endure extremely dense fogs and when the rising smoke met a cold, damp, air stream thick 'smogs' formed. These thick, yellow smogs sometimes descended and persisted for days. They were real 'pea-soupers' that turned day into night and at times it was impossible to see to the other side of the road. Chemical emissions, such as ammonia, mixing with the damp air of the river valley were thought to be a contributory factor. A large metal foghorn, mounted on the superstructure of the new bridge and operated by means of compressed air, was sounded to warn approaching high-masted ships of its looming, unseen presence. On raw, damp, bone-chilling nights I vaguely recollect lying awake in bed listening to the eerie, mournful, fog-muffled, deep-toned, diaphonic blaring that occurred at monotonously, regular intervals. It was so loud that it seemed to be right outside my bedroom window.

The heavily polluted river, between the two bridges, was over three hundred feet wide (97m.) in places and it formed a long, northward sweeping bend that enclosed a roughly triangular piece of land known as 'The Ironmaster's District'. A network of railway lines and marshalling yards separated it from the grid-like pattern of our streets. Further downriver, beyond the Transporter Bridge, lay Smith's dockyard with its crowded berths and its tall crane jibs that leaned at all kinds of crazy angles. The Ironmaster's District was packed with grimy iron and steel works; blast furnaces and coke ovens that reached up into the smoke-filled sky. Towering, bottle-shaped, cooling towers belched out clouds of white steam and smoky noxious gases poured from tall smokestacks adding yet more filth to the already vile, foul-smelling air. At night, as the furnaces were charged, fierce flames and an eery hellfire glow emanated, and the lurid glare lit up the underside of the clouds, turning the whole sky a dirty orange. The ugliness of the scarred landscape was offensive to the eye but I assumed that this was the colour of the night sky everywhere.

The smoke-laden air left a permanent layer of smut over everything, settling on the washing that hung on the thin, rope clothesline that was strung across our tiny backyard. In the background there was the constant rattling and clanking of rail locomotives and heavy freight wagons being shunted; works hooters blared and screamed at shift-changing times and every day, prior to the sounding of the hooters, the streets were filled by an army of grey, tramping, flat-capped men. These were the ones lucky enough to have a job to go to and their segged and steel toe-capped working boots clattered on the stone setts echoing back from the grimy brick walls. Hissing steam poured from pipes and boilers; steam hammers clanged; drills whirred and the whole combined to produce a deafening and hellish cacophony. The hustle and bustle and the frantic activity never ceased and after a while people became inured to it. The endless din became part of the fabric of our lives.

On the northern bank of the river stood the huge British Oxygen Company and close by lay the busy Furness & Company shipbuilding yard, with its massive dry docks and slipways. Lord Furness had created the shipyard in 1918 from an area of reclaimed marshland. The activity had recently increased as it had received government orders for the construction of large numbers of naval vessels and the increased employment was in marked contrast to the prolonged and catastrophic slump of the inter-war years. At that time orders had all but dried up and unemployment on Teesside had been more than double the national average with one in three men out of work. Now things were picking up and on the south bank further down river, Smith's Dock also found itself in the same boat (if you'll pardon the pun). Both shipyards were soon to be involved in constructing frigates, landing barges and the like.

The biggest economic event to take place on Teesside in the pre-war years had been the amalgamation of a number of large works that now formed the Imperial Chemical Industries (ICI) Limited. This vast and sprawling complex lay to the south of Billingham just across the river from us on the Durham side and was the largest chemical complex in the country. Four of the largest companies prior to their amalgamation had been the German firm, Brunner Mond; Nobel Industries; United Alkali and the British Dyestuffs Works and the new chemical giant had played a major part in providing a wide and diverse range of products for the British Empire. With its many oil refineries, distillation towers and flaming flare stacks, it was now working flat out and the light oils; lubricants; glycol; kerosene and high-octane aviation fuels were to be of vital importance to the Allied Air Forces in Western Europe.

These activities were to make it a prime target for the German bombers, as its products were essential to the war effort. Nitrogen was needed to manufacture explosives; fertilisers were vital to a much-needed increase in wartime food production and 'Perspex' (formerly called Resin X), the first transparent plastic in the world, was produced here. The bomber and fighter pilots would now have the protection of Perspex cockpit canopies and 'blisters' whereas in the past they had endured the bitter cold with open cockpits. Nothing was wasted. Hundreds of thousands of tons of high-octane aviation fuel were being manufactured from coal and creosote and the coke oven gas was used within the works and in the domestic grid.

The effluents, which had been pouring into the local waterways for years, had turned the mudflats along the margins of the Billingham Beck a sickly, bluish-grey in colour. The polluted waters of the tidal beck then emptied into the river Tees turning it a dirty, greyish brown in colour. Under the riverbed, a little way downstream lay vast caverns and tunnels from which huge amounts of salt had been excavated, processed, refined, packaged and sold as 'Cerebos Salt'. The firm later added 'Bisto' gravy powder to its list of products which became household names with 'Bisto' still going strong after a hundred years. The murky waters of the river formed swirling eddies that we called 'whirlpools' before it swept the few short miles eastwards past Seal Sands to flow out into the vastness of the grey North Sea.

In recent weeks Mam had seen khaki-clad squads of soldiers working on the nearby area of waste ground, which the council called the Newport Recreation Ground. We called it 'The Common'. The soldiers belonged to the Royal Scots Fusiliers and the King's Own Scottish Borderers (known as Kosbie's) and they were in the process of raising huge, hydrogen-filled, barrage balloons. The Kosbie's seemed to be small men who wore Glengarry bonnets with a pompon on top and they were nicknamed 'the bantams' by the local people. The balloons, which were about sixty feet (19m.) long, looked to me like great, fat, floating pigs with huge ears. The bloated, greyish-white balloons were often called 'Blimps' after the well-known First World War windbag who went by the name of Colonel Blimp. They were attached to a winch by means of a long, gleaming, steel hawser and each was strategically placed with its nose facing into the wind. They were raised to a height of about 5,000 feet (1,520m.), and the thick, mooring cables were strong enough to bring down low-flying aircraft. When it was windy we could hear them twanging and humming and in high winds they had to be storm-bedded, which involved anchoring them down to heavy, concrete blocks.

On one never-to-be-forgotten stormy night, one was struck by lightning brightly lighting up the area. Just prior to the blaze, eerie bluish-white lightning had been seen arcing from one steel-wire cable to the next. There were also odd-looking contraptions called Thompson-Haslar units that looked like a large metal bin with a funnel that emitted black, oily smoke and they were mounted on the back of a special, wheeled trailer pulled into position by army vehicles. The smoke units were being tested and would later be used, taking into account the prevailing wind direction, to screen the industrial sites. Incidentally, Gran's niece, 19 year old Katie McNeil, who was living with her mother (Gran's younger sister, Maud) on Cannon Street, got to know one of the Scottish soldiers and two years later they were married in the local church.

The Common covered a large part of the open area at the Newport Bridge end of Cannon Street and a long wooden fence, constructed from upright railway sleepers, hid the railway lines. Here, workmen had dug a network of nine feet (2.75m.) deep, interconnecting, slit trenches that were lined with wood, and the roof was supported by timber props. Along the sides where low wooden benches, or 'forms'. Rows of wooden, double-storey, bunk beds had been installed and the local people entered the new, underground, air-raid shelter by means of a concrete ramp, which led down to thick, metal, blast-proof doors. The tunnels were lit by rows of electric bulbs powered by a generator and the timber-framed roofs were covered with corrugated metal sheeting, which had a deep layer of soil on top. In an emergency an exit could be made by means of wooden ladders that were fixed to the sides of steel-lidded, brick lined shafts placed along the tunnels at intervals.

These and the brick street shelters were to be used by hundreds of local people.

On another part of The Common there was a wide, twenty feet (6m) high, cement-coated wall buttressed at both ends that, in the not too distant past, had been part of a handball court. It was called Nugent Court, after Councillor Nugent who had taken the welfare of the local people to heart and had suggested building it to occupy the unemployed at the time of The Great Depression. The game of 'Fives' involved hitting a ball with the flat of the gloved hand, hence the name, and it had once been quite popular. The aim was to score points by hitting the ball into marked areas. On the far side of the common there were rundown allotments with the fences and sheds patched up with roof felt, bits of rotting wood and rusty corrugated metal sheeting. Close by stood a pigeon park, now in a state of disrepair, with the white paint of its wooden lofts flaking and peeling – all symptoms of the recent hard times.

Groups of poorly clad, grim-faced men in flat, greasy, cloth caps regularly gathered on a corner of The Common, most wearing off-white, 'art silk', mufflers tied in a tight knot above collarless shirts. Many of them had the gaunt grey-faced look of the long-term unemployed defeated by too many years of hardship and poverty. Depressed and broken in spirit they felt that they were of no use to their families or anyone else and they could be seen slouching around at the street corners or on that particular area of the common day after day. Several had hacking coughs, spitting great gobs of phlegm on to the ground or sucking on an empty tobacco pipe and staring blankly at nothing. A few, fortunate enough to have a few halfpennies (0.1p) in their pockets, played pitch and toss in the constant hope of winning a few more coppers to spend on beer, fags or baccy. A couple of scruffily clad lads stood cavy for them (acted as lookouts) giving warning should the other type of 'copper' appear.

Our house backed on to The Common and one day the 'rozzers' (a local term for policemen) turned up in force. The hapless illegal gamblers scattered and one tried to make his escape by climbing over the wall into our backyard where Mam was hanging out the washing. She was heavily pregnant and the man's sudden appearance startled her making her cry out, at which Dad

15

dashed out through the kitchen door. He was really angry and grabbed hold of the man saying, "Bugger off sharpish mate or ah'll punch yer bloody lights out."

As a young man, Dad had brought home numerous presents from his postings in the Far East, one of them being a large tortoise that we kept as a pet. A beautiful ivory model of the Taj Mahal at Agra, that he had brought back from India, stood on the sideboard and could be lit from the inside. One of my earliest memories is of bleeding profusely after pushing George down Booth Street on his three-wheeler trike. We had been to visit Gran, who now lived round the corner on King George Street, when I slipped, and as I landed on my left knee a sharp piece of gravel cut deeply into it. I still have a small pyramid-shaped scar to show for it. In another incident I was wearing semi-transparent, rubberised pants that were elasticated and fitted tightly round my chubby thighs and, desperately needing to go to the lavatory I could hold on no longer. I passed water, which soon saturated the Terry towelling of my inner pants and, when it could absorb no more, the 'pee' could be seen slowly filling up the 'see-through' pants. I remember the lovely warm feeling of it before it seeped out and turned cold as it trickled down my legs.

My maternal grandmother, Florence Emma Bradford, a small, fifty-year old widow, lived a little closer to the bridge than us. Her 15 years old daughter, Irene (always known as Renee) was a small, slim, attractive, auburn-haired girl. At the age of eleven she had been a bridesmaid at their wedding and many years later she told me that just prior to the wedding she couldn't be found. It seems that - being a gamine young creature - she had been playing in the dirty back lane in her woollen, hand-knit, one-piece, swimming costume and was too preoccupied to respond to her name being called. Gran eventually got hold of her, stood her in the sink and washed her down and, once into her white satin bridesmaid's dress she looked sweet and innocent. A great bond of unspoken affection had developed between my parents and Mam's winsome young sister. Dad, used to call her his 'Little Princess', and he spoiled her rotten.

Gran's eldest son, John, was twenty years old and was serving his apprenticeship as a plater at the Britannia Steelworks, a large, steel-plate, rolling plant in the Ironmasters District. In February of the previous year he had joined the Territorial Army attending meetings in the Drill Hall every week and going on weekend training camps. The part-time soldiers were known colloquially as the Terriers or, as some said, 'Saturday Night Soldiers'. Uncle John had joined chiefly for the excitement, the sense of adventure and the glamour of the uniform, which seemed to attract the girls. The extra money was also very welcome. In late autumn he received a letter from the local office of the Ministry of Labour and National Service on Grange Road stating that he was now liable for conscription into the regular Army. He was to report to the Wesley Hall in Middlesbrough town centre where a medical examination would be carried out. He turned up at the huge and imposing, red and white brick, Victorian chapel known locally as Big Wesley as directed and being small but strong and healthy he passed A1.

Soon afterwards his call-up papers - with a four-shilling (20p.) postal order to cover his travelling costs - were delivered by a boy in a black uniform with red piping, a belted pouch and a pillbox hat who was often seen in the area on his red, Post Office bike. In the meantime, Gran fed him well, as like most women of the time, she considered it her duty to wait on the men hand and foot. Uncle John was just one of the thousands being 'mobilised' and on the seventh of February he made his farewells. Travelling with several other young men to the Army Barracks at Richmond, North Yorkshire, he swore the oath of allegiance; 'took the King's shilling'; was read the Riot Act and became number 4390218 with the rank of Private. After being vaccinated he was issued with a uniform and kit, which included two enamelled tin plates; an enamel mug; a knife, fork and spoon - soldiers for the use of - and was put into the Fifth Infantry Battalion of the Green Howards.

The recruits were broken down by hard work and strict discipline before being built up again into an efficient fighting unit. They learned to work as a team, which was to stand them in good stead when they eventually went into battle, and as an unmarried private he was paid just fourteen shillings (70 p) a week plus bed and board. Each week during the long basic training he managed to send part of his meagre pay to his mother. A few weeks later following the outbreak of the war he was sent on embarkation leave. He sailed from Southampton as part of a naval convoy - with a fighter escort overhead - bound for the French port of Cherbourg. It was too dangerous to take the shorter, more direct route to Calais through the Straits of Dover, as the ship would have been within the range of German bombers. On disembarkation, in bitterly cold weather, army lorries took them to Fresnay, near Le Mans, and then up to the Rouen area that had been selected for the deployment of the British Expeditionary Force. With its forward headquarters at Arras the BEF was fulfilling its promise to come to the aid of France in the event of war with Germany. The 5th Battalion of the Green Howards then moved up to the Belgian border that had seen so much bloodshed in World War I.

The regiment had been raised in 1688 when it was known as the 19th Regiment of Foot. Fifty years later the Hon. Charles Howard, the youngest son of Charles, the third Earl of Carlisle, the builder of the magnificent Castle Howard near Ripon, became a Colonel. His regiment wore green facings on their red coats they became known as The Green Howards, whereas most of the foot regiments took the names of the counties from which the men were recruited. In Yorkshire there were the 'East Yorkshires' and the 'West Yorkshires' but the Green Howards were allowed to keep their name because of their association with the Howard family. Sadly, after some three hundred years, they have now become part of the Yorkshire Regiment.

Gran's other sons, Archie and Harry, were aged thirteen and eleven years old respectively. Her other twenty-six-year old daughter, Hilda, and her son, Jimmy, were living with Gran's younger sister, Ruby, in Croft Street (just three streets away) having left her Irish, Roman Catholic husband, John Nolan. His faith frowned on mixed marriages at that time and throughout her turbulent and unhappy marriage there had been prolonged and bitter conflict with many verbal slanging matches and ugly name-calling. Gran, who was a forthright God-fearing woman, declared, "I've got no time for the Nolans with their hypocrisy, boozing and excessive religious humility and John's mother is a hard-bitten, intolerant, religious bigot. I'll never forgive her for bawling after them in the street 'I hope you die in your bed and rot in hell you Protestant bitch!' just after their marriage in the Register Office. She called

Jimmy a bastard because to her mind the marriage was not legal saying, 'If you are not married by a priest you are not married at all'."

There was a fair amount of resentment of the Irish at that time as there had been more than a hundred IRA bombings on the British mainland. Large numbers of Irishmen had come over here to take jobs left vacant by the men who had been called up and many of them were living in the Cannon Street area where their priests were all-powerful and highly respected. The notorious 'Irish charm' and 'gift of the gab' won the hearts of many of the English girls, which led to more resentment. Aunt Hilda had fallen for John Nolan's smooth talk and they had married in 1934 - the same year as Mam and Dad - and had rented a house on Tomlinson Street just round the corner from Gran. When in drink, John Nolan was inclined to violence and they separated in 1936 after he had been sent to prison for theft, leaving Hilda on her own to bring up their young son.

Gran was a granddaughter of John Knights, a Suffolk-born sea captain, whose ancestors had been farm labourers for centuries. In the winter months he worked as a fishermen and the boats often called in at the young, up-and-coming port of Middlesbrough. It was on one of these calls that young John met his wife-to-be. In the 1860s he had settled in the developing boomtown which had grown dramatically from the tiny hamlet of 1830 to become a large iron and steel-producing centre. The Prime Minister, William Gladstone, called it 'an infant Hercules' and Professor Asa Briggs, in his essay on 'Victorian Towns', stated that "Six solid, broad-brimmed, broad-fronted, broad-bottomed Quakers cleared a swamp and made a city". The town's motto 'Erimus' meant 'We Shall Be'.

John Knights then worked on the colliers that sailed up and down the East Coast and, reputedly became quite wealthy as he moved up through the ranks to command various ships. It was said that in later life he lived in some style in large and impressive houses in the more affluent parts of the town with one story alleging that he had a sock full of gold sovereigns hidden up his chimney. Back in East Suffolk, one of his sisters had married a local ship owner, but he was involved in the smuggling of contraband goods and after his arrest by the Customs men, spent several years in Ipswich gaol.

Great Grandfather, Henry Knights (about 1920).

Their eldest son, Henry Knights was Gran's father, and he too was a merchant seaman. In 1886, at the age of just nineteen years, he married a twenty-year old local girl called Caroline Martha Wanless who we always knew as 'Granny Knights'. She was a live-wire and a real character who was not averse to the odd tipple or a regular 'flutter on the gee-gees'. By the time Gran was born, the family had fallen on hard times and were living in dark, damp, and squalid conditions in a hastily and cheaply erected terrace of tiny, back-to-back houses called Linthorpe Mews just south of the railway lines. The original town had been confined to a low-lying, riverside site to the north of the railway that often flooded and was later always referred to as being 'over-the-border'.

The population at the time of the 1841 census was 5,500, which almost doubled over the next twelve years and by the turn of the century had reached 80,000. The spill over into the area south of the railway had been left to too many small firms that had thrown up the maximum number of houses that could be squeezed onto any given plot. This led to overcrowding and unsanitary conditions and the area became a breeding ground for all kind of diseases. The emptying of chamber pots into the gutters did not help matters and, by the time Gran came into the world, the town had suffered three serious cholera epidemics and the infant mortality rate was extremely high.

Gran, the oldest of eleven children who were all small in stature, was born in one of these run-down, cramped and draughty houses that had only two rooms - one down and one up. Each measured 15 feet 5inches (4.7m) by 11 feet (3.4m), the roof let in the rain and the peeling wallpaper was black with mould. The only natural light to enter the ground floor room came from a small window in the tiny pantry and the back door led into a tiny yard with an ashpit and privy. A narrow alley with its walls and pathways coated in a vile green slime - barely wide enough to allow a wheelbarrow through - ran between each pair of houses.

The outside privy consisted of a wooden board with a hole in it, beneath which was a layer of ashes. Gran, as a young girl, had suffered much embarrassment and indignity when the night soilmen came at the most inopportune moments. Digging out the excreta and ashes from under her bare buttocks with long-handled shovels, they took the fully loaded wheelbarrow through the alleyway into the narrow street where it was trundled up a ramp and emptied into a wooden cart pulled by an old nag. Gran was to say later, "I don't know how the poor men tolerated the foul, obnoxious stench that was always behind them."

In 1906, when she was just sixteen years of age, she eloped to get married leaving home wearing work clothes on top of her best clothes so as not to arouse suspicion. She knew - all too well - that her mother was 'dead set' against the marriage to her 26 years old husband-to-be who was weather beaten and had skin like brown leather as a result of working on the river Tyne in all weathers. Granny Knights called him a foreigner, as she was barely able to comprehend his broad Geordie accent. He had been blinded in one eye by having sand kicked in his face as a young boy. The couple had married at Trinity Church, North Ormesby on the eastern edge of the town. Granddad always called her 'Lol' and they had a hard but happy life for more than thirty years before death intervened.

My maternal Granddad, Archie Bradford, hailed from South Shields, County Durham, and was a chronic asthmatic but he nevertheless managed to find fairly regular employment. He worked mostly as a dock labourer or as a lighterman on the two rivers with his job involving the unloading of ocean-going ships on to the lighters. The ships being of too deep a draught had, of necessity, to be anchored in the deep channel in midstream. A lighter was a kind of wide barge with a shallow draught on which the goods were taken to the wharves to be lifted ashore by cranes and derricks. He worked long hours over many sweltering summers and chilled-to-the-marrow winters, until two years before the war, he died after one too many asthma attacks. Granddad would 'fear no more the heat of the sun nor the furious winter's rages'. He lived just long enough to see his two eldest daughters wed and the first three of his grandchildren come into the world, these being - Jimmy, me and George. Three years prior to his untimely death he had promised Renee that he would take her to see the opening of the 'Newport' Bridge, but she developed several, huge, septic abscesses on her neck and was bitterly disappointed. Boils were common amongst the undernourished children of the area at that time.

Gran, a graduate of the school of hard knocks like many another at that time, had had a very hard life. It had been a long grim struggle for survival throughout the late 1920s and 30s; the years of the terrible world trade depression and, as a result, she had 'lost' five of her eleven children. It appears that great poverty invariably leads to a higher fertility rate as having lots of children improved the odds of them reaching maturity. Three sons and a daughter died in their infancy, one of them being her firstborn son,

Archibald, named after his father and a little later, a much loved, gentle and delicate daughter - named Florence after her mother - died at the age of only eleven years. She became ill after a rusty nail sticking up through the paper-thin sole of her boot, punctured her foot. The tiny black spot under her big toe became infected leading to the septicaemia that killed her.

For many years Gran had lived on the edge of an abyss of uncertainty; just one of a warren of people who had to endure real hardship in squalid and wretched conditions. At times the family's meagre reserves were all but exhausted. Existence was sharp edged and it was very easy to cut yourself on it. She never knew from one day to the next if Granddad would get a day's work in or where the next meal was coming from. When a domestic article broke it was never thrown away, as there wasn't the money to replace it: it had to be mended. She had to make a couple of shillings stretch a long way often living from hand to mouth. Fortunately for her, her eldest daughters were in work as domestic servants enduring interminably long hours for miserably low wages. Like many sisters they didn't always see eye to eye and Gran, losing patience with them, would say, "Can't you two go five minutes without arguing?" Mam worked as far away as Leeds for a time, but they managed to send a little money home to keep the family's head above water. After marrying they were obliged to support their own families, but, luckily, Uncle John had started work as a trainee crane driver in the Teesside Bridge works on leaving school in 1933 and Renee became a domestic servant on leaving school four years later.

During the long hard years of 'The Depression', Granddad used to walk down to the nearby Newport wharf early every morning to see if the foreman was taking on any men and, if he was lucky enough to get a day's work, Renee would take him his 'bait' (food) tin and a can of cold tea at the midday break. The work was hard and could be dangerous or even fatal. Gran's elder brother, John, had died of suffocation after falling into a container of red ore powder. Gran was tough, resilient and stubborn and, although entitled to poor relief, she was far too proud to accept any form of charity. Although close to destitution at times, she would never beg, suffering her many and repeated hardships in silence. She would never let others see her emotional pain and gradually this rigid, grin-and-bear-it stoicism became the norm. She just got on with it because if you didn't you went under.

Gran had an inner strength that seemed to be a strange mixture of fatalism, resignation and faith and she somehow managed to maintain her dignity and the small decencies of life, accepting whatever fate threw at her. Although close to despair at times, she was never completely vanquished, saying, "There is always someone that little bit worse off than you." Sadly, the long years of grinding poverty, unremitting toil and repeated knock-backs gradually hardened her soul and the long years of struggle turned her into a sad and bitter woman in her twilight years.

Her neighbours - although rough and ready - were a plucky, strong-willed, independent lot, who were never servile. Desperation has a way of binding the poor together and the people of that close knit community helped each other out in order to make ends meet. There was a powerful sense of belonging and they knew they could call on 'Florrie' for help in times of crisis. The strong helped the weak and the elderly but most of them were worn out by the age of thirty-five and were old at forty-five. They believed and hoped that better times were just round the corner and things could only get better, unaware that there would be many more years of hardship, self-sacrifice and personal loss before their living conditions would improve.

The Bradford family's fortunes had fallen such a long way. They had been relatively affluent before the General Strike of 1926 and the lockouts by the bosses that followed it. It had been a disastrous time for all when the dockyards and the local steelworks had fallen suddenly and strangely silent. Gran said, "The toffs don't give a damn about the conditions that the working class have to endure." However, the local landlords did their best to keep relatives in houses just a few doors from each other. A clannish, law abiding, hard working lot, they stuck together through thick and thin and, apart from the family, their only balm was God and the church. Religion was their prop and hope of eternal salvation, offering material as well as spiritual help. It offered the promise of a final, blessed release from their earthly hardships and misfortunes. Marx had called it 'the opium of the people'.

The many family burials, baptisms and weddings over the past thirty years or so had taken place at the local parish church of St. Cuthbert that stood close to the pair of tall, stone obelisks that flanked the approach road to the Tees (Newport) bridge. The church had first opened its doors in March 1901 and Mam was a voluntary Sunday school teacher there. When at home, Dad played the organ and often helped with the putting on of plays as well as organising the scout gang shows in the wooden hall that stood in the earthen yard of the church.

The church, with two, sombre, square, twin towers at its westernmost end, was never a beautiful edifice. It stood dark and severe-looking, but solid and strong - an enduring refuge in times of adversity and an appropriate symbol of the gritty fighting spirit of the poor, long-suffering folk of our crowded neighbourhood. There were, inevitably, a few slackers; people who did not try to help themselves, unless it was to something going for nothing or that did not belong to them. The church still stands tall and proud, but it has been forced to change with the times. It now has an upper floor lined with slot machines and 'one-armed bandits' and the ground floor is used as a sports and leisure centre. If the gamblers were to raise their eyes they would see, above their sacrilegious heads, the beautifully carved and painted roof bosses. I suppose it is better than demolishing it - but only just!

On my father's side, Great-Great Granddad was a true cockney who had moved north in search of work. His son was born in Middlesbrough in 1846 and became an iron shipwright. Granddad, Thomas Allen Wright, was also born in Middlesbrough some thirty years later and was brought up 'over the border' in an area known as the 'Far Marsh'. He became a master shoemaker and married Emma Peart at the Parish Church of St.Hilda on January the first, 1902. Two years later he died of a heart attack at the age of only twenty-seven - just four days before my Dad, his second son, came into the world. His death left my paternal grandmother as a twenty-four years old, pregnant widow with a young child. She was living in a street nearby at the time of my birth but I don't know if she ever laid eyes on me, as it seems she was ostracised by our family following her second marriage.

2. Evacuation

By April 1939, the threat of war had grown and the Government announced a scheme - called Operation Pied Piper - to evacuate some two and a half million children. Some adults, not directly required for the war effort, were also to be sent from the danger areas and would include many mothers, the elderly and the infirm. The lion's share of the cost was to be borne by the Government, but part of it was to come from the parents - if they could afford it. The Women's Voluntary Service for Civil Defence, known by the acronym WVS, had been formed a year earlier. Its first Chairwoman, Lady Reading, had been a VAD nurse in the last war and she was charged with organising a vast network of women from widely differing backgrounds. They were asked to drive home to the people what air raids might mean and what to do when they started. Along with the Red Cross and others, they had to see that the scheme ran smoothly

The word 'evacuate' means 'to empty', and it became an exercise in emptying the towns and cities likely to be targeted; the emphasis at the sending end being to get the evacuees out as quickly as possible. The fact that they were dealing with young and vulnerable human beings was often overlooked and the upheaval sometimes led to great distress and emotional pain. Powerful blood ties made it difficult to break up the clannish family units as life had little meaning to them except in terms of flesh-and-blood relationships. There was much fear of the unknown as mothers realised that they would be delivering their loved ones into the hands of 'borrowed parents'. They would be living with complete strangers that they knew nothing about. Many were extremely reluctant to let their children go, especially since so many sons, husbands and brothers had left to join the forces.

Governmental pressure was brought to bear on the wavering mothers and they were made to feel selfish and uncaring. It was implied that only bad parents would allow their children to stay at home to face the dangers of enemy bombing. In many families the father was unemployed but they were proud men who hated having to go cap-in-hand to the National Assistance Board. It meant that they would have to eke out a meagre living from the pittance provided by the means-tested scheme known as the dole. They received dole money for each child and if the children were sent away, many poor families would lose it and find it very difficult to survive at all.

There was now much more government intervention in people's lives and during the year leaflets had been issued setting out the details of the mass evacuation plan. Mothers of pre-school children could accompany their children to the relative safety of the countryside if they so wished but, all were required by law to register first. What thousands of mothers had secretly dreaded had come to pass! Schools were to be evacuated en masse, including many of the teachers, and the redbrick, Victorian School on Greta Street, Middlesbrough was just one of the many involved.

Poisonous gas, which had been used by the Germans in World War One, was the greatest fear and the Government made plans to provide the whole population with free gas respirators. It was a mammoth task. Millions were boxed up prior to distribution and in Middlesbrough they were to be given out from the blue-painted, wooden, police-boxes dotted around the town. It was the responsibility of the Civil Defence Wardens to collect the gas masks from the police boxes and deliver the cartons to every individual living in their designated area and they carried out an important population census at the same time. The schools handed out gas masks to the children and practices at using them were regularly carried out. The under fives were to get a special, bright, red and blue model - known as a 'Mickey Mouse' mask - that was designed with the aim of making the toddlers more willing to wear it, but these were not issued until later in the year.

In readiness, rehearsals were carried out involving my uncles, Archie and Harry, and my young cousin Jimmy. They lined up in pairs and practised marching, as part of a long crocodile formation carrying their gas masks in small, strong, buff-coloured, cardboard boxes that were suspended on a long loop of string. Plans to raise the school leaving age had recently been suspended and Archie was just about to start his final term in school when Gran decided that he should go and take care of the boys.

Teachers were called back early from their already shortened summer holiday on 26th of August in one of the hottest and sunniest summers for years. The very next day there were violent thunderstorms. Were they an ill omen? Government leaflets advised parents on what the children should take, i.e.: - a change of underclothing; night clothes (in the form of a man's shirt in Archie, Harry and Jimmy's case); shoes or boots, plimsolls (known, to the boys as 'sand-shoes'); two pairs of socks or stockings; shirts or blouses; a cardigan or pullover and a cap or hat. They should also have a toothbrush; a comb; a towel; soap, a face cloth; a pocket-handkerchief and a warm coat or mackintosh. Many mothers felt embarrassed at being too poor to provide a number of these articles. Gran and Renee cut up old shirts and muslin flour bags - that had been bleached and boiled to soften them - for the boys to use as 'hankies'. Most boys never wore caps or hats and many didn't wear underpants either. The soles of their boots had toe and heel plates and were covered in metal studs to prevent them wearing out too quickly.

On 31st of August further notices were sent to every household stating that the evacuation was imminent and each school was given a number. The names of the children, with their school number, had to be written clearly in block capitals on a cardboard label or on a piece of thick, brown paper. This was tied on to the lapel of their coats and they were repeatedly told their school number in case they got lost in the crowds. Initially it seemed to be great fun and many of them thought that they were going on holiday to the country or the seaside. Most of the parents believed that the war would soon be over.

Gran became more upset as the day of the evacuation drew near and, the night before they were to leave, the boys had a good bath and a scrub in the tin bath in front of the fire. After they had gone to bed, Gran sat staring with unseeing eyes at the changing shapes in the coal fire trying to put tomorrow out of her mind, but to no avail. She had already 'lost' her husband to chronic asthma and John was in the Army; now her other two boys and her grandson were going away and she had no idea of where or to whom they would go. She asked herself, 'will they go to nice people who will understand their mischievous ways? Will they be

28

able to tolerate their likes and dislikes? Mind you, they're not fussy eaters and Archie will keep them in order. He's a level headed lad.'

Evelyn was also planning to go away with her two youngsters and at the thought tears welled up in Gran's eyes, but she managed to pull herself together. She had to stay strong for the children's sake. At least Hilda and Renee would be staying so she would not be entirely alone and at last, after banking up the fire, she took herself up to her single bed in the tiny box room above the larder. It took her a long time to get to sleep - there was just too much to think about - and she slept fitfully and woke often.

A mass exodus of over six thousand evacuees from Middlesbrough began on the 8th September 1939. It was now mid September and Archie was told to report to Newport Road Primary School with the two boys. He climbed from his warm, familiar bed for the last time and it would be nearly eighteen months before he saw it again. Hilda brought Jimmy over to Gran's house and lots of children left for school that morning with little idea of what all the fuss was about. The only thing that they were sure of was that they were being sent away to places in North Yorkshire, which were thought least likely to be bombed. Most were dressed in their 'Sunday best' clothes with their faces pink and shining following a vigorous rub with a well-soaped flannel. Their hair was neatly combed and plastered down with water so that many of them barely recognised each other. The innate pride of most of the working class mothers saw to it that they were wearing clean white vests and socks - 'just in case they got knocked down or something'. Many had no boots - only sandshoes. These were fine on the pavements and the tarmac of the local roads but were not really suitable for the mud of the countryside.

The crocodile of children, carrying their bag or case and their gas masks, snaked its way along Newport Road, which still had iron tramlines sunk into its cobbled setts. Most of the cases were made of cheap cardboard reinforced at the corners but some of the very poor kids had brown paper carrier bags, or even pillowcases and many of the them were beside themselves with excitement. The long 'crocodile' followed a slow moving, loudspeaker van to the railway station with the scene reminiscent of a modern-day Pied Piper of Hamelin. Most of the children would never forget the feel of the small cardboard boxes that bounced against their legs and the day they left home with their scant belongings would dwell in their hearts and minds forever.

At the head of the column a teacher carried a name placard on a pole and the staff wore armbands on which their school number was clearly displayed. The younger children laughed and chatted as they skipped along. Some were even carrying buckets and spades. Sympathetic ladies handed the children fruit and sweets and shouted encouraging remarks and these acts of kindness helped to reinforce the holiday-like atmosphere and excitement. Dozens of mothers trailed behind dabbing their eyes trying to make the most of the last precious minutes as the thought of parting from their loved ones was heart-rending. Most had shed copious tears in the privacy of their own homes before steeling themselves to face the final parting but they were prepared to make this great sacrifice as long as it ensured a safe future for their children.

As they walked up Sussex Street, the children could see the high, three hundred yards long, arched roof of the Victorian railway station. The excitement and babble of voices increased as they walked up the long, cobbled, carriage drive to the forecourt. The entrance was partly obscured by heaped-up sandbags and, on entering, they found themselves in the central concourse. Here red buckets of sand, stirrup pumps and fire extinguishers stood at the foot of the sandstone walls on which signs and posters exhorted the public to shop at Dickson & Benson, Upton's, Newhouse's Corner, Amos Hinton's, or Saltmer's and another read 'Binns Store for Everything'. The scene on the crowded platforms was one of noisy, echoing, chaos as concerned parents, shouting teachers and excited children bumped and jostled each other. Guards' whistles shrilled and doors slammed as steam and the smell of smoke filled the air and anxious teachers pulled their charges back from the edge of the crowded platforms.

WVS. ladies in soft, large-rimmed, felt hats and greeny-grey, woollen jumpers and skirts tried their best to maintain some sort of order. Grey and red wool had been woven into their uniforms as green was thought to be an unlucky colour on its own. Most of them were middle-class and they were vulgarly known in our area as 'Widows, Virgins and Spinsters'. They handed bottles of 'pop'

30

and brown paper bags of raisins, nuts and oranges to the children. Nurses attended to children who had fallen and hurt themselves while others saw to those who were upset and crying. Policemen took distressed children that had become separated from their group, back to where they belonged with one or two carrying tiny tots in their arms. Muffled messages blared from loudspeakers and echoed back from the high arched roof as teachers urged their charges to take their seats quickly or to desist from playing with the doors.

Archie made sure that Harry and Jimmy stayed close to him and Gran and Hilda checked that the boys had their pack of sandwiches and hard-boiled eggs for the journey. They also checked that their stamped and addressed postcards were safely tucked away. A few food items (e.g. tins of corned beef; pears; peaches; baked beans; 'Carnation' milk; a couple of bars of Cadbury's chocolate and a packet of biscuits) had been packed to help out their hosts during the first days. Several mothers found that they could not control their feelings of anxiety about where and to whom their children were being sent - it was all too much - and, bursting into floods of tears, they took their children back home.

Much tearful last minute hugging and kissing took place through the open carriage windows and the boys turned scarlet with embarrassment on being kissed in front of all these people. As salty tears coursed down Gran's and Hilda's cheeks wetting the boys faces, things went from bad to worse when Gran shouted, "Be good boys and always wash behind your ears. Be very brave and try not to cry." Archie kept well back while all this was going on.

Most of the tough, hard-bitten fathers of our neighbourhood found it difficult to express love and affection as they had been brought up to believe that crying or the showing of physical warmth in public was a sign of weakness or effeminacy in 'real' men. They were typical of the northern males of that time who felt that pouring tea or pushing prams was woman's work and therefore outside their domain. However, some found it necessary to blow their noses loudly, which, of course, caused their eyes to water. There was much frantic waving and buckets of tears flowed as the heartbroken parents were left on the station platform not knowing when or where they would see their children again. The older children leaned out of the carriage windows and waved as the train carried them away from their loved ones. The train left platform one heading for Darlington, a small town some 15 miles to the west and once on their way, the teachers and carers led the children in singing. They tried hard to keep up the 'holiday mood' and to take the children's minds off parents and home, singing - strange as it seems - popular songs of the previous war. Songs such as, *Ten Green Bottles; Roll out the Barrel* and *It's a Long Way to Tipperary* were easy to remember and join in with.

At Darlington, which was a mainline station, the evacuees had a long wait as their specially laid on London and North Eastern Railway (L.N.E.R) train was shunted into the sidings. Extra carriages that were full of local children and some that had been sent down from the industrial areas of Tyneside were coupled to it with much clanking of chains and bumping of buffers. They had a long wait while the train was rescheduled as priority was given to trains required for troop carrying and the transporting of essential war workers. Hundreds of lumpy kit bags were piled high on the porters trolleys and soldiers were helping their pals to remove their harnesses and bulky packs that weighed several pounds as they could not get through the narrow carriage doors of the crowded troop trains with them on. The teachers and carers accompanied groups of children to the toilets passing the large advertising posters that adorned the walls promoting common commodities of the time, such as Swan Vesta matches; Lifebuoy toilet soap; Tizer the Appetizer and Vimto. Others stated, 'The blackout is now in force and no chink of light must show after dark'.

During the long wait the children were again kept occupied by means of guessing games and singing to help pass the time. Amidst the hustle and bustle of a vast array of people on the move, the WVS ladies were kept busy handing out large mugs of hot steaming cocoa poured from huge white enamelled jugs. These were regularly refilled from the gleaming brass taps of the large aluminium urns that stood on four-wheeled trolleys. Several of the children had opened their food packs within the first half-hour of the journey and a few had made themselves sick and had to be cleaned up by their harassed teachers. Red-capped, military policemen wearing armbands and white-blancoed webbing belts mingled with the crowds on the look out for improperly dressed soldiers. Whenever they found one they put him on a 'fizzer' (i.e. a charge). Khaki, navy-blue and light blue uniforms were everywhere as hundreds of soldiers; sailors and airmen milled about.

The train finally set off again on its journey to York with the slamming of the heavy carriage doors accompanied by loud cheering from the children. It was a journey south of about forty miles and a lone fighter plane circled above them. The train made stops at Northallerton and Thirsk, to drop off groups of children accompanied by a few teachers and parents. From Thirsk onwards the gleaming tracks were perfectly straight for twenty miles. It was one of the longest straight stretches in the country with no stations or halts on it at all and the *Mallard* had set a world speed record of 126 mph on it only fifteen months earlier. Built in the year I was born, it was the pride of the railways and Archie had once seen the great, streamlined, giant locomotive as it passed through Newport Halt station. Being the eldest, he had been made responsible for the children in his compartment and as they passed four miles to the east of the village of Kilburn he tried to interest them by pointing out the shape of a huge white horse on the hillside. It was 305 feet long (about 100m.) and its surface covered roughly an acre making it the largest in Britain. It had been carved out some eighty years earlier and had been refilled with fresh chalk and lime every year since. However, the powers-that-be soon ordered it to be hidden from view with camouflage netting and turf as it was thought to be too good a marker for the enemy with so many bomber airfields in the vicinity.

Some of the children spent a good part of the journey sucking on short bits of woody, liquorice root (known as 'Spanish wood') completely unaware that it was a laxative. Others repeatedly wet their black liquorice stick with spit before dipping it into a paper packet of yellow lemon crystals, which they called khali (pronounced 'kay-lie'). It fizzed and stuck to the wet liquorice before they sucked it off. Harry sat enjoying the adventures of Desperate Dan (who ate cow pie); Korky the Cat and others in his *Dandy* comic while Jimmy was deeply engrossed in looking at the pictures of Big Eggo (the Ostrich) and Lord Snooty and his Pals in *The Beano*. *The Dandy* had first come out in the December of 1937 and *The Beano* seven months later with both comics costing 2d (less than 1p). They were then the size of a newspaper, with each containing 28 coloured pages. The evacuees soon grew tired of counting the fields or the telegraph poles, which began to make them feel dizzy as they whizzed by the carriage windows. Many of them had never seen cows or fields of stubble before.

One scruffy little boy, after a prolonged spell of picking his nose and eating it, suddenly rushed up to the carriage door and managing to pull the leather strap from its brass peg, he lowered the window. He then unashamedly peed out of it, and children looking from carriages further down the train had to rapidly take evasive action. One or two of the little girls that had been too excited or too shy to ask to go to the toilet at Darlington station were unable to control themselves and wet their pants. Some of the older boys on seeing a large sign that had 'WHISTLE' printed on it started whistling and the occasional argument and scuffle broke out making the frightened little girls cry.

Another snotty-nosed kid spent part of the journey pulling on the leather strap on the door, thus making the window go up and down and allowing gusts of smoke to rush in. This continued until a little girl screamed in pain when a piece of grit blew into her eye. Archie had to make several attempts before he got it out with the corner of his, muslin handkerchief on which. 'Spiller's Fine Flour' could be faintly seen. His well meant ministrations left the little girl's eye looking red, raw and watery and turning on the lad who had caused it, he shouted, "If yer touch that strap again I'll give yer a good clout round the lughole. Do yer understand?" Meanwhile the unfortunate victim, feeling homesick and sorry for herself, sat snivelling and whimpering.

It came as a great relief to Archie when the train crossed the narrow railway bridge over the wide waters of the River Ouse, from which he caught a glimpse of the old fortified city of York. The great steam locomotive slowed as it entered one of the four soaring roof arches that made up the cavernous, crescent-shaped station. The long line of carriages clanked and rumbled as they slowly rolled to a halt and amidst loud hissing and great clouds of steam they found themselves alongside platform two. An attempt to obliterate the York signs, by brushing white paint over them, was only partially successful, the aim being to confuse the Germans, should they arrive unannounced but it seemed more likely to confuse the British! Many heavy doors clattered open and out poured the mass of sweaty, travel-weary kids clutching their cases and bags. The teachers made sure that they had their gas mask boxes with them, as if they lost them, the law stated that their parents could be fined £5, which was a lot of money in those days. Archie had not enjoyed having this new and unaccustomed responsibility thrust upon him one bit and he resented being lumbered with those two, badly behaved young tearaways. It had seemed to him at one time that the living nightmare of the long journey would never end.

On leaving the train a number of the children gaped wide-eyed at the vast, brightly painted station and, just for a moment, they were speechless as they gazed in awe at the great curving girders studded with hundreds of round-headed rivets. The huge windows of the arched roofs soared over their heads supported on long rows of cream-coloured, iron columns, each one crowned by a Corinthian capital with gilded acanthus leaves. These curved away in long avenues to the far end of the fifteen, stone-paved platforms and between each hung a graceful, iron-framed lantern on a long black chain. They were completely unaware that beneath their feet lay a Roman cemetery and the trains, which then travelled at more than a mile a minute, ran above streets on which Caesar had once ridden his horse. York, then named Eboracum, had once been a great military centre.

The walls on the western side were honey-coloured and had circular openings above a row of graceful sandstone arches. Between the middle two was a large double-dialled clock with its faces angled at forty-five degrees enabling it to be seen from either end or from the platforms opposite. The clock and his stomach told Archie that he could do with a snack and with his mouth watering he walked down to an iron, vending machine intent on buying a bar of delicious Fry's chocolate. He was too late and lost his two pennies (1p) into the bargain as the machine was empty and a sailor was walking away eating the last bar. For security reasons there was now no ship's name on the sailor's cap band - only HMS. Soldiers, sailors and airmen milled about on the crowded platforms.

The group, with their bags and cases, were ushered together by Mr Lamballe, the young teacher who had travelled down with them, and they gathered around a skinny man in a dark pin striped suit carrying a clipboard. From it he read out the names of those who were to be taken by motor coach to Haxby, a small village with a population of about 1,400 souls that lay four miles to the north. Following him along the platform they passed a large waiting room, a magazine kiosk, a large, round, two-faced clock and the wide stairs that led up to an elevated, white-painted, wooden, signal box. Behind its large glass windows they caught a glimpse of long rows of shiny metal levers. The ticket collector, in his black serge uniform with shiny brass buttons, glanced at the proffered paperwork before the group made their way into a rectangular, lofty-roofed, stone concourse, the walls of which were covered in posters advertising Ovaltine; Bovril; Fairy Toilet Soap; Oxydol; Venos cough cure; Rinso; Spratt's Dog Food and the like. They passed below another fine, circular clock mounted on the wall above W. H. Smith's bookshop. A large, enamelled, metal sign advertised 'ROWNTREE'S ELECT COCOA' in white letters on a blue background, proclaiming that they were 'MAKERS TO H.M. THE KING' in gold letters. In the centre there was a black and white picture of an immense factory with a tall, smoking chimney. At one end of the concourse was a large cafeteria and, at the other, the ticket and booking office.

Emerging from the station they found themselves on the pavement beside a stretch of covered roadway that ran under a high-roofed portico; its weatherworn stones blackened by years of locomotive smoke. Nearby a queue of shiny black taxicabs waited but, due to the rationing of petrol, they no longer left their engines idling and there were fewer in business. It seems that taxis firms were only allowed enough pool petrol - which was now stained pink to make it easier to tell if it had been stolen - for a few hours of work each day.

Above them stood an impressive stone balustrade and below it a row of wide, stone columns flanked the arched exits that led out onto the station approach road. This was lined by a long queue of motor coaches with the drivers waiting their turn to take the hundreds of evacuees to villages on the outskirts of the city. On the far side of the road, was a steep, grassy embankment that sloped up to the almost white stone battlements and walkways of the city walls. Mr Lamballe told them, "That magnificent wall is of Roman and medieval origin and it almost encircles the oldest part of the city. To your left is the huge, Victorian, ashlar-built, four-storey *Station Hotel* owned by the LNER and it has a hundred and eighty elegant rooms and beautifully landscaped gardens." It is now called *The Royal York.*

On noticing a stone statue on a plinth at the end of the road, Mr Lamballe told them something of the early days of the railways, saying, "That statue is of George Leeman a highly successful 19th century railway pioneer and entrepreneur who succeeded the flamboyant George Hudson - 'The Railway King' - as Lord Mayor of York. Hudson, George Stephenson and others had first met in a small York hotel run by a Mrs Tomlinson, and at this meeting, they planned the formation of the Yorkshire and Midlands Railway Company. Hudson went on to make a fortune from the railways but after serving for some years as the MP for Sunderland, he went bankrupt. He was accused of shady share dealing which led to his downfall and he ended up in York Debtors Prison".

Many of the children, becoming bored at this, started to chant, "Why are we waiting?" and, after waiting for some considerable time (under yet another large clock) their coach finally pulled in. It was a Leyland single-decked bus, with a half cab, able to seat thirty-five passengers. The motley group of grubby, sweaty and tired evacuees clambered onto it and the tearaways made a beeline for the back seat, so as to be as far away from the teacher as possible. Archie, being bigger and older than the rest, managed to get himself, Harry and Jimmy onto it first and the coach drove off, turning right by the statue. It entered the inner city through a wide-arched, battlemented gateway in the wall with the magnificent, redbrick council offices with their Dutch-gabling to their left. After crossing Lendal Bridge that spanned the two hundred feet (65.6m.) width of the fast flowing river Ouse, an old, three-storeyed, battlemented, stone tower with arrow slits caught the attention of some of the older children.

After driving up Museum Street they beheld York Minster for the first time. Archie gazed up in wonder at the magnificent west front of the thirteen hundred years old edifice. The stained glass of the great west window, with its beautiful fourteenth century limestone tracery, held within it the shape of a great heart. The pair of doors within their recessed, stone ribbed Norman arches, were dwarfed by it and it was majestically flanked by graceful, two hundred feet tall (60m.) stone towers. Turning left along St. Leonard's Place the bus slowed at Exhibition Square where Mr Lamballe pointed out the World War One tank on display there. A solid iron cannon, a relic of the Boer War, stood nearby on the lawn of the King's Manor school. The coach passed out of the city through a gap in the wall and to their right was one of the four medieval gateways into the city. Bootham Bar had four round towers with arrow slits and crenellations and its portcullis was still in situ. Mr Lamballe explained that, "At one time the decapitated heads of traitors were put on public display here to act as a deterrent to any other would-be malefactors." Jimmy asked, "What does 'deecappywhotsit mean and what's a mallythingy?" to which Archie retorted, "Shush. I'll tell yer later"

As they travelled up Gillygate they passed a horse-drawn Corporation dustcart and Mr Lamballe told them that Gillygate was named after a church dedicated to St. Giles that had once stood there. The driver then bore left onto Clarence Street where the road divided again and, bearing right, the coach rattled up the long, straight Haxby Road. On the left they saw the immense, imposing facade of the six-storey Rowntree's cocoa and chocolate factory with its tall, brick chimney and huge, square, clock tower which were well-known landmarks. Its myriad windows were blast-taped and the factory and playing fields covered an area of some two hundred acres. Adjoining the main factory building was a large wood pulp yard where paper and packaging for their sweets and chocolates had been made for years; their most recent being Kit Kat bars and Black Magic chocolates. The driver told Mr Lamballe that the Rowntree family had generously donated tons of free cardboard to York City Council, which was used to make thousands of gas mask boxes for the local people.

Here, the river Foss meandered along very close to the main road in places and across the fields the kids could see Lock House, a Victorian lock keepers cottage built in the glory days of an earlier canal navigation scheme. The coach climbed a slight incline and bumped over the gated level crossing of the York to Hull railway line, known locally as the Haxby Road Crossing.

They then came to Joseph Rowntree's model village at New Earswick, within which most of the roads were named after trees. Tall trees shaded the neat houses and it had its own school. The driver, a local man, said, "Joseph, who died fifteen yeers back aged eighty-nine, were an employer o't'paternal and benevolent sort and 'e were noted for his philanthropic and avuncular care of the workers. 'Is village' were built in t'early yeers o't'century, to 'ouse 'em at affordable rents." To the north of Rowan Avenue, there was a mile or so of open countryside and several of the fields had long rows of shiny brown ridges and furrows - the result of recent ploughing. Mr Lamballe told anyone who cared to listen, that "That is an example of how pasture land is now being dug up in order to produce food crops. It is happening all over the country and it means fewer cows will be kept, which could lead to milk shortages"

The sunlight on that late afternoon was soft and golden and the scents of early autumn wafted in through the partly open windows. On the right was a farm with its stables set back a little from the road and the driver said to Mr Lamballe, "That's Dolly Ward's place. The next one up, wi' its front facing towards York, is called Crompton Farm and it belongs t't'Suttill family. That row of semi-detached houses, that were built six yeers back, is Crompton Terrace." Not that anybody was listening.

On their right the golden light of the setting sun was reflected in the windows of a white house in the distance, temporarily blinding the boys. The driver said, "That's another 'Lock 'ouse' and it were built around t'yeer 1800. It stands beside 'Axby part o' t'aud canal, which formed part o' t'Foss Navigation scheme. It became unviable after t'local railways were built. The barges used ter transport coal and lime from York and it carried stone, timber and farm produce to it. It were thought that it would 'elp ter prevent flooding on t'marshy land t't'east and north of 'Axby". Jimmy whispered, "What did 'e say?" and Archie again told him to be quiet.

The coach then passed two railway cottages on the left, the second one being where Mr Barnes, the signalman lived, before bumping over the white-gated level crossing of the York to Scarborough line. This line had opened in the July of 1845 as part of the then new Yorkshire and North Midlands Railway and just north of it, on the left, stood a small, single-storey house roofed with red-clay pantiles, where Mr Dicks, the other signalman, lived. It and the redbrick signal box had been built at the same time as the railway. On it was a sign stating that it was '3 miles, 27 chains' from York station, but this was removed when the threat of invasion became very real. This was the Haxby Gates Crossing, often called the Hilbra Crossing, and it stood just within the southern boundary of Haxby village.

The coach was now on York Road and running off it to the left, was Hilbra Avenue and, a little further up, Eastfield Avenue (a cul-de-sac). There was a row of seven, large, detached, exclusive houses, all of differing design. After this, elegant Eastfield House - a fine gentleman's house with large bay windows flanking its impressive Georgian doorway - could be seen set back within spacious gardens with two fine trees flanking its York Road entrance. It was surrounded by an ornately patterned, red brick, buttressed wall and just after it a narrow lane led up to Eastfield Farm.

A little further up the road they passed on their left a long terrace of large, late Victorian town houses faced with unglazed yellowish bricks. On the opposite side there were a number of large private residences with ornate, wrought iron or heavy, wooden gates leading on to long concealed drives. These were screened from the road by high walls and trees and as Harry and Jimmy knelt on the back seat they noticed that some of the 'posh' houses had monkey-puzzle trees in their large gardens. To the north of these they could see the extensive parkland and gardens of Haxby Hall and on the left stood a few more large houses, including the local bobby's house with its blue paintwork.

At the top end of York Road was a grassy roundabout with a tall, leafy pine tree in the centre and the driver explained "That were planted forty-two yeers ago ter mark t'Diamond Jubilee of Queen Victoria." The motor coach turned right then, almost immediately, right again onto the gravelled driveway of Haxby Hall stopping in front of the majestic residence with tall chimneys, that stood out from the much humbler dwellings near it. Built around the year 1700, it stood on the corner facing the traffic island behind a long brick wall. Its ivy-covered walls contained many high, small-paned, sash windows criss-crossed with adhesive brown paper strips and behind it were, what had at one time been, a double coach-house, stables and several outbuildings. It boasted neat, well-kept gardens and its large, rectangular, ornamental fishpond was still stocked with carp. The first village air raid siren stood on top of one of the outbuildings but it was soon to be moved to another site.

As the feet of the weary and bedraggled boys and girls crunched noisily over the gravelled driveway, a few paused for a second to gape in awe at the impressive building. However, most were now sullen, silent, and too exhausted to bother as they slouched and shuffled towards the entrance. They passed between four fluted pillars that supported an elegant, semi-circular, iron-railed, stone balcony. The heavy solid-oak door of the Georgian building stood ajar and immediately ahead was a wide stairway with plush carpets at the top of which, directly above the spacious landing, was a huge and magnificent, gilt-framed, glass dome. The fine cupola could be seen best from the rear of the building. An important looking lady in a tweed two-piece suit led them into a large, high-ceilinged room to the right of the entrance hall. Wall mirrors and pictures in gilded frames adorned the handsome reception room with its elegant décor and white stucco mouldings which soared to a height of some fourteen feet. On the ceiling intricately wrought cornices, medallions and rosettes hinted at the opulent lifestyle once enjoyed by its former residents.

A Mr Kenneth Ward, a prominent architect with a thriving business in York, was the present owner of the Hall. He, his wife, Ethel, and their three children had been obliged to relinquish their fine residence when it was requisitioned by the Health Authority of the Flaxton County Council, who were now using it to house a number of wartime amenities including a First Aid post. It was also used as a centre for the local branch of the British Red Cross Society with a Mrs Sullivan, the wife of Colonel Sullivan, being its Commandant. The Sullivans resided at a large, old, detached, double-fronted, bay windowed house called 'The Firs' at the western end of the village.

The reception room was soon packed to the doors with children, teachers and a number of local people. The crowds of children milled around as another group of evacuees had just arrived from Hull and as they shouted to each other across the room the rising babble echoed back from the high ceiling. The overtired and fractious evacuees quietened down a little when they were given steaming hot soup, pies, sandwiches, cakes and biscuits with a choice of Rowntree's cocoa, tea or soft drinks. The 'eats' were set out on a line of wooden trestle tables covered by freshly starched and ironed, brilliant-white cloths that several of the local housewives had kindly helped to set out. Some of the children were shy, some had queasy tummies but all were grubby and dishevelled as most of them had not seen soap and water since the crack of dawn. Since they largely came from the poorer areas of the industrial towns, their cheap clothing and tear-streaked faces did not make them appealing to the locals and many of the boys had no handkerchief or never used one. One or two had 'snot' around or dangling from their noses and a number of them were in the habit of drawing their coat or jumper sleeve under their noses so that the cuff looked as though a slug had slithered over it.

A number of the rougher lads liberally peppered every sentence with a few choice swear words. Archie, Harry and Jimmy - although from a similar background - had been brought up to believe that swearing was wrong; and even more so in the presence of women or girls. Many - with their best clothes now soiled, crumpled and stained - felt utterly dejected and homesick as it dawned on them how far away they were from their families and loved ones. A few were not bothered in the least and were just glad to be getting away from their uncaring parents and their squalid homes in the slum areas. Many smelled of sweat and urine, and one or two of the younger children had soiled their pants. For most of them the adventure and glamour of it all had faded some considerable time back.

The children had then to endure what seemed to them a long and boring welcoming speech given by a Mrs Butterfield from a platform set up at the far end of the room. She was, apparently, an important village dignitary and a local parish councillor and her husband, Mr Ralph Butterfield, was also a local bigwig in the community. He was a County Alderman, a parish councillor who held a managerial post on the National Coal Board and was an honorary officer of the Flaxton area ARP Committee. They were 'pillars of the community' and their sixteen years old son, Billy, was just starting a college course in York. The family lived in a large, detached bungalow on The Avenue; a crescent shaped road that was lined with the older, detached houses and bungalows of the more affluent members of the village. The exclusive private residences along it had names rather than numbers, and it ran off the eastern side of York Road before curving round to rejoin it just north of Jones's little grocery shop. They were fine houses but the surface of the road left a lot to be desired, as it was rough and full of potholes and, being a private road, the residents had to pay for its upkeep. Behind the houses cows grazed contentedly in the grassy fields.

The children were eventually ushered into an untidy line and led into the elegant library where rows of crowded bookshelves rose up to the ceiling. Here they had their heads inspected by the middle-aged District Nurse, Mrs Ethel Lealman who was also the highly regarded midwife. She lived with her husband and thirteen years old daughter in a nice, modern, detached house on Station Road. On hearing some of the local women calling the evacuees 'dirty little tykes', she thought to herself 'Maybe they are justified' as on closer inspection, many were found to be verminous. Several had skin infections, such as scabies, impetigo and eczema and some of the worst cases were sent immediately to an isolation unit that had been set up in Chapel House, a former Methodist Chapel in the centre of the village, which had stood empty for some time. Nurse Lealman had a large, evil-smelling, brown bottle of thick dark liquid called 'lethane', which was the main nit-destroyer of the time, and with it she anointed the heads of several children making them smell worse than they had before. This, along with Derbac soap, soon sold out in the local shops.

The more 'well to-do' women wore a wide variety of the felt hats, usually with the rim pulled down over one eye, that looked like small trilbys with feathers inserted under the band, as these were fashionable at that time. A few were wearing animal fur coats or tippets around their shoulders and others had fox furs with the heads still attached. Much to the consternation of one of the ladies, a scruffy lad suddenly pointed at her fox fur before shouting, "Look lads, it's biting its own arse!"

The mouths were full of jagged white teeth and they had glassy staring eyes, which terrified some of the younger children who - thinking they were alive - burst into tears and hid their wet faces in the coat of the nearest person. There was no question that cleanliness and general appearance played a large part in the selection process.

A few stepped forward and chose the most attractive children before registering them with Mrs Horn, the local Billeting Officer, who had a bespectacled lady called Mrs Riddolls stood beside her. She was the wife of the much-revered Dr. Riddolls who had catered to the medical needs of the local people for many years. Pretty, little, curly-haired girls that looked like Shirley Temple were among the first to be led away. The cute child star had captivated so many hearts in her Hollywood films and her latest, 'The Little Princess', was showing at the Gaumont Cinema in Middlesbrough in the week that war was declared. Archie had been told to stay close to Harry and Jimmy in case they were put into separate lodgings but, the way things were shaping up, he doubted if any of them would even be picked.

There were problems in matching evacuees with foster parents and the people willing to take an evacuee dwindled to zero. It seems that they had found nothing to attract them to the remaining children. Archie, Harry, Jimmy and the rest felt angry and humiliated at being picked over like articles in a rummage sale and then thrown back. They stood subdued and huddled together feeling fed up, rejected and homesick. One sad looking little girl with lank, mousy hair sobbed uncontrollably crying out. "No one wants me or loves me and I want to go home."

Maybe the would-be hosts thought that a big lad like Archie would eat too much and would be too expensive to look after. By 7.30 p.m. as dusk fell, the young children were starting to feel drowsy and Mrs Horn announced, "I'm afraid that you will have to sleep here tonight. But rest assured that arrangements are being made for you to be billeted tomorrow morning."

A few of the local residents stayed to serve the children with biscuits and mugs of cocoa. Thin, biscuit-like, flock-filled palliasses and bedding were brought out and laid on the parquet floor and the children spent a long, lonely night in unfamiliar surroundings. Two local ladies had agreed to stay overnight but they were complete strangers and the children were badly missing their homes and families. Several of the younger children were crying and could not be consoled as it dawned on them that there would be no mother or father on hand in the foreseeable future: no one to comfort and soothe them. No one to kiss a bruised elbow or a skinned knee to make it better.

That night many of the little ones pulled the blankets over their heads and cried until their pillows became wet. They could not understand why they had been so cruelly rejected and the tiny tots whimpered and sobbed uncontrollably for their mothers. A few woke to find their pyjamas, sheets and mattresses soaking wet! This was a common occurrence amongst new evacuees and it surely didn't deserve punishment! Some authorities had set up special hostels to send them to. Prolonged bedwetting was to cause the billeting officer and some foster parents quite a problem and urine-stained sheets and mattresses hanging out to dry became a common sight in the village. If they so wished, foster parents were entitled to claim financial compensation for the ruined bedding and several did so.

The next morning, the children were given a choice of milky porridge or Kellogg's cornflakes, followed by buttered toast and marmalade with cocoa or milk. After breakfast, more local people arrived and a few more children were selected and taken away. The ones left were led in a sad procession from door to door by the small and chubby Mrs Horn, who worked in the council offices in York and had the legal authority to make people take at least one evacuee if they had an unused bedroom. Most of the local folk accepted this unusual situation with good grace and were happy to accept these little strangers into their homes. Sadly, the lines of dejected children became a common sight as Mrs Horn tried to get someone to take them in, if only for the night.

The procession stopped outside 10a, York Road, which was the second from last house at the northern end of the long terrace of town houses passed by the coach on the way here. At the turn of the century an influential man called Samuel Sutton, a JP and parish councillor, had financed the building of these quality houses. The fine old house was now the comfortable home of a couple of middle-aged spinsters who, for quite a while refused to accept an evacuee, asking vehemently, "Why should we have instant parenthood thrust upon us just because we have a vacant room? We are quite content as we are, thank you very much!"

"If you refuse you will be breaking the law. You have a spare bedroom available, therefore you are obliged to take at least one person" Mrs Horn retorted, until, with much reluctance, they chose Harry from the sad looking group. In their opinion the wiry, good-looking, flaxen-haired, eleven-year-old was the best of a poor lot. But Archie objected strongly, shouting, "He can't go there! We're supposed to stay together." He was told that few people had the room or the inclination to take three children and he was powerless to do anything about it.

There were complaints about 'the well off' not taking their share of evacuees and a week or so earlier the *Yorkshire Evening Press* had carried a story with the headline, 'Haxby Vicar's Protest'. The person concerned was the Reverend K.J.L Donald, the Vicar of Haxby, who had lived in the large Vicarage on Moor Lane for the last seven years. It stated that he and his family had been told that they must take in four evacuee children with the vicar pointing out that, "In the event of an air raid the children will have be left alone in the house. My wife and daughter will often be engaged elsewhere on ARP (Air Raid Precaution) duties. It has been agreed that it would be more sensible in the circumstances to take in two mothers who could always be there with their babies".

The next day a car arrived with an adult and three boys and the Vicar pointed out that there must be some mistake, so the boys were taken away. A few minutes later they returned accompanied by a policeman who said that the family *must* take them in and they did so. They had just given the children lemonade and biscuits when another car arrived and the boys were taken away for a second time. The next day one hundred and twenty three evacuees arrived rather than the hundreds expected and the Vicarage was not required after all.

Shortly afterwards the tongues of the village gossips began to wag and, in response, the Vicar sent a strong letter to the newspaper speaking out strongly about the wicked talk in the village concerning his alleged refusal to take in evacuees. He was very angry and ashamed of them for holding the church up to ridicule and scorn and rebuked them publicly for their 'cruel and foul gossip' advising them to desist and to 'keep their tongues from evil speaking in future.' One of them had been a certain Mrs Harris who complained about almost everything and we shall learn more of her shortly.

Earlier intakes of evacuees from Middlesbrough, Hull and London had been received at the village school and others had been taken to the recreation hut in the adjoining village of Wigginton. Some had walked to their new homes and a few had been driven there in the shiny black Flying Standard car that belonged to a teacher called Miss Curry. She was only a young lady but she had been given a position of great responsibility after being called from her first teaching post in Malton to co-ordinate the teaching of the evacuees. The car had cost most of her life savings but she thought it well worth it and considered it essential if she was to carry out regular checks on them. She was extremely proud of the car with its sinuously curving mudguards that flowed into the running boards below the front doors.

Eventually, Archie and Jimmy were accepted by a man and wife called Smith who were in their late twenties, and they were taken to a nice end of terrace house on the outskirts of York. The house was not far from Rowntree's chocolate factory and they started school in New Earswick soon afterwards. The Smiths had a large back garden, in which their small white 'Scottie' dog raced around yapping and wagging its tail ten-to-the-dozen. But, for some reason, they stayed there for only a week.

They were then moved into a house on the eastern side of York Road with a young married couple called Souter. Mr Souter had a motor bike and one day, for what he called 'a special treat', he put on his goggles, gauntlet gloves and tight-fitting, leather 'flying' helmet. He loaned Archie a pair of uncomfortable, ill-fitting, round-lensed goggles, as helmets were not compulsory at that time, and with Archie on the pillion seat, they set off on a bumpy, white-knuckle ride into York. Archie was terrified and clung on for dear life with his arms tightly around Mr Souter's waist as they jounced over the (un)level railway crossings. This hair-raising experience put him off motorbikes for the rest of his life. It was learned shortly afterwards that Mrs Souter was pregnant and so, as their spare bedroom was required for the baby, the pair were moved yet again.

A married couple from nearby Strensall village agreed to take Jimmy, who had an obstinate, headstrong and wilful nature, but he did not want to go. He was determined to stay with Archie and he adamantly refused to settle. Being given to sudden outbursts of temper if he felt he was being wrongly treated, he cried constantly - kicking them, the door and the doorjambs - when they attempted to take get him into the house. He would drop to the floor and throw a tantrum, kicking and screaming when told to do anything. The separation of close relatives seemed, in the circumstances, insensitive or even cruel and it caused much unnecessary heartache and emotional pain. Many children, like Jimmy, who were abruptly uprooted from their parents at a very tender age, experienced great emotional trauma. The well-meaning family could not cope with him and, after a few days, to his great delight, he was re-united with Archie.

In the meantime, Archie had been billeted in an early 1930s red brick, semi-detached house on Wold View Terrace at the north eastern edge of Haxby village. It was one of a row of twelve semi-detached houses on the western side of Usher Lane built by a local man, Tom Pulleyn. On the opposite side of the lane there was open countryside and from the front upstairs windows the rolling Yorkshire Wolds could be seen in the distance. The houses had a small front garden and a much longer garden to the rear and behind them were grassy fields.

The house was rented by the middle-aged Mr Harris and his wife, who was a tall, large boned, sandy-haired, domineering type of woman with a generous bosom and heavy horn-rimmed spectacles. She had the reputation of being a right battleaxe - a real virago - who led her pleasant, good-natured husband a dog's life and he scarcely got a moment's respite from her constant nagging. She had come from the Leeds/Bradford area and her husband was a local man who had been born in nearby Wigginton. His father, being an illiterate farmhand, had signed his birth certificate with a cross; a common occurrence in those days.

The middle-aged couple had a grown up son who was in Canada with the RAF. Before the war it had been agreed that billeting allowances should be paid and it would appear that Mrs Harris saw this fostering 'lark' as an easy and tempting source of extra income. She had only two small bedrooms vacant but she was to take in another three evacuees in the early weeks of the war, plus two more not long afterwards. One of the 'spare' rooms was just a tiny box room containing a three-quarter sized bed that left no room for any other furniture.

Foster parents were well paid for taking in evacuees, receiving ten shillings and sixpence (52½p) for a single child and 8/6d for each additional one. The payments steadily increased and by the February of 1940 the Government announced that foster parents would receive 12/6d (62½p) a week for an unaccompanied evacuee aged between fourteen and sixteen years of age; 10/6d (52½p) for those between ten and fourteen and 8/6d (42½p) for children under ten.

A month later Archie celebrated his fourteenth birthday with a small tea party and his mother (my Gran) travelled through from Middlesbrough bringing with her sweets and a tin full of delicious homemade cakes and 'fadgees'. Gran's home-made fadgees (bread buns) had a lovely flavour - the likes of which I have not come across since. By this time Mrs Harris had acquired another big thirteen-year-old lad, called Albert Crabtree, and two seven and eight-year-old girls - all of them from Middlesbrough. Before the war Albert's elder sister had been in the same schoolclass as Archie's sister, Renee. The two little girls were called Dorothy ('Dot') Sirman and Thelma Nicholson. Mrs Harris' income had more than doubled and she was now receiving a total of £2.10.6d. (£2.52½) for agreeing to take in the five evacuees. This was more than her hard-working husband was earning as a labourer at nearby Church Farm. For a time, at a later date, she was to have six children billeted with her.

Archie Bradford and Albert Crabtree (standing), Harry Bradford and Jimmy Nolan (sitting), Haxby 1940.

The parents of the evacuees were expected to pay this, if they could afford it. It was means tested, and Gran (who was a widow) and Hilda (Jimmy's mother) were not required to pay the full amount. Some mothers were annoyed at having to pay for their children to live apart from them and took them home. The foster parents could also claim for damage to furniture or bedding. The local authority was authorised to pay the foster parents five shillings (25p) a week for each child that they nursed through a minor illness. Shoes and clothing were to be provided by the parents, but if they could not afford it, the local authority would pay for them. On the one hand it cost foster parents, like the Harris's, nothing; on the other hand, it disrupted their way of life and brought a certain loss of privacy.

The house had round, dark-brown, Bakelite switches with white mica surrounds, that with just a flick instantly flooded the room with white light. There was no hissing or smell of gas and no matches were needed, whereas at home Archie had been accustomed to the dim light of the white and fragile gas mantles. After years of washing at the kitchen sink a bathroom was a real luxury. The water was heated by means of a cast-iron boiler behind the fireplace and there was an indoor, flush toilet with a wooden handle suspended on a chain, which Archie repeatedly pulled just for the fun of it. He was intrigued on seeing and hearing the sudden gush of water from the overhead cistern as it rushed into the pan, but Mrs Harris gave him an earful for wasting water. The evacuees had never experienced such luxuries before.

Not only that, they could now step out of the back door into a grassy garden whereas at home, they had stepped from the back door into a concrete, brick-walled yard or directly onto the grimy pavement at the front. It took them some time to adjust to the spaciousness of the lush green fields and they revelled in the clean, fresh air and the quietness and beauty of the countryside. Back home nature had been buried beneath tons of bricks and concrete and the squalor of the dirty, crowded streets was still fresh in their minds.

Having strange children in the house was undoubtedly tiring and nerve-racking for the new foster parents but most coped well and made them welcome while others cracked under the strain. Making room for the large number of evacuees was difficult but lucrative and Mrs Harris looked forward to collecting her money from the post office every week. Archie, Albert, and Jimmy were told that they were to sleep in the double bed in the back bedroom, while Dot and Thelma had to sleep in the three-quarter sized bed in the box room. Mr and Mrs Harris continued to sleep in their large and comfortable double bed in the front bedroom. On Jimmy's first day, even though he was pleased to be back with Archie, he clung to him when they were alone in the bedroom and sobbed his heart out for his mother. Archie tried to console his distraught young nephew, as they gazed out at the wet, misty fields saying, "Don't cry Jimmy. I promise that I'll look after you and I won't let anyone hurt you." It proved to be a hard promise to keep!

3. Exodus

Before the war broke out, George and I were attending the Settlement House Nursery School where Mam had been working as a voluntary part-time helper for the last year or so. The nursery was in a Victorian townhouse with massive rooms and large double bay windows that stood behind an elegant wrought-iron gate and ornate railings. Set back behind its low brick wall it faced out onto busy, grey-cobbled Newport Road that ran in a west to east direction and had been nicknamed Poverty Row at the time of the Depression. The Settlement itself was once described as an oasis in an urban wilderness. Just behind the big house was a long, cobbled, back lane called the Bull Alley that led to a large slaughterhouse and, as the nursery was at the rear of the house, we could not help but hear the lowing and the clattering of hooves as the cattle were driven down it to their deaths.

Our playroom had a large area of south-facing, glass windows that let the sun in and the floorboards were kept smooth and highly polished so that we didn't get splinters as we played on it. My best friend at the time was a little lad called Eric Ward, the youngest of ten children, who lived in a crowded two-up, two-down, back-to-back, terraced house nearby We played together most of the time and where one was the other was sure to be found. He had five sisters and two brothers still alive and his eldest sister, Edna, was thirty years old by the time he came into the world.

We were well cared for by the nursery assistants - who we called 'Lady' for some reason – and they read lovely stories to us from *The Blue Fairy Book* and suchlike. Every day after dinner we were tucked up for an hour's sleep on little canvas beds that could be folded up and stacked away. My favourite assistant was a cheerful and pretty sixteen years old called Kathleen Begley who laughed a lot and was always singing classical songs. She had a lovely soprano voice that was delicate and high and 'Lady Kathleen' used to sing *One Fine Day* from Puccini's opera Madam Butterfly for us. My other favourite was *O, My Beloved Father*.

In the summer months just before the war, Eric's fifteen years old brother, Len, and his mate Bobby, used to come to the nursery

53

playroom every day. They would appear just as the Lady's were clearing up the toys and books that we had scattered everywhere. Their excuse being, "We have come to take Eric home," but once there they were in no hurry to leave. Their true motive was to try to get off with the two attractive nursery assistants. Unfortunately, their efforts were of no avail as the two girl's interests lay with older and more 'mature' youths.

Separating Russon's Coal Merchant's yard from us was a high brick wall behind which there was stabling for their eight huge draught horses and room for the flat coal carts. The coal deliverymen worked long hours and at the end of the day they would bring the horses and the coal-begrimed rulleys back to this yard to be hosed down. In the summer evenings the coalmen had to walk their horses across the Newport Bridge to the rough, coarse-grassed, pastureland on its northern bank. They then had to make the long walk back, as they were not allowed onto the buses in their coal-blackened state and, by the time they'd had a bath and changed their clothes, it could be nine o'clock. To give themselves an earlier finish they were prepared to pay lads, like Len and his mate, 4d (1.7p) a time to ride the heavy horses over the bridge. Once there they tethered them, left them to feed and ran all the way back to take another one. This arrangement benefited both parties as it gave the boys a bit of extra pocket money and the coalmen had time to go for a drink or to the pictures.

The Settlement was a charitable organization that had, over the last forty-seven years, provided a great deal of help to the poor and needy folk of our area, which was officially classified as socially deprived. We, of course, were totally unaware of this; there always seemed to be someone worse off than us and we didn't think of ourselves as poor; we just didn't have much money. Our parents were proud and tried their best saying, "If you have love and care you are rich indeed."

Over the years hundreds of women had received aid and support here when opportunities for them were extremely rare. Apart from material help, they provided lectures, courses, and books to help them to better themselves, raising funds which were used to provide clothing, day-trips and free holidays. The Settlement had set up several youth organisations and it had a thriving cycling club and Mam and Renee often took part in the concerts they put on. Mam regularly attended the mothers' meetings and the Bible reading classes and their motto was "What Live We For But This". Plans were underway to evacuate the children to the safety of a nursery in the countryside. Mother, who believed in the family as a sustaining force, was concerned for us and the thought of an indefinite separation filled her with horror, therefore she applied for and got the job of assistant cook at the new place.

It was mid September by the time we caught the rattling, trackless trolley bus that had the letter 'O' on the front. It was called a 'trackless' because it no longer needed the tram lines, being electrically powered by means of a long, twin poled arrangement on its roof that connected it to a network of paired overhead electric wires. Mam, my little fair-haired brother and I sat on the hard, slatted seats until we got to the terminus in Exchange Square, where we met up with a nursery assistant and a few other children. I was pleased to see that one of them was my pal, Eric, and we walked with them to the nearby railway station. We were so excited, holding hands as we hopped and skipped along, and we were really looking forward to the coming train journey. Mam led us past the smoke-blackened stones of the sandbagged booking hall, walking us through the central concourse to the white-edged, stone flagged platform. Our voices echoed back from the iron girders and glass panels of the grimy roof that soared to a height of some sixty feet (18 m.) above us.

Mam, on realising that the carriages were of the non-corridor type, took George, me, Eric and the three other toddlers she was in charge of, to the lavatories on the platform. We gaped, wide-eyed with wonder, taking in the sights and strange sounds but I was a bit apprehensive on passing the huge, shiny, black steam locomotive. It reminded me of a fiery dragon resting in its lair hissing faintly as it slowly breathed in and out. As the fireman in the cab opened the door of the firebox, an orange glow illuminated his red sweating face and the glare of the burning coals reflected back from an array of shiny copper pipes and brass gauges. As he wielded his long-handled shovel to throw coals from the tender into its gaping maw, it seemed to me that he was feeding it. The great shiny beast stood creaking and groaning as pungent fumes rose up as oil came in contact with hot iron. White jets of steam squirted out from cylinders down by its gleaming pistons and the metal rims of its massive wheels reflected the light. The minute droplets of steam that landed on my face were reminiscent of the spindrift on a windy day in summer when Mam had taken us to the water's edge at Redcar beach. At this point Mam helped us up the steps and into a carriage.

Steaming on past the wooden platforms of the tiny, outlying, sub stations of Ormesby and Nunthorpe, we caught a glimpse of Ormesby Hall surrounded by its fine parkland. Mam said, "It was here, on a fine day just over two years back, that the Right Honourable Neville Chamberlain addressed the assembled crowds seven weeks after he became Prime Minister." The Hall had been the home of the Pennyman family for four hundred years and Ruth, the second wife of Colonel James Pennyman, had left wing leanings and was known to her friends as 'The Red Duchess' although she never actually joined the Communist party. Colonel Pennyman's grandfather had helped to raise the money to build Holy Trinity church in the market square in nearby North Ormesby. "That's the church which your Gran got married in." Mam had said, as she pointed it out in passing.

As we stopped to pick up a few passengers at Great Ayton, Mam said, "The old village is about a mile away and it was here that Captain Cook's family used to live. It's only five years since his parent's cottage was sold, taken apart stone by stone and shipped out to Melbourne in Australia. You'll no doubt learn all about him when you start school." From here the train gradually climbed onto the lower slopes of the Cleveland Hills and we caught a glimpse of a towering, stone obelisk silhouetted starkly against the blue sky. It stood on the crest of a high hill on nearby Easby Moor and Mam said, "It was erected in honour of Captain Cook, the famous explorer."

The train halted for a few minutes at Battersby Junction where we could see a row of tiny railway cottages, each with a pigsty behind it. As we clattered onwards and upwards towards the high moors, we gazed out on a patchwork of pale-gold, stubble-

56

covered fields, thorn-hedged green meadows and isolated farmsteads.

As Mam dandled George on her knee, Eric blurted out, "Ah'm not coming to the new nursery school with yer, like." It seems that arrangements had been made to billet him in a nearby village and, taken aback by the news, I sat thinking about it as I gazed wistfully out of the window as we gradually climbed towards the higher moorlands. Lush shoulder-high fronds of green bracken, some of it just starting to turn brown, caught my attention as it formed a mosaic on the brilliant green, sheep-cropped, grassy slopes. We then beheld the fawns and browns of sere, bent grasses; the russet of reeds and the yellow of gorse that clad the airy heights of the beautiful North Yorkshire Moors.

It was a glorious day and sweet, heady scents of sun-warmed heather and gorse wafted in through the partly open window. We, still with the young child's capacity for wonder, were awe-struck and entranced by the vast openness of it all. Journeys are always exciting to young children and I was loving this one. We climbed steadily up to broad uplands where great clumps of sunlit purple heather stretched away as far as the eye could see. I gazed out on a vista of purple hills and the vivid, green hues of stream and river valleys. I was enthralled and exhilarated by the wide, limitless expanse of these treeless uplands, as this was my first experience of such hazy and gloriously melting distances. It was so different to the urban world we knew and I had never dreamt that such wild and lovely countryside existed. As bright, sparkling, crystal-clear streams rushed and tumbled down beneath a wide unclouded, Indian summer sky, it was the start of a lifelong love affair with nature.

George, nestling up close to Mam's soft and rounded, Mother Earth figure, was lulled to sleep in the warmth and comfort of her lap as she sat with her head against the padded headrest quietly and sweetly singing a soft and gentle lullaby. The words of which went something like, "Golden slumbers kiss your eyes. Smiles awake you when you rise. Sleep my darling one, gently sleep and I will sing a Lullaby." One or two of the younger children, who had been woken much earlier than usual that morning, also nodded off; lulled by her quiet singing. The soporific, rocking of the carriage and the rhythmic, clackety-clack sounds of the train as it rolled over the jointed rails added to the languorous atmosphere but I sat there wide-eyed with childish wonder. I was not at all apprehensive about leaving home, as I knew that 'our Mam' was going to be with us.

By the hamlet of Kildale, the track ran close to the meandering course of the upper Leven as we rattled along through the beauty of the bracken-clad heights of Commondale Moor. Occasionally the train stopped at tiny rural halts to let the odd passenger off and we saw greyish-white, greasy-fleeced, Swaledale wethers scattered far and wide across the moors. At first I thought they were boulders until they moved. Most of the hardy curly-horned sheep continued their endless chewing as, unperturbed, they stood gazing blankly at our train as it thundered by on that fine sunny early autumn day. Their continual grazing had given the grassy areas the look of neatly mown lawns and they seemed to be making a better job of it than any lawnmower.

The train steamed on by sleepy moorland farmsteads and narrow winding lanes before we passed close to the relatively large village of Castleton and on to Danby station. On the hilltop we could see a number of tall, steel-framed towers unaware that they were top-secret radio transmitting stations. From the train I could see the steep earthen banks of the narrow, meandering upper reaches of the River Esk, as it wended its way down to Whitby. From here the track ran on embankments and passed over small stone road bridges on its way to the tiny, quaintly named hamlet of Howlsike. High above to the south, we could see the beautiful purple heather-clad heights of Danby Moor.

Descending slightly, we passed the patchwork fields of Fryup Dale before halting briefly at the little station at Lealholm Bridge that had a small stone-built stationhouse with crowfoot gabling. We rattled on by yet more small oddly shaped fields around which a network of dry-stone walls dipped and arched following the contours of the land. In the damp, boggy areas the grass was tussocky with clumps of brown rushes and the stones were moss-covered. Black-faced, white-muzzled Swaledale ewes scattered, running stiffly on long grey-mottled legs as our train clattered by before it crossed a five-arched, stone-built viaduct. Close by stood humpbacked Beggars Bridge with its old weatherworn stones and

Mam told us that we were close to the picturesque moorland village of Glaisdale.

"Smugglers and wandering traders have used these old moorland tracks for hundreds of years carrying their wares in pannier bags slung over the backs of their patiently plodding packhorses. The tracks are paved with sandstone slabs in parts, and are called trods or pannier ways and these ancient tracks cross many miles of high wild moorland that lead to and from this old bridge. The low stone walls forming the parapets lean outwards so as to allow for their wide bulky packs." Mam explained.

On the far side of the River Esk another stone-slabbed trod wended its way through the oft-flooded area known as The Molly Mires. Here the greenery of birch, hazel, beech, rowan and alder formed lovely Arncliffe Wood - a remnant of the dense forests that had once covered the whole of Yorkshire – before the trod emerged at the pretty village of Egton Bridge. We crossed the shallow waters of the river Esk on yet another bridge and Mother told us that, "Nearby, on the fast flowing river bed, there are several narrow stepping stones that are about a yard-long. The middle part of these sandstone slabs have been worn down by the feet of countless travellers. The iron road bridge over there replaced an old stone bridge that was swept away by raging floodwaters about nine years back."

At Grosmont station, which was to feature in the television series *Heartbeat* many years later, Mam lifted us out on to the platform with our luggage. A black clad porter, after shouting, "All change for Pickering", brought George's pushchair to us from the guard's van. As we waited an elderly lady standing next to us said to Mam, "Seventy years ago this village were part of a booming ironstone refining industry with several blast furnaces in full production. The ore was mined in t'Rosedale area and were brought 'ere on a purpose-built railway to be converted in ter pig iron. It were just one o't'several ventures that failed due t't'decline in t'quality and quantity o't'local ore-bearing seams. Until 1850 it were called 'Tunnel' because George Stephenson built one 'ere." We had to change trains as the line branched with a line going off to the fishing port of Whitby. The elderly lady said, "Ah'm goin' to Pickering an all. D'yer mind if I travel with yer?"

"Not at all," Mam replied. Boarding the train, we slowly huffed and puffed over the level crossing, passing the old Station Tavern and, as we passed St. Matthew's church, the lady said, "That were built by t'local ironmasters and mine owners tha knows and this railway were once a lifeline to all the little villages along it." The line now ran close to the course of the Murk Esk and beside it we saw abandoned sidings, ventilation shafts and cottages.

As we climbed up through a lovely wooded area towards Beck Hole, the lady said, "There are several whinstone quarries round 'ere that are still being worked and Beck Hole used to be a thriving drift-mining community with two blast furnaces, two inns and thirty stonebuilt workmen's cottages." It was now just a tiny hamlet at the confluence of the Eller and the West Beck and below us, through the canopies of the alders that clung to its steep banks, I caught sight of a pretty, stone-walled, humpback bridge and a shady beck with tumbling waterfalls that glinted in the sunlight.

The lady said to Mam, "In t'early days o't'line, there were a steep bracken-clad incline and on reaching it, engine were attached to a thick hemp rope that were five inches in diameter. This passed around a ten feet diameter (3 m.), horizontal, wooden drum at t'top and t'other end were attached to two huge, iron tanks on wheeled platforms. These were filled with water and their weight made 'em descend, which pulled t'coaches up. It took just over four minutes to reach t'top and the ascending carriages passed t'water tanks going t'other way. The tanks were emptied int't'river before being pulled up agen by 'orses."

"Sometimes rope snapped," she continued, "and it were replaced by a wire hawser. Then there was a bad accident when t'wire broke sending a load of herring careering down t't'bottom and t'place stank o'fish for weeks. There was a fatal accident in 1864 when t'rope snapped and t'coaches raced back down t'incline killing two people and injuring many others. So, plans were drawn up to prevent it happening agen and the four mile stretch of line to Goathland that we are now on was laid in 1865. The old incline were on t'other side o't'Eller Beck" It was a glorious day and the sun reflected on the waters cascading over two lovely waterfalls which the lady said were the Thomason and Water Ark Fosses. On reaching a relatively new station called Goathland Mill, named after an old watermill that once stood there, the train stopped for a while.

I was discovering so many new and exciting things and it seemed to me like a magical journey through an enchanted land. Passing on again by the pretty village of Goathland the steam train headed south into Goathland Dale and the wild and narrow gorge of the Eller Beck. Many years later Goathland was to become known as Aidensfield in the popular T.V. series *Heartbeat* and it was called Hogsmeade in the Harry Potter film, *The Philosopher's Stone*. On the open moors we saw several heather-covered hurdles before the line began the long drag up from the Raindale area to Fen Bog where I was spellbound by the stunning views and refreshed by the purity of the moorland air.

The lady from Pickering said, "Those 'urdles shelter t'sheep from t'snow in winter and in t'grouse-shooting season men with guns conceal themselves be'ind em. In t'early days train and t'carriages, which were converted stagecoach bodies fitted on a chassis with iron wheels, 'ad to be pulled up 'ere by 'orses and passengers 'ad to disembark and walk alongside. Just up theer behind t'ridge of Wheeldale Moor, there's a wide, two miles long bit o' roadway called Wade's Causeway or T'Auld Wife's Trod. It's sixteen feet wide (5m.), paved with sandstone and pebbles and it follows t'line of an auld Roman road."

Beside the single-track line the sun glinted off the clear purling waters of the lovely Pickering Beck as the lady said to Mam, "At times, when it's swollen by t'run-off from t'peaty moors after heavy rain, it's a deep brown in colour, like cold tea. The word beck comes from the Norse 'bekk', meaning a stream and in these parts a small waterfall is called a foss." A little further on, to the east, lay the huge natural amphitheatre called the Hole of Horcum. The line skirted this strange but natural phenomenon that was quarter of a mile across and four hundred feet deep (130m). Mam said, "I've heard about that. Some call it The Devil's Punchbowl and local legend has it that, Wade, an angry Anglo-Saxon giant, was having a row with his wife, Bell. He scooped out a handful of earth to throw at her and left this deep depression and, having missed her, the resulting heap of soil formed the high hill called Blakey Topping a mile or so further east." She then frightened us by adding, "Some say it was the devil himself who dug out the great hollow." The deep grooves near the bottom looked to me like gigantic fingermarks. Round here nature was wild and untamed and perched high up on the eastern flank of the marshy hollow Mam pointed out the old *Saltergate Inn*, saying, "The Devil was once trapped in its kitchen and a peat fire was lit to keep him in and it has been kept alight ever since."

My imagination ran riot and I prayed that the fire would never go out. In reality, the 'Hole' had been formed by the power of glacial melt-waters and collapsed springs following the last ice age. Above it masses of blooming heather turned the rolling moorland purple with tall sere grasses and reed clumps standing out in fawn and umber. I glimpsed isolated stone cottages and farmhouses and the beauty and serenity of it all took my breath away.

After skirting the high bluff of Pickering Moor the train began a long gradual descent. In places the steep sides of beautiful Newtondale rose up to about 450 feet (146m.) and the lady said that in the old days the trains had rolled down here under their own gravitational pull. The slopes of the deep and lonely gorge were clothed in lovely trees and shrubs and Mam said, "I've never seen such glorious autumn tints." The beauty of this remote eleven miles long stretch made a powerful impression on my young mind. I was seeing Mother Nature in her natural state and her clean vibrant colours and leafy grandeur contrasted so sharply with the grime of our mucky neighbourhood. As the train thundered on by Forestry Commission conifer plantations, Mam said "Those trees were planted in the same year you were born."

Steaming onwards we passed close to a flat area on the eastern side of the line where a derelict, partly overgrown, track bed led off to mounds of fallen stone. The area was gradually being colonised by grass, weeds and scrub as Mother Nature slowly reclaimed her ravaged flesh. An old dried up reservoir overlooked the former mine workings and ruined stone buildings. There was an air of neglect and melancholy about the place and fragments of rotten wood swung back and forth on creaking, rusty hinges. The ugly scars were sad reminders showing where the bowels of the earth had been ripped open and turned out in the frantic search for iron ore; the ore on which my hometown's very existence had once depended. Close by an old 50 feet (15.2m) tall, stone chimney, that had once been an airshaft for the underground workings, still dominated the skyline. It was demolished for safety reasons some twenty-one years later and the stones and rubble were used to fill in the 300 feet (91m.) deep pit shaft.

I was to learn later that a successful entrepreneur of the time, James Walker of Leeds, had set up the enterprise. He had put a great deal of his time and money into it but, in 1866, after years of hard work for little return, it failed. In an unfortunate series of storms, the mine and its expensive machinery was repeatedly flooded. High above on the cliffs stood a dark, derelict, square tower, which seemed to teeter on the very brink of the precipice. The elderly lady said, "Yon ruin is Skelton Tower. It's all that's left of an old shooting lodge that once 'ad stables on its ground floor. It were built for an allegedly dissolute reverend gentleman of that name."

The train began to slow by a tall white signal post at the point where the single line became a double track and we passed over a narrow level crossing by a wooden coal storage hut. We then rumbled over a wide wooden-gated level crossing that stood close to a tall, brick-built, signal box that had small-paned, blast-taped windows. Just past the ticket office, we pulled in alongside the neat and tidy stone platform of a little station called Levisham Halt. On the platform were a couple of paraffin lamps mounted on cast iron posts that had been freshly painted in cream and maroon.

A few people got off and, as the red and white arm of the signal went up, we continued on our journey. Crossing over the points, the double line became single track again for the next six miles and the train rattled southwards on a long flat straight stretch bordered by the tree covered slopes of Blansby Park. Here the valley widened out and the track had several bends and we could lean out of the window and see the steam and smoke-shrouded engine and, in the other direction, the guard's van. High above stood the curtain walls of Pickering Castle.

Pickering Beck was always in sight and we finally rumbled over it and into Pickering Station where a wooden newspaper and magazine kiosk stood at the end of a long platform. The walls and doorways were piled high with sandbags that almost reached the glass roof. The great black engine gave out a long echoing hoot as, with an agonised squeal of brakes amid billowing clouds of steam, it slowly clinked and clanked to a halt. To a staccato clattering of carriage doors, we climbed down onto the platform to be met at W.H. Smith's bookstall by Miss Florence Thorne, the auburn-haired, middle-aged matron of the new nursery school who had travelled down from Middlesbrough a week or so before to get things organised.

We followed her slim figure out of the station through a wrought-iron gate to a single-decked motor coach where the driver loaded our cases and we set off. My friend, Eric, was on the seat behind us as the coach turned right at the level crossing and travelled west on the main road through the villages of Middleton and Wrelton and then north to the pretty little village of Cropton. After passing the *New Inn*, the road forked to either side of a large chestnut tree with a low wooden seat encircling the wide girth of its gnarled old trunk. Miss Thorne said to Mam, "The local gentry and landowners used to assemble here prior to the start of the Sinnington foxhunt, which was a regular event before the war. They met here in their brightly coloured jackets, riding breeches and hard black hats to partake of the traditional stirrup cup at the Inn over there."

Bearing left onto the Rosedale road, we travelled down Cropton Bank with, on our right, a grassy mound that was once the site of a Norman motte-and-bailey castle. Heading north, we passed through a pleasant river valley lined with sunlit meadows and hedges close to the weir at the confluence of the river Seven and Sutherland Beck near Blackpark Lodge cottage. There were two other mothers on the coach with their children as we drove up the narrow country road for another four miles, passing the Inn at Hartoft End on our right. Beautiful spruce and pine-clad slopes rose up on our right-hand side before we pulled in at the large inn on the square in the grey, stone-built village of Rosedale Abbey. Small groups of people were waiting as Miss Thorne, the mothers and a few of the children got off and the driver collected their bags and cases from the luggage compartment. I was quite upset to see that my pal, Eric, was one of them. However, young children adapt quite quickly and I soon got over it.

After a few minutes of talk and introductions, Miss Thorne got back onto the coach and we went back the way we had come. Near Blackpark Lodge a wooden gate led onto a narrow stony road that passed between the tall sentry-like conifers whose tangy aroma scented the air. At the side of the tree-shaded track - that led up to a large, stone-built farmstead called Spiers House - small brightly coloured birds darted about. We climbed ever upwards through the hushed beauty and solitude of the forest until the coach turned right by the big farmhouse that stood in an open area of wide grassy meadows. Crossing over a stream we turned right again to travel south along yet another stony track. It was a gloriously sunny early autumn afternoon and sunlight filtered down to lose itself in the depths of the dense, dank forest.

Sutherland Lodge in the 1940s; bothy to the right of the house.

Climbing up from a gurgling runnel the track passed between hundreds of densely packed green giants that stood as tall and straight as guardsmen. Tiny black and brown birds with a striking white nape patches flitted in and out and Miss Thorne said, "Those shy little birds that you see there are coal tits."
Halfway down it a short track led eastwards to the rear entrance of Sutherland Lodge some three-quarters of a mile from Spiers House.

A short gravelled drive, big enough for a car to turn round on, ran along the back of the house that had no formal gardens as such. There was just the odd grassy area to the south and east, otherwise it was hemmed in on all sides by the deep, dark vastness of the silent forest.

On our arrival, the driver unloaded our luggage and carried it through an old nail-studded oaken door leaving it in the passageway. From here a narrow servant's staircase led straight upwards and a door on the left led into a large kitchen. We were warmly welcomed and shown round by the deputy Matron Miss Rosemary Waters, a tall well-made young woman with short fair wavy hair that was parted in the middle. Mam told us later that she was the daughter of a doctor in Liverpool. Mam was shown around the huge old-fashioned kitchen at the eastern end of the house where there was a large well-scrubbed wooden table in the middle of its stone flagged floor. A large and heavy-looking, dark-coloured Welsh dresser stood against the back wall and a wide stone fireplace and chimneybreast occupied most of the gable end. In front of it was a range of fire irons and an old wooden rocking chair stood to one side.

"Ere I'll 'elp thee with thy baggage." said an elderly, bow-legged man. Mam then left to go off with the man who was wearing a soft, checked flatcap; a waistcoat; riding breeches and leather gaiters. We learned that he was called Spaven and he carried her luggage along an earthen path that led through the trees to her lodgings. Mam said later that the trees had a tangy smell similar to carbolic soap. Between them she caught glimpses of lovely wooded hills stretching away into the distance. She was to lodge in an old stone farmworker's cottage, called Keldy Cottage, which stood in a forest clearing about a mile away. Her cosy bedroom lay directly beneath the red pantiles of its steeply sloping roof and she said that the view from her dormer window was magnificent. Spaven, who took care of Mrs Stancliffe's horses, lived with his daughter and her husband in a large stone house at the far side of the meadow to the east of Sutherland Lodge. It had been the estate gamekeeper's house at the turn of the century. In time, we learned that Spaven was a little too fond of visiting the local hostelries and he sometimes arrived back a bit tipsy after sampling the potent 'ale' available at the *New Inn* at Cropton and we would see him reeling around like the top of a spruce tree in a gale. He was a smallish man of medium build and it was said that he thought more of his beloved horses than he did of people. He was convinced that they were sometimes plagued by witches saying, " T'osses 'ave bin found first thing in t'morning agitated and lathered in sweat after bein' 'ag-ridden durin' t'neet." As a preventative measure he hung small stones that had a natural hole through them above each of the stalls. These were known locally as hagstones.

Although we were to see Mam every day, she was kept very busy in the kitchen, but on most days she would stay with us for a while when her work was done. We were taken to her cottage on her off-duty days and this helped us to adapt more readily to the sudden changes in our life, but in the early days, we cried a lot when she was obliged to leave us.

Sutherland Lodge with its impressive double gabled ivy clad frontage stood on rising ground and had magnificent views to the south. It overlooked dense green forests, rolling countryside and the green fields round Cropton way. The eaves of the house had intricately carved bargeboards with a series of alternating diamond and bow shapes cut into them along their whole length. Slender delicately carved wooden finials crowned the apexes of the gable ends with, below them, a matching, inverted finial. High up on the gable at the western end there was the gauntleted, forearm of a knight grasping a short dagger on a stone shield with the word PERSE engraved below it. It was probably the crest and motto of a noble family, with the word meaning 'perseverance'. We would need a good deal of that in the times to come.

Three stone steps led up to a pair of studded solid-oak doors with ornate wrought iron hinges that were flanked by stone buttresses. Above them an elegantly carved Gothic arch framed a lead-latticed, stained-glass window with a leafy stemmed rose (the flower of secrets) in the centre of it. A pair of finely carved, but grotesque, winged gargoyles - which always frightened me - jutted out on either side of it. At the side there was an old-fashioned, brass bell pull and directly above the doorway there was a slim, stone-mullioned, three-sided, oriel window.

Kitty (in old age) in the Gargoyle doorway, Sutherland Lodge.

A wide gravelled drive ran along the front of the house and we were told that the upper west wing was for the exclusive use of the resident Stancliffe family. From the drive, a wide flight of steps flanked by low stone walls led down to a rustic fence that surrounded an open paddock where a couple of horses were contentedly grazing on the meadow grass that was still lush and green.

Part of the house had been requisitioned on behalf of the Middlesbrough Borough Council to be used as a nursery school for evacuee children below school age. It was about a mile and a half north east of Cropton as the crow flies but, in reality, it was three miles or so by road and Forestry track. It stood in a small clearing at the southern edge of the vast Cropton Forest where English kings had once hunted deer and wild boar.

Much of the land had been in the care of the Forestry Commission since 1930 and they had provided much needed work for the local people and others who came here from other parts of the country. A huge area of land had been planted with conifers, although many of the indigenous trees remained and rhododendron shrubs grew in profusion along the edges of the forest tracks. Our new home (built in 1870) had originally been a shooting lodge belonging to a Lieutenant Colonel Daniel Thompson, a retired veteran of the Crimean War.

The fine three-storey stone building, with its eleven-bedrooms, had later been the property of the Ringer family who were much involved with fox hunting and grouse shooting. They had made good use of the long range of stables and kennels that stood to the east of the house but most were now unused. A couple of the stables housed the horses of the present owners, Captain and Mrs J. Stancliffe, who had bought the house between the wars. They were deeply involved in local church and village affairs and regularly attended committee meetings, although Mrs Stancliffe's husband, like so many others, was away serving with the army.

Mrs Stancliffe, a refined and attractive middle-aged lady with dark curly hair, was always kind, gentle and ladylike in her dealings with the nursery. We thought her very posh as her daughters Susan, aged seventeen, and Rosemary, aged fifteen, were away at a private boarding school. Her parents lived in the family residence called

High Hall in the pretty village of Thornton-le-Dale two miles to the east of Pickering, where her mother was a leading light in the local Red Cross and Women's Institute. They owned several farms and a good deal of the land in the area.

Mrs Stancliffe employed a young German Jew as her housekeeper and her living quarters were in the topmost room of the ivy-covered tower. To me it seemed like a scene from a fairytale. Apparently she had recently been reported for letting a light show after dark as the blackout regulations were being strictly enforced and a light had been spotted at her high narrow window. Malicious rumours concerning the Jews were circulating in some quarters and there were real fears of infiltration by secret agents. Stories concerning the unseen presence of German sympathisers were 'going the rounds' and the press called these fifth columnists 'the enemy within'. It was said that they not only sympathised with, but were also prepared to work actively for, the enemy and suspicion became greater if they were German nationals. This atmosphere of mistrust may have had a bearing on the governess being reported and she was fined and sternly reprimanded at Pickering Magistrates Court.

Within a few months all German nationals were to be classed as aliens and interned. Most were kept behind barbed wire patrolled by armed soldiers in requisitioned hotels and guesthouses on the Isle of Man while their credentials were examined, but most turned out to be genuine refugees escaping Nazi persecution.

Mother had had a good deal of experience as a domestic servant, having worked for middle class families in a number of large residences over the past ten years. This stood her in good stead as she assisted Mrs Winnie Ruonne, an excellent cook who always managed to feed us well even in those increasingly austere times. She was a small plumpish lady with small-features and a pale freckled complexion and we always called her Dinner Lady. She was actually a middle-aged woman but her round baby-face made her seem much younger. She always wore a white wrap-over pinafore and a white, elasticated mobcap that hid most of her gingerish-coloured hair, which she plaited into a thick pigtail, that hung down her back.

Her husband was a railwayman, who lived in a cottage close to Pinchinthorpe Station, some forty miles away near the old market town of Guisborough on the edge of the North Yorkshire Moors. His cottage lay in the lee of Roseberry Topping, a 1,057 feet high, formerly round-topped hill, the peak of which had literally been 'under-mined' some years earlier. Miners digging for sandstone, jet and ironstone caused it to collapse leaving a steep cliff face on its western side that, from a distance, made it look like a Roman soldier's helmet.

Dinner Lady saved up her off duty days so that she could go and stay with her husband from time to time and they had a young daughter called Mary living in Pickering. Mam and Dinner Lady worked happily together in the cosy warmth of the kitchen where there was a large open stone fireplace and a Yorkist range of cream coloured, enamel-coated ovens. They rose early and were in the kitchen getting things ready for breakfast long before we got up. As the porridge bubbled away in a huge pan the great black kettle steamed on the hob and the distinctive mouth-watering aroma of homemade bread and cakes often permeated the whole house.

Across the corridor from the kitchen was a large well-stocked storage cupboard with its shelves full of tins of ham, soup, baked beans and the like. There were even 7lb tins of bully beef in it. At the other end of the kitchen there was a walk-in scullery and a large copper for washing the masses of dirty laundry that we produced every day. A local woman used to come in on a Monday to do this and she came the following day to do the ironing. Whole days were set aside for particular domestic tasks at that time.

A doorway led out into the side yard and diagonally across the yard there was a stone-built coal store and the garage, where Mrs Stancliffe's kept her big shiny-black Humber car. Next to it was a tack room with a converted bothy on the floor above, and beyond that lay the stables and kennels. It was not until many years later that I learned that the sensuously curving pantiles on the roofs had been brought to this country from Holland as ballast in the old sailing ships. On the end of the kitchen there was a small lean-to conservatory with a few tomato plants still growing in it.

On my first night I was put into one of eight small beds set up in the large ground floor dormitory that had a polished wooden floor and no carpets. There was a small rug by each bed and a wooden frame covered in a layer of thick black material was placed over the windows at dusk. It took me a long time to get to sleep and, in the dead of night, I woke with a start not knowing where I was, I felt lost and frightened in the unfamiliar blackness and had the urge to go to the 'lav' (as we always called the toilet). Trying desperately to 'hold on', I searched under the bed for the po (chamber pot) only to find there wasn't one. I had not been there long enough to know the whereabouts of the bathroom and, in any case, there had always been a smelly po (often called a jerry) under our bed at home; a necessary evil as the 'lav' was outside. When we went for a pee or a kack during the day we always said, "I'm just going down the yard." Unable to hold it any longer I wet the bed and, fearful of the consequences, I cowered under the covers on the damp warmth of the saturated sheets. These were going cold as I lay there full of shame and guilt and I thought the reek of ammonia must surely be noticed and I would be found out, but nothing happened. I lay there choking on the fumes that rose from the stinking palliasse wishing it would go away but, like me, it had nowhere else to go. Trembling with cold, I tried to smother my sobs in the now wet pillow. I lay there - a lonely home sick ashamed four-year-old who badly needed his mother - shivering in the darkness for what seemed like hours until, exhausted, I dozed off wrapped uneasily in a ragged veil of sleep.

The following morning, when 'my crime' was discovered, nothing was said and I was bathed and dressed by Miss Waters who was a caring, sympathetic and likeable young woman. The thin mattresses on our small metal framed beds were filled with straw and chaff and were, fortunately, easily emptied, washed, dried and refilled and when Mam came to work that morning and learned of my 'accident' she gave me a big cuddle, a hug, and a kiss.

"I couldn't help it Mam, it just came." I mumbled tearfully.

"Never mind darling, just forget about it. Things will soon get better." she said in her consoling way. It was not an unusual occurrence, nevertheless, I was to live with the guilt and shame of it for some time to come.

A few days later the gaunt-featured and prim Miss Thorne took George and me to have our hair cut in Pickering. Her auburn hair, parted on the right, was severely tied back giving her a stern appearance but she was nice to us although firm when necessary. Spaven brought out and yoked up the trap. In retrospect, his surname seemed a little inappropriate for a man in charge of horses as the word 'spavin' is defined as 'disease or distension on the inside of the hock of a horse'. Miss Thorne sat with us in the trap, owned by the well-to-do Stancliffes but it was always readily available for our use, and she referred to it as a Governess cart.

It was our first time in a pony and trap and we loved it as we sat on the hard, wooden side seats of the highly polished carriage. The wooden-spoked wheels were twice my height and the burnished brass rail at the front gleamed in the autumn sunshine as Spaven busied himself with the harness of the pony. As we set off the rhythmic rippling of its sleek, glistening flanks fascinated me as the muscular haunches twitched constantly and it swished its long tail about to stop the swarms of tormenting, stinging gadflies from settling. The sharp resinous tang of pine-scented air mingled with the faint leathery smell of horse.

We travelled on a different route this time, and as we headed south on the long straight forest tracks, we sat quietly drinking in the stillness and gazing at the dark luxuriant greenery as we watched the small red squirrels collecting nuts and cones to store up for the winter. The forest was mostly made up of sentinel-like spruce trees with greyish-brown flaky bark, but the pine trees had more deeply fissured, crusty-looking trunks. The brooding stillness was broken only by the gentle rustling of leaves and the rhythmic and leisurely clip-clop of the iron-shod hooves of the sleek brown-haired mare. A slight autumnal haze hung over the leafy vale and we could hear the soft murmuring of a beck. Spaven said, "It rises at a spring two and a 'alf miles from 'ere up Raindale way and runs into t't big dammed lake up by Elleron Lodge and from there it flows a mile or so through t'forest to this point."

The bay mare crossed the sparkling beck at a shallow ford, or the water-splash as we called it, beside which was a stone footbridge with white handrails. The ford nestled in the depths of a small valley and a little way past it, to the right, a path led up to Kelton Banks Farm. "Mr Ward owns that farm." Spaven told Miss Thorne. "It used to belong t't' Sparks family before they moved in to Cropton and they keep several Shire 'osses stabled theer. They do various jobs on t'farm as well as pullin' t'snowplough, which is kept in readiness in case it's needed locally durin' t'winter. Less than six yeers back we 'ad t'worst snowstorm in livin' memory and most o't'villages were cut off for weeks on end."

The narrow twisting road climbed up a steep bank between tall, overgrown hedgerows before we turned right on to the Cawthorn-Cropton road, which was known locally as Cropton High Lane. We travelled for a few hundred yards beside wild briar bushes that were heavily laden with blushing hips. "In t'winter months this road often gets blocked by deep snowdrifts," said Spaven. As we got closer to Cropton the tightly packed conifers gave way to mixed woodland interspersed with ploughed fields and grassy meadows. We turned left into the top end of Cropton village and on our right a narrow earthen track led up a grassy slope to the church gate. Behind it lay an old graveyard with its grassy hummocks and leaning headstones clustered around the pretty parish church in which Mrs Stancliffe was a Sunday school teacher - as Mam had been at home.

We thoroughly enjoyed that lovely carriage drive of about eight miles and the sights and scents of the countryside kept us entranced. The leaves whispered in the gentle breeze with the odd one spiralling silently down and Miss Thorne called them 'harbingers of autumn'. The trees seemed, to me, to be sad at their loss. Apples were ripening in the orchards and blackberries hung in red clusters in the hedgerows. Once in the small market town of Pickering we were taken up Potter Hill and as we walked past the Memorial Hall, Spaven told us that, "It were formerly a corn mill. Two and a 'alf yeers back the abdication of Edward the Eighth were proclaimed from t'wide steps ower yonder. Lots o't'local lads joined Territorial Army or one o't'voluntary Defence Services 'ere and the Green Howards, who were granted freedom o't'town not long back, 'ave a camp just up t'road."

We walked over the level crossing and up the hill to the old stone building called The Vaults where Fred Pickering's barbershop was at one end and the rest of it was Turnbull's Animal Feed Store. Spaven informed Miss Thorne, "Fred's dad, also called Fred, were a barber in t'town for many yeers and t'aud building were originally

74

a bank and then a spirit vault for t'Scarborough and Whitby Brewery." It stood on 'an island' at the top of the Market Place with the pathway going right round it and we had our hair cut in the bobbed style of those days. The barber put an enamelled tin bowl on my head and cut up to it and I vaguely recall the masculine scents of bay rum hair oil and shaving soap. I remember the click and snip-snip of the scissors as my fair locks tumbled to the floor and as we came out the old, octagonal-shaped clock on the square, church tower struck four. The slim, weather-cocked spire of St. Peter and St. Paul's church pointed skywards and below it, over the porch, a sundial had the date 1817. We giggled when we were told that the top part of Potter Hill, facing east, was once called High Backside. We were taken to the Central Café that was above a tobacconist's shop just across the road and were treated to a lovely iced fairy cake with half a glazed cherry on it, and a glass of orange fizz.

The long fine sunny spell came to an end and October was very wet with heavy and persistent rain that rushed down the forest runnels to swell the waters of Sutherland Beck. The streams became engorged to overflowing as the seemingly endless rains drained down from the saturated uplands. As the appalling weather continued unabated the once shallow beck became a deep, raging torrent that raced down the narrow valley to join the roiling waters of the seven-mile stretch of the river Seven. Now in full spate, its source was high up on Danby Head on Glaisdale Moor.

Lower down it became a man-deep torrent that angrily thundered, foamed and surged southwards threatening to sweep away the picturesque old footbridge at Nutholme. This small, wooden, suspension bridge spanned the turbulent waters close to the former home of William Scoresby. Miss Thorne told us that, "In the late 18th Century, he had set out on the long walk across the wild, open moors to Whitby where he found fame as a captain on the whaling ships and devised the first crow's nest as a lookout point near the top of the tall wooden masts. He was a seaman, an explorer and a scientist and wrote a notable book on the North Polar whaling industry but, gave it all up to become a humble village curate and a preacher." Further downstream the muddy, engorged river caused extensive flooding when it burst its banks in the low-lying area around the village of Sinnington.

On those cold, dark and dreary days the staff kept the paraffin lamps lit all day and the doors and windows were kept tightly shut as the incessant rain lashed against and streamed down the windowpanes. The wind howled, rattling the tall sash window frames as it boomed and echoed in the wide, stone chimneys. The lashing rain saturated the land and clattered on to the portico roof making the glass sing before it rushed down to flow along the old cast iron guttering. It drip-dripped interminably from the trees and bounced high in the puddles, as the packed soil of the pathways became sodden and slowly turned to ooze.

4. Little Man You've Had A Busy Day

Around that time two new twenty-year-olds called Catherine Todd and her friend, Mary, joined the nursery staff. Ten years earlier, when Catherine was only ten, her mother had died in the family home at Berwick and she was sent with her younger sister to a children's home in Scarborough. After leaving school she worked as a housemaid in Leeds, then in the early thirties, she got a job as a housemaid at Queen Margaret's Girls School for well-bred, young ladies on Filey Road, Scarborough. It was a private school: a kind of finishing school for the well-off where she became a close friend of another maid who came from Middlesbrough. Mary, a tall, slim, dark-haired girl, went home on holiday taking Catherine with her. The family was living on Cannon Street when war was declared and the pair went to a Keep Fit session at The Settlement Club where they heard that staff were urgently required. They applied and in early October were delighted to learn that they had obtained posts at Sutherland Lodge. Catherine was 5 feet 4 inches (163 cms.) - quite tall for a young woman in those days - slim, fit and attractive with soft mousy hair (with a 'kink' in it) that rested on her shoulders.

The two young women really loved children and, from the outset, Catherine used to sing us to sleep at night after tucking us in and giving us a hug and a kiss. These little gestures of affection were much appreciated by the children who, like me, were so far away from home. She used to sing a song that began, "Little man your crying, I know why you're blue." and went on to say, "Time to go to sleep now, little man you've had a busy day." Another part went, " You've been playing soldiers, the battle has been won; the enemy is out of sight. Come along that soldier put away your gun, the war is over for tonight." It continued with, "Ship ahoy little sailor your bound for Blanket Bay, the Isle of Dreams is now in sight" and "Time you should be dreaming, little man you've had a busy day." It ended with, "God bless you darling and goodnight." but by that time we were usually fast asleep. I learned later that the lyrics were from a song recorded by Kitty Masters - a popular and well-known singer of the time - who was a vocalist with Henry Hall's BBC Dance Orchestra. During the thirties the band, with its signature tune of *Here's to the Next Time*, was often heard on the wireless and we called Catherine 'Kitty' from that time on.

We took to her and came to love her and she returned our love a hundredfold. She turned out to be a sensible, capable and level headed young woman who believed that children are precious and should be protected and loved if they are to become stable adults. When we had to stay indoors Kitty kept us entertained and happily occupied playing music, singing and dancing for us and her youthful exuberance and enthusiastic nature ensured that we did not mope or brood about home too much. She kept us busy drawing and playing with wooden blocks, toys and games and she devised guessing games that lifted our spirits and encouraged us to think for ourselves. When we were with her we scarcely noticed the rain that fell pitilessly day after dull, dismal day.

North side of the bothy in 2003.

The cosy day room was in the bothy on the floor above the tack room and in it we sat on tiny wooden chairs that were arranged in a circle around her. In times long past, the bothy was the place in which the unmarried farmhands used to sleep and eat and to get to it we had to go up a narrow wooden staircase and through a door to the left of the landing. A nice log fire burned in the grate of the open stone fireplace behind a wire-mesh fireguard and on the green-painted, wood panelling of the dividing wall there were brightly coloured pictures of children at play. A row of five tall, elegant, mullioned windows faced north and beyond the garage, the stables and the soggy meadow the deep dark forest crowded round us in all directions.

Mary and Kitty read to us and we learned to chant 'Incy Wincy Spider' and many others popular nursery rhymes. We sang children's songs like *Twinkle Twinkle Little Star*; *I Had A Little Nut Tree* and Hickory, *Dickory Dock* and I particularly enjoyed singing "You push the damper in and you pull the damper out and the smoke goes up the chimlee (as we called a chimney) just the same" at the top of our voices. We made atishoo sounds and flopped down giggling when the music stopped as we played 'Ring-a-Ring-a-Roses', never realising that we were re-enacting the sneezing that was a symptom of the bubonic plague that three hundred years back had caused thousands of tragic and painful deaths.

At other times Kitty read us stories from *Aesop's Fables*, *Grimm's Fairy Tales* and *The Arabian Nights*, that told of wicked giants, flitting fairies, fearsome ogres, fire-breathing dragons and the like. There were men in turbans wearing slippers that curled up at the toes and huge genies that came out of little oil lamps and little children got lost in deep forests and were in danger of being eaten up by gnarled old witches. Our reactions to them told Kitty much about us and the tales helped us to learn right from wrong.

In the cosy warmth of the dayroom I felt loved and secure but some of the tales frightened and thrilled me at the same time. I would sit there wide-eyed, totally engrossed and enraptured by Kitty's lilting and mesmerising voice as her stories weaved their magic spell. Sitting there transfixed and wide-eyed, I soaked up their atmosphere like a sponge and I will be forever grateful to Kitty who was one of the first to fire my young and vivid imagination. From that time on - in my mind - I was able to transport myself into enchanted realms as she had given me the key that opened the door to fantastic new worlds and hidden treasures.

The room across the landing contained several small, camp beds, each with a feather-filled pillow and a straw-filled palliasse. There were white cotton sheets and warm woollen blankets on every bed and the row of tall, narrow windows were shuttered against the fury of the raging tempest. The regular routine of The Settlement Nursery School was continued here and we were kissed and tucked in bed for a nap every day after our midday meal, which we ate at the tiny tables in the day room. We always called it dinner and never lunch because we had been brought up to believe that only posh people called the midday meal lunch or luncheon. Every time we turned over in our little beds the hooked wire springs made a metallic, twanging sound and this, of course, encouraged us to try to outdo each other to see who could make the most noise until we got a telling off.

Sometimes, after Kitty had read scary stories to us, I could not get them out of my mind, and I was reluctant to be laid down. The low, dancing flame of the paraffin lamps threw out a soft light and had a distinctive smell but the guttering candle threw grotesque, shifting shadows and, where they were deepest, I 'saw' horrible monsters and weird phantoms lurking, flitting and floating. Stifling my terrified whimpers I would curl up under the bedclothes and try to shut them out. Were they the product of an overactive mind or due to some trick created by the light and shade?

Upstairs in the main house, there was a spacious bathroom with a large white enamelled bath enclosed within highly polished, wooden side panels and in its capacious depths Kitty and Mary bathed us every night. Kitty always dipped her elbow in it to check that the water temperature was not too hot and one child was bathed while another was being dried. We were then put to bed, either in the large downstairs dormitory in the west wing of the house, or in a smaller room above the kitchen, in which Kitty slept. Here she was able to keep an eye on four kiddies - usually those that required more care or supervision than the rest. I enjoyed the climb up the narrow, back staircase to that little bedroom and I liked sleeping there, as I always felt more comfortable and secure with her around. The room had once been used as living quarters for the maids that worked in the grandeur of the old country house.

At bath times, Kitty and Mary had been told by Miss Thorne to examine our heads for lice and to check our bodies for signs of scabies. This happened more often after a puny little child arrived from a slum area of Middlesbrough where he had contracted scabies after sharing a bed with an infected person. He was showing the classic symptoms of the nasty and unsightly, contagious skin disease that was quite common in those days. It was caused by a female parasite, the itch mite (Acarus scabiei), which burrows into the skin to lay its eggs. When the eggs hatch, the small mites, in their turn, burrow through the skin, usually at night, causing red, papular eruptions that itch severely. The eruptions occur most commonly in the webs of the fingers, on the wrists and buttocks and in the groin; hence the examinations. When the child scratches a secondary infection is liable to occur often leading to impetigo.

The little boy was kept apart from us to prevent the disease spreading and was given hot baths in a small bathroom off the downstairs passageway. Kitty had to scrub his back and buttocks to lay open the lesions and we could hear him crying pitifully throughout this painful process. But she had to be cruel to be kind and, if it had not been done, further complications could have arisen. A yellow emulsion called benzyl benzoate was then very gently applied and the messy stuff, which covered a good part of the skinny boy's little body from the neck downwards, took about ten minutes to dry. A second application was applied the next day to make certain that the mites had been killed off. Her heart went out to him, but the disease was caught early enough to prevent impetigo and he soon recovered and Kitty often hugged and cuddled him in the days and weeks that followed.

By Halloween the rains eased a little and were succeeded by thick clinging white mists that often lingered all day. The trees of my 'enchanted forest' looked spooky in the dim, dreary light and the bushes became indistinct and assumed nebulous and ghostly shapes. The raw, chilly fogs that shrouded the damp and drearily dripping forest were known locally as roaks. Kitty and Rosemary entertained us with games with apples suspended on a string, which we tried to bite, or we played at apple bobbing where we tried to get one from a barrel of water using only our mouths. She dressed us up as witches, ghouls, ghosts and vampires and made lanterns from hollowed-out turnips, the fleshy insides of which were not wasted: they were kept and cooked for dinner the following day. It was scary in the darkness of the bothy with the lights out and we were glad when they lit the candles in the hollowed out turnips.

I felt sad on seeing the number of trees that had been brought down by the gales as I looked on the fallen giants as my friends. On the afternoon of November the fifth the gardener built us a bonfire from tree cuttings and deadwood and Mam told me that, "In the distant past bones were burned to ward off evil spirits, hence the name bonfires."

We were only allowed to have a fire during the hours of daylight and the fallen softwood branches and twigs, known locally as 'kids', spit and burned well due to the resin in them. Once the fire was well established we roasted jacket potatoes and the delicious, golden butter dripped down onto our chins and bibs. The fire had to be put out before dusk, which arrived just before teatime at that time of the year. We then sat in the semi-darkness of the bothy and watched wide-eyed as Kitty lit sparklers and a small box of indoor fireworks that were the Stancliffe family's 'leftovers' from the previous year. Soon all fireworks were banned completely.

Kitty was well able to cope with most of our childish problems and small emergencies and she had an uncanny knack of knowing when things were troubling us. She got to thinking and started to get us up to go to the toilet during the night, thus greatly reducing the bed-wetting. The weak and pitiful little boy (the runt of his family) who had had scabies used to tremble and shake on being taken from his bed during the chilly nights and Kitty felt so sorry for him. She would often wrap a warm blanket round his thin little body and hug him close until he settled and she lavished on him that little bit of extra love and attention that she knew we all so desperately needed.

With the air heavy with the odours of cabbage and onions, we would often catch sight of Mam in the kitchen amid great clouds of steam. There was a constant clatter of pots and pans and rich, fragrant smells of tasty, savoury stews often assailed our nostrils making our mouths water. As she baked fresh bread and cakes, her hands were often white with flour and we came to associate her presence with the aroma of lovely food. More often than not when I saw her, she was smiling and she had a way of tilting her head as she spoke. She was to stay with us for just a few, short, precious weeks but it had to come to an end and, as the time for her to leave drew near, there was a deep sadness in her speech, which is often the case before a parting. Her face was often red and blotchy from crying but we never saw the tears that undoubtedly dripped into the stew.

She knew that we were being well fed and looked after and had settled in well and that pleased her, but sadly for George and me, she was obliged to go. On the day of her departure there was much hugging and crying on both sides and she tried to hide her tears but I could see the slight movement of her throat as she swallowed them. She was unable to afford the rent on Keldy Cottage for any length of time even though she had managed to sub rent our house in Middlesbrough while she was away. But she now felt that she should be there when Dad got a forty-eight hour pass, as the train journeys were too slow for him to come here. Her doubts and fears remained unspoken and we were told much later that leaving us had broken her heart, but she knew in her heart of hearts that she had done the right thing in getting us away to safety.

That was the bad news. The good news was that my pal Eric had rejoined us, as for some reason, he had failed to settle, and I was delighted that he was back. Three mothers and eleven children from Hull had been evacuated to the former ironstone-mining village and all of them had returned home within the space of two weeks. Eric's mam, Winifred, who mother knew quite well, said to her, "Rosedale Abbey is in a lovely setting but it's bleak and remote. Eric was billeted with a Mrs Dowsland at a big stone-built place called Abbey House and just after he got there I got a letter from her. In it she said that Eric was a nice little fellow and she asked for his birth certificate. During the recent wet spell she asked me to send him a pair of Wellington boots and when the parcel arrived she said that his face had been a picture. He was thrilled to bits at the thought of wearing them, as he would now be able to help her to get the ducks in. That Sunday they had duck for dinner and Eric asked her if it came from Albert Park in Middlesbrough. That was the only place that he had ever seen ducks before."

Not long afterwards, as we were playing outside on our tricycles, the garage doors were stood open and there was a damp, musty smell from within it as Mr Bentley - Mrs Stancliffe's chauffeur - polished the car. At that point something exciting caught our attention and we dashed off into the playroom to see what was happening but Eric had forgotten his trike leaving it by the garage doors. He was devastated to find that the car had been backed out flattening it and scratching the gleaming, chromium plating on the car's rear bumper. The trike was a wreck and he was lucky that he hadn't been sat on it at the time

It was around this time that we were told by Miss Thorne that, if the Germans came, they might use 'nasty smells to make us feel ill' and we had to practice putting on our newly issued Mickey Mouse gas masks. They had a bright red, rubber bit at the front and the circular eyepieces had blue rims but some of the children were frightened of them and hated the choking, claustrophobic feeling and the rubbery smell. Eric and I thought it was just a funny game and we collapsed in fits of giggling when the red floppy bit fluttered as we breathed in and out.

There were large storerooms and wine cellars beneath the house, which were reached through a doorway in the kitchen that led to a flight of stone steps. The cellars, with their whitewashed walls, were always cool, during both the summer and the winter and many foods, such as cheeses, apples, salted sides of ham and jars of preserves, were stored down there. There were no fridges in those days and eggs were preserved in buckets of isinglass, a kind of gelatine that was obtained from fish. Kitty assured us that if we were bombed or attacked from the air we would be quite safe down there. However, I always had an illogical fear of what might lurk in the darkness down the steps behind that spooky cellar door.

In mid December it turned bitterly cold with severe frosts. The muddy ruts of the forest paths became as solid as rock and light snow flurries drifted down from time to time. On duty the nursery assistants wore a thin, floral-patterned cotton housecoat that buttoned up at the front to protect their every day clothes but it didn't keep them warm and these 'uniforms' had to be bought with the money that they managed to save from their meagre wages.

In the run-up to Christmas thoughts of home crowded in and Kitty kept us occupied to take our minds off it. We coloured in strips of paper, which we then made into links using a paste made from flour and water until we had a long chain. Kitty hung these up in the bothy dayroom along with the colourful strings of twisted tissue paper, which Mrs Stancliffe had provided. We beamed with pride when the staff hung up the paper lanterns that we had helped to colour and glue.

The stairwell was wide and deep enough to hold a seventeen feet tall (5.2m.) Norway spruce from the forest and it was decorated using cotton wool as snow and a fairy was placed on the top. On it we hung a few of the long, light-brown, spruce tree cones that we had collected during our forest walks. We were lucky, but many families had to do without Christmas trees that year, as all timber was now badly needed for the war effort. We painted Christmas scenes and Kitty pinned them up on the walls and we repeatedly asked her, "How many days is it to Christmas?" We were so excited and impatient for Father Christmas to come but, just before Christmas, we were sad to learn that Mary, Kitty's closest friend, had decided to go home at the end of the year.

5. Haxby

On the last weekend in September the Government decreed that everyone had to be registered and at Haxby they had to go to the Hall to do so. Everyone had to carry his or her identity card at all times. The adults ID cards were green; the children's were buff and they had to be signed and held by a parent or foster parent. They were to be shown, on request, at police or armed services checkpoints that were being set up close to factories, crossroads and military installations. There were scare stories of airdrops by German parachutists and rumours of infiltration by German spies.

The evacuees came under the jurisdiction of the Ministry of Home Security and Mr and Mrs Harris were informed that certain wartime requirements must be complied with. Many people with gardens dug a hole and erected Anderson shelters, bolting together the six corrugated, steel sheets to form a short curved tunnel and adding flat pieces at the back and at the doorway end. They then covered them with sandbags and earth but residents who earned more than £250 per annum had to pay for them. People earning below that got them for nothing but Mrs Harris didn't want one.

They were told that they *must* prepare a place of refuge for the expected enemy bombing and decided that the girls would go in the gas cupboard under the stairs with Mrs Harris. Mr Harris had fitted up an electric light bulb, and once in it, the first thing she had to do was turn the gas off at the mains. Bottles of tap water and Mrs Harris' spare soda water dispenser were put in it and a small cache of biscuits and sweets was kept on the shelf in case of emergency. The boys would go under the heavy parlour table with Mr Harris who had moved it into the corner of the room farthest from the window but it was to be some time before they were put to the test.

Mr Harris was annoyed to read in the paper that thousands of well-to-do people had fled to Canada. 'At least the King and Queen had stayed at Buckingham Palace' he thought. By this time, Archie had written their new address on one side of his and Jimmy's pre-stamped and addressed postcards using Mrs Harris' scratchy-nibbed, wooden, dip pen. It was now compulsory to carry your gas mask at all times and farmers working in the fields; workers walking to or getting the bus to their shops, offices or factories; housewives doing their shopping; and children going to school all had them. In fact, the cardboard, gas mask boxes were everywhere.

Soon afterwards, Mrs Harris sailed down Usher Lane with Archie and Jimmy in her wake with the small flotilla changing tack at Mr Morse's large brick-built house on the corner. Behind it were a forge, workshops, a smallholding and some small hayricks stood on the open area between it and the first pair of houses. All summer long the hay had blown about and by now it was entangled in most of the garden hedges. Crossing the entrance to North Lane, they passed a large white house and a row of small cottages, each with a small front garden; a short cobbled stone path and a low front wall surmounted by short, spiked wrought-iron railings. Then came Jack Widd's old farmhouse and the outhouses that he used as workshops, all of them built with thin, white-flecked Haxby bricks. Jack was a tall, slim and gaunt-featured, well-liked, middle-aged man with a longish, aquiline nose and high cheekbones, who wore a checked, flat cap and generally had a merry twinkle in his eye. He had arrived in Haxby from Thornton-le-Dale as a thirteen years old lad in 1908 and had worked extremely hard over the years to make his small farming business viable.

The group then passed the frontages of a couple of large, stone houses with double bay windows, the last of which had recently become the home of the Wards; the owners of Haxby Hall who were to stay there for the duration of the war. They walked alongside a low brick wall topped by ornate, wrought iron railings, behind which stood a large, redbrick, Victorian building. A large, cylindrical, two-faced clock surmounted by a red and gold crown overhung the wall supported by intricate, black, wrought iron tracery. Mrs Harris said, "That fine clock was erected in 1903 to commemorate the Coronation of Edward VII the previous year. You will be starting school here next Monday if plans for taking in the new evacuees have been sorted out by then." Just past the school, there were three old, two-storey, terraced houses with grey tiled roofs and next to them was a grocer's shop with a red pantiled roof. A hand-painted sign on the board above its window declared 'P. Bryant and Son' and Mrs Harris said to Archie, "The houses beyond here replaced a terrace of old cottages called

Younghusband's Row. The Bryant's son, John, is just a teenager but he helps out in the shop and his sister, Barbara, is your Harry's age."

Haxby School commemorative clock

At the back of the shop, the small post office had a wooden counter with a wire mesh screen above it, which stocked everything from postage stamps to sealing wax. Posters and signs indicated that it sold Waverley pens; packets of nibs; lead pencils; crayons; Stephens' ink; blotting pads; boxes of chalk; notebooks and many other associated materials and it was here that the boys handed over their postcards to Mrs Mary Bryant, to be sent home. It was the only means of letting their parents know where they were billeted and, in the event of postcards being lost in transit or not posted at all, the local billeting officer sent the names and addresses of all evacuees to the relevant authorities who informed their schools.

The main part of the shop was a general dealers and grocers with signs advertising such mouth-watering things as Sharp's Kreamy Toffee, Huntley and Palmer's Biscuits, Tate and Lyle's Golden Syrup and Heinz Tomato Soup. It even stocked Veritas asbestos gas mantles, which were still being used in many of the local farms and cottages. A large red, black and white, tin sign adorned the front of the shop under the window, proclaiming 'Smoke Craven A for your Throat's Sake' and a very tall man with a deep voice was serving. He was wearing a blue and white striped apron and had salt-and-pepper hair cut in a crew-cut style, which the boys thought looked like a steel-wool scouring pad. Mrs Harris said, "That's Philip Bryant, the shop owner who lives in the two rooms upstairs with his wife and son. They bought the shop from the Wardles not long before the war started." The boys waited while she collected the weekly cash that was paid for taking in evacuees and stocked up with several packets of Park Drive cigarettes - her favourite brand.

In October Haxby endured the same thunderstorms that we were having twenty-five miles further north and the fields, lawns and grass verges became quagmires. Autumn had arrived with a vengeance. Wearing their rain macs, the new and apprehensive evacuees turned up at the village school carrying the ever-present gas mask boxes. Archie, a tall, slim, handsome lad with fair wavy hair, looked very smart in his three-piece, pinstriped, long-trousered suit with padded shoulders. It was unusual for a schoolboy to wear a suit with a white shirt and tie in those days, but Gran had bought it especially for the evacuation. He would be fourteen years of age in a few days time and had been given special dispensation allowing him stay on at school for an extra year beyond the usual school leaving age to take care of his brother and young nephew.

Western end of Haxby School in 2002.

The façade of the building was faced with smooth red bricks with bluish-grey chasing and it stood lengthways on a few feet back from Front Street. There was a wide, tall-pillared, gateway at one end of its low wall behind which was a narrow strip of lawn and shrubs. The date 1876 was etched on a rectangular sandstone plaque and a narrow doorway with a glass fanlight, led into the girl's cloakroom, which separated the headmaster's house from the school. The house consisted of the large gabled-ended, east wing, and a two-storey extension with a dormer window on its steeply pitched, grey-tiled roof. On the grey-slate roof of the school there were small, louvered belvederes.

The ornate cast iron gates and railings were painted black and in the days to come Jimmy would often drag a stick along them to make a loud clattering noise which he thought sounded like a machine gun. By the following year these railings, along with those in front of many of the local cottages and houses, had gone with only short, metal stumps left to show where they had once been.

Gangs of workmen wielding oxyacetylene torches cut the lot down ostensibly, to aid the war effort. Wortley House, a large and elegant red brick building at the western end of the village, was the only building in Haxby to retain its fine cast iron railings. Several doctors had resided in it over the years and it seems that the railings were hidden within a thick privet hedge and are still there.

In 1890 the school had housed just over a hundred pupils up to the age of ten. Eleven years later the leaving age was raised to thirteen and the school was extended at the western side and at the rear. The addition of a new infant department increased the accommodation to two hundred and twelve with the children being of mixed sex and ranging from five to thirteen years of age. Most of it was built of white-mottled Haxby brick, with smooth red bricks used only for the façade, cornerstones, and around the windows and doorways.

The playground at the side and the rear was covered in tarmac with a brick wall, about four feet tall, separating the western side from the terraced houses. At the rear there were brick outbuildings, which contained the toilets with their vitreous china urinals and wash bowls. One was used as a bike shed and coal and coke for the boiler and stoves was stored in another. The rear windows of the headmaster's house looked out onto his garden and part of the playground beyond it and when he was not in the school he was still able to see what was going on in that area. Even as he was changing his clothes, the children's misdemeanours could be seen and the trick was to keep out of sight. If you were smoking or up to any kind of mischief you could not be seen round the corner by the cycle bays.

Mr Fox had replaced the former head, Mr Atterton, who had been very strict, and he was now the church organist and choirmaster. He was imbued with a deep love of Yorkshire county cricket but his views were almost feudal and he believed in the authoritarian hierarchy of things, pointing out that God had put some on earth 'to hew wood and draw water'. In Haxby, with its plethora of farms and smallholdings, there appeared to be a preponderance of the latter who he reckoned would grow up to have little brain but no lack of serviceable brawn. To his mind, every person had their preordained place in the structure of things and should count their blessings and be content. This then was the ethos that Archie, Harry and Jimmy now found themselves in.

Mr Fox was considered by most of the villagers to be kind and helpful and was generally well liked. However, he was perceived as a figure of fear by many of the evacuees who saw him as an all-powerful, Godlike figure. It seemed to Archie that his 'new' school was controlled by the threat of his demeanour, just like the one at home where the threat of corporal punishment had been effective in keeping the boys in line. The rougher townies thought that Mr Fox put discipline before affection and they did their best not to attract his attention. His favourites appeared to come from middle-class backgrounds, which the poorer children considered to be posh. The girls from them were better dressed than the herd and tended to be rather prissy but, to the head's way of thinking, they had a much better chance of passing the Grammar school examinations so that he could add their names to the honours board in gold letters.

When evacuees were despatched to his room for punishment, his very presence created an aura of dread. Caning on the fingers and palms of their outstretched hands was the common practice but if caned on the backside they would emerge red-faced trying hard not to cry. Some sat on the hot radiators as that was supposed to ease the stinging pain that felt like cuts from a rapier and a few wet themselves before they even got there. Mr Harris said to Jimmy, "If yer gonna be caned, rub an onion on yer 'ands, it'll deaden t'pain." The girls, who were cowed and shy in his presence, were never caned; being made to stand in the corner facing the wall with their hands on their heads was usually punishment enough. Sometimes they were kept in at playtime to write repetitive lines such as 'I must not talk in class' or to catch up on any missed schoolwork.

He appeared to believe that obedience and discipline were the chief objectives and was not averse to giving the lads a clout round the ear if he saw them misbehaving. He always gave *his chosen few* his special attention and most of the others were consigned to the domestic servant or tillers of the soil categories. It was said that he had been known to use sarcasm to humiliate and belittle certain unfortunate children in front of his grinning clique.

In the labour intensive farming community, change was very slow and tended to be viewed with suspicion. Most of the local pupils were polite and obedient, but generally of a plodding and amiable disposition, and not particularly inquisitive. Their main interests seemed to lie in husbandry, horse care and the working parts of tractors and many felt that being at school prevented the *real* work from getting done.

The headmaster felt that the children should not question God's will, they must know their place and be content to stay in it: after all, ducks can never be swans. From a very early age it had been instilled into most of the working class town children that they were inferior to the middle and upper classes. Their parents and grandparents had been grateful for any droppings from the rich man's table and this innate belief stemmed from their fear of long term unemployment and the constant threat of starvation. They believed that their 'betters' knew what they were doing and that they must accept their lot in silence and not upset the status quo. They thought that they should not try to climb out of the gutter, as that was their rightful place and Mr Fox did not go out of his way to dispel these ingrained working class tenets. However, as Oscar Wilde had once said, "Even though we are in the gutter some of us are looking up at the stars."

On their first day, the children were brought to the school by a foster parent, who after giving their details left them to it. The school was badly overcrowded due to the recent heavy influx of evacuees and the teachers were finding it hard to cope. The children were gathered together to be addressed by the headmaster in the crowded 'hall', which consisted of two classrooms made into one by folding back to the walls the tall, hinged, wooden panels that ran in a metal groove in the wooden floor. Mr Fox was a tall, bald, sallow, sparely built man with a long straight nose and a not unpleasing demeanour.

After welcoming the new children, he spoke of loyalty and patriotism in the difficult days that lay ahead, pointing out that, "We must be prepared to make sacrifices for the national good and must man the oars and pull together through the rough and stormy waters that we will inevitably have to face. Even though we will be buffeted by gales and tempests, we must stay firm and never, ever, rock the boat." Of that 'vessel' full of infants and youngsters cast loose in a raging storm how many were likely to survive? They were all in the same frail boat. How many would find a way through the hazards unscathed? How many would founder and be scarred for life on this parlous part of their voyage through life?

The children then recited the Lord's Prayer and Jimmy, not knowing the words too well, found himself mumbling, always a word or two behind the rest until he finally caught up at "Ever and ever, Amen" and they ended up in, *almost*, perfect unison. They were introduced to their class teachers and to Miss Clapham, the acting head of the infant department. She and Miss Johnson then led out their motley band of infants and marched them in a straggly line of pairs along Front Street. Turning right up a snicket (the local term for a narrow alleyway), they came out on the back lane near St. Mary's Church hall. After what the headmaster had said, the children - at least the ones who had bothered to listen - were rather concerned and puzzled. Jimmy, for one, didn't think he would be strong enough to row a boat in a storm without rocking it as he had never been asked to do anything like that before and besides, he couldn't swim!

St. Mary's Church hall was a long red brick building on North Lane, onto which its central double doors opened, and it stood within the church graveyard, almost directly behind the Anglican Church. Mr Harris told them later that, "It were built and used as t'Church of England school from t'mid 1850's till 1876 after t'auld brick-built school, which were once a barn, got too small and dilapidated. That's that auld building down South Lane behind Westow House and t' *Tiger Inn*, which for a while, were t'First World War Memorial 'all. In 1908 St.Mary's 'all were vastly improved and it 'ad a tall bell tower set back from t'main entrance. That red brick 'ouse next door to it were where t'headmaster lived. It were t'village school till t'new Board School were built and it's now used for t'Sunday school an all."

Miss Clapham had come with the kids from Hull but she was to stay at Haxby for just a few weeks. Quite strict, she was not averse to punishing minor misdemeanours by means of a few whacks on the bottom with a table tennis bat, as Jimmy found out the hard way. In the tiny, one storey, shingle-roofed building, now

94

packed near to bursting, the internal rooftrees and rafters were fully exposed. To ease the pressure the children were sometimes taken out for lessons in the nearby fields, weather permitting. Archie, Albert, Harry, Jimmy, and the girls walked back to Usher Lane during the dinner break but children with parents or guardians at work took sandwiches to school.

The children were streamed on ability and not just by age and Jimmy's group teacher was now Miss Johnson who had come with the children from Middlesbrough. She was billeted in a large detached house on York Road almost opposite Harry's billet. There were now so many in the church hall, that there were not enough desks and several children had to sit on the long low benches that lined the walls. In Jimmy's group alone, there were forty-nine pupils and this combination of large numbers and lack of space made it difficult to teach any of them effectively.

The teachers muddled through but the children did not learn much in the formal sense, however - when not in school - they were unwittingly absorbing the wonders of nature and the life of the countryside. For most of those from the industrial towns, being transported to such quiet, wide, open spaces was an exciting experience, as many had never seen green fields or real live pigs, sheep and cows before. Although a few had kept hens in their backyards, many were not even aware that milk came from cows; they thought it was made in a factory.

Sadly, there was a certain amount of prejudice and resentment in the village and some of the local children were told not to talk to the 'dirty vaccies' and never to bring them home with them. The older children were put into groups in the care of Miss Curry, Miss Rutter, Miss Francis and Miss Welsh from Hull. There was also Mr Lamballe, Miss Burns and Miss Morton, who was a tall, thin, loud-voiced woman whose hair was tied back in a bun.

Miss Burns was a forty-somethingish woman of Amazonian proportions who was mannish in her manner and was of the no-nonsense, shut-up-and-sit-down sort. She kept a cane across the front part of her desk as a deterrent to those who might hold thoughts of misbehaving. The latter three had come from the same school as their charges and therefore had knowledge of their educational standards and knew something of their family backgrounds, which proved to be of value in putting them into the appropriate teaching group. It also gave the children a sense of continuity.

Archie was placed with the 'bigger' children being taught by Mr Fox. Harry was with Miss Welsh who was lodging with the Midgeley family at Manor Farm in nearby Wigginton. His numbered, wooden peg was just one of a long, low row in the corridor The textbooks had to be shared between two or more children and the exercise books were cut in half with the guillotine in order to provide enough to be going on with. Powdered ink was mixed with water by an ink monitor who poured it into the old white porcelain inkwells that were covered in fine spidery cracks. These were placed in the round holes in the front part of the old desks that were scratched and ink-blotched. Over the years, their fixed wooden seats had been polished to a high gloss by countless bottoms. Designed for two, they now had to accommodate three. The lumpy, powdery liquid, into which the wooden pen's scratchy, steel nib was dipped, made it difficult for even the neatest to write without 'blotting their copybook' and the blotches had to be mopped up with (increasingly scarce) blotting paper or chalk. The pencils were cut in half to double their number but even then there was barely enough.

The Misses Morton and Burns were to return to Middlesbrough after a couple of months and Mr Lamballe was called up into the RAF after three months, which left the overcrowded school with just four teachers to care for the children whose ages ranged from five to fourteen years.

At playtime, the feet of the excited children clattered noisily on the wooden floorboards. Freed from adult restraint, the energetic, bright-eyed children poured out onto the playground with the rougher, rowdy, snotty-nosed townies shoving and pushing each other on the way out. The hubbub was sometimes augmented by the sudden roar of a low-flying Spitfire while, at other times, the deep vibrant drone of a bomber filled the air as the village was close to several airfields situated on the flat Vale of York. It was bedlam in the playground and there was a good deal of high-pitched shouting, squabbling, and sometimes fighting but, if the fighters were caught, they generally received six of the best from Mr Fox. Caning was the norm in those days and they would come away red-faced and dry-voiced with their arms crossed over their chests and their smarting hands held under their armpits.

The younger teachers were by this time exclusively female and they found it difficult to control some of the rougher elements from the towns. At break times the boys tended to play football or other boisterous games, while many of the girls played hopscotch. The younger children mostly played games of 'tig' and the rhythmic slap-slap-slap of a skipping rope could usually be heard. The older boys seemed to spend a lot of their time chasing after the rosy-cheeked, lithe-limbed girls who raced around, their hair tousled, tossed and blown in the wind created by their own velocity. One minute they were giggling, the next screaming when the lads caught and tickled them, pulled their pigtails or applied painful Chinese burns to their wrists.

"And what may I ask is your name?" said the gruff-voiced Miss Morton, on catching Archie indulging in these 'wicked' activities, even though she knew full well who he was. Although he received a good telling off, she thought to herself, 'I suppose boys will be boys.' She was a strict, but fair, bespectacled woman in her early sixties and she knew Archie, as his elder sister, Renee, was working at her home while she was away. Her large house, with its leaded, stained glass, bow windows was in Cranford Gardens in Acklam - a middle class part of Middlesbrough - and two years earlier she had taken Renee on as a domestic servant and a maid-of-all-work. She had just left Newport School but she was worked hard and was expected to take care of Miss Morton's elderly parents. She had to do the gardening and mow the large lawns with a big, heavy rotary mower that was difficult for a teenage girl to manoeuvre. When Miss Morton returned home she gave Renee an old push bike to save her paying to get there on the bus, and Renee came to know her very well and became quite fond of her. However, the low wages and the long, unsocial hours were hard to bear as it meant that she could not go to the local dances like the other girls of her age. She didn't stay long; finding a better paid job as a trainee overhead-crane driver working shifts in the steelworks.

On the fourth of October the Minister of Agriculture coined the phrase 'Dig for Victory' with the aim of making the country more self sufficient with regard to food production. The people were relieved when the Home Secretary announced that it was no longer necessary to carry gas masks at all times; however, it was still law to have them close by and readily available. Many cinemas and places of entertainment had refused admission to those not carrying one but Archie, Harry, Albert and Jimmy found the boxes quite handy when playing in Widd's field using them as goalposts or wickets. Some stores did brisk business selling decorative covers to those who could afford them.

In mid October Mr Harris sat at home quietly reading the *Yorkshire Evening Press*. He liked the paper because it had made a stand against appeasement in the pre-war years but he was shocked on learning that a seventeen and a half years old Haxby lad, Ken Cornelius, had been killed. A couple of days earlier the battleship HMS *Royal Oak* had been torpedoed with the attack coming as a complete surprise. It seems that a German U-boat had managed to penetrate the home base defences at Scapa Flow in the Orkneys, which had been considered a safe haven. Ken was one of 883 men who lost their lives with only 396 surviving. He had lived with his parents and sisters on Hilbra Avenue before joining the Royal Navy and his father was the manager of Samuel's the Jewellers, on Coney Street, York where he had hoped that his son would follow him into the trade.

Sadly, his nineteen year old friend, Arthur Long of Chestnut Grove, New Earswick, was also killed. They had both worked at the Rowntree's factory and had been at the same school as youngsters. Arthur had joined the Royal Marines two years earlier and had been posted to the *Royal Oak* at Whitsuntide that year and Ken, who had joined the Royal Navy as a boy entrant eighteen months back, had written home only the week before telling his parents that he was very happy. The news came as a devastating blow to their families as they were just callow youths who had barely started shaving. Sadly, many more were destined to go to the grave before their distraught and grieving parents.

At Halloween, as a few, light brown, crispy leaves still clung to the oak and beech trees, the grass was crisp, white and crackly underfoot as the first frosts of the winter arrived and there were no bonfires to warm your hands on this year. The Battle of the Atlantic had begun and an increasing number of Merchant ships were being sunk by German U-boats leading to national food shortages. Farmers were offered financial incentives to plough up more land for crops and radio broadcasts and the national newspapers urged the public to grow more vegetables. People were encouraged to apply for allotments at low rental rates and Mr Harris did so and was allocated one at the western end of Front Street in the low-lying area by the Wyre pond and Sandy Lane. It was an area that was prone to flooding after heavy rain but his allotment was to be the main source of vegetables for his evacuees in the years to come. He was to spend many happy hours down there and he sometimes took the boys to help him with the weeding and digging.

Harry, although reluctantly accepted, had settled in well and was enjoying life at the spinsters' large, Edwardian, four-bedroom townhouse, built around the year 1906 by the local building firm of S. R. Pulleyn. The elegant terrace, faced with yellowish Scarborough Buff bricks, consisted of seven blocks of four houses and there was a wide grass verge between them and the main road. The Walkers, at the end house, were the spinster ladies' closest friends.

The floor inside the entrance hall was attractively tiled in black and white and on the first landing was the door to the bathroom with its large white-enamelled tub and gleaming brass taps, from which cold or steaming hot water was readily available - a novel experience for Harry. On the upper landing there was a tall, deep, clothes press made of dark wood and in his bedroom was a brass knobbed bedstead. The doors of the tall, sturdily built wardrobes had full-length mirrors and there was an aroma of lavender bags and camphorated mothballs.

There was thick, plush carpeting throughout and the house was comfortably furnished in turn of the century style but there was an air of mustiness and faded gentility about it. The furniture, although of top quality, was rather dark and heavy and the wooden tables, that were built to last, had thick solid legs. These, along with the well-padded horsehair chairs and the elegant chaise longue, were kept spotlessly clean and shiny, as Miss Law vigorously polished them with beeswax and sweet-scented Mansion polish several times a day.

Harry's billet (2nd from end) on York Road.

The front parlour had a deep, luxuriant carpet into which the feet sank and its high ceiling sported intricately carved plaster medallions and stucco cornices. The ladies had turned it into a splendid and comfortable haven in which to escape the wartime anxieties. Their fine china and crystal 'treasures' were displayed in an elegant, glass-fronted, rosewood cabinet and the hearts of the middle-aged couple swelled with pride on surveying its smart interior, but Harry thought it looked like a museum. The frilly-edged, white cotton antimacassars laid neatly over the headrests of the easy chairs had been there since the Edwardian days when the house was built and antimacassar oil was used on gentlemen's hair. In one corner stood a highly polished, roll-topped, walnut escritoire and in the other Miss Barker kept her deceased father's gramophone in its rosewood cabinet. A lovely, delicately carved, Victorian tea table with hinged leaves stood against the wall with an elegant, finely-crafted, silver table lamp on it. A stuffed, speckle-chested, tawny owl sat inside an ornate glass display case in one of the alcoves.

The Adam-style fireplace had a flower-patterned, pale green and yellow-tiled surround and sported elegant, white marble side jambs within which a black-leaded, wrought iron grate shone. A large, well-burnished, copper coalscuttle; shiny brass tongs; various fire irons; a small brush and a porcelain-handled steel poker sat on a rack on the tiled hearth. Behind a gleaming brass fender there was an ornately decorated, wooden fire screen. A maroon, velvet cloth with a tasselled fringe hung down from the high, wooden mantelshelf, on which stood a dark, wood-encased, old-fashioned, chiming clock flanked by a pair of fine, antique, ceramic vases. Round brass switches on the wall served to turn on the ceiling lights that were enclosed within brightly coloured Art Nouveau glass bowls.

There was a small, well-tended, low-walled front garden and at the rear was a spacious kitchen with an old fashioned, blackleaded, cooking range. A door led into a long, back yard that had redbrick outbuildings along one side with a washhouse and coalhouse at the far end. A wooden gate opened onto a back lane with a wide back lawn with neat herbaceous borders on the other side of it. It was here that the pair loved to potter about when the weather was fine and in the far corner was a tall, gnarled, wide-girthed, oak tree, just one of an avenue of them that ran behind the terrace of houses. A small wooden summerhouse stood in the other corner.

The opulence, and the high living that went with it, took some getting used to and Harry couldn't believe his luck at finding himself in such unaccustomed luxury. The spinsters' lifestyle had come as something of a shock and a revelation to him. Beyond the back garden lay the village football field and, to the south of it, there were extensive orchards that were heavy with juicy apples, pears and plums on his arrival. Not far away in the area known as The Headlands (named after the place where the plough horses turned in the old days) there were tennis courts. The cricket field was reached by means of an earthen pathway and an old railway carriage served as a changing pavilion. Opposite the house there was a brick-pillared gateway that led into the grounds of Haxby Hall and its surrounding wall was topped with long capping slabs of York stone. Behind the wall the landscaped gardens, lawns and parkland covered some twenty-two acres, making it a tempting prospect for play and future exploration. Back in Middlesbrough, Harry had had little choice but to play on the common, in the streets or in the grimy back alleys.

Over the past few weeks, he had been well fed and cared for by the childless, middle-aged couple, who were known to keep a very good table. Having affection to spare, they lavished it on him and they grew to love and coddle their 'darling handsome boy who had hair like thistledown'. Inordinately proud of him, they fondled his golden locks, doted on him and treated him like the son they had never had. Even so, Renee had found him in tears and wanting to go home as it was clear that the spinster ladies were unfamiliar with the needs and ways of an eleven years old working class boy. Miss Law was inclined to be obsessive about germs and cleanliness and was excessively anxious concerning his personal hygiene. In their desire to care for his crop of wavy, pale-gold hair, they made him bathe every day - much to his disgust. At home he had been accustomed to sitting in the tin bath in front of the fire once a week and this bathing-every-day-business came as a shock to his system.

They were typical English spinsters leading a quiet sheltered life and - being quite well-to-do - they had never had to work for a living. The only employment they had ever known had been as housekeepers to their parents in the early years of the century when children left school at the age of thirteen. Miss Barker had posted Harry's stamped-addressed postcard to his mother the day after writing it out with her elegant, wide-nibbed, Waverley fountain pen. He was given the best food available; much of it supplied by Miss Barker's brother, Arthur, the owner of Westfield Farm, which was close to Sutton-on-the-Forest, a village a few miles to the north west. Other friends and members of her family were thought to own farms in the area and they too brought farm produce that was in short supply elsewhere.

6. Kitty

When Christmas Eve, which was on a Sunday, arrived at Sutherland Lodge, Mam paid us a short visit, but Dad was not able to get leave from the Army, and, unseen by us, she left presents with the nursery staff. At bedtime we excitedly climbed the wide, plush-carpeted staircase to our dormitory and hung our woollen socks from the mantle piece above the small cast-iron fireplace. A small glass of ginger wine and a sugared mince pie were left on the tiled hearth for Father Christmas but, due to an excess of excitement, it took much longer than usual to get to sleep and we tried *too* hard. Kitty had said, "The sooner you go to sleep the quicker the morning will come," but to no avail. We had tried to be good in the days leading up to Christmas, as Miss Thorne had told us, "Santa Claus brings bags of cinders to children who have been naughty."

Kitty had told us that, "The Sandman comes every night and puts sand in children's eyes but nobody ever sees him." And eventually - on that night of all nights – he must have crept up on us unnoticed for when we awoke on that most wonderful day of the year we saw that the glass and plate were empty. Santa Claus had been! What other proof did you need? Kitty rubbed our faces and wiped the remnants of gritty 'sand' from our eyes with a warm, damp flannel and, full of childish glee, we emptied our bulging socks on the coverlets. George and I found a few sweets and nuts, an orange (still available at that time), a bar of milk chocolate and a nice big, shiny, rosy-red apple. Huddled over our presents, I found that I had a popgun and some brightly painted lead soldiers and George got a nice colouring book, and crayons. Christmas morning's magic never failed to thrill us.

The rationing of food hadn't started yet; therefore Dinner Lady was able to cook us a huge and delicious roast goose for our Christmas dinner and we had slices of it with roast potatoes, Yorkshire pudding, vegetables, and thick, rich, steaming gravy in the bothy. We sat on tiny, rail-backed chairs at low tables covered with green-checked, gingham cloths where we pulled crackers and drank lemonade. The main course was followed by hot, rich plum pudding with lashings of steaming hot custard but George and I missed our Mam and Dad terribly on this our first Christmas away from home, even though the staff did their utmost to try to take our minds off it. It never entered our self-centred minds that the nursery assistants, who were also far from home, might also be missing their parents.

We were too excited to sleep when we were tucked in for our afternoon nap and we were so delighted when Father Christmas came to our tea party. We never suspected that he was actually Lol Bentley, the chauffeur and odd job man who was the husband of old Spaven's daughter and lived in the big house across the field. The Christmas tree, cut from the top of a spruce tree in the nearby plantation, was now fully decorated. The staff had hung up the little parcels we had made earlier, along with shiny baubles and strings of silver tinsel and under it were the presents from our parents.

Sutherland Lodge Xmas, 1939

We were given presents from Santa's sack and every child was handed a toy or a book. We wore paper hats and played games by the roaring log fire. We gorged ourselves on cheese and biscuits, hot mince pies, cakes, sweets and crisps and had a slice of the white-iced, Christmas cake, until we were near to bursting. We laughed and giggled uncontrollably when Eric burped loudly after drinking too much gassy lemonade. Old Spaven's grandson and the two teenaged Ward girls who lived at Kelton Banks farmhouse came and joined in with our games and carol singing.

Our photograph was taken, and I was all eyes when the man ejected the burnt out flash bulb. We sat on low wooden chairs and I was behind my friend Eric, who held his new cowboy pistol. Eric was two months younger than me, but he was tall and well built for his age and I thought that he must be older than me as I was at that stage of development when children judge age by height. I reasoned that adults are taller than we are, therefore, that makes them older. Our George was safely ensconced in the arms of Miss Waters and Kitty stood next to her holding the hands of Mary who was kneeling on the carpet in front of her. We had a lovely Christmas in the company of people we loved and who loved us in return.

The whole of January 1940 was bitterly cold and the snow fell thick and fast and the ground was frozen rock hard. We had dense, freezing mists as an exceptionally cold wave gripped the whole of Europe and the snow lay thickly on all the roofs. The windows were often covered with intricate, lace-like, frost patterns and there was even a thin layer of ice on the inside of the glass at times as the icy conditions persisted for weeks. The bare branches and twigs of the deciduous trees were pure white and were three times thicker than normal due to the hoarfrost that coated them. Woodland birds were twice their normal size due to their feathers being puffed out to retain body heat; with their heads tucked under their wings they looked like little fluffy balls. Many did not survive the cutting Arctic winds of that long harsh winter when temperatures as low as -2°F (-19°C) were recorded in the area. We overheard Tommy Gibson telling Miss Waters that, "One of our bombers was so affected by the thickness and the weight of ice on its wings that it crashed three miles away on the moors over by Spaunton."

The icy wind wailed as it knifed through the trees and the tops of the conifers rocked and lashed about wildly. We were kept indoors cosy and warm as a huge spruce log crackled and spat in the fire-grate throwing out blue and yellow flames that licked around it and roared up the wide chimney. The Reverend Illingworth, the vicar of Cropton and Middleton, had some difficulty in reaching us through the deep snowdrifts. After we had sung a hymn, he asked us to close our eyes and put our hands together to pray for the thousands of British soldiers and airmen, who, he said, "…are having to endure atrocious weather conditions of frost and deep snow as they prepare to defend France and the Low Countries from an expected German attack. The training is going badly as their gun mechanisms, their lorries and they themselves are frozen stiff as quite often a foot of snow falls overnight."

Uncle John was among them, and the vicar said a prayer which went, "Pray for all who serve in the Allied Forces by sea and land and air; pray for the peoples invaded and oppressed; for the wounded and for the prisoners. Remember before God the fallen, and those who mourn their loss." We were too young and full of the joy of life to really understand what it was all about.

The walnut-encased wireless that sat on a shelf in the kitchen was often on and its fretted speaker was carved in the shape of a sun and sunbeams. On it Kitty heard that the River Thames had frozen over for the first time in sixty years and, during slight thaws, when winter deigned to ease its icy grip, huge icicles hung like long daggers from the eaves. We were only allowed outside for short spells, wearing our warm Melton coats, knitted mufflers, woollen balaclava hats and Wellington boots. In Middlesbrough we would never have had a hope of possessing such warm, top quality overcoats, which had been bought with funds raised by generous-hearted benefactors.

We snapped off icicles and sucked them and sometimes we used them as swords and had mock fights until someone, inevitably, got hurt. Bursting into tears they had to be comforted by the staff. We made slides on the frozen puddles and played out until the frost nipped at our fingers and turned our noses red. Our legs became mottled and changed from red to purple after prolonged exposure to the wet snow and the icy air. After crunching through the deep snow, we kicked the verandah steps to remove the thick chunks from the soles of our wellies. Taken inside, we were given hot soup and steaming mugs of cocoa or Bovril as we sat in front of the fire. The tops of my wellies had chafed my legs, so Kitty gently smeared the red, raw places with a soothing salve. Later that month the worst storms of the century swept the country with several trees being blown down and the becks were frozen so solid that we could walk and jump up and down on them with no danger of falling through.

Winter dragged on and it often grew dark, making it seem later than it really was as snow fell softly and silently. Large flakes floated and spun in the air as the snow hid our deep footprints and the dense forest was hushed as the house lights came on in the gathering gloom. When Jack Frost bit at our noses and the icy air hurt our lungs, Kitty ushered us inside. The blackout curtains were drawn and the rooms were flooded in golden light and we warmed ourselves at a fireplace built not for coal but for a raging log fire. At bedtime Kitty rubbed our chests with Vick or camphorated oil and the pungent, soothing vapours crept up from under our wincyette pyjamas to clear our clogged up nostrils. She always gave each of us a kiss after tucking us into our beds that had been warmed by means of glazed, earthenware ginger-beer flasks filled with hot water. There was much human warmth and loving-kindness in that isolated place so far from home and it helped to make the upheaval a little more bearable!

Those northern winters were harsh indeed and in February the countryside lay asleep under a creased and rumpled white sheet. A wan winter sun reflected back from the freshly fallen snow that thickly blanketed the grounds as Kitty got us warmly dressed to go outside following a long spell indoors. Wearing thick socks under our wellies, our woollen balaclavas were pulled over our heads to keep our ears warm. Long knitted scarves were crossed over our chests and pinned at the back and we had thick coats and warm mittens on as we excitedly ventured out squinting into the blinding glare. Kitty used her tiny, Kodak Coronet Brownie box camera to take a photo of us next to the horse-drawn snowplough. It had cost her seven shillings and sixpence (37½p), which was a lot of money in those days when her weekly pay was only around £1.10shillings (£1.50). Not many people had cameras and she greatly treasured it and I still have that tiny black and white snapshot. Kitty brought out the Stancliffe's beautiful, highly polished, wooden, sledge, named 'The Yankee Clipper' after a fast 19th century British Naval cutter that had won the 'Blue Riband' in sailing schooner races across the

Atlantic. She sat on it with two excited, giggling kiddies at a time sitting between her legs and, starting slowly, it picked up speed as it slid down the long, arrow-straight snow-clad forest drive. Kitty tugged on the rope and dug in her heel to make it shoot round the sharp right hand bend at the bottom and this was repeated over and over again, until every one had had at least one turn. It was a long hard trudge for her as she repeatedly dragged the heavy sledge back to the top of the track that was like a long white gash as it cut through the avenue of dark green trees. Giant spruce trees with their distinctive greyish-brown trunks lined the sides of the woodland track in their serried ranks, towering above us like majestic, sylvan gods. Masses of glossy, dark green, waxy-leafed, rhododendron shrubs crowded the sides of the track beneath them. It was great fun and, in between our turns, we threw snowballs at each other while Kitty trudged back to the top where we clamoured impatiently for another go.

Kitty was an attractive young woman who always kept herself neat and well groomed and she liked to varnish her toes and fingernails in bright colours when she could get it. She was always cheerful, but around that time she seemed to be happier than usual and she positively glowed. It seems that she had been going out for some weeks with a chap called Alan Brown who was a Forestry Commission worker and the first time she came across him she had been taking us for a walk in the forest. After hearing someone whistling a happy tune, she had caught sight of him up a tree wearing a flat, cloth cap and a red shirt. She learned that he was living with his parents in one of four, rented, red brick cottages that had been built by the Forestry Commision in 1930. It was officially called Sutherland Beck bungalow, but the locals always called it Peep o' Day bungalow as *Peep o' Day* meant dawn. It stood at the edge of the forest about a mile west of Sutherland Lodge and to get there you had to walk down a gradually descending grassy track that continued on to join Cropton Bank. The walk, a right of way used by the postman and local tradesmen, involved the opening and closing of five wooden field gates.

In the fields next to it was Peep o' Day farm, the home of old Willie Hammond, a little, wiry man with a bushy moustache who usually wore a flat cap and a dark three-piece suit of thick,

108

hardwearing, fustian. When it was wet he wore an old mackintosh with no buttons that was tied round the middle with a bit of coarse binder twine and on his feet he had hobnailed boots. His leather gaiters only served to emphasise the bandiness of his legs. Born at Levisham seventy years earlier, he had run this small farmstead for more than forty years and he often drove his horse and four-wheeled wagon into Pickering to get his horse shod at Fletcher's Forge on Smiddy Hill. By that time he was as deaf as a gatepost and his fifty-year old, eldest daughter, Hannah, a spinster lady, had kept house for him since his elderly wife died. They had an evacuee from Middlesbrough, called Frank, billeted with them and nearby there were other farmsteads called 'Rising Sun', 'Flowers o' May' and 'Cuckoo's Nest'. These lovely poetic names had given rise to a local song called 'Spring in Ryedale', written by Mr F. Austin Hyde, a former headmaster of Lady Lumley's School in Pickering. The chorus of which went something like:-

"The rising sun brings the flowers of May
See the cuckoo's nest at peep o' day."

We learned that Kitty, one of life's givers, had been going to the threepenny (1¼p) hop (dance) at Cropton village hall on her evenings off and she had grown fond of Alan. She and Miss Waters would get us bathed and tucked into bed, before they set off along the track to Peep o' Day bungalow to meet him. They then took the short steep path down from the bungalow to the beck, where Alan and his dad often fished, crossing a narrow wooden bridge before walking up the hill into Cropton; which took about thirty minutes. They enjoyed and keenly looked forward to the dances and on those dark winter nights as snow lay thick on the ground, they were sometimes accompanied by fifteen years old Andy McDonald, the son of the Keldy Castle gamekeeper who lived in one of the cottages.

Glad to be out of the cold and the darkness, she would change her shoes and leave her favourite green coat in the warmth and brightness of the cloakroom. It was at the Saturday night hop that Kitty, after mingling with the locals, had first spoken to Alan. She had been wearing a homemade, checked, cotton frock with puffed out, leg-of-mutton sleeves and on her feet she had blue, Cuban-heeled, court shoes. The young people were dressed in their best clothes, with most of the girls wearing floral-patterned frocks and peep-toed shoes. The youngsters enjoyed the high-spirited fun in the cosy atmosphere of the small hall but many were obliged to dance together, as there was an acute shortage of males with most of the men away in the forces. Footloose and fancy-free, they performed the popular sequence dances of the time, including the lively Gay Gordon's; the Valeta; the St. Bernard Waltz; the robust and regimented Military Two Step and the energetic Dashing White Sergeant. In between there were various old-time Viennese waltzes, foxtrots and quick steps.

Alan was a good dancer and had a passion for it and, during the strict tempo quicksteps, he would throw in a few twiddly bits and chassés. Kitty was not so good but she enjoyed the soft, sentimental, romantic dance tunes, such as the haunting *Laura* and the recent hit *A Nightingale Sang in Berkeley Square*. The music issued from an upright piano in the corner of the wooden-floored room that was played by a middle-aged lady reading from sheet music. The village hall was on the main street and was known locally as the Reading Room, and the pianist's husband, who had a motorbike, brought his wife over from Elleron Lodge way on the pillion seat every week.

Kitty and Alan held each other very close moving as one as a slow foxtrot, to the tune of *Falling in Love with Love*, was played. The atmosphere was romantic under the dimmed lights and in the warm, intimate and cosy setting they let the music take them as he gave her a peck on the cheek, which was looked on as quite daring in those days. The last waltz was always danced to the tune of *Who's Taking You Home Tonight*, and whoever was chosen as a partner for this was generally recognised as your best girl. Alan chose Kitty. Just before midnight everyone stood to attention while the national anthem was played as Sunday was still observed as a day of rest. Everyone knew almost everyone else and the hops were always pleasant and friendly occasions. They were a much-needed antidote to the social isolation of the big house in the forest, and they helped folk to forget their wartime anxieties for a little while.

Kitty was pleased to learn that Alan's work was considered important to the war effort and his job was - like that of the farmhands - a reserved occupation that exempted him from military service. Whenever they had time off work they would meet up. Alan, who was ten years older than Catherine, was a strong, but smallish (five feet five inches) man with straight brown hair that had gingery flecks in it. His teeth and fingers were stained brown with nicotine from the Robin and Player's Weights cigarettes that were his favoured smokes. He had come down here from the mining village of Chopwell, a typical County Durham pit village, in 1930. It had one long street lined by miners' cottages and stood close to the ugly steelworks perched on top of the hill at Consett. He had moved with his parents and younger sister, Nancy, when times were hard following the Slump, when droves of young men were desperately seeking employment and the work prospects in forestry looked promising. His dad, an ex-miner called Joe was a small, jolly, placid man who was, like many another at that time, unemployed.

Alan was a rugged, tough and resourceful man, like most of the miners and steelworkers of the North East who were reputed to be as hard as the things they produced. His friends called him Geordie, and Kitty soon learned that he had a quick and fiery temper when aroused. He and Joe had been glad to take any employment, especially when it included a cottage and a bit of land. The bungalow, and the smallholding that went with it, consisted of three fields at the front and one at the rear and it had a large garden where they could grow vegetables and keep a few pigs and hens. Alan's mother, Minnie, was an outspoken geordie with a really broad accent, who was inclined to speak her mind, even if it sometimes hurt the people around her. Alan was her favourite and his older brother, Fred, was still working in a coal mine in Durham. His eldest brother, John, had been killed in Italy just four days before the armistice was signed on the eleventh hour of the eleventh day of the eleventh month of 1918. His sister had obtained work in the hotel trade in the pretty village of Thornton-le-Dale.

Kitty told Mary that, "A woodman never works in the forest alone. They work in gangs for safety reasons as a man could easily wound himself in some isolated spot and lie there for hours before being found. Two men use a long saw with a wooden handle at each end to fell the great softwood trees when they reach maturity and the job is essential to the war effort as timber is in great demand for making pit props, telegraph poles, railway sleepers and such. The small side branches are used for fencing and for rustic work and they also have to know how to handle the big, powerfully muscled, Shire horses that are used to drag the felled trunks out of the forest. Harnesses and chains are attached to a long timber shaft fixed between two huge wooden wheels and the straight, newly felled giants are slung beneath this contraption which is then pulled along by the horses. It is a tough and often dangerous job."

The minor roads and the forest tracks leading to Sutherland Lodge were often blocked by deep snowdrifts and when snow blizzards sealed in the house Kitty's walks to Cropton had to be curtailed. Often completely shut off from the outside world, the roads and forest tracks had just been reopened by soldiers stationed in Pickering. With the wind whipping the snow into their faces, they had dug through the deep drifts in the more exposed areas. The powdery snowdrifts, blown through gaps in the hedges by the easterly winds, were known locally as stowerings. Squads of soldiers were also sent out to help the local farmers to dig out buried sheep that had been sniffed out by the hard working Border Collies. At times the snow on the surface of the drifts froze so hard that the soldiers were able to walk over them. They said it felt really strange to be walking on top of buried hedges and stone walls. It was said to be the coldest winter of the century.

When a slight thaw set in Mam visited us again, and the taxi had great difficulty in getting through the slushy lanes and the rough, snowbound, forest tracks. She had come down on the train with her friend, Winnie Ward, who she had known since The Settlement days. She showed Mam a nice letter she had recently received from Miss Thorne, in which she had written, "I'm pleased that you sent him such warm and sensible clothing for this time of the year. Eric was delighted with the skittles, the comics and the sweets. He asks such intelligent questions about everything he sees." Eric had shared some his sweets with me and we had great fun playing with the skittles in the bothy.

By this time I was getting the feel of the countryside and was slowly but surely changing from a child of the town into a child of the forest. Like many children of my age, I seemed able to identify with the intangible forces of nature, *feeling* as much as I saw. It would appear that the developing child is often open to influences that adults are not and I would sometimes sense that 'other' spirit world that lies just beyond this one. Young children, at times, have an uncanny intuition about such things and I believed that all natural things had good or evil spirits within them. I felt that the tall green giants were my friends spreading out their long arms to protect me. It may be that the young child retains fleeting recollections of their soul's early origins and this may enable them to look through a tiny chink in the door to see things older folk are blind to. I seemed to dwell at times in a private, secret and mystical world of my own; a world that, sadly, becomes buried and lost forever as we grow up. There are many psychic things that can never be explained and it may be this that causes young children to behave so unpredictably at times. It seems that I had several invisible friends that I openly talked to and played with.

On Shrove Tuesday it was still dark as we got out of bed to be washed and dressed and the thickly forested countryside was still snow covered and the cold thin air was crisp, clear and bracing. It was just getting light as we sat down to our breakfast of cornflakes with hot milk and toast and marmalade in the dayroom. The Robertson's marmalade jar had a golliwog on the label, which led to arguments as to who should have it, so Kitty devised an alphabetical rota of our surnames. This, of course, meant that I was last on the list to get one, which was to be the case throughout my schooldays.

At teatime we watched wide-eyed as Dinner Lady expertly tossed pancakes high in the air and flipped them over before we ate them steaming hot and covered in sweet, sticky, Golden Syrup spooned from a large yellow tin with the word 'Tate's' enclosed within a red diamond shape. Miss Thorne told us that, "In Pickering it is the custom to ring the pancake bell at 11 a.m. on this day and on hearing it all the shops close and the children have a day off school."

113

It was dark again by our bedtime but then, to our amazement, on a day soon afterwards, it suddenly changed when something called double summertime - that was a mystery to me - came in. It was still dark at breakfast time but light until well after we were put to bed and, not understanding it, I presumed it must be part of God's magic, as nobody else could make night and day change as suddenly as that.

For parents wishing to visit their children the L.N.E.R (London and North Eastern Railway) had started to provide cheap day returns at weekends and Mam - sometimes with Dad when he could get leave - took advantage of these special offers. They visited us as often as they could afford to, which was not as often as they would have liked. It was such a long and difficult journey to get to and from Sutherland Lodge and they had to set off very early in the morning to catch the train from Middlesbrough to Pickering. The trains were slow and stopped at every station and they then had to catch the Helmsley bus and travel the two and a half miles west to Wrelton village. It was four miles on shank's pony through Cropton to Sutherland Lodge but occasionally, if they were in luck, they managed to hitch a lift on a passing farm wagon. On bitter raw days, as rain swept across the fields and forest, they arrived bitterly cold with the wet penetrating to their very bones and they were glad to dry out by the flames of a nice log fire. They then had to face the long walk back or share a taxi with other visitors, which they could seldom afford to do and taxis were getting harder to find due to the petrol rationing.

In the hard winter months this was often the case and Mrs Stancliffe would sometimes ask Spaven to take them to Pickering station in the pony and trap. The Lodge was in an ideal setting for us but it was far from ideal for our parents who often arrived back at Middlesbrough railway station well after midnight. By that time the last bus had gone and they either walked or hired one of Hornigold's cabs at the taxi rank if they could afford it. Around this time Miss Thorne had written to the parents suggesting that they should group together to hire a bus saying she would arrange a meeting with Mrs Moffett, the Nursery Schools secretary, but nothing came of it.

In the early part of the year catkins hung on certain trees and shrubs. The willow catkins were small, soft and fluffy, like a rabbit's paw; the alder catkins were dark and hard while the hazel catkins were long and pendulous with a dusting of yellow pollen when they first appeared in late January. They reminded us of lambs' tails, as they shook in the gentle, chill breeze and, as the winter days passed and the severe weather eased its icy grip the birds began to sing. New life began to stir as the cold earth started to warm up and we noticed the first faint hints of spring. Green shoots of snowdrops pushed through their icy blanket to hang their white, droplet shaped heads and Spaven said, "They're known as Fair-Maids of February round these parts." Soon after yellow, mauve, white and lilac crocuses thrust their way through the yielding earth.

On Palm Sunday, at the start of Holy Week, we were presented with small raffia crosses and Spaven said, "If yer keep 'em till this time next yeer, yer'l 'ave gud luck." On Good Friday we ate thickly buttered, home-made hot-cross buns and on Easter Sunday Miss Waters hid hard-boiled, 'pace' eggs that had been dyed in bright colours around the grounds and we had to search for them. We then re-enacted the age-old custom of rolling them down the grassy slope at the edge of the paddock to see who could get the farthest. "Even the ancient Egyptians exchanged eggs as fertility symbols at this time of the year," Kitty informed us. Being too young to know what that meant, we were more interested in the fluffy, yellow chicks that were hatching out in the warmth of the incubators.

On Carling Sunday we ate the delicious, brown-skinned peas, known as carlings. Dinner Lady had soaked them in water overnight and then fried them in butter and we called them sheep droppings, because that's what they looked like to us. Miss Thorne, who hailed from South Shields, told Kitty, "It is an old northern custom, which stems from a time of severe famine. It seems that many, many years back the River Tyne was frozen over and no ships could get in with food. The first one to get through was laden with these peas. They had a great public feast to feed the starving people and the story lives on in folk memory."

In their due time, the green daffodil shoots budded, burgeoned and bloomed and there were large clumps of them around the stout, stone walls of the old house. They nodded their bright yellow trumpets and rocked in the wind as Spaven said to Kitty, "Don't bring yon snowdrops or daffy-down-dillies in t't'ouse. Flowers that 'ang their 'eads are unlucky indoors and they stop t'ens eggs from 'atchin out." Pale yellow primroses and deep yellow celandine broke through and peeped from under the hedgerows around the paddock where the horses would soon be put out to graze.

The swelling buds created a green haze as the emerging foliage misted the hedgerows and shrubs beside the forest tracks. Mrs Stancliffe told Kitty that, "During the lambing season, catkins are put round the fireplaces of some of the local farms as they swear that it aids the birth of the animals. Some of the country folk secretly cling to the old nature worship and this is a clear example of their belief in sympathetic magic. These customs have been handed down for generations and it doesn't do to discourage the ancient, and (to them), still resident, vegetation spirits. Many of them still believe in the spirits of the trees and the water and the sky and the plants and animism - the attribution of a soul to living objects - is said to be one of the oldest religious beliefs. To the Brigantes, the ancient Celtic tribes of this region, stones, water and trees held real spiritual significance and pools, springs and rivers were regarded as entrances to and from the underworld. Many of the villages and farms are said to have their resident 'wee folk' and some say that creatures such as hobs help with tasks as long as they are not spoken to or interfered with in any way. There are stories circulating of folk being spirited away by the little people." Old Spaven added, "Aye, not far from 'ere at Fairy Call Bridge near Lastingham, fairies used ter blow out t'lanterns on t'carriages and other strange beings, such as bargests, if seen, foretell of a death in t'family".

We enjoyed taking short cuts through the dense, dark forest under the tall shady trees where, year upon year, the pine needles had silently drifted down to form thick soft, spongy, brown carpets for us to bounce up and down on. We would often see Mr McDonald, the Keldy Castle estate gamekeeper, in his thick, checked, tweed suit as he patrolled the woods in leather gaiters with a double-barrelled shotgun bent open and resting over his forearm. To him and the local farmers, a gun was like a third arm. After the long cold winter we enjoyed playing in the open fields on the fringes of the forest and were taken along the grassy track to the forestry workers' bungalows. Here we saw the frisky, high leaping of the gambolling lambs and thought it odd that the dirty grey, slow moving, black-faced Masham ewes could give birth to such frolicsome snowy-white offspring. We loved to see their long tails shaking rapidly from side to side as they pushed under their mothers' body to suckle. Willie Hammond said, "Yon ewes are t'remnants o't'vast number of lambs born 'ere two yeers back." In the early spring sunshine, when everything was new, the dazzling whiteness of their wool stood out sharply against the lush, bright-greenness of the grass.

So, in these idyllic surroundings, I experienced the bliss of being and I loved the miracle of spring, the season most propitious to all living things. Wild violets, primroses and the blue periwinkle were now in flower and on April Fool's Day, we played silly tricks on each other. George and I received birthday cards from our relatives and family friends in Middlesbrough delivered from Cropton post office on foot by Ez Thorpe who wore a black, serge uniform and a flat-topped cap with a shiny black peak and a silver badge. He even worked on Christmas Day, walking long distances between the scattered farms regardless of the weather unless the roads were completely impassable. His full name was Ezekiel and he had a sister called Tabatha; names taken from the Bible, as was the practice among many rural families. He and his brother, Cai, were fully qualified tailors who made quality suits working from their home close to the church in Cropton but the orders were not regular enough to make a living from it - hence the postal job.

I was five years old on the fifth of April and George was three on the following day, which fell on a weekend that year. They were soft, warm, days of changing sunshine and cloud and we were delighted when Mam and Dad came to visit us and stayed for a special birthday tea in the bothy where we had jelly and custard and fancy cakes. Mam usually managed to make the long, difficult journey about once a month, and whenever Dad managed to get leave and come with her, we were over the moon. We ran about on the springy turf of the lawns, and when he dropped to the grass we clambered all over him. We were given pick-a-backs and never gave him a minute's respite. It is amazing what young children can make otherwise sensible parents do and we were in raptures of delight and scarcely left his side. When he was with us we felt safe and secure and all was well with the world but, all too soon, it was time for them to leave again. Each parting became harder to bear and Mam tried her best to hide her pain, not letting the tears round her heart to come to her eyes in case it upset us. No doubt she let them flow once we were out of sight.

We were taken to see Mrs Stancliffe's recently born foal, with its big, mournful, brown eyes and long eyelashes, as the shiny-coated mare grazed on the lush, new grass within the rustic fencing of the paddock. The foal stood wobbling on long stiff legs, as it tried to nuzzle up to the black teats on the mare's under-belly and its skin was as smooth and sleek as the skin of a mole. The mare was usually harnessed to the trap when old Spaven took it on errands but she was enjoying an extended break from her duties after her eleven-month pregnancy.

The harnesses that hung on the walls of the stable had an acrid smell of leather and linseed oil and Spaven talked of horsey things while stroking and gentling the whickering mare as she stamped her forefoot and snorted. He tried to explain things to us but, on receiving the inevitable "Why?" in response, he became so exasperated that he gave up. The horses were huge beasts to us but he lifted us up to help with the grooming using the body or the dandy brush. He loved his 'osses' and looked on them as close friends and I liked the feel of the mare's warm, sweet breath as I held out a few pellets in my cupped palm. I loved nuzzling up against her and stroking the long soft hair of her mane and the top of her long muzzle.

We would carry in small bundles of wheat or barley straw when the soiled bedding needed changing and we were sometimes given the job of stirring the bucket of bran mash and mixing in the thick gooey molasses that old Spaven had prepared. In the winter he warmed it up for them. Twice a week he took a handful of linseed, put it in a pan and boiled it up and when a crust formed on top of the oil he let it cool before adding bran and oats. He said this helped to give their coats a lovely glossy sheen and he warned us never to stand directly behind their back legs as they might suddenly take fright and kick out. On the insides of their legs we couldn't help but notice a network of thick veins that were so pronounced that we thought they might burst at any moment

Tommy Gibson brought the tall, round milk churns to the kitchen of Sutherland Lodge every morning in his little van. His farm and small dairy were on the western side of the Wrelton to Cropton road opposite the stone quarry. Spaven sometimes collected our meat from Mr Wilf Brown's little butcher's shop at the side of his large stone house across the street from the school in Cropton but, more often than not, it was brought in Mr Brown's van. He delivered meat to several of the local villages, including Appleton-le-Moor, Spaunton and the pretty village of Lastingham. Legend had it that at Spaunton a buried horde of gold and silver lay waiting to be found. Square-towered St. Mary's at Lastingham was seven hundred years old and it boasted a unique, apsidal, vaulted, Norman crypt built on the site of an earlier shrine to St. Cedd. It seems that Abbot Stephen of Whitby had intended to build an abbey here, but local robbers and outlaws forced him to move to the relative safety of York.

Mr Brown was a tall, bald, stocky man who played for the village cricket team. His free-range Leghorns and Sussex hens rootled in the grass for grain on his smallholding behind the house and he kept pigs in sties, killing, preparing and dressing the meat himself. Mrs Nell Brown, his wife, a small, jolly woman in her forties, was an ardent member of the WVS and was responsible for finding billets for the evacuees in the village.

On those warm, sunny late spring days the twittering and trilling of a variety of small birds could be heard as our walks took us through green woodland glades. The tick-tick of the tiny jenny wren and the black-hooded bullfinch issued from the depths of leafy thickets and the low cooing of collared doves could be heard. The midges danced and bit in the damp umbrella of shade beneath the deciduous trees. As the sun shone through the trees dappling the ground it lit up the leaves making them translucent so that from below we could see every vein in them. I thought, 'if they have veins then they must have hearts' and as Mam used to say, "You can see the hand of God in every living thing"

Sometimes we saw buff-coloured hen pheasants with their tiny, dun-coloured chicks making weak, whistling cries of alarm as they scuttled for cover. Occasionally the clattering flight of a wood pigeon would startle us as it flew up shattering the peace and hush of the forest. The noise it made was like that of a roller blind being released and we would catch a glimpse of white as it flew off. We nibbled on tender, pale green leaves of hawthorn and called them bread and cheese, as they were said to give as much sustenance as a plate of bread and cheese, but they never tasted like that to me.

Even in that idyllic setting things were not always of a pleasing nature. Sometimes we had to pass a gaggle of orange-footed geese, with the gander being called a steg in these parts. I had been terrified of them ever since one had hissed and chased after me honking loudly with his neck fully outstretched as his cackling concubines joining in. As I ran like billy-oh, blinded by floods of tears, he had torn my trousers with his vicious, stabbing beak and bruised my arm with his powerful wings. That incident established a life-long wariness and distrust of them. Kitty said, "They make good guard dogs because they honk whenever anyone approaches." All the same, I liked to see the fluffy, white-downed goslings as they crossed the paths near the Forestry bungalows. At other times we glimpsed them on the wide grassy firebreaks between the trees.

Another frightening experience occurred when we were confronted by a tall cross-eyed tramp, who occasionally turned up pushing an old pram that held all his worldly possessions. He had a dirty, straggly beard and long matted hair and wore torn and filthy clothes. We cowered behind Kitty's skirts as she assured us that, "He is a well-educated man who has fallen on hard times and he is quite harmless." But we were not so sure and kept well out of the way when we saw him begging at the bungalows. When he knocked on our kitchen door, Dinner Lady always gave him something to eat in return for small jobs, such as chopping up logs into sticks for the fire.

On the spruce trees the pale green tips of the year's new growth contrasted sharply with the dark green of the older leaves. A large area of the forest had recently been cleared and squads of soldiers were erecting Nissen huts. Army officers were moving into the recently commandeered 'Keldy Castle', which was a few minutes walk away from Sutherland Lodge. The site was being made ready to receive the many infantry soldiers who would soon train here. Metal stovepipes stuck up through the semi-circular, corrugated 'tin-roofs' of each hut that would soon house eight soldiers. Large areas of the moors had recently been made inaccessible to the public as they were to be used for military manoeuvres and as firing ranges.

Keldy Castle was not really a castle at all, but it had been made to look like one. It was really a large, castellated, country house with landscaped grounds, gardens and terraces. A long drive led up to an arched doorway with a two-storey wing at each side and well-groomed lawns swept down from colourful shrubbery. The wooded estate covered some 7,000 acres that included some fifty farms and smallholdings. Purchased by Sir James Reckitt, the founder of the nationally known firm of Reckitt and Colman, at the turn of the century, it had a well-stocked fishpond with its own boathouse. Their products had been household names for many years and included the widely used Reckitt's blue bags for washing clothes and the world famous Colman's mustard. However, its huge factories at Hull and Norwich were soon to be bombed by the Luftwaffe.

The main house had been rebuilt to Sir James' specifications and had the look of a traditional castle. Its battlements surrounded an inner courtyard, and rows of merlons and embrasures crowned every parapet and corner tower. We were taken through the trees to the fishpond where we expected to see frogs basking on the shiny, lily pads. As we got there we heard them croaking, snoring and bubbling contentedly but we made too much noise and they rapidly plopped into the pond. We saw the wriggling tails of lots of little black tadpoles as they swam about in the shallow, sunlit water. Sadly, the Army caused extensive damage during the war years and the 'castle' had to be demolished in 1956.

When Mam visited she often brought us goodies in a wicker picnic basket and if the weather was fine she would bring out the HMV (His Master's Voice) wind-up gramophone, inside the lid of which was a picture of a small white terrier dog sat with one ear cocked towards a large horn. She had a pile of twelve-inch, black, 78 rpm, shellac records in thin, plain brown, paper sleeves. Holding one by the edges with her fingertips she placed it on the turntable, and taking the arm from its cradle she swung it out and carefully lowered the needle onto its edge. After some crackling, we would hear children's songs like *Old Macdonald had a Farm, This Old Man* and *Girls and Boys come out to Play*. Three of the nursery rhymes I recall were Hickory Dickory Dock, Wee Willie Winky and Lucy Locket. When a record ended I was fascinated by the scratching sounds as the needle swung back and forth in the grooves round the hole in the centre.

Mam loved to read to us and we were told lovely stories about giants, magic carpets that flew through the air and suchlike. With my curiosity aroused, my imagination grew wings and took flight and I sailed away into realms of fantasy. I was scorched by the flame of her enthusiasm and influenced for life and it was from her and Kitty that I learned the magic of words and acquired those gifts of laughter and quiet listening that are so precious to a growing child. We were given plenty of TLC (tender loving care) and I grew to love the place and the people, feeling warm and secure even when mother and father were not there. They say that absence makes the heart grow fonder and it was true of Mam and Dad. With Dad away in the army most of the time their love had not had chance to fade; it was still as shiny and new as on the day they married and it was obvious to all when they were together.

During these visits we often wore ourselves out running around on our knobbly-kneed, stick-like legs. Leaping about like the newly born foal that had recently been let out to grass, we ran laughing across the meadow playing vigorous games of 'tig' or hide and seek. When I hid in the deep, dark, spaces under the drooping branches of the rhododendron shrubs, I could see out but no one could see me. I have fond memories of Mam in her favourite dark-blue, cotton frock with the white spots playing a kind of pat-a-cake routine on George's hands. She would hold my hands as I put my feet on her and walked up her body and, on reaching her chest, she would swing me over backwards so that both feet landed back on the ground. George would pester for a go, and the performance would be repeated, with lots of giggling, until Mam said, "I'm worn out and will have to sit down for a bit." A playground had been set up on the flattened rectangle of packed earth near the house and they pushed us on the swings and the seesaw until they had to rest again.

They spread an old blanket out on the lush grass of the meadow and we sat snuggled up cradled in their warmth and loving presence. Sweet natured, gentle Mam lavished on us all the hugs and kisses that she had saved up since her last visit and those poignant moments are stored in the depths of my psyche never to be forgotten. At times they threaten to burst my heart asunder but the memory of her all-encompassing love never fades. It is like a pale ghost of the past that is greatly treasured and very precious to me. She always spoke softly and quietly from the heart and was awash with tears at the first hint of sentiment. Mother would often tell us exciting stories of battles and miracles from the Bible, which she knew off by heart. We were loved and contented, surrounded by good and caring people and in our secluded valley we were as happy as kings. The gory details of the war mercifully passed us by and we were blissfully unaware that violent battles were about to flare up across the English Channel. We were loved and cared for and that was all that mattered.

On first hearing the mellow, disembodied call of the cuckoo in the distance, Kitty said, "He is the welcome harbinger of summer." Nature was coming into her own and the old horseman, Spaven, still a believer in the old country superstitions, showed us the thin hazel twigs, woven into the shape of a cross, which he wore under his shirt. "They ward off t'witches thar knows," he said to Dad, before adding, "If yer turn t'coins in yer pocket yer'll allus 'ave money until t'cuckoo comes agen next yeer." Dad called him 'that owld gadgie.'

We usually wore short sleeved smocks, that had a pair of pockets in the front just below waist level, to protect our clothes and these often bulged out due to being full of all weird and wondrous items. We kept anything and everything that interested us, picking up many things, such as worms, twigs, leaves, dried-up acorns, conkers, cob nuts, marbles and bits of string. Kitty often said, "Waste not, want not." So we took her at her word.

I loved the month of May when there were hardly any biting and stinging insects about. Mam visited us again, coming down with Eric's mam, Winnie, who told her that Eric's elder brother, Len, had recently been rescued from the sea. "It happened on April the twenty-ninth, just one day before his sixteenth birthday. He had signed on as a cabin boy on the SS *Whitetoft* and the steamship was part of a convoy coming back from Liege in Belgium. It was the practice in foggy conditions, for a man in the bows of the ship to guide them. Each ship in the convoy threw a barrel overboard attached to it by a rope and, as it trailed in their wake, the ship behind had to keep it in view. Unfortunately the lookout man lost sight of it in the dense fog and she foundered after striking a submerged rock just off Robin Hood's Bay. The ships had been carrying a consignment of captured German rifles and were bringing them back here to be tested for quality. Luckily the *Mary Ann Hepworth*, the Whitby lifeboat, arrived in time to rescue them."

Masses of white mayblossom tipped with pink, weighed down the boughs of the hawthorn bushes and, from a distance, it looked as though they were covered in a thick, dusting of icing sugar. The rich, heavy scent permeated the warm, still air as wild briar and dog roses blushed pink and white in the burgeoning virescence of the hedgerows. Wild hyacinths were in flower as the tall spikes of foxgloves opened their spotted bells that we called Witch's Thimbles. Beside them tiny green fern fronds were unfurling and the air was full of musical birdsong, which we were coming to recognise. We loved to hear the lovely song of the thrush; the gregarious pipit; the tiny brown tree creepers; the colourful coal tits and the pink-chested chaffinch and other woodland birds that made up the daily choir. They had paired up and were laying claim to their territories as upright red and white 'candles' of blossom adorned the chestnut trees down the lane.

Kitty took us to a nearby smallholding along the hard packed earth of the forest paths to see the newborn calfs, which tried to suckle on our fingers. By now, we were becoming increasingly able to recognise our whereabouts by the different shapes and colours of the moss, lichen and algae on certain stones and trees. We were told that the frilly grey lichen on the trunks of fallen trees indicated that the air was very clean. Kitty took great care of us and tried to ensure that we came to no harm but inevitably, the occasional fall resulted in a grazed elbow or a cut knee. One or other of us would trip over the exposed, raised roots of the spruce trees and the hurt needed to be kissed better, before being washed and smeared with Zam-Buk herbal balm.

On one occasion as we were out walking I tarried, wandering along in a daydream as usual, lagging further and further behind. Something caught my attention and I wandered off the path and into the gloom beneath the closely packed spruce trees. The further into the depths of the forest I ventured the trees seemed to hold a deeper, more ominous darkness. To a child life is full of curiosity and wonder and I was looking for the red toadstools with the white blotches on them on which the elves and fairies sat. Kitty and Mam had shown us pictures of them when reading Hans Christian Andersen's fairy tales.

The 'other world' was very real to me and I suddenly found myself in a darkly green, twilight area where a deep chill seemed to emanate from the wild and primitive giants around me. The air was dank and drear as a brooding, menacing stillness reigned and a feeling of melancholy and apprehension crept up on me. The light grew ever dimmer beneath the dark overhanging boughs and I seemed to sense a low and growing, heavily breathing presence. I heard indistinct, stealthy movements; there were eerie echoes and strange whisperings in the air and faint utterances seemed to be coming from behind me. I felt that a dark mystical power was very close and that the aura of latent danger was not of *this* world. My heart was beating fifty to the dozen and chills ran up my spine as I sensed that someone, or something, malignant was very close and watching me. That was it; I froze; petrified with fear; my throat tightened in terror and the horror threatened to stop my breath. I could not shout out or bring myself to turn round; afraid to raise my eyes in case ghastly spectres were hovering near.

At that moment, to my vast and utter relief, Kitty found me! Suddenly the voices were gone and a deep hush descended on the forest. It was like the deathly silence that followed the firing of the gamekeeper's gun and you could have heard a pin drop. All of the evil lurking things had fled at Kitty's approach. As she gave me a big hug and a cuddle, she tenderly wiped away the tears that burst forth to stream down my cheeks with the corner of her housecoat. I sobbed uncontrollably; trembling like an aspen on legs that had turned to jelly and they were still rubbery when we rejoined the others. Had the fire gone out at the *Saltergate Inn* letting the devil loose? Was it the voices of lost souls in limbo that I heard; an evil spirit of the woods; the old tramp; the gypsies (who were said to steal and sell children) or just a figment of my highly vivid imagination?

Adults tend to forget the wealth of a child's imagination: they often have the capacity to feel extremes of fear and excitement in response to what adults consider mere trifles. The world of childhood can be a place of frightening fantasy and strange happenings and to a child unseen forces are still strong and readily accessible. They know the allure of witchcraft and magic and understand the eternal themes of love, truth, power and death and some are able to 'see' things that adults cannot. There are some things that can't be logically explained and, for a while after that terrifying experience, I did not sleep well and had bad dreams, peopled by ghosts, witches, hobgoblins, dryads and evil ogres. On future walks in the 'enchanted forest' I made sure that I stayed close to Kitty and I never wandered off the beaten track alone after that.

On those late spring mornings the newly risen sun gently warmed and gilded the mellow old stones of the big house. When the blackout blinds were removed and the shutters were opened its rays warmed my bed and formed golden rectangles on the wall. I would lay watching as they crept, almost imperceptibly, across the flowery patterns on the expensive, embossed wallpaper sedately measuring the relentless passage of time. I remember thinking that, because the sun could move by itself and did not have to be pushed like Eric's tricycle, it must be alive. It seemed to me that it must be intelligent because it wanted to do good things like making us warm and helping things to grow. I *knew* that God must have been controlling it.

Colourful chaffinches twittered as they decorated their nest with bark and lichen after building them with moss, feathers, grass and sheep's wool. As the sunny days lengthened and warmed up, the cows and horses were left out to graze overnight in the fields. In

126

what seemed a never-ending task, little birds flitted back and forth with grubs and worms to repeatedly fill the gaping maws of their tiny, naked offspring. On one of our morning walks, we were upset to find speckled, broken eggshells in lovely pastel shades of grey and blue. Close by were the wrinkly-pink, featherless bodies of two tiny nestlings, their heads with their pale yellow beaks looked far too big for their scraggy necks. The poor things lay broken on the ground having fallen from the nest. We called all newly hatched birds 'gollies'.

The breath of summer was just touching the budding trees as the smooth, light-grey twigs of the ash trees belatedly opened their black leaf buds to put forth fresh, lime-green foliage. These and the red-leaved oaks were usually the last of the trees to do so. Soon pendulous bunches of tiny, green, single-winged seedcases, which we called keys, would form. The verges beside the lane became crowded with tall stemmed umbrellas of white-flowered cow parsley and Spaven showed us how to dig out the soft white pith from their thick stems to make peashooters. As spring gently eased into early summer, the 'owld gadgie' said, "Yer must never 'andle yon 'emlocks, or t'deadly nightshade that we call Devil's flowers. Yer see them giant 'ogweeds towerin' above t'others over yonder. Well, they 'ave tiny white 'air-like spines on t'stems that carry poisonous sap. Don't touch 'em, or yer skin'll cum out in 'uge blisters."

On the following Sunday the mothers came out again and Eric's mother told my Mam that Miss Thorne had written to her again asking, 'Could you bring him a pair of leather, crepe-soled sandals as sandshoes are no good on the rough, stony forest roads. Sandals are light and cool and protect the feet. The weather is simply lovely out here and the children are outside a lot of the time. They roam the fields gathering flowers and are as happy as kings. Could you bring Eric some cool summer clothes?' adding, 'He was sick one day after his tea. Possibly the heat had upset him, as he has not ailed otherwise. He is a most intelligent boy and asks hundreds of questions like, Where does lightning come from? Why doesn't it strike trees? Why does God make the sun shine? and so on.'

Even in those austere times, hard pressed working class mothers, like ours, tried to maintain the old traditions. Although she was finding it hard to make ends meet, Mam still managed to bring us at least one item of new clothing at this time. It was a long established Yorkshire custom to wear something new, and preferably white, in honour of Whitsuntide and that Monday, as the dreaming valley lay warm, calm and hushed, was to be no exception. Mam brought George and me a new white shirt. The sun beat down from a blue and cloudless sky that formed a perfect backdrop to the vivid, green foliage of the trees. The stillness and beauty of the place were overwhelming and on days like that it was hard to believe that there was a war on.

In the sunny dining room the windows were wide open and Miss Thorne had brought bunches of yellow-flowering broom into the dining room. Yet another Whitsuntide custom in these parts, it was believed to bring good luck. We were served delicious roast lamb with freshly picked home-grown vegetables and the first, sweet-tasting, new potatoes of the year, all smothered in rich, brown gravy. This was followed by thick and steaming, creamy custard poured over a slice of hot, tangy, 'goosegog' pie that was two inches deep (5cms). " I have used only freshly picked, early gooseberries and have baked it specially for you little ones, so be good bairns and eat it all up," Dinner Lady said. She maintained that gooseberries were good for the liver and stomach.

7. Winter into Spring

A number of households were issued with letterbox red buckets; one to hold sand and the other water. Certain houses also received a stirrup pump and a long handled scoop enabling them to deal with incendiary bombs. One person had to pump while another directed a jet of water from the nozzle at the end of a short hose. Houses with a stirrup pump were obliged to display a white card showing the letters SP and they had to make it available to neighbours as and when required. At the Harris household the buckets were kept by the tap on the outside wall by the back door

By November 19th no bombs had fallen on England but floating mines had been dropped in the Thames estuary. A bomb, jettisoned by an enemy aircraft over the Shetlands, had killed a man making him the first civilian casualty of the war. Even by December, no bombing had taken place and the Americans called this period the *Phoney War;* Churchill called it the *Twilight War.* Some parents, thinking that the bombing would never happen, took their children back home.

In Haxby the villagers got used to seeing a variety of aircraft passing overhead. Among them were small, single 'propped' Lysanders with diagonal wing struts that were nicknamed Flying Carrots due to the shape of their fuselage. The aircraft, with their strangely shaped wings and odd-looking wheel 'spats', that were actually 150-gallon (568 litre) fuel tanks, had only recently appeared in the area. Grasshopper-like, they could take off and land in the length of a football pitch, and the spats had been fitted to extend their range. They were based at nearby RAF York, which had formerly been a small civilian airfield known locally as Clifton.

Whitley bombers, which had come into service two years earlier, were quite often seen and heard as they were based at RAF Linton-on-Ouse. This airfield had been specially built in 1937 and the first two bomber squadrons had arrived there in the April of the following year. It was not until after the war that Archie learned that aircraft had flown from there to drop millions of propaganda leaflets on German cities in the first few days of the war. This process was known as nickeling and many of the crews thought that the sorties were a costly and dangerous waste of time. Most of them said, "The only thing that Chamberlain's bits of paper achieved was to supply the Germans with free lavatory paper."

The boys soon came to know the distinctive drone of their Armstrong Siddeley Tiger engines, the failure of which was the cause of several aircraft crashes. The large airfield lay eight miles north west of the village and stood to the west of the A19 trunk road that ran north from York to Easingwold and on through Thirsk to their home on Teesside. It had three new concrete runways and in the month before Christmas King George VI had visited it - the first of several royal visits.

At that time the BBC Home Service mostly had talks, news bulletins or Sandy McPherson playing the organ. Weather forecasts had been stopped to prevent the Germans using them to plan bombing raids. Jimmy liked to listen to *Children's Hour* (which only lasted half an hour) after tea each day. Archie was too old for 'that childish stuff', as he called it. Derek McCulloch, who was known as Uncle Mac, presented the programme, which began with "Hello children everywhere." The Gracie Fields hit *Goodnight Children Everywhere* was based on the programme and in it was a moving line that went 'Your Mummy thinks of you tonight' which upset Jimmy every time he heard it.

Their favourite programme - the English speaking Radio Luxembourg - had been shut down at the start of the war. They used to enjoy listening to the high-pitched singing of a group of children known as 'The Ovaltineys', who had become very popular, as they extolled the virtues of Ovaltine - a hot, milky, chocolate-flavoured, bedtime drink. They often joined in with the catchy words of the wireless jingle that went; 'We are the Ovaltineys, little girls and boys'.

At Christmastime the school holiday was reduced to just over a week. To the east the distant rolling hills of the Yorkshire Wolds were covered in a thin dusting of snow and looked chilly and forbidding. Over the last few weeks, Jimmy had changed. He was no longer the tear-stained object of compassion of earlier; he was now a lively and mischievous lad with a hearty appetite. Archie told Gran, "Our lot felt a bit embarrassed on going into school recently. We only had a few measly biscuits and rock cakes to take in for the school Christmas party, while Harry took in much more than us and he had much better stuff an all. But we still enjoyed the free-for-all and did justice to the eats."

No lights were to be seen twinkling on Christmas trees in people's front windows that year due to the blackout restrictions. Brightly lit displays were not allowed in the shop windows, as had been the case in previous years. After dark the village lay hushed and submerged in a deep, stygian blackness that is hard to imagine these days. No light reflected upwards from the earth's surface which made the stars appear exceptionally bright and far more numerous. The church carol services were held behind blacked-out windows and the cheerful atmosphere created by the twinkling Christmas lights - that had always been part of the magic of the festive season - was lacking. It was meant to be the season of good will to all men but there wasn't much peace on earth this year.

Even though far from home, Archie, Jimmy and the others enjoyed their Christmas dinner of roast chicken, roast potatoes and all the trimmings. They wore paper hats, pulled crackers, and at 3 p.m. they sat and listened as the King stammered his way through his Christmas speech. It was an annual tradition that families all over the country keenly looked forward to. Mr Harris was in the habit of singing or humming snatches of the popular songs of the time, one of them being the recently released *Moonlight Serenade*. The records of the up-and-coming Glenn Miller band were being played on gramophones all over the country at that time and the young child star, Judy Garland, had just made a record that was very popular. The song had featured in the recently released Hollywood film, 'The Wizard of Oz' and was called *Somewhere over the Rainbow*.

That first Christmas away from home was, inevitably, tinged with sadness, as memories of home and happy times were still strong. On Boxing Day, Gran and Aunt Hilda visited bringing with them new clothes and presents. For Archie there was Richmal Crompton's latest book, *William and the ARP* and the *Hotspur* annual and Harry got the *Dandy* and the *Beano* annuals. For Jimmy there was a homemade, wooden truck made by an uncle. They brought what nuts, fruit and sweets they could afford (which was not a lot). As they were not offered a meal at the Harris household

131

they made an excuse to take the boys out to see Harry who was by now was well settled in at his spacious and superior billet on York Road.

On arrival, they were cordially greeted and made to feel welcome by the amiable Misses Barker and Law who were as old fashioned as Toby jugs and as English as roast beef. They hung up their coats and placed their hats and gloves on the wooden stand in the entrance hallway and then the spinster ladies, displaying their innate generosity, gave the boys small but top quality Christmas presents. After the usual pleasantries they sat down to a plateful of delicious sandwiches filled with lean York ham or cold goose that had been cut into dainty, crustless, triangular shapes. Afterwards they indulged themselves by tucking into the hot mince pies and fancy cup cakes that were set out on white, lace-edged doilies placed on finely patterned, gold-rimmed, china plates. No expense or trouble being spared.

The table was overlaid with a real, embroidered, white linen tablecloth and the serviettes had Christmas themes on them. They drank tea from almost translucent, white china cups decorated with tiny pink roses that matched those on the tea plates. This was poured through a sterling silver tea strainer from a white porcelain teapot and everything was of the finest quality. Cream was poured and sugar lumps were taken from a china basin using silver tongs and they did not require much pressing to accept generous second helpings. This was followed by a large slice of rich and fruity Christmas cake covered in marzipan and thick Royal icing. It was a feast fit for a king and they were fit to burst and Archie didn't feel it was right to wipe his mouth on such fine quality linen serviettes. They couldn't help but notice that Miss Law kept her cutlery wrapped up in white tissue paper and assiduously avoided using the same teaspoon as the others. Steaming glasses of spicy hot toddy warmed them through before they set out off on the long, chilly walk back to the Harris's house. The mothers then had to undertake the journey back to York Station on the rattling number ten bus.

It was not a very happy Christmas - what with the bitter cold; the long hours of darkness; the uncertainty about the future; homesickness and the knowledge that food rationing was to come into force on Monday, January 8th 1940. Plans to bring it in had been put back several times already and Mr Harris commented, "It'd 'ave come sooner but for t'*Daily Express* and its anti-rationing campaign." Personal ID cards would have to be shown to obtain or renew a ration book.

At that time the newspapers were full of stories about evacuees with most of them trying to assure the parents that all was going well and there was no need to take them home. On certain days it was so cold that the frost and the freezing fog lingered till midday and in January the gardens and fields were frozen solid. The trees stood naked and dormant, stripped bare by the cutting winds of the coldest winter for many years; the hooked twigs at the ends of the creaking oak boughs seemed to claw at the low scudding clouds. The biting wind brought flurries of stinging hail and snow and the intricate tracery of the branches was starkly silhouetted against the steely, battleship-grey of the sky. As fresh flurries of powdery snow threw a thin white sheet over the cold hard earth, parents wrapped their children up and sent them out to every shop in the village to buy as much sugar, fats, and tinned foods as they could lay their hands on. They were stocking up their larders before the dreaded rationing began.

The people had registered with the local grocery shop of their choice in November and this entitled them to a ration book. The books were issued from behind the high wooden counter of the single storey rates office on Front Street, which was painted black. The colour matched the mood of Mrs Harris as she queued to collect hers, her husband's and those of her five evacuees. Along with the icy weather, it was a time of heavy shipping losses and military successes were few and far between.

The small wooden building stood next to a large, imposing, ten roomed, two-storeyed, red brick building called Spring House which was next to the *Red Lion* public house. Each evening and at weekends the pub was chock full of servicemen and locals. Its smoke-filled rooms and tab-end littered floors had an exclusively masculine atmosphere and there was always an air of stale beer about the place. A respectable woman would never dream of frequenting it except to work as a barmaid or as a cleaner. Drink could shame a man but, in those days, it was positively scandalous in a woman.

The adult ration book cover was buff, the junior book blue and the baby book green in colour and each page covered a certain period of time and was divided into small, coloured, numbered squares. The coupons were not vouchers that you could buy things with but they allowed you to buy them if you had the money. Schoolchildren were to have free milk, and the younger ones were to get free cod liver oil, concentrated orange juice and malt. This meant that in future orange juice would become available to those who needed it most. Up to that time it was more likely to be found only on the breakfast tables of the affluent. Malt was a sweet, thick, dark-brown, gooey stuff that came in a brown glass jar.

Mrs Harris collected her entitlement of it every week from the rates office. Rationing was to give many of the evacuees a more balanced diet than ever before, with a subsequent increase in protein, minerals and vitamins and their health gradually improved as a result. The first foods to be rationed were butter and bacon (or ham) and each person was allowed 4 ounces (113 grams) per week. At the end of December, it was announced that sugar was to go on ration starting at 12 ounces (240g) per person per week. This was a heavy blow to people who baked their own cakes (as most housewives did at that time). To Mrs Harris, who liked a lot of sugar on her cornflakes and enjoyed regular cups of hot, strong, sweet tea, it was devastating. Rationing was to change everybody's life in one way or another but Archie, Harry and Jimmy didn't notice much difference as they had been on rationed food since birth due to a lack of money.

The blackout curtains stirred in the cold draught from the kitchen window and the ill-fitting frame rattled in the wind. Sleet spattered against it and streamed down the glass causing the white disc of the moon to wobble and shake as Archie took a peep round the dark material. It was around this time that he first heard the hateful voice of 'Lord Haw-Haw' on the crackling wireless receiver. The American born, Irish renegade's real name was William Joyce and his arrogant, grating nasal drawl created a feeling of revulsion in most people and he was hated across the whole nation. Broadcasting on Radio Hamburg, his irritating voice could be heard saying "Jairmany Calling, Jairmany Calling" nearly every night straight after the nine o'clock news as he broadcast his anti-British and pro-Nazi propaganda.

He often mentioned details of places and events that had taken place here quite recently and only people living in those areas could have known such facts. His broadcasts sent people in to a rage but they put up with it because they were desperate for news of the war from any quarter. The BBC Home Service tended to censor or suppress bad news. Before the war Joyce had been Sir Oswald Mosley's Deputy and Propaganda Director and had been among the Fascist thugs at the rallies at Olympia and had fled to Germany when war was declared. People thought that spies or Nazi sympathisers must be feeding him local information, which caused them to become even more suspicious of each other. When Gran visited the boys she said, "It makes me feel ashamed to think that that swine was living not far from us before the war."

Archie, Jimmy and the rest returned to school on the first Tuesday of the new year. The bitterly cold east wind nipped their noses, ears and fingers making them glad to get into the relative warmth of the classroom. As mounds of dirty frozen snow lined the roads all the nineteen to twenty-seven year old males learned that they were to be called up. One of them was Mr Lamballe, the young teacher from Middlesbrough. It was to be a month of snowstorms alternating with clear skies and severe frosts.

There were days when it was so cold that the rain froze solid almost as soon as it hit the ground and one of Archie's pals from Hull said, "My mother actually saw several ships trapped in the ice in the Humber estuary." The kids made slides in the playground and some were caned by Mr Fox for making them on the pavements. The lads enjoyed skating on the ice-covered ponds and on the frozen puddles at the side of the road. Several households, including the Harris's, suffered electric power cuts and the leaks from the burst water pipes flooded people's houses when they thawed out.

After yet another hard frost, the paths were like sheets of glass and Mrs Harris made her way along very gingerly. She was glad to get through the door of the CWS (Co-operative Wholesale Society) store to register for her butter and sugar with the manager, Mr Tom Widd, who was the brother of Jack. She now had in her possession seven ration books and was looking forward to the time when her dividend (known as 'the divi') would be paid out. The windows of the Co-op faced onto Front Street; formerly known as 'The Village' and it stood on the corner of the narrow opening that led up to North Lane. Initially the shopkeepers cut out the coupons from the ration books but later they were stamped in order to save time and paper. People had to register with a dealer for each type of food and were then obliged to collect their goods from that one named dealer only.

The Haxby Co-op stood almost opposite the old Wesleyan Chapel - the front part of which was now Walker's fried fish and chip shop - and it had originally been a humble wood and corrugated zinc hut on that same site. Mrs Harris was looking forward to collecting the rations of bacon, butter and sugar for her foster family. She would now get one and three-quarter pounds (0.8kg) of bacon every week but, at the end of the month, it was doubled with the cost increasing to 2/- a pound and she couldn't afford to pay that. Jimmy told his Mam, "We never see much of all the butter and bacon that she gets."

In the icy-cold, overcast days of February, snowdrifts built up on the verges and thick blankets of it garlanded the leafless hedges. As Mr Harris sat by the kitchen fire looking through the *Yorkshire Press* newspaper he became very angry, which was unusual for him. He had just read that the privileged members of the York Conservative Club had sat down to a sumptuous twenty-first annual dinner. This had taken place in the elegance of their neo-Gothic building at Lendal and the report stated that they had enjoyed cocktails; hors d'oeuvres; fillet of sole; roast pheasant; mutton; woodcock; baked potatoes and all the trimmings. He was fuming at the unfairness and injustice of it. The common people had been told to tighten their belts or do without as the ever-increasing food shortages and rationing had started to bite. He said to no one in particular, "There seems to be one law for t'masses and another for t' privileged few."

The Government decided that from the 25th of that month the clocks should be moved forward an hour. In the autumn of 1939 the clocks had not been put back as had always happened before. This was done partly with the aim of reducing the rising number of road accidents caused by the total blackout even though there were fewer cars in civilian use due to the petrol rationing. The speed limit had been reduced to 20 mph during the hours of darkness and the few cars that were seen in Haxby at that time belonged to professional people like the doctor. Nearly all of them were black with gleaming, chromium-plated bumpers, handles and headlamps. Drivers made signals with their arms and hands and car headlights and cycle lamps now had to be hooded or screened to reduce the chance of them being seen from the air. The masks had one or two narrow slits that directed the beam downward and some people fitted cardboard headlight masks but these gave out barely enough light to see by. Rear lights had recently become compulsory on pedal bikes and Mr Harris put a thin, worn-out sock over his front lamp and tissue paper over his backlight to dim them.

Several pedestrians were injured due to the icy roads and the blackout. As people groped around in the blackness ghostly shapes would often loom up in front of them. Some people slipped on the ice, but walking into lampposts or each other was the biggest cause of injury. Torches soon sold out, Ever Ready batteries were in short supply, and even these had to be dimmed by wrapping tissue paper around them. White rings were painted around roadside trees, lampposts and pillar-boxes. The pavement kerbstones were painted white and, for the first time, white lines were painted down the middle of the main roads. The front part of the mudguards of cars, lorries and buses were painted white and folk were advised to wear something white at night.

The cattle, only recently let out into the fields, turned their backs to the chilly north easterly gales as meat became rationed, not by amount but by value, and each person was allowed one shilling and ten pence (9p) worth a week. Rabbit, poultry, fish, brawn, sausages, pies and meat pastes were not rationed, but were in short supply and often not obtainable at all. When they were, long queues quickly formed. The evacuees stayed indoors vying with each other to hog the fire and irritating the irascible Mrs Harris in the process. It was a bright but cold Easter as wild garlic - often called ramsons - flowered white under the newly budding trees. The yellow of the daffodils and the blue of the forget-me-nots complemented each other as they flowered by the hedges and in the weak sunshine the odd bumblebee foraged lethargically amongst the crocuses.

The six o'clock news on the World Service began with the words 'London Calling, London Calling' and on it the people learned that German troops had invaded Denmark and Norway by sea and air. Later in the month, on Churchill's orders, British troops landed and pushed the Germans back and retook the port of Narvik. The good news helped to raise the morale of the British populace for a while after so many setbacks but this rare success was short-lived as, by June, the British forces were again forced to mount a hasty retreat. A Nazi sympathiser, Major Vidkun Quisling, proclaimed himself head of the Government in Oslo and ordered all resistance to cease. His name became a synonym for traitor. Even though the Germans occupied Norway the people appreciated our support and were grateful to Britain for allowing their king and queen to live here in exile. After the war, as a token of their thanks they sent a huge Norway spruce to be erected in Trafalgar Square; a gesture of gratitude and friendship that continues to this day.

Across the road from the Thompson's, the family in the last of the houses on Wold View Terrace, a muddy, rutted track led to a deep pond that was reputed to be bottomless. Beside it stood the tall, skeletal framework of a rusty, old wind pump with twisted metal vanes that had once been used for irrigating the fields by means of sluices and water channels, a method of water control that had been practised since time immemorial.

Just past the Thompson's house there were four older semi-detached houses just before the entrance to Crooklands Lane, which was a narrow cul-de-sac branching off to the left through the fields. On it stood two red railway carriages that had been joined together to form the home of Mrs Alice Howes who was a Shaw before her marriage. She lived in them with her son and four daughters, one of whom was to marry a RAF corporal who was billeted at Claremont Farm in Wigginton. Continuing on past Crooklands Lane there were two bungalows and two larger and fairly old houses called Golland Cottages. From there the road, with a deep drainage ditch beside it, continued north to the stream called the Golland Dyke before turning eastwards towards Strensall. Beside it were thorn-hedged meadows and fields of root crops and corn. At Strensall there was a large army barracks, with extensive firing ranges that had been established here as the number of streams in the area made it unsuitable for an airfield.

To the north of the houses on Usher Lane there was a large meadow, known as Widd's Field, and in the middle of it was a large, shallow pond. It was here that Archie, Albert, Harry and Jimmy often played football. On a warm evening in mid April they stopped their kick-about to gaze in awe as three Armstrong-Whitworth Whitley bombers came into view. The shape of the lumbering twin-engined, aircraft were familiar to them by this time. As one them flew quite low over their heads, they swore that they had seen the leather-helmeted, tail-end Charlie, and they told the kids at school that, "He waved at us as he sat behind his Browning guns in the cramped, power-operated, tail turret."

They wondered what it must be like to be up there in the bitter cold of the unheated gun turret as they had heard that the crews had to wear thick woolly underwear, two jumpers and heated jackets. They tried to picture what it would be like flying over Germany with flak bursting all around as you apprehensively scanned the sky for enemy fighters. During the month, echelons of these heavy bombers flew over the village as they went out in tight formation on dangerous round-the-clock bombing raids. To their crew of five they were known as 'flying coffins'. When they returned at night, the navigation and landing lights at Linton airfield were switched on just long enough to allow them to land without attracting enemy intruders.

The Whitley bombers were instantly recognisable to the boys because of their strange nose-down way of flying and they had long, slender, camouflaged fuselages that tapered towards their twin tail fins. As three of them passed over, their red, white and blue roundels stood out clearly in the golden light of the setting sun. Mr Harris said, "They're most likely flying out to Norway ter bomb t'airfields at Stavanger and Oslo." The enemy, who seemed invincible at that time, now occupied these airfields.

Cheese become rationed and no bombs fell on mainland Britain until the ninth of May and many parents, lulled into thinking that there was now little danger, called it the Bore War. They reckoned that the Government - through lack of action – must be trying to bore the enemy to death. The expected air raids hadn't materialised and many mothers had taken their children back home. One of these was Albert Crabtree, who, having reached the age of fourteen years, left school and went back to Middlesbrough to get a job. Donald Barrett, an eight-year-old lad from Newcastle, replaced him. For some reason he was nicknamed 'Ducky' and he now shared the bed with Archie and Jimmy.

The spectral looking Prime Minister, the Right Honourable Neville Chamberlain, was frail with a face as grey as old linen as he sat in the House of Commons. Faith in him was at an all time low and his former supporters and the opposition were calling for his resignation. One member shouted out, "In the name of God, go!" They had had enough of his eight months of insipid wartime leadership and many of the MP's refused to serve under him. He was to pay the price for his dithering and his policy of appeasement. It had to be Churchill; the man who had repeatedly warned of the dangers of Hitlerism. Even then they had vacillated and not shown the necessary urgency. The country was still woefully under-armed and inadequately equipped and they were fortunate to have been given the time to catch up. After many long years in the doldrums, Winston Churchill finally reaped his reward.

On May the tenth, in a moment that changed the course of history, he was asked by the King to become the leader of a new coalition government. On that very day the Germans attacked in Belgium and Holland! Winston Churchill took up the challenge. Appointing Lord Beaverbrook as Minister for Aircraft, he called for a vast increase in aircraft production. He was a natural leader whose thin wispy hair, pugnacious jaw line and projecting lower lip indicated a dogged tenacity and his poetic grace and power of words were to instil the people with fresh hope. A birth defect in his palate had created a certain sibilance; nevertheless, his stirring speeches were to revitalise the flagging morale of the nation. You can only express your visions with feeling and clarity if you passionately believe in them - and he did. He became the voice and the driving spirit of a beleaguered Britain. With his shoulders rounded and hunched like those of a boxer in the ring, he vowed that this country would fight on, growling, "We will never give in!" Addressing the House of Commons, he said in a grave voice, " I have nothing to offer but blood, toil, tears and sweat. We have before us an ordeal of the most grievous kind. We have before us many, many long months of struggle and suffering".

That month, Sir Oswald Mosley, the leader of the British Union of Fascists, was interned and all potential spies and enemy aliens were rounded up and had to appear before a tribunal. Those classed as A were considered to be a high risk to security; B meant that their loyalty was suspect and they were subject to certain restrictions; C meant that they posed no risk at all. Most of the C's consisted of Jews who had fled from the Nazi persecution. The authorities were taking no chances and most of the internees were sent to the Isle of Man, well away from any military installations, and were kept behind double-stranded, barbed wire fences patrolled by armed soldiers. Many of the high-risk detainees were shipped off to Canada and Australia and all refugees living on the East Coast had to report at their local police station on a daily basis and had to observe an 8 p.m. to 6 a.m. curfew. Large numbers of them had an intense hatred of the Nazis, and were willing to fight for this country, and volunteered to join the various arms of the Forces.

Mosley was imbued with the same arrogance as his Nazi 'heroes' and had assumed the same haughty, hands-on-hips posture as Mussolini. He had long admired his hubris and pompous mien and had become a close associate of Hitler himself. Diana, a beautiful, married woman, who was one of the six aristocratic Mitford sisters, had left her husband fifteen years earlier to become the mistress of the philandering Mosley and they had married in Berlin in 1936 in the living room of the Nazi Chief of Propaganda, Dr. Joseph Goebbels. Goebbels' small physical stature had led to him being called the Poison Dwarf by the British public. Hitler was a guest at the wedding and only a month previous to the outbreak of the war the Mosleys had been his guests at a performance of Wagner's *Gotterdammerung* in Bayreuth.

It was a known fact that Diana's sister, Unity, was a dedicated Fascist. Beguiled by Hitler, she had insinuated herself into his circle of friends and admirers. When war broke out her world fell apart. She sat in a park, put a revolver to her head, and was seriously brain-damaged lingering on in a sorry state for years before dying from the resulting meningitis at the age of just thirty-four. Diana was put in Holloway prison for three and a half years where she slept under an old fur coat.

Mosley had founded the BUF in 1932 following his ejection from the Labour Party where he had once been a cabinet member. They were secretly funded from Italy but many of the members were little more than thugs and bully-boys. They assumed a para-military look, wearing black shirts, riding breeches and field boots; and were often jeered and stoned as they held their anti-Semitic marches that usually led to violence on the streets. Their insignia was a lightning flash inside a laurel wreath similar to that of their heroes - the jack-booted, SS, and they claimed that the Jewish refugees had infected Britain.

Britain still placed enormous faith in its Senior Service and the Royal Navy was extremely proud of this title and of the people's trust in them. Global power had previously been measured in terms of numbers of ships and the Royal Navy was still the largest fleet on the oceans. We also had a huge merchant service, on which Britain's economic survival was dependent, with 60% of our food being imported in 1939. Her enemies - knowing this - had amassed a vast fleet of U-boats and had sunk over 140 ships since the turn of the year. There had been no phoney war for the seamen; they had been in the thick of things from the start. The Germans reasoned that if they could stop food getting in the people would starve and might even give up. Their new tactic of laying magnetic mines was proving to be very effective with many ships being lost when their magnetic field detonated the mines as they passed over them. The Battle of the Atlantic was not going well for us.

On a day towards the end of May when the countryside was beautiful and freshly green, the schoolchildren were given the day off to enjoy the local Empire Day activities. The British Empire still spanned the globe and they hoped that the celebrations might bring about a resurgence of national pride. That Friday the local air raid wardens; the St. John's ambulance-men; the Boy Scouts; the Girl Guides; the WI, the Home Guard and contingents of soldiers and airmen, marched through the village with a military band playing patriotic music; such as *There'll always be an England,* which reverberated from the walls of the old houses lining Front Street. As they paraded proudly along in their colourful uniforms, they passed

142

the streamers and buntings that festooned the houses. Union flags adorned the shops and hung from almost every bedroom window. The marchers smartly saluted the civic dignitaries on passing the dais on the village green where a balmy breeze fluttered the Union flag on its pole. In St. Mary's church, where yet more large Union flags hung, the Rev. Donald delivered a stirring sermon on national loyalty and good citizenship.

Later that day as the villagers gathered around their wireless sets, they were given a sharp reminder of the parlous war situation. The Harris's listened in silence as King George VI broadcast to the nation saying in grave tones, "Let no one be mistaken, it is no mere territorial conquest our enemies are seeking. It is the overthrow, complete and final, of this Empire and of everything for which it stands".

On Sunday evening, a service from Westminster Abbey was broadcast with the new Prime Minister and the King amongst the congregation. In his address, the Archbishop of Canterbury said in a voice tremulous with emotion, "Let us now pray for our soldiers in dire peril in France." This unexpected statement came as a surprise and shock to the whole nation. They were completely unaware that the BEF and her allies were in any sort of trouble. The Government had led them to believe that the troops and the Royal Navy would soon put Hitler in his place. The dreadful news had been withheld so 'as not to further lower the morale of the British people'.

In France the balloon had gone up, as they say, and Archie's brother, John, was among the 400,000 men in retreat. France had entered the war with a vast army but only about seventy vintage aeroplanes and the BEF only had a few lightly armoured tanks. The Germans had far superior numbers in the air and on the ground and our RAF's Fairey Battles were no match for their ME 109s that could reach speeds of 350mph and carried twin cannons and a machine gun. Following horrific losses of men and machines, the obsolete aircraft were withdrawn from service.

It was some days before the British public was informed of the devastating mass retreat as the media had been ordered to disclose nothing until the evacuation of the troops was well under way. Many acts of great courage took place in the face of overwhelming odds as the bore war came to an abrupt end. The ferocious German blitzkrieg (meaning 'lightning war') and a surprise attack through the hilly, wooded Ardennes region split the Allied Forces and the huge French army. The Germans dropped paratroopers behind the Maginot line that the French had put such faith in and their troops simply by-passed it.

The disorganised French divisions had been in the wrong place at the wrong time and in the French High Command many of the leaders were old, argumentative and did not see eye-to-eye. Marshal Petain, who was eighty-four years of age, and General Weygand, who was seventy-three, were former World War One heroes. There was incompetence, muddle and lack of communication and the ill-equipped troops were no match for the Germans and they soon cracked under the savage onslaught. France accepted defeat and the newspapers were quick to point out that, "France has lost every war that it has fought for the last two hundred years. Greedy men in high places have sold out their country for the promise of power. Like a fungus on the bark of a tree the corruption has spread rotting the healthy wood beneath. The muddy grey-green uniforms of the Wehrmacht have swept across the land like a plague of locusts ravaging and destroying everything in their path."

Desperate appeals to save the Army came from General Lord Gort and the BEF Commander-in Chief was sacked soon afterwards. Anthony Eden, the new Secretary of State for War, held urgent consultations with Winston Churchill who ordered the mass retreat to Dunkirk. Thousands of weapons and vehicles had to be abandoned and the Germans made use of many, but most were purposely destroyed or rendered unusable. Mr Harris read in his newspaper that 'The soldiers have had things far too easy, following eight months of drinking limitless amounts of cheap plonk, NAAFI beer and whisky. They have indulged in too much *horizontal refreshment* with the Mademoiselles in the estaminets - as Major-General Montgomery had so controversially put it - without being called on to fight. When it came to it they were found wanting.' In truth, they fought hard and well but rifles and Bren guns were not much use against the enemy's heavily armoured tanks and it seems they had been let down by both their allies and their leaders.

While the retreat was in progress Anthony Eden broadcast an urgent appeal inviting the men who had been obliged to remain at home to 'do their bit' by forming local defence units. He offered them the opportunity to serve their country in its hour of need and gave those who - because of age or work - could not join the Services, the chance to hit back should the invasion come. Participation would be voluntary and unpaid but, eventually, a full uniform and rifle would be issued.

An LDV (Local Defence Force) unit was set up in Haxby under the leadership of Captain Tom 'Ticker' Pulleyn, the local builder. The tall, dark-haired, well-built Sergeant Fred Jefferson, who was an executive at the Rowntree's factory, became his second in command. Married with a nine years old daughter and two young sons, his large, tree-embowered house stood almost opposite Harry's billet on York Road. The small group of volunteer youths and men registered at the police house and were issued with khaki coloured armbands: the only thing that distinguished them from the locals. Initially they met in the old Memorial Hall in South Lane where they learned aircraft recognition, how to dismantle and put together a Lewis gun, the use of hand grenades and how to deal with local emergencies.

Vast numbers of rifles had been left behind at Dunkirk, so for a time they had to drill, march and carry out military manoeuvres without them. Initially their job was to help the police and rescue services and to carry out tasks such as roping off and mounting guard on factories or danger areas. They learned traffic control and took their turn on night duty, even after a long spell of work on their everyday job. When on standby, they had an emergency telegraph line to Strensall camp, and slept in the old, brick-built Memorial Hall. Some wags nicknamed them the Look, Duck and Vanish brigade.

Mrs Harris never seemed to have a cigarette out of her mouth and there were brown nicotine stains on her teeth, the hairs on her upper lip and her fingers. Of a domineering nature, she was of a dyspeptic disposition with pitiless eyes and her mouth was usually turned down at the corners. Very strict and bad-tempered, she soon made it known who was the boss of the household. She made it abundantly clear that the house was to be kept neat and tidy at all times and woe betide anyone who did not abide by her rules, including her henpecked husband who was expected to set a good example to the young ones. On going to bed she always had with her a large glass bottle of water with a metal soda siphon attachment at the top. It seems she suffered from acid indigestion or some such stomach disorder, which may have been the cause or maybe a consequence of her irritable nature. It was made plain that her condescending to take evacuees had been an act of sheer kindness on her part and they were never allowed to forget it.

She generally wore an expression of disapproval, along with a faded, flower-patterned, crossover type of pinafore dress that fitted her portly figure where it touched. She had a capacious bosom to match her ample backside and hips. On her feet she generally wore fluffy-topped, carpet slippers and there were metal hair curlers in her pale-gingery hair except when she went to the shops. She then kept it under a hairnet, arranged in a victory roll that framed her flaccid, heavily-jowled, sallow face. The freckles on her face and arms reminded Jimmy of rust disease or brown mould on the whiteness of the lilies in the garden. Vociferous and acerbically outspoken, she was accustomed to getting her own way.

Mr Harris, by contrast, was a small, strong, wiry man of a quiet retiring nature and gentle manner, who was 'put on' no end, by his large, domineering wife. He was a thoughtful, good and kindly man who seldom retaliated when she provoked him. Trying his best to keep the peace, he plodded on uncomplaining bearing his burden unto himself. He had submitted to her will over the years, surrendering far too readily and too often. She seemed to have taken his quiet good nature as weakness and had repeatedly berated and belittled him. Maybe she blamed him for putting her through the agony of childbirth as she seemed to be one of those people who seek to hurt others because they have been hurt themselves. In her quest for retribution she used her vitriolic, lashing tongue as a weapon to humiliate him.

She would have been slimmer when they married and there must have been an attraction and passionate warmth between them. However, there had been a gradual decline from a trim prettiness to a shapeless, slow-moving comfort by the time she has reached the age of fifty. It would appear that the rows, the destructive bickering and the constant nagging had done their damage. The regular lambasting had led to a cold anger and a deep bitterness that lurked just below the surface of Mr Harris' apparently placid demeanour. Unhappiness and frustration had taken root and had grown between them like some dark, malignant flower. The fruit of their loins had left to join the forces and it was very seldom that he came home. Jimmy said later, "'E came 'ome on leave just t'once in all t'time I were billeted there."

Mr Harris kept his sadness and anger locked away and was determined not to let her see his emotional pain. They lived under the same roof but love seemed to have gone out of the window. He let the nagging flow over his head, saying "Yes dear" or "No dear" at regular intervals and he tried not to let it get to him. She often became infuriated by what she took to be his cold indifference and, at times, she literally shook with frustration and rage. Over the years he had closed up within himself and an icy bitterness and a distance had grown between them as too many sacrifices can turn the heart to stone. The marriage appeared to have become a hollow pretence kept up for appearance's sake; it was an example of the awful effects nagging can have upon the happiness and peace of mind of a husband. Mrs Harris kept herself to herself and only went out when she had to shop or go to church.

Mr and Mrs Worthington and their four years old daughter lived next door but one and kept two brown and white spaniels which gave the house an unpleasant animal smell. Mr Worthington was a short-sighted, neat and short-bodied, rather pompous man, who seemed to consider himself a cut above the locals. He was inclined to be secretive and taciturn and the boys found him bumptious, lugubrious and unfriendly as he peered through wire-rimmed spectacles that had really thick, round lenses. Jimmy said, "They look like the bottom of pop bottles if yer ask me."
His wife was a chatty person, who was always pleasant and amiable with everyone and they had come from the same area of West Yorkshire as Mrs Harris. This gave them at least one thing in common and they were the only people she ever socialised with.

Mr Harris loved to work in his garden and he spent most of his leisure time either there or at his allotment. During the warm

147

days of spring and in the heat of early summer he spent many hours digging, hoeing, planting and weeding. When heavy drops of rain plopped onto the large green leaves of the rhubarb at the bottom of the garden, he would shelter in his cluttered potting shed. He had inherited most of the accumulated junk in it from his father and things had been made to last in those days and nothing was thrown away. Old tools stood in rusty tins of oil and sand and the wooden handle of an old chisel looked more like a shaving brush as it had been hammered so often over the years.

The shed stood at the end of the wide path that ran between the houses and Mr Harris could usually be found sitting on a wooden stool obscured by the rank, malodorous, bluey-white, tobacco smoke that emanated in great clouds from his beloved and badly charred old pipe. As he worked, he was in the habit of holding it tightly clenched between his tobacco stained teeth, which had left deep indentations in the mouthpiece. He often used its stem to point things out to the boys. His wife would not let him smoke his stinking' pipe (as she called it) in the house and he had to 'go out in t't'shed' in all weathers.

He kept his garden - with its seemingly haphazard assortment of shrubs and flowers in a cottage garden style - very colourful and pleasing to the eye for the greater part of the year. He took great pride in doing a job thoroughly and in the spring, the summer and into the autumn, passers-by - their noses assailed by sweet scents – would comment that it 'looked a real picture'. The borders and rockery were full of flowers of every size, shape and colour and the neatly trimmed lawns were as smooth as bowling greens. In the summertime the side of the shed was a riot of colour as masses of sweet peas climbed up its trelliswork filling the air with their powerful, heady scent.

If only his home life had been as sweet. The shed was one of the boltholes where he was wont to make his escape and in it he found temporary relief from his wife's loud voiced, ill-tempered vituperance. He also had his allotment close to the Wyre pond that was crowded with bulrushes at the margins. By early autumn, their tall, deep-brown heads would become ragged and untidy and their cotton-like seeds would float away on the wind. He was only too happy to get away from her to spend the weekend 'digging for victory' and by the early summer his lettuce, onions, peas, tomatoes and runner beans were coming on nicely. He said to Jimmy, "I weren't surprised that we 'ad such a bad winter cos t'onions 'ad thick skins on 'em last yeer. They 'ave thin uns if it's goin' ter be a mild un."

The green pea pods were filling out and the runner beans were sporting their first bright-red flowers. These were tied in with coarse twine and supported on tall sticks that Archie and Jimmy had helped to collect from the hedgerows. His neat rows of vegetables were very much needed and he knew how important they were to the health of his recently enlarged brood. Many vegetables had been in short supply since the fall of France and in those dark days of increasing shortages and wartime austerity they were a godsend.

At other times when the atmosphere at home became too unbearable, he would make his escape to the Workingmen's Club. Once settled in his seat he would tamp down the dottle of Condor baccy in the bowl of his pipe using the flat bit on the end of his penknife. He would then light up and slowly sip his pint of mild to make it last while enjoying a much needed spell of peace and quiet. He needed to be free of her from time to time to reassert his independence and separateness. The club, with its pungent, smoke-laden air, was tucked away just off Front Street up a lane not far from the main school gate.

Sometimes he would make an excuse to pay a visit to the home of his good friend, Harold Mann, who was Miss Barker's cousin. Sometimes they would go to the club together and Harold agreed that the venomous tongue of Mrs Harris had poisoned their marriage. He said, "If she'd lived in t'seventeenth century she'd a been a prime candidate for t'Scold's Bridle or t'ducking stool." Harold lived with his tiny, sweet-natured wife, Nora, and his son, Brian, and his four-year-old daughter, Margaret. His old bay-windowed, end-of-terrace house called Beech View was on York Road not far from the traffic roundabout and he was the ARP warden for that area. With its white chasing, it stood on the corner of South Lane facing the Haxby Hall outbuildings. It seems that when young Brian had been taken to the village school for the first time he had not liked it one bit and had run home and his mother had to take him back but he was now well settled in.

Both men had been hard-working farmhands for most of their lives and Mr Harris had started his working life at the turn of the century. His mate, Harold, an honest broad-faced man, had started work for the Suttills at Crompton Farm at the age of thirteen, moving later to George Tindall's place. Even though he had been permanently lamed by a kick from a bullock as a young man, he had managed to obtain regular work. He had met his wife when she was working as a maid at The Laurels. He now covered certain parts of the village delivering the milk from a pony cart that belonged to the dairy at Church View Farm. The milk was carried in heavy, twelve-gallon (55.6 litres), aluminium, milk churns, which he managed to move by leaning them over on their bottom edge whilst twirling round the tight fitting circular lid with both hands. Wearing his brown-cotton, overall coat, he was as regular as clockwork and he had a habit of jingling the coins in the leather moneybag that hung on a strap across his chest and over his left shoulder. He ladled the milk into the assortment of jugs and containers that were offered up to him by his customers, which included Mrs Harris.

Abel's Farm had been in the hands of the same family for many, many years and was run by the very able (no pun intended) and respected 'aud gaffer', Robert, who was sixty years of age. Aud being a term of affection used for both humans and animals and it was pronounced 'ord' locally. Abel's was mainly a cattle farm, but they also reared sheep and grew mangolds, beet and potatoes and grew hay and corn in fields on the outskirts of the village. The farm and its dairy were situated on the south side of Front Street a little to the south west of Church Farm.

Church Farm was owned and worked by the two ruddy-faced, middle-aged, brothers Harry and Ernie Britton. Ernie was generally known as Jock. Both were thickset men of medium height with short, red necks. Their skin looked like creased leather and they had hands like shovels and they never bothered about appearances. What was the point in dressing up to get mucky? At the age of twenty-eight, Harry had fought in the Great War and had, coincidentally, been a private in the same battalion of the Green Howards that Uncle John was now in. Their sister, Maud, was their housekeeper. Down the lane at its juncture with North Lane, the brickwork had been rounded off to a height of about ten feet (3m.). Above it the layers of bricks had been stepped outwards to leave the top part as a normal right-angled corner. This strange, cleverly worked out, bricklaying allowed the farm vehicles to enter or leave the narrow opening without damaging the wall or the carts.

The wall at the juncture of Church Lane and North Lane, Haxby

Harold had put in a good word for Archie and as a result, he got part-time work at the farm. He worked there during the long, late spring and summer evenings and on Saturdays and during school holidays, which earned him a bit of extra pocket money on top of the sixpenny postal order sent to him from home each week. The Abel's still used horses - not tractors - for all their farm work. Tom Parrot, their affable and easy-going horseman, lived in at the farm and he and his wife, Elsie, who was the housekeeper there, had befriended Archie. Tom, who had recently become a member of the local LDV unit, really loved his horses and the job held for him an exhilaration and vitality that could not be matched anywhere else. Even though it meant rising early to bait the horses and long working days, Tom was happy. He would talk softly, gently and affectionately to his beloved horses and they would prick up and turned their ears to listen to him. They were a team and a good horse ploughman, like Tom, often walked more than ten miles every day and could plough an acre (about the area of a football pitch) in an hour. Archie loved working in the fragrant summer fields where there were no jarring mechanical noises, just the snorting and stamping of the horses and the occasional command from Tom who seemed to have an uncanny power over them.

He warned Archie never to touch the lump on Monty's back, "It contains a ganglion of nerve endings that are close t't' surface and it's excessively sensitive. That pony 'as a certain spark in its eye that speaks of fire in its heart" If touched on it, Harold's skittish milk cart pony would go berserk and race around kicking out at any person or thing. Archie often helped Tom to muck out by raking up the old straw and putting fresh clean bedding down. He liked feeding and grooming the heavy farm horses and was happy to help with the loading and carting of the hay. In the baking heat of early summer, he would roll up his shirtsleeves and get stuck in.

He was not so keen on some of the other jobs. It was no fun getting up very early in the morning during the Easter break when it was still chilly with flurries of hail and sleet. Setting the spuds nine inches apart in the drills was backbreaking and singling the sugar beet meant being bent over all day - often in wet and muddy conditions. Leaving a space of three inches [8 centimetres] between each young beet plant was known as 'thinning'. The seedlings between every third plant had to be pulled out to allow the plant to grow to a decent size by the autumn. He hated it but it was vitally important that the country's sugar requirements should be met in those times of heavy shipping losses. The pulp left after the sugar had been removed was used to make cattle pellets. By late spring, as the tempo of natural life was quickening, the weather turned unseasonably hot.

8. Grove House

By late May, the rhododendron shrubs were coming into full flower beside the forest tracks and many of the mauve and pink blooms were the size of my face. It had been decided that Sutherland Lodge was too close to the newly opened army camp and they feared that it might become a target for enemy aircraft. It was also too far off the beaten track making it difficult for our relatives to visit. As Mam had remarked, "It's a beautiful spot but it's too out of the way." Plans were made to move us out, but one little lad was to stay behind to live with the Wards at Kelton Banks Farm as they had taken a great liking to him.

On a fine, sunny day Robinson's motor coach and a pantechnicon arrived and took everything and everyone to the newly set up nursery school at Grove House. This was about three miles east as the crow flies, but seventeen miles by coach along the winding country roads. Mr Robinson also ran a daily bus service between the villages of Cropton, Lastingham and Rosedale. Our journey took us south along forest tracks and narrow lanes to Cropton and Wrelton before turning on to the Pickering road. From there we travelled up the A169 Whitby road as far as the Lockton turn off where a narrow road dropped down from the wide sweep of the moors descending into a deep green valley where it crossed a narrow stone bridge beside an old watermill. The coach then climbed the steep hill into the isolated hamlet of Levisham with its quaint stone houses, farms and wide grass verges.

From there we travelled along a narrow sunken lane between high earthen banks topped with thorn hedgerows and dry-stone walls before traversing an open, unfenced grassy area where cattle grazed. Here the road swung sharply to the left and down a steep incline becoming a leafy lane that emerged at a little railway station. We had passed this spot on the train eight months earlier. Grove House stood about a hundred yards to the east of the level crossing. It was about 35 miles from home and 6 miles north of Pickering tucked away in a beautiful wooded valley on the southern edge of the rugged North Yorkshire Moors. One elderly local when asked, "Why was the station built so far from the village?" replied with laconic country logic, "Ah suppose they wanted it close t't'railway line."

Levisham Crossing, taken from Grove House in 2003.

The large, stone-built house was said to have been converted from an old farmhouse around the year 1856, the work being done on the orders of the Reverend Robert Skelton who was the Rector of Levisham and the Vicar of Rosedale. The house was built with locally quarried, golden sandstone, which had become blackened by the smoke from the steam trains that had passed close by for more than a century. The reverend gentleman had been obliged to sell his former residence, Levisham Hall, and most of his local properties to pay off his debts on becoming bankrupt. It was alleged that his financial problems were caused by ill-advised investments, womanising and heavy drinking. James Walker, an entrepreneur from Leeds, bought his former estate and by 1859 he, his wife and their six children were in residence at the Hall.

By 1881 Grove House had become the home of seventy years old Robert Hansell, a local iron ore proprietor from Rosedale who lived in it with his wife Hannah, the daughter of the Reverend Skelton. Their thirty years old, unmarried daughter, Jane, acted as their housekeeper. At the time of the 1891 census the house was unoccupied standing silent and sadly neglected. After it was reoccupied, a large two-storey extension was added at the eastern side and, at a later date, a female member of the Rowntree's of York bought it. They used it as an occasional holiday home and it was rented out to family and friends when they were not in residence.

In the 1930s another member of the family married a Mr Wilkinson and they used Grove House as their country residence. Their wedding reception, a huge affair with many well-to-do guests, was held there shortly before the war. The senior signalman's eldest son, Ernest Artley, who was eight years old at the time, was entrusted with the job of opening the large, five-barred, wooden, entrance gate for the well-heeled wedding guests as they arrived in their smart, shiny motor cars. The Wilkinsons gave up the house when it was requisitioned for our use.

The gravelled lane crossed the railway line close to a brick signal box and the station buildings could be clearly seen from the house, as there were no trees to block the view at that time and we were able watch the steam trains coming and going. There were two old, semi-detached, stone cottages almost opposite the booking office, which were set back behind small front gardens on the far side of the line. Jack Pickering, the junior signalman, lived in one of them and a short distance north of his signal cabin there was another, narrow, gated level crossing linking two farm tracks.

On arrival we followed the spare and sprightly figure of Miss Thorne from the coach, which had pulled up under the luxuriant, green foliage of a towering beech tree. Kitty held open the heavy, white painted gate and we skipped up the gravelled drive that was edged with neatly trimmed lawns and flowerbeds. In some parts of the garden there were glossy-leafed rhododendron shrubs that were adorned with masses of huge, red, multi-floretted blossoms. A lovely, variegated holly shrub, with white edged leaves, stood on the lawn near the station goods yard. In the borders the last few spikes of purple-flowered honesty were going over and flat, round, green seedcases were forming. In time these would become large and opaque and we called them silver pennies. Their grey-green leaves were spear-shaped and in the borders tulips and primulas were still in flower.

Grove House

Grove House, a solid, thick-walled, seven-bedroomed, residence within twelve acres of gardens and shrubbery, nestled in the lee of a steep wooded hillside. Deep in the valley amidst the peace and quiet of lovely countryside, the only other buildings were the stationhouse and the two old cottages on the far side of the track. It was a wonderful old Victorian gentleman's house and its grandeur and scale was in stark contrast with our working class house that could have fitted into one corner of it. There were only fourteen children - aged from two years up to six - in the nursery when the war started, but that number had grown to twenty-four as the bombing raids on Middlesbrough had increased.

Our little band of infants and toddlers entered the house through a solid oak door that led into a square, stone-built porch with a crenellated parapet. The side windows had wooden shutters on the outside and above the inner door was a rectangular, stained glass window. When the sun shone it cast red and orange-coloured patterns onto the plush carpet below the intricately wrought iron chandelier that hung over the long corridor. Passing dark brown wainscoting we came to the foot of the wide staircase with its intricately carved newel post. Its risers and treads were thickly carpeted and the banisters were made of pitch pine. Turning right we passed through a finely carved, panelled door into a large private lounge, which was to become our playroom.

The long room had two wide, large-paned, sash windows with wood panelled reveals. The thick walls were also wood-panelled and the windows looked out onto a long, wide, paved verandah with a glass roof that was supported on square wooden posts. It formed an open sided portico and French doors led on to it. On the far side four stone steps led down to a gravelled area, beyond which there were more well tended lawns and colourful flowerbeds. The large, square windows were not blast-taped as they had blackout screens and sturdy wooden shutters to protect us from the battering rain and howling gales. Carved, forward-facing lion heads adorned the top corners of the fluted architraves of the windows. Apparently, lions' heads featured prominently on the Rowntree family crest. The high ceilinged room had beautifully moulded medallions and cornices and on the south wall was a wide, stone chimneybreast with a magnificent marble fireplace built to hold a blazing log fire. There was a wire-mesh fireguard to ensure that we did not come to any harm.

Behind the playroom lay the dining room, which also had a fine but smaller fireplace. A doorway led from it into a wide, stone-built, glass-windowed porch that faced south onto the grassy garden at the rear of the house. Ten yards (9m.) away from the porch was a smooth-barked Locust tree, also known as Silver Chain or White Laburnum - a tree of light and graceful proportions which had long slender branches and two feet up from its base it forked and its leaning trunk made it easy for agile youngsters such as us to climb. It was just one of the many exotic and beautiful ornamental trees and shrubs in the spacious surroundings of the grand old house that we were to come to know every inch of. Some of the shrubs were rare species brought from foreign lands by wealthy owners, which was apparently the fashionable thing to do in Victorian times.

To the left of the front hallway was a large cloakroom and behind it lay a stone-flagged kitchen with low beams that had large metal hooks in them. In the centre stood a heavy wooden table scrubbed almost white and a deep, square, vitreous china sink stood under the blast-taped window of the scullery next door. It was a much smaller kitchen than the one at Sutherland Lodge but this time we had the whole house to ourselves. Behind the kitchen there was a large larder that kept the food cool in the summer months.

The grand staircase had a gracefully curving balustrade and there were beautiful stained glass windows above the landing half way up it. At the top there was a large bathroom and our metal-framed beds had been set up in the dormitory, which was in the wing that had been added to the house some forty years earlier. Five large bedrooms, in which the nursery staffs were to sleep, led off a long corridor. The rooms had a small wrought iron, black-leaded fireplace with a mantle-shelf supported on delicately fluted, wooden columns and there was a fender with a brass rail around each hearth. The bedrooms were directly above the kitchen and larder and their small-paned windows were all blast-taped.

At the southern end of the garden there was an overgrown pond where we sometimes saw dark-grey, white-billed coots that dived and stayed under the water for so long that we thought they must have drowned. We were not allowed down there on our own so Kitty took us to see the small, brown, chestnut-cheeked little grebes, commonly called dabchicks, with the female carrying three tiny, fluffy chicks on her back. She had a small whitish patch on each cheek where the beak joined it and her nest actually floated on the water amongst the reeds. There were small, furtive waterhens with white-streaked flanks and red beaks tipped with yellow that looked as if they were wearing red garters on their green legs. They are, more correctly, called moorhens and we watched them as they dived for food. Emerging mayflies performed their strange up-and-down dance above the placid, pearly sheen of the water, where hundreds of gnats formed smoky clouds. A long, rustic fence separated the garden from the station goods yard. The wooded slopes above the house were clothed in a mixture of conifers and deciduous trees.

The large, three-bedroom, stone-built, stationhouse stood just south of the pair of cottages and its gable end abutted the northbound platform. The door of the paved yard at the back of the house led directly on to this 'up' platform. Near it was a cast iron, Rowntree's, 1d (0.5p) chocolate dispensing machine and close by was a wrought iron bench with a wooden seat. The gable end of the house had a clock let into it at about shoulder height. It had a big, round, white dial faced with black Roman numerals proclaiming in black letters that J. Sidebottom & Son of Buxton had made it. The front door of the stationhouse was reached through a wicket gate and a footpath that led west from the platform. Late tulips were in flower in its little front garden where the door to the kitchen was set within a rectangular stone porch. The front windows overlooked the fields beside the railway line.

The station house and cottages in 2003.

The kind and good-natured, senior signalman, Mr Walter Artley, lived here and on rising his first job was to wind up the platform clock from within his second sitting room. The family called that room The Office, as it had formerly been the station booking office. A door from the first sitting room led into the kitchen where a wooden clothes maiden, that was raised and lowered by means of cords and pulleys, hung from the ceiling above a gleaming black-leaded fire range. The fire consumed lots of wood, but there was plenty of that to be had nearby.

The stairs led from the kitchen to the bedrooms where ceramic pitchers and ewers were used for washing. Walter lived with his wife, Dorothy, and their four children, namely, Ernest - aged twelve; Monica - ten; Sheila -aged eight and two years old Clifford. Mrs Artley, a friendly and caring lady, played the organ in Levisham Chapel-of-Ease every Sunday. She also played for the services held in the tiny 'Valley Church' in the summer months. This lay at the bottom of a steep path in the deep ravine between the villages of Levisham and Lockton that became very muddy and slippery in wet weather.

There was a neatly cultivated flower and vegetable garden behind the stationhouse and it had an outside brick coalhouse and a privy with a flush toilet. A narrow beck ran past the bottom of their long garden before it swung west to drain into Pickering Beck. In dry, calm weather the beck could be heard as it babbled quietly over the water-worn pebbles of its stony bed. The Artleys kept a few black-faced Masham sheep and we would often hear the lowing of their black and brown Holstein cows as they grazed in the meadow. The smelly cow byre and the stables were situated in a range of wooden buildings at the far end of the field. The excess milk was carried across to Grove House in large, two-gallon, white enamelled jugs to be sold to Dinner Lady.

On balmy early summer evenings we could hear Mrs Artley calling the cows in as sound carried a long way in the quietness of that deep valley. The animals would amble along with their distended udders leaking milk and after we got to know Monica, she would occasionally take us into the warm, cosy atmosphere of the byre. We liked to watch Mrs Artley as she sat on a three-legged stool with her head resting against the cow's side calmly milking them by hand. The milk from the limpid-eyed cows would squirt noisily into the white enamelled pails. The cows seemed like huge beasts to us but they had a nice warm, sweet smell close up. Occasionally, as a special treat, we would be given a glass of the warm, creamy milk, which was at its richest and most plentiful when the meadow grass was lush and green. Mrs Artley used to separate the lumpy curds from the thin watery whey when she made cheese in an old contraption that had a wooden barrel fixed to a cast iron wheel. To rotate it she turned the handle on the side and the whey was given to the pigs.

The stables housed Charlie their loveable little black pony, Daisy, their roan horse and her foal. They called the partition between their stalls the skelbeast. The cow byre was known as the shippon - terms that lingered from a bygone age. They kept a few clucking and scratching hens and reared a couple of pigs that were killed at Christmas to supply the family with sufficient ham and bacon for the year to come. The small-paned windows of the station house and the railway cottages were, of course, criss-crossed with sticky blast tape and oil lamps were used to light the place.

Levisham village was one and a half miles away up the steep gravelled lane, which - during high summer when the stones were dry and sunlit - became a dazzling white ribbon. The village could be reached by a shorter but steeper route as a rutted, earthen footpath led off the lane just above Grove House passing behind the range of stone outbuildings that were used to store coal, garden tools and suchlike. It continued eastward behind one of the larger outbuildings that housed the electric generator before swinging left to climb steeply through mixed woodland and hazel shrubs. It emerged into open fields halfway up the hillside and - with a blackthorn hedge to the left – it led up to a barn. Here it turned right following the grassy line of a disused iron ore tramway before climbing steeply up to a wooden bench, which had been put there to celebrate the Coronation of King George the Sixth three years back. From it there was an excellent view of Newtondale and the railway line running through it and Newton village could be seen perched on the opposite hilltop. From the bench the path continued beside grassy fields before emerging on a lane that entered Levisham village close to the Chapel-of-Ease. The 'squire' of the manor house at that time was a Mr Baldwin, the co-founder of the Paton and Baldwin wool manufacturing and knitting pattern empire, a firm that was a household name at that time. Their head office and factory were in Darlington, some fifty miles to the north west and Mr Baldwin had lived in the Hall with his family for the last sixteen years.

The Hall was actually little more than a large, three-storey cottage with a stone porch and double bay windows that were castellated at the top. It was full of quaint nooks and tiny rooms and its commanding position gave it fine views of the Lockton valley and the countryside to the south. It stood behind the tiny Chapel-of-Ease at the top end of the main street next to Low Grange Farm that had the date 1802 engraved on it. Around the turn of the century the wife of the future Lord Baden-Powell had hired the Hall for an extended holiday with her young family. At that time her husband, Robert, was a cavalry officer fighting in the Boer War. He was involved in the defence of Mafeking, which was under siege and he became famous after founding the Boy Scout movement in 1908 and the Girl Guides two years later.

On those glorious summer mornings the golden light of the sun, as it rose over the high ridge to the east, bathed the dark fringe of trees on the opposite hillside turning them a bright green. The dawn of a new day was the signal for choirs of birds to break into gloriously cascading waves of song. While the big house was still immersed in half-light and sombre shadows, we were roused, washed and dressed. The strengthening power of the ascending sun slowly burnt off the dew on the meadow and her rays dissipated the mists from the valley, as we sat down to breakfast. This usually consisted of thick, steaming porridge, made with Scott's Porridge Oats that had a dollop of jam or treacle on it. We then filled up on thickly buttered toast and marmalade. Every morning, after breakfast, Kitty sat the younger children on a row of little ceramic chamber potties that we called pos (pronounced pose) or jerries. They were sat outside on the verandah, if the weather was dry and warm and, if it was cold or wet, they would be sat inside until they had done their 'duty' leaving the windows and doors open because of the pong. We older children were able to go to the toilet by ourselves. The large dormitory had a polished wooden floor and an elegant tiled fireplace and it was in here that most of the younger children slept.

The older ones, including myself, were allowed to stay up a little later than the rest and we slept in the playroom. At midday we had a hot savoury meal with plenty of potatoes and vegetables depending on the season of the year, as there were no freezers to keep food fresh in those days. A sweet of sago, tapioca (that we called frogspawn), rice pudding, jam roly-poly or plum duff followed. After our meal we were laid in our little beds with the window shutters closed and this was our regular nap of an hour or so to allow our food to digest. In the half-light the ugly leonine faces above the windows frightened me and I hid my head under the bedclothes. If we were naughty and refused to lie down or if Eric and I disturbed the other children by talking, we were made to stand in the corner with our faces to the wall. We were often told off but were never smacked. After our nap we would sometimes be taken for a walk along the path that started not far from the kitchen door.

Pretending to be soldiers or airmen, we chattered and babbled on. Aeroplanes were all the rage at that time and we zoomed about with our arms outspread dodging round the adults. We no doubt drove them mad making aeroplane noises as we bombed and killed hundreds of nasty Jerries (Germans) in our imagination. My three years old brother, George, was quite content watching a snail pushing out one feeler at a time as it emerged from its shell or in pushing the large, fluffy white toy Scottie dog along. With its short fur and stubby upright tail, it was mounted on a steel framework that had four small, solid, rubber-tyred, tin wheels. It had a tubular steel handle with which to trundle it along and 'our' George really loved it. Eric preferred to pedal around on the flat-seated tricycle that had replaced the one wrecked at Sutherland Lodge.

In the evenings, tired out and grimy but well fed, we were put in the magnificent antique bath that had bright, shiny copper taps and beautiful polished mahogany side panels. It could comfortably accommodate three adults within its massive tub, but the staff had to go sparingly on the amount of water they used, otherwise we might have drowned in it. It was so different to the long, zinc-coated tin bath we had been accustomed to at home on our weekly bath night. At home the anodised tub had been placed in front of the kitchen fire and it took several pans and kettles of boiling water to fill it. Here we had scalding hot water at just the turn of a tap and it was still a great novelty to us: we had never seen such luxury, even at Sutherland Lodge! Amid great clouds of steam four or five of us would splash about in it and, with our little naked bodies glowing pink and warm, Kitty would dry us. I was kept snug and warm wrapped in a huge, soft, fluffy white towel and she gave me lots of hugs and I loved her very much. We would have done anything for her. She was pure of heart and would never dream of hurting anybody's feelings; in fact, there was not a hint of deceit in her make-up.

We knelt by our beds every night to say the prayers that Kitty had taught us, such as, " As I lay me down to sleep, I ask thee Lord my soul to keep, If I should die before I wake, I ask thee Lord my soul to take! Amen" and "Gentle Jesus meek and mild, Look upon a little child, Pity my complicity, Come to me when I die. Amen." After that we were tucked into our beds, scarcely aware that there was a war on outside our cosy, sheltered, little world. At times, as I lay tucked up in bed, I could hear the barking of a dog fox and the quietness was sometimes rudely shattered by the painful death cries of some small animal in the woods. When woken by the wind as it rattled the wooden shutters during heavy rainstorms, I would lay in the darkened room listening to the sounds of the rushing water in the flooded beck. In dry weather water just trickled down the runnel beside the lane that led up to Levisham village but, at times like this, it became a gushing torrent. Gusts of wind would buffet the sturdy old house as they howled round it like the spirits in hell. As the thunder rumbled and growled and the lightning flashed I would hide under the bed covers frightened but enthralled by the awesome power of nature. Kitty got us to count the seconds between the flash and the thunder when we were unable to sleep and this helped to take our minds off it for a while. She said, "You can tell by the time between them whether it is moving away or not"

We would get quite excited when we were told that 'the parents are coming out to visit the bairns'. We would sit and wait expectantly in the roofed shelter or on the seat of the wrought iron bench on the station platform and listen eagerly for the first faint train whistle to come from the quiet remoteness of the Newtondale Gorge. In the goods yard there was a big warehouse where coal for the trains was stored, but our coal was delivered in a lorry that came from Pickering. Nearby was a small wooden hut with a stovepipe chimney sticking up from its sloping roof in which paraffin and oil were stored for use in the lamps on the platform, in the stationhouse and in the booking office.

The Artley children by the hut on the platform in 1940.

So we chatted and fidgeted as we impatiently waited. It was so still and quiet that we could hear the Artley's sheep as they ripped up and chomped on the tussocks of grass in the field beyond the fence. Behind us the hundreds of colourful roses - that grew in profusion in the rich soil by the diagonally sloping slats of the fence - scented the air. The colourful flowerbeds were edged with white-painted stones and the hanging baskets and tubs on the platforms were well tended and kept extremely neat and colourful. In recent years, Mr Artley had entered the annual Best Kept Railway competition, winning the much-coveted first prize on a number of occasions. We got excited on hearing a faraway whistle and feeling a slight vibration under our feet. The puffing sounds became louder and the shiny-black, steam train appeared round the bend. Clouds of black smoke and hissing white steam belched out to veil the signal box as the train slowed down.

Our tremulous excitement increased as the great engine rumbled to a halt. The heavy doors slammed back and the parents and relatives stepped down onto the platform. Mam was there with Dad in his civvy clothes, which meant that he had a week's leave. I raced towards them to be scooped up into Mam's loving arms and she hugged me ever so tight and smothered me in loving kisses. George was still in the garden with Kitty, as he was too young to be wandering about on the platform. I did not understood why there were tears running down Mam's cheeks when we were so happy

It was a warm sunny day at the beginning of June and Dad played football with us in the field. When he took off his jacket and rolled up his sleeves we were reminded of his army service in China and India as a young man. His strong, muscular, sunburnt arms, with their haze of fine fair hairs, were covered in colourful red, black and blue tattoos. On one arm there was a tattoos of his army badge, on the other there was a naked woman with a snake wrapped around her that extended from the back of his hand to his elbow and when he clenched and unclenched his fist it looked as though she was dancing. After working up a good sweat he took his shirt off unveiling the great eagle with widespread wings that was tattooed across his chest. It looked as though it was flying when he tensed and relaxed his pectoral muscles.

He told us fascinating stories about his sea voyages to foreign lands where he had seen dolphins and flying fish and he talked of his army service in China, Egypt and India, saying, "In India we had servants and lived like gentlemen. The charwallahs made and served us tea and punkahwallahs cooled us with fans made from palm fronds. The atmosphere was very dry and hot. Darzis made us new clothes and dhobiwallahs did our laundry, washing our clothes in the river in which huge venomous snakes could be seen swimming." He told us that, "There were numerous beggars in dhotis (loin clothes) and the sacred cows wandered about the streets wearing garlands of flowers round their necks." He showed us pictures of some of the animals he had seen, such as elephants, Bengal tigers, monkeys, peacocks and hyenas. "July was the rainy season," he continued. "It was heaviest in the evenings when it really lashed down and it went on for weeks - often with spectacular displays of lightning. At other times the blazing sun bleached our hair and our uniforms as the bullock cart drivers took us past banana plantations and beneath coconut palms and we paid them in rupees and annas" He told us about the Red Fort in Delhi and 'The Black Hole of Calcutta'; he had seen so many wonderful exotic things that we could only dream about.

After a while we grew tired of sitting and were eager to run about again and Dad said "The Indians played us at football in their bare feet on rough sand and gravel pitches." He dribbled a rubber ball around us pretending to be the new blond-haired, Middlesbrough football sensation, Wilf Mannion, and I was supposed to be George Hardwick, the brilliant left fullback with the film star good looks reminiscent of Clarke Gable. A local lad, just like Mannion, he was to captain the England team after the war. Before the war, Dad had been among the cheering crowd at Ayresome Park football ground when the twenty years old Mannion had scored four goals for the 'Boro' in a dazzling exhibition of his footballing skills. The Boro were in the top division of the Football League and on a bright sunny day two weeks before the Christmas of 1938, Dad had seen them thrash the tangerine-shirted Blackpool team 9-2. He had been there when they had recently beaten Portsmouth 8-2 when Mannion had scored a brilliant hat trick. He was Dad's hero

Soon afterwards, the mayblossom faded and fell and the elders produced their pinky-white curds. Blatant, blood red blotches of wild poppy splashed the lush, greenery of the roadside verges contrasting sharply with the pallid umbels of the hedge parsley. The air on that sultry afternoon became oppressive as dark, cumulus clouds massed and heaved up behind the western hillside. The light faded and ragged rain clouds raced overhead as the wind rose. As the storm increased in fury the wind shrieked and howled like a multitude of lost souls and the tops of the trees thrashed about wildly as the rain clattered down in stair rods onto the portico roof making the glass sing before it cascaded down into the guttering of the verandah. The beck that was normally just a trickle, became a deep raging torrent and rainwater dripped incessantly from the eaves until, suddenly, the violence of the summer storm abated as quickly as it had arisen.

On that unusually dull and chilly summer day mother came to visit us again but Dad was not with her as all leave had been cancelled. She was wearing her soft, round, dark-blue, narrow-brimmed hat, her favourite light blue, white-spotted frock and her navy blue coat, but I sensed a deep sadness in her, and a whole range of emotions seemed to flit across her honest open face. The

168

smile that usually lit it up was missing this time and she looked as pale and melancholy as the clouded, battleship-grey sky. In the dim half-light of the hallway I could see that she was close to tears, which made me feel sad in return. We were not to know that she had just learned that her younger brother, Private John Bradford, was in retreat to the French coast. His battalion was fighting a rearguard action with their backs to the sea as thousands of French, British and Allied troops were surrounded by the Germans and trapped on the long flat beaches near Dunkirk. Some sought refuge in the high, bone-coloured, sand dunes that rimmed the beaches in which even marram grass struggled to survive.

I was to learn later that the German Army had smashed its way through neutral Holland and Belgium in just four days and in the near rout towns and villages had become flaming ruins. Major General Erwin Rommel, in command of the 7th Panzer (Armoured) Division, deploying some 1,800 tanks, had broken through the last of the French defences and turned back an Anglo-French counter attack at Arras in which Uncle John had been involved. His thrust to the Somme had severed the BEF from the French forces to the south and he had then taken the ports of Saint Valery and Cherbourg. With most of the inadequate British aircraft shot down or badly damaged, he took the airfields. The Wehrmacht had swept across northern France driving the BEF before them before thrusting north towards the coast. Britain's 'invincible army' was in full flight, caught in a pincer movement. The whole front crumbled, and the Belgian Government capitulated. As the Germans advanced in persistent drizzle towards the flat and marshy coastal plains, Uncle John was among the troops vainly struggling against overwhelming odds to hold the defensive perimeter line on the canal that ran from Burgues, through Furnes to the Nieuport area to the east of Dunkirk. The name must have reminded him of the Newport area of Middlesbrough where he had grown up and he must have wished that he was back there.

Later he told Gran of the long queues of soldiers, wearing greatcoats or dripping groundsheets, on the crowded beaches as the rain was driven on by a cold northerly wind. Shivering with cold and fear they waited patiently for their turn to be taken off. The canals and roads were choked with wrecked lorries and the fields flooded as Luftwaffe bombs breached the dykes. Abandoned harrows, rakes and spades spoke of a more peaceful time.

Winston Churchill gave the go ahead for a massive rescue bid. More than a hundred thousand soldiers were quickly taken onto ships at Dunkirk harbour and, providentially for a time, they were hidden under a dense bank of fog. The men waded, shoulder deep, into the sea to meet the flotilla of small boats that had made the parlous Channel crossing to bring men directly home or to ferry them to the waiting ships. When the fog lifted the new, twin-engined, Messerschmitt 110 fighters - some with rows of jagged shark's teeth painted on their noses - machine-gunned the town and the harbour. Terrifying, screaming, crank-winged, Junkers 87s, known as Stukas, swept down like dark, howling birds of prey. The Luftwaffe had fixed sirens to their wheels and on the tails of the bombs and they strafed and bombed the waiting ships, the small boats and the long, orderly, zigzag lines of soldiers. Dazed and wounded men sat or lay on the open beach crying out for water or medical attention. It was pure mayhem. The RAF was conspicuous by its absence having lost half of its obsolete aircraft within the first forty-eight hours. It was a sad tale of heroic failure. Broken bodies littered the beaches like squashed fruit and the sweet, cloying, gut-wrenching stench of putrefaction was everywhere. The tides ran red and black with blood and oil as hundreds of khaki clad bodies floated face down in the filthy water.

Gran and her daughters, who had seen the bloodstained stretchers on the cinema newsreels, were relieved on learning that John was safe. He had been among the last to get away, being taken off the mole onto a ship that had made the parlous trip out and back a total of nine times already. Totally worn out he had curled up on the deck under his greatcoat collapsing into a sleep of utter exhaustion for the whole trip. He was in a sorry state and later the passage home was just a hazy memory. On arrival on the south coast there was not a breath of wind or a cloud in the sky. Like thousands of others he arrived hungry and unshaven sporting a week's growth of stubble. Just twenty-one years old, he was unspeakably weary with eyes that were red-rimmed and bloodshot. When he disembarked under the grey barrage balloons at Dover he was half starved with his sodden uniform ripped and filthy. He sat on the pavement with his back to a garden wall alongside other bedraggled soldiers, some of whom had no uniform at all wearing old rags that they had managed to pick up. The people opened their hearts to the lads of the battered army and brought out jugs of tea and plates of food. They were beaten but unconquered in spirit as they waited to be sent home on much-needed leave.

All told nearly 350,000 British, French, Belgian and Polish troops were brought out and the *Daily Mirror* banner headlines called the whole evacuation 'Bloody Marvellous'. By some miracle, most of the army had been saved to fight another day. People living on the south coast had witnessed the bombing, the fires and the great pall of black smoke that hung over Dunkirk.

Many scheduled trains were cancelled in order to get the men away from the coast. The troops had priority and more than three thousand special trains were laid on. Uncle John was given a blank postcard on which to write his Christian name, home address and 'Am safe'. On receiving it Gran was over the moon. The station platforms were crammed with soldiers and the WVS did sterling service with their sandwiches, fruit and steaming tea urns. John was sent to a rest camp for a couple of days to be re-equipped and to recuperate a little before being given a seventy-two hour leave pass. Once home his mother and three sisters greeted him with tears of joy and relief. He slept long and late and soon made up for his recent lack of food. People bought him beer in the *Newport* pub and the returning 'heroes' were allowed into dances and cinemas without paying. On visiting Archie, Gran said, "I was so worried when John was sent abroad but he has experienced the utter madness of war at first hand."

He now knew the horror and pity of seeing friends killed in combat and had gazed repeatedly on the repulsive face of death. He had left home little more than a boy but had returned a man. On leave he refused to talk about it saying only that it was too close and too painful to think about. He just wanted to blot out of his mind the dull, stupid expression he had seen on the faces of the dead and it would be some time before he laughed out loud again.

The Green Howards were based at Richmond in North Yorkshire and on being recalled to duty at the Alma Barracks he was promoted to the rank of Corporal. In French the name meant strong hill. The camp was situated not far from the Norman castle with its hundred feet high, rectangular, thick-walled keep, which stood on a rocky promontory overlooking the River Swale. Sturdy curtain walls surrounded the inner bailey and what had been the outer bailey was now the town's cobbled market place. A tall 18th century stone obelisk, which had replaced an earlier ancient market cross, stood in its centre with winding alleys and narrow streets - called 'wynds' in these parts - radiating out from it. The Norman Holy Trinity church with a strange arrangement of shops built into its walls was later to become the regimental museum.

The ranks of Uncle John's battalion had been sorely depleted by the debacle in France. He, and hundreds of other men of the defeated army, retrained and soon afterwards were posted to Blandford in Dorset becoming part of the 50th Northumbrian Division. They had learned some harsh lessons in France and here they continued to hone their new skills. They lived under canvas in long rows of bell tents, sleeping with their feet to the central pole. The battalion was made to work hard and the men were brought to a high state of fitness. Their uniforms had to be spotless, with razor sharp creases, and their packs had to be correct in every detail. Their rifles and brass buckles gleamed in the sun as they went out on long route marches in full kit and the locals became accustomed to the sound of their heavy, steel-shod boots crashing down onto the metalled roads. Carrying heavy packs they manoeuvred and streamed over tough assault courses; they dug trenches, hacking into the earth with their heart-shaped trenching tools. They suffered frequent air raids and carried out regular duties; including the guarding of the nearby prisoner-of-war camp.

We saw troop trains passing through Levisham station crammed with grim-faced soldiers, hollow-eyed from lack of sleep, many of them with bandaged heads or their arms in slings. These, like our Uncle John, were the lucky ones and they waved to us from the carriage windows no doubt delighted to be going home on leave. The humiliating retreat to and from Dunkirk had been an unmitigated disaster. England had not been so vulnerable since the Napoleonic Wars and the Government came perilously close to caving in with many people feeling that the war was all but lost. The country was at rock bottom and now stood alone against the might of the all-conquering Germans. In mid June German troops marched up the Champs Elysees for the first time since 1871. A bloody battle on English soil could easily have been next as England was now within easy striking distance of the Luftwaffe in occupied France. In a stirring speech Winston Churchill said, "Let us brace ourselves to our duty…'

At Grove House time passed peacefully and the long hot, blazing summer days were followed by short, hot, sweaty nights. We always seemed to have long, hot summers in those early war years and we played in the sunshine blissfully unaware of what was taking place across the English Channel. One day we were playing out on the daisy-covered lawn vainly attempting to catch grasshoppers when a German Dornier bomber roared by very low overhead. It was black and huge with two machine cannons sticking out of its transparent nose turret and it seemed to be following the railway line northwards and the sudden ear splitting noise shocked and frightened us. It was there and gone in no time, leaving the air pulsating, before we even realised what had happened. We were terrified and in a panic, crying our eyes out as. Kitty hurried us - a little too late - into the doubtful safety of the dayroom.

9. Salad Days

Balmy, sunlit days followed one upon the other and we made chains from the daisies that were scattered across the green, neatly trimmed lawns. Bees buzzed busily working tirelessly as they went from flower to flower pollinating the plants. "They carry the pollen in sacs on their legs and they collect the nectar in their crops. From it they make sweet golden honey," Kitty told us. "A bee has to visit thousands of flowers to make just one spoonful of honey." Colourful butterflies fluttered by or basked in the sun with their wings raised or widespread, as pale-blue damselflies, with long, thin bodies, whizzed about on shimmering, translucent wings. On the horse chestnut tree, the green, spiky seedcases were starting to fill out and little bunches of tiny green berries had succeeded the great white curds of the elderblossom. In the verdant tranquillity of that sequestered, sylvan setting it was hard to believe there was a war on.

On certain mornings our grey-haired gardener-handyman, who wore a flat cap; a waistcoat; green corduroy trousers held up by a broad, brass-buckled, leather belt and heavy boots, was fuming after finding the lawns covered in freshly-excavated molehills. He called the moles nasty mouldiwarps; the Artley's cows were kine, neats or oxen; rabbits were coneys and wood pigeons were cushats. The speech patterns of more than a hundred years back were alive and well in him: he was a throwback to an earlier way of life that was fast disappearing.

We would often glimpse colourful birds and sometimes hear the faint hollow knockings of woodpeckers in the woods. In the meadow we picked the wild flowers that grew in abundance and breathed in the summer scents of new mown rye grass and foxtails. We held buttercups under each others chins believing that if they reflected the yellow of the petals it indicated that that person liked butter. We were delighted when we glimpsed baby rabbits with their bobbing white scuts from the playroom windows when no one was about. They hopped and bounced contentedly across the grass on their soft padded feet but made a dash for cover when anyone approached.

Above a thickly wooded area beside the lane up to Levisham there was a south-facing grassy bank that was warmed by the sun in the afternoon and well into the long summer evenings. On the other side of the road was a gulley, known locally as a griff. The silver birch and scrub oaks, which struggled to grow on it, were small and stunted and did not cast much shade making it ideal for the adders that thrived there. The old gardener called them northern vipers, adding, "Snakes won't rest under an ash tree or on its leaves. It 'as magical properties and an adder can be killed by a single blow from an ash stick." He always kept an ash walking stick by him and he told us that, "Snakes are cold-blooded reptiles and can only raise their body temperature by getting 'eat directly from t'sun or by absorbing it from sun-warmed surfaces."

The area was known locally as Adder Bank and Miss Thorne had sternly warned us never to go up there. This was partly due to the danger the snakes presented and also because there was a dangerous, boggy area nearby. However, when no one was watching we sometimes skipped up the lane and across to a small tree by the side of the road that was easy to climb. From our perch we watched the snakes basking in the hot afternoon sunshine. One day, when Kitty wasn't looking, we sneaked out through the small wicket gate near the goods yard as we had seen some adders - now in their bright summer colours - near the railway crossing. They lay on the warm stones between the railway sleepers and we dared one another to jump from one heavy wooden sleeper to the next. In our ignorance and innocence we did not see the danger. Jack Pickering, on spotting us from the high window of the signal cabin, shouted, "Hey, you kids, get off that line!" Kitty heard him and came running out to us. We shouted and yelped in sudden fear when a snake, that had horrible reddish-brown eyes with a thin vertical slit for a pupil, reared up baring its fangs as we leapt over it.

Miss Thorne told us later that, "They are the only snakes in Britain that have a poisonous bite, but fortunately this is rarely fatal to humans. In the spring they slough off their winter coats, dragging them off by slithering under brambles and thorns, which allows their bodies to grow. The adults can grow to a length of just over two feet (60 cm). The males are a light shade of grey with black zigzag markings down their backs - the females have brown markings - and they feed on field voles, mice, lizards, frogs, nesting birds and eggs." Whenever we found one of their colourless, discarded skins we kept it and put it in our smock pockets along with our other 'treasures'. One day I heard a tiny piercing scream and saw the back legs of a frog hanging from the wide mouth of one of the flat-headed adders. I hit it with a stick and the frog made its escape. Although they are reptiles, we knew that they gave birth to live young and this took place within their nests in the autumn. We had seen the young ones from our perch up in the tree. In the cooler days of cloud and rain they became sluggish and slow moving, which made them easy meat for foxes, hawks and other birds of prey? Kitty said, "They hibernate over the winter."

The local farmhands, in their thick corduroy trousers, sweated in the enervating heat as they led their horse and wagon down the steep 1 in 5 gradient to the station. They had their shirtsleeves rolled up showing their bulging biceps. The heavy, wooden wagon was filled to the top with rolled up fleeces. We had watched the Artley's black-faced Masham sheep being dipped. Gangs of men travelled from farm to farm to carry out the shearing. Grabbing and unceremoniously upending the sheep, they used metal-bladed hand clippers to remove the greasy, matted fleeces in no time. "It's a soap-like substance called lanolin that makes their wool so greasy," Kitty told us. Afterwards they looked more like skinny goats than sheep and we laughed at them as they looked so small and funny without their woolly coats. Their thin necks and near-naked pink skin was nicked and bleeding in places.

Soon afterwards we were taken to a local farm to see a big, fat, Large White Yorkshire sow that had recently farrowed. She lay on the straw and bracken that covered the concrete floor of her spacious, shaded shelter. The sty was well drained and airy and care had to be taken to see that she did not suffer from sunburn. She had smooth white skin with just a few, fine, fair hairs on her back and pigs are unable to cool themselves by sweating. The sow had to lie down on her side very carefully as she had eleven, tiny, pink piglets fighting and climbing over each other to nuzzle at the double row of six teats on her fat underbelly. After weaning, ten of them were taken away by the 'men from the Ministry'.

In the heat and glare of late June the earthen paths became hard, dry and dusty and the air was filled with the sweet heady scent of the new mown hay that lay in thick, yellowish-green swathes slowly fading in colour as it dried out on the shorn and baking fields. The hay had been waist-high before it was mown down in long, rhythmic sweeps by the sun-glinting scythes of the sweating and cheerfully singing farmhands. In their occasional breaks from work they would whet (sharpen) the long, curving, cutting edges using a coarse grained stone. From time to time, wielding two-pronged pitchforks, they tossed and turned it and left it to dry and this ancient, tried-and-tested method was known as tedding. Soon afterwards to our delight, the clover, vetch and trefoil scented hay was gathered up into ridges (known as windrows) by men using light and beautifully crafted wooden hay-rakes. The windrows that covered the hillside slowly changed from green to golden brown in the unrelenting sunshine that burned down day after day. We thought that the ridges of soft, sweet scented hay had been put there especially for us to roll around and play in.

Shortly afterwards, in the sultry heat, the summer-scented ridges were raked in and piled up to form haycocks in which we made dens before they were carted away by the farmhands. The aroma of rowans, sometimes called mountain ash, scented the air as they were in full blossom at that time of year. The great, placid carthorses sweated in the shafts of the wagons as they plodded back and forth between the hayfields and the stackyards with their mighty haunches rippling and shining in the summer sun. Sweating, pitchfork-wielding farmhands tossed the hay on to the large open wagons. The great, wooden-spoked wheels, with their iron-rimmed tyres, rumbled and crunched over the stones embedded in the hard packed earth as they wended their way up to Levisham village between high earthen banks that were topped by dry-stone walls or quickthorn hedges. These ancient, deep and narrow, sunken lanes were known locally as 'holloways'. The men and the horses were glad to get out of the blazing sun into the welcome shade of the tree-embowered lane where shafts of sunlight struck through breaks in the luxuriant canopies to turn the fern fronds a brighter green.

The hay gradually filled up the barns where it was kept and used as fodder over the winter months with the excess being made into large gable-ended hayricks in the stackyard. These were built and thatched with great care and pride to be looked at and enjoyed; an art passed down through generations of fine craftsmen. The thatching protected them from future onslaughts of wind and rain. We found hay everywhere; bits of it littered the lanes and the verges and it was tangled in the hedgerows for weeks.

In mid summer, when the sun shone on both sides of the hedge, we cast short shadows and this now occurred at around 2 o'clock due to the double summertime that was now in force. I thought that the shadows were inside us and that the sun made them fall onto the ground. Occasionally I was allowed to play with the Artley children on the swing that they had set up in their field and I enjoyed being taken up on to the high, almost treeless, moors well away from the army's training areas. We would help Mrs Artley to pick the small wild strawberries, and at a later date, the ripe and juicy bilberries. The latter were covered in a grey powdering of yeast and, after they had grown to purple ripeness on the low, ground-hugging plants, they turned our tongues and fingers blue. Sometimes I ate too many and ended up with a stomach ache. Later, when they were ripe, we picked the small, wild, hairy 'goosegogs' (gooseberries), which Dinner Lady used to bake delicious steaming hot pies for us.

The airy vastness of the high moors could be beautiful or utterly bleak. Up there in the bracing air, the great enveloping silence was occasionally broken by the plaintive bleating of the hardy Swaledale sheep. At other times it was the haunting, plaintive call of the shy and wary curlew, with its long downward curving beak, that we heard. It was hard to see them in their camouflaged plumage, even when they were close by, as they were barely visible against the russet-brown of last year's dried up bracken. They seemed to prefer the marshy areas of the moors. The ling was springy beneath our feet and the twisted, black, woody stems of the old heather had a dry, dusty smell. I chased after the green, chirruping grasshoppers that were easily alarmed and leapt away in a long curving flight. Occasionally the sudden, clattering explosion of a red grouse would startle us as it sprang up with whirring wings from right under our feet. The male bird, about the size of a small chicken, had dark reddish plumage with a bright red wattle over its eyes and white leg feathers. To me its call sounded like "Go back! Go back." Scattered over the moors we saw large, ancient, standing stones and cairns that were composed of heaped up stones. There were heaps of piled up peat turfs, some as tall as six feet, that the diggers had left to dry out as the use of peat as a winter fuel was quite common. There were tangled patches of reddish-brown, dead bracken everywhere and amongst it the newly emerging shoots were just starting to unfurl looking like small, brilliant green, question marks.

The Artleys owned two defunct, but clean, furnished, railway carriages that were kept in the goods yard sidings and their paying guests sometimes came with us. We called them the 'camping carriages' and the family had been renting them out since before the war. They also provided bed and breakfast and an upstairs bathroom in the stationhouse at a rate of six shillings (30p) a week and at times the house was so full that the family had to sleep in the wash house at the bottom of their yard. Many guests came back year after year to enjoy their hospitality and wholesome fare and some became family friends. They came here to escape from the anxiety of the war-threatened towns and cities for a little while. Here they could walk and enjoy the soothing peace and tranquillity of the deep forests and could relax in the glory of the open moors and the quietness of the countryside. It was an enchanted place unspoilt by man. Some got lost when the weather suddenly turned hostile and only the hardy Moor Jocks (sheep) were able to endure the harsh conditions. The Artley children used to come in to the nursery school where they played with us for hours on end. Clifford was closer to our George's age than the other three.

The Dog Days begin around July 3rd and end about August 11th when the Dog Star, Sirius, the brightest star in the heavens, rises and sets. The Romans believed that dogs went mad at that time of the year and the old gardener said to Kitty, "Tell 'em not to touch t'dog roses in t'edgerows as they're 'armful. If they were to put their fingers on their eyes or ears afterwards they could go blind or get an earache." adding sagely, "When t'Dog Days be clear t'will be fine all t'yeer" and that year they had been and it was.

Eric and I were forever asking questions about the animals and plants that we saw. We had become watchers of the natural world and we were learning the names of the animals, the trees and the plants by observation. As day succeeded day and week followed week I was becoming more aware of the power and order of nature and the law of 'kill and be killed'. At times I got things mixed up, as children do. In the morning I would watch the sunlight creeping down the western hillside and it seemed to me that it was pushing the shadows ahead of it: I thought that it was shoving the darkness into the ground in the valley bottom. Later, as it set in the west, the shadows came up again stealing away the colours and filling the air with darkness and that made it night. To my childish reasoning that was why it was dark under the ground all the time. In those pleasant surroundings, many of these early observations of nature were to stay with me and many of the lessons learned were to have a profound influence on the course of my life.

After Kitty moved to Grove House with us, Alan would cycle over to Newton-on-Rawcliffe, where he left his bike and walked down the steep path to call on her. Even when she could not see him she knew he was coming as he whistled loudly everywhere he went. Whenever she was with him she was radiant and her face lit up with pleasure. If the weather was fine and sunny he often took her for long loitering walks and they would sit in the quiet of sun-drenched glades or linger in the dappled shade of the wild woods. Here they walked arm in arm quietly talking as only lovers can and, with no one there to see them, they would gaze into each others eyes and share a kiss or two. Their liking became a fondness that blossomed into full-blown love - a love that was to transform their lives and bring them lifelong joy and happiness.

Warm-hearted Kitty tried so hard to make up for the maternal love that she knew was missing from our young lives: she seemed to instinctively sense how important it was that someone should love and care for us. Maybe she had known the emotional pain on being put into a home as a child; maybe she too had lain awake at night afraid of the dark and its secrets; maybe she had once yearned for a parent to hug and cuddle her and kiss away the dark forebodings. She was so kind-hearted; there was not a malicious thought in her.

Sometimes, if the weather was kind, she took us up the track that started close to a tall, white, railway signal post on the other

180

side of the railway line. After a short, flat stretch of grass-seamed track we crossed the little footbridge that spanned the shallow waters of the boulder-strewn Pickering Beck. Its white-painted, handrails reflected the glare of the sun and as we peered down the clear waters gurgling over the smooth stones threw off scintillating and shifting darts of light. Below the surface the fast-flowing stream shook its long, green tresses of waterweed. Ugly flatheads and spiny sticklebacks darted about on the bottom but we left them for another day. The stony path gradually became a narrow hard-packed earthen track that climbed the steep hillside. It became very muddy after rain and near the crest there was a hairpin bend. The path came out on a hedge-lined lane that led into the pretty village of Newton-on-Rawcliffe that stood three hundred feet (100m.) above the railway line.

The old gardener-handyman had told Kitty, "A couple o' yeers back there were a long drought. All of t'wells, cisterns and ponds in t'area went completely dry. To our amazement, a mile long iron pipe were constructed and taken from up theer down t't spring near Levisham Station. Five hundred gallons (2,250 litres) of water an 'our were pumped up t't'uge trough they'd set up next t't'main street. Some o't'farmers and all o' t'ousewives brought all sorts o' containers to it to be filled. The farmers even brought t'cattle theer ter drink from it. The crisis passed when a terrific summer storm broke. There were terrific thunder and lightning, with huge 'ailstones that lay an inch deep an' caused a deal o' damage t't'crops."

In the middle of the village was a large grassy green close to the *White Swan* public house that stood on the eastern side of the main street next to a row of small stone cottages. We walked down to the duck pond that was close to the road and had a raised grassy bank where the sun twinkling on its wind-ruffled surface fascinated me. A little further down the road was another small pond, the two being separated by a muddy farm track down which the local farmers had brought their cattle during the drought. This track was often churned up into an ankle-deep morass in wet spells. We liked to see the ducks preening and up-ending; cutting themselves in half and turning the water murky with their dabbling. We fed them bits of stale bread and were delighted on seeing the flotilla of fluffy ducklings that paddled like mad in their mother's wake sending widening ripples across the sun-glinting surface.

We were happily enjoying the warmth of the sun and the peaceful village scene when we suddenly became aware of a wild and strange looking boy staring at us intently from the other side of the road. He had long, filthy, matted hair that hung down to his shoulders and was wearing dirty, ragged clothes. Even though he was fully dressed the story of Tarzan sprang to mind. Kitty had shown us pictures of him and had told us of how he had been raised by wild apes. She told us that the strange boy lived with his parents in a shack in the woods and his name was Maurice Milderstone. She added, "He never mixes with or speaks to anyone. The family are reclusive and probably of gypsy stock." We felt a bit scared and uncomfortable with him there and asked Kitty to take us back to Grove House.

We hurried back to the top of the path and as we set off down to the railway in the valley we kept looking back to make sure that the wild boy was not following us. The view from the top was magnificent; far below Grove House looked as if it was floating in a sea of bright green foliage, with the tree canopies on the steep slopes above the house at their full and luxuriant best. We were glad to get back down that day. Sometimes the Vicar of Newton-on- Rawcliffe used the same steep path when he came to conduct short prayer services for us. The Reverend Tibbit, the middle-aged vicar of the church of St. John, was an eccentric bachelor and his church stood at the bottom end of the village, towards Headlam Lane. His hurrying cloaked figure could sometimes be seen followed (at a safe distance) by groups of local children who pursued him, insolently shouting, "Tib, Tib, Tib, Tib!" He completely ignored them, abstractedly muttering, "Boys will be boys."

Kitty occasionally took some of us older children for a longer walk taking ham salads, meat pies, biscuits and pop prepared and packed up for us by Dinner Lady. One day she took us on a walk through the woods and up to Levisham village on the path that came out near the duck pond. We spent some time in the Chapel-of-Ease searching for the little wooden mouse that was carved on the cover of the baptismal font. It was the trademark of Robert

Thompson, the carpenter from Kilburn. As we noisily emerged, we disturbed the rooks nesting in the tall pine trees and their raucous cries added to our irreverent din. A farmhand was guiding a herd of cows up the main street with a stick and we took care not to stand in the wet cow claps as we passed by Glebe Farm and the village Institute. Eric trod in one and we made sure that we stayed upwind of him for a while.

We saw a number of deaf and dumb children who had been evacuated here from Middlesbrough and were pupils at the special school set up in the old village schoolroom. The old school at the top end of the main street had closed when the war started and it stood just across the lane from the Chapel-of-Ease and next to the big house that had once been the village Inn. The old Inn, actually two houses made in to one, was now a guesthouse. It stood by the village green, where the main road divided, and it was packed with paying guests at this time of the year. Most of them had had to make the long climb up from the station, their train usually being met by a young lad who lugged their cases up the steep hill for them. It was so popular that seven huts containing beds had been erected behind it.

The present incumbent, the Reverend Frederick Newby Kent, had only been here for six months and he was often seen tinkering with, or roaring about the lanes, on his beloved Francis Barnett motorbike. We hopped and skipped down the steep lane, with its 1 in 4 incline, that led down through the woods to the bracken-clad slopes of Levisham Beck that had its source - a mere trickle - in the bosom of the moors in the Hole of Horcum.

The waters of the tiny fast flowing stream, leapt, fell, and leapt again between its steep banks. It gushed over coruscating waterfalls, which held small rainbows in their spray. The crystal clear waters then bounded and tumbled ever downwards before splashing and gurgling past the picturesque, stone watermill that stood beside the old stone bridge. The mill had once been the property of the Reverends Skelton and there was a deep rock pool where fat trout with dark markings along their sides basked - until we disturbed them. Lower down the brook flowed less rapidly as it levelled out and beside it tall clumps of bright green ferns grew in abundance. The stream, with its grassy banks kept close-cropped by

183

the wandering Masham sheep, flowed through the quiet isolation of the lovely Levisham-Lockton valley before emptying itself into Pickering Beck near Farwath.

We trooped along with jam jars and fine-mesh nets on the end of canes as the birds twittered and powerful scents of flowering honeysuckle and wild garlic assailed our nostrils. We tried to catch the red-breasted sticklebacks and the spiny-backed bullheads, that we called 'flatheads, that zigzagged about erratically leaving a muddy cloud when we lifted the stones from the bed of the stream. We were wary of the ugly, bewhiskered, stone loaches and left them alone. We had a picnic on the soft velvety grass, with juice dripping from our chins as we bit into luscious, shiny-red tomatoes that the gardener called love apples. Kitty poured sparkling lemonade from glass bottles that had a thick wire contraption, to which stoppers made of white pot were fixed. We ran and frolicked in the warmth of the sun that beat down from a clear blue sky. The grassy banks and the bracken-clad slopes were a vivid green and the clear waters sparkled in the sunlight. Salad days indeed!

The picturesque little church of St. Mary was reached by means of a steep track that led off from the Levisham - Lockton road. It stood within its crowded graveyard where the mortal remains of Mr Barnes Wimbush, a former owner of Levisham Hall, had lain mouldering for more than thirty years. The summer sun lit up the crusty grey lichen on the gravestones. The small square tower, at its western end, had been added forty years back and it was tucked away in the verdant folds of this green and pleasant vale. In times long past, it had stood close to the old Whitby to Pickering road; which was called Sleights Road on old maps but it was now little more than a narrow bridle track that led down to Farwath. We entered the church through a small stone porch and Kitty pointed out some intricately carved Anglo-Saxon remnants embedded in its walls. Once inside our high pitched voices were thrown back as hollow-sounding, spooky echoes that agitated the dust motes and it felt as if we had stepped into a past age; a time before our time; and we suddenly became subdued and quiet. It seemed as if the past was trapped within its ancient walls where a deep and timeless silence reigned. We were reluctant to disturb the reverent hush of the long years and the shadows in the corners seemed to waver and stir. It was hot and sunny outside but it felt dank and chill in there.

On the floor of the chancel there was a very old grave slab with what looked like a crusader's sword incised upon it; its history was a mystery lost in the mists of time. The Skelton family vault stood within the brass altar rails where the two Roberts, father and son, had been rectors. They had moved into the Hall soon after it was built in 1792 and had extensively rebuilt the church to the glory of God in the year 1802. Their memorial hatchments could be seen on the stout stone walls on either side of the rounded Saxon arch that separated the nave from the chancel and altar. We were glad to get out of the gloom of that dusty old place and, emerging into the balmy air, we were dazzled by the sun's blinding rays. Bees buzzed busily, green grasshoppers chirred cheerfully jumping away as we tried in vain to catch them as the scent of wild flowers filled the air.

Full of exuberance and the joy of life we skipped and raced around on the yielding springy turf. On such brilliant and heavenly summer days as these we seemed to be imbued with endless vitality. The days were long and lovely and I experienced moments of dreamlike rapture and a quickening of the senses. I was enjoying a free and open way of life and seeing the natural world at close quarters was giving me some conception of the interdependence of all living things. We were so lucky to be growing up in such idyllic surroundings and my soul was nourished and lifted by it. Although unaware of it, I was getting an inkling of the kindredness and balance of all natural things and experiencing the full gamut of emotions, from love, joy and wonder to fear, guilt and helplessness. I was starting to appreciate the sheer God-like beauty, power and majesty of nature and to realise that I was just a tiny part in the great interlocking pattern of things. I watched and learned as the days came and went and the harsh realities of the war scarcely touched us in our lovely sheltered world.

We heard the tinny clatter of gunfire more and more often. Once the Army training camp became established at Keldy Castle the peace and quiet of the Newtondale valley was never quite the same as soldiers charged around in combat dress taking part in military exercises and mock battles. They were being trained for combat prior to being posted to one of the war zones and we often saw soldiers crouched and running with their rifles in the trail position. Their silhouettes were clearly outlined against the skyline. The distant machine gun fire from up on the moors sounded like tearing cloth and we felt the earth-shaking crump of the shells against our eardrums. They sent up plumes of black smoke that drifted away on the wind and the deep thud of the powerful guns was accompanied by the metallic clattering of caterpillar tracks. Tanks, heavy armoured vehicles and Bren gun carriers rattling by added to the general cacophony.

The sudden roar of a train as it thundered through drowned out all of them and we would sometimes come across soldiers in woollen hats, their faces blackened with burnt cork. They held their rifles in front of them as they crawled across the fields on their elbows and sometimes we would see them laid on their bellies under the hedgerows with their Enfield .303 rifles poking through the gaps. As our little column passed we tried to keep in step as the soldiers did and Kitty said, "You must never pick anything up, especially shrapnel and spent bullets, no matter how interesting it might seem." It all seemed so exciting to us.

Before the Army arrived most of the country sounds had come from the birds and the farm animals, although, at harvest time, the chugging of the steam traction engine and the threshing machine could be heard as they were taken from farm to farm in rotation. The placid, lumbering carthorses had clip-clopped along these quiet lanes for generations and the magnificent draught animals still trundled their loaded wagons down to the station and carted goods up from it and we would hear the ponderous rumbling of their heavy, metal-shod wheels. The contrast between the military din and the soothing, age-old country sounds was stark but in the evenings the peace and quiet returned.

Mam came to visit us without Dad as the threat of invasion was very real and all leave had been cancelled. She told us that, "In mid August large numbers of German planes based in Scandinavia had crossed the North East coast to bomb our airfields. The sirens sounded night after night and I spent most of my time in the underground shelters on the common where we make tea, have singsongs, and play cards to pass the time away. Dad got a forty-eight hour pass and he told me that he had been kept really busy firing at the German bombers. He said 'you should have seen the strings of red and orange flak as it snaked up into the night sky. It was an awe-inspiring sight and sometimes it formed an s-shape as we swung our long gun barrels round. Even if we didn't hit the blighters it made them fly higher making their bombing less accurate'."

One Sunday the Artley family was walking down the lane from Levisham on their way back from the service in the church-in-the-valley and they were quite alarmed when a young soldier suddenly jumped out from behind a bush. Pointing his rifle at them, he belligerently shouted, "Halt! Who goes there? Friend or foe? Advance and be recognised". His gleaming, double-edged bayonet was fixed to the business end of his rifle leaving the empty, canvas frog dangling from his webbing belt. When they explained that they lived at the railway station he looked a bit sheepish and allowed them to continue. It seems he had only recently been posted to the area and was a little overenthusiastic. Kitty and Rosemary sometimes got bored on going all day without seeing anyone, so to break the monotony they used to pop over to the stationhouse sitting room for a chat with the Artleys. Here they could share in the latest gossip over a nice cup of tea and listen to the latest war bulletins on their mahogany-encased wireless set.

We saw troop trains crammed with soldiers that clattered through without stopping as sparks flew from the wheels and the acrid smell of oil on hot iron hung in the air. The men leaned out of the carriage windows waving and shouting to us but what they said was blown away on the wind and drowned by the train's roaring passage. We stood by the maroon and cream waiting room and vigorously waved back. Quite often the trains were hauling weapons and ammunition wagons as apparently there were ammunition dumps located somewhere further up the line. When the tarpaulin covers of the heavy, clanking flat-backed trucks blew back we sometimes caught a glimpse of a camouflaged tank or the protruding muzzle of a huge gun. Posters on the notice boards asked everyone to 'Be like dad and keep mum', while others warned that 'Careless talk costs lives', 'Keep it under your hat' or 'The walls have ears' which I never understood. In my mind I 'saw' walls literally with ears sticking out of them. There was, at that time, a fear of imminent invasion as the victorious Germans now occupied the defeated countries on the other side of The Channel; nevertheless, we felt safe and secure here with all the soldiers and weapons around.

On our walks with Kitty during the nutting time of late summer and early autumn, the days were still warm and we crunched over the thick carpets of dark brown, bristly-cased, beech mast that lay beneath the trees that clothed the hillside. The nuts are only produced in large quantities in hot dry summers, like the one we had just had, and the deer, (which we glimpsed from time to time) the squirrels; the blackbirds; the pheasants; the dormice and the badgers loved them. In the damper areas the boughs of the hazel shrubs were heavy with clusters of green frilled, brown cobnuts and the pockets of our smocks bulged as we crammed in as many as possible. The old gardener-handyman called them 'filberts'. In the background we could hear the faint tinkling of trickling rills and the woods echoed to the knocking sounds of the tiny, stubby nuthatches. When collecting the nuts they take them to a convenient crevice, like those in the deeply fissured bark of the pine and the oak trees, and wedge them in, and proceed to hammer away at them with their small, straight beaks until the shell cracks and they can reach the kernel. Kitty said, "In Celtic times, the hazel was known as the tree of knowledge and its nuts were said to be the ultimate receptacles of wisdom." Maybe we were gaining in wisdom, for we ate plenty of them.

As the lush fruitfulness of autumn crept on the weather turned chilly and thick, shifting mists often blotted out the hillsides. Locally, the potatoes and the harvest had been safely gathered in and the corn stubble had turned from burnished gold to a dull grey. Before the war it had been burned and the ashes had helped to enrich the soil but now it had to be ploughed in due to the blackout regulations. In the low autumn sunlight, the leaves of the deciduous trees stood out in various tints of gold, yellow, red and brown contrasting sharply with the dark leaves of the evergreens. We saw red squirrels racing back and forth hastily gathering up the nuts before scurrying away to hide them before the winter set in.

On certain days the valley was shrouded in thick white swirling fog, which lingered all day and there was frost on the grass in the early mornings as the year moved inexorably on. The ripe crab apples, sloes, and blackberries were picked and Dinner Lady used them to make delicious jams and jellies in huge bubbling, steaming pans. Eric and I, by this time, were having lessons with Miss Thorne as, by rights, we should have been starting school. We 'played' with water, plasticine and sand, not realising that we were learning the basics of volume and measurement. Miss Thorne poured equal quantities of water into a short wide glass and a tall thin glass saying. "Which glass has the most water in it?" We both thought that the tall glass held more than the other one as we were still too young to understand conservation of volume. She said, "The mind is a treasure house that should be kept well stocked and once knowledge is safely stored the world can never take it away."

In early autumn, a ten years old girl, called Anne-Marie Calvert, entered our lives. She had been evacuated to Levisham village with her mother, and her brother, Richard, after their house was damaged in a raid on York in early August. The anxiety and worry caused her mother to bring her children to this relatively safe, secluded spot. They did not see a great deal of their father as he was busy in his gent's outfitter's shop in York and had to take his turn on firewatching duty. After a while, her mother decided that the children would fare better at their former school in York. She heard that one of the platelayers' cottages at Levisham Station had become vacant. She made an application to rent it and the family moved in so that the children could travel on the early morning mail train that came through from Whitby to York at 7.50a.m. The three eldest Artley children also caught this train but they got off at Pickering as they had been attending school there since Levisham School had closed.

One day as dew lay on the grass, Mrs Calvert came along the lane beside the nursery school. Seeing George and me playing close to the gate, she came in and asked if she could take us to see her goat. Permission was granted and we were taken across the level crossing to her cottage but were quite apprehensive when we came face to face with the large, hairy, bearded beast that loomed over us with his mouth agape. He had a huge head and his orange tongue flapped about between large brown teeth. It seems that he would try to eat anything and, as he chewed on our smock sleeves, we feared that he might eat us. I didn't like the devilish look in his close set, dark, blankly staring, rectangular pupils and I felt again that creeping fear that I had experienced in the forest; a kind of horror that comes over you as a child when something beyond your comprehension happens and you find yourself helpless to do anything about it. A powerful musky odour emanated from the goat and Mrs Calvert said that this was attractive to female goats, but it was repulsive to us and it was to put me off all things caprine for life.

I was allowed out to play with Anne-Marie, if her mother was also present, and on one occasion she said to me; "Mother has made a lovely stew with lots of fresh vegetables from our garden. Would you like to come over and try some?" Being a growing lad and always hungry, I didn't take much persuading even though I could hear the horrible goat bleating nearby. The stew was simmering away in a black pot that looked to me like a witch's cauldron and there was an iron bar fixed to the wall, which was hinged and could be swung out over the open fire. It was called a reckon in these parts and the stew pot was suspended from it. "Sit yerself down luv," Mrs Calvert said as she ladled out the stew. It was delicious but there were lots of tiny bones in it as it was wood pigeon stew. On the stone-flagged floor of the kitchen lay several peg rugs, which the family had made from strips of old clothing that they pushed through a piece of hessian sacking with a wooden prodder and my favourite rug had the shape of a Spitfire worked into it. A glass-shaded paraffin lamp hung from a hook in the ceiling.

Ann-Marie would sometimes go 'wooding' with her family in order to make logs, which they piled up by the back door. The bundles of twigs and small branches that were used as kindling were known locally as kids and these were put in the oven of the cast-iron range to dry. She used to pick up any pieces of coal that fell from the tenders of the passing trains or from the farm wagons as they carted it up from the station to Levisham village. One day she took me up their narrow staircase to see her tiny bedroom with its sturdy metal bedstead that had shiny brass rails with knobs on the corner posts and she had a real feather mattress. Under the bed was the ubiquitous ceramic, chamber pot and I caught a whiff of stale pee that brought back memories of home. There was a wooden

190

washstand with a blue and white, glazed earthenware pitcher and ewer and a pewter candleholder stood on a chair beside the bed. The lavatory was outside and she said to me, "I hate having to go down there when that bad tempered goat has got into the garden," before adding, "When the soldiers are down by the beck training they sometimes come to the kitchen and say 'Any chance of a drop of tea missus?' They bring their tin mugs and Mum fills them up but if their sergeant appears they quickly chuck it away."

We would sometimes see her near Grove House picking bunches of wild flowers that she would take to school. Each day, when the mail train came through, the incoming mailbag was passed out to Mr Artley or Jack Pickering who, between them, worked half a day on and half a day off. The bag of outgoing mail was collected from the platform by the guard. Jack worked the signals and issued the tickets and whenever a train came through he would collect a large metal hoop, below which hung a small leather pouch containing the 'tablet'. The train driver would lean out and place this hoop over the arm of the man on duty and this important safety procedure ensured that no two trains could be on our stretch of line at the same time. The tablet was then placed into a device in the signal box, which caused the signals to change thus reducing the chances of an accident. The 'tablet' was replaced when the next train came through.

The busiest day was Monday when Mr Artley scuttled here and there in his shiny-peaked black cap and black waistcoat regularly pulling out his large Hunter watch on its gold chain to check that everything was on time and running smoothly. He was not the stationmaster but he often stood in for him as the man lived in the Goathland stationhouse travelling down on one of the trains each day to check that all was well before leaving on the next up train. The platform was all hustle and bustle as it was market day in Pickering and there were large numbers of local people going there. Many of them had made the long walk to the station from the surrounding farms and villages. Like the Moor Jocks, these North Yorkshire folk were a strong hardy breed and took it all in their stride. The farmhands and the women of Levisham and the various outlying farmsteads eagerly looked forward to these weekly shopping trips into town.

191

Steam train alongside the signal box.

When he was not too busy, Jack would sometimes get a few of us older children together and take us into the signal box, saying "Yer can 'elp me ter change t'points if yer like." As he pulled back one of the ten, tall, shiny metal levers, we 'helped' by holding on to it with him. We loved to look out of the blast-taped windows as a great hissing black steam train thundered past making the signal box tremble under our feet.

One Monday Kitty took a few of us on the six miles journey to Pickering and Eric and I were delighted to be part of this special treat. The track south of Levisham station beyond the two tall signal posts became single track and it ran straight as far as the hamlet of Farwath. After that it was all bends with the line crossing and re-crossing the beck as it passed the lovely mixed woodland that clothed the steep slopes on either side. The last mile was almost straight and flat as it passed a signal box that stood close to the Newbridge level crossing before it pulled in under the long glass-topped roof of Pickering station after passing another signal box at High Mill. Behind this signal box was a huge, round turntable where the locomotives were swung round to face in the opposite direction.

High above on a limestone bluff stood the extensive ruins of an early Norman castle. Kitty said, "It was built on a high mound that was surrounded by deep ditches and a moat. At one time it was an important royal stronghold and from it several medieval kings, including William the Conqueror, are said to have hunted the deer, wild boar and game that were abundant in the vast forests that covered this area." Eric and I were already planning to play games involving kings and knights when we got back to Grove House. Not far from the castle stood the Nissen huts of 'Castle Camp' where a local battalion of the Green Howards was based and Kitty said, "A Major Chadwick, who owns a coal haulage business in the town, has recently been heavily involved in recruiting local men."

At that time steam trains still ran from Pickering to all four cardinal points of the compass; east to Scarborough; west to Kirby Moorside and Thirsk; south to Malton and York and north to Whitby and Teesside. After Kitty had handed over our tickets to be clicked by a man in a black uniform with brass buttons, she took us out of the station and walked us along the street and up the hill. We joined the hustle and bustle of the crowds that milled around under the brightly striped awnings of the stalls that lined the market place gazing in wonder at the clothes, crockery, vegetables and sundry items that could still be bought in spite of the increasing shortages. We stayed close to Kitty as she moved amid the myriad sights and smells, including odours of wet fish fresh from Whitby. It was a new and exciting experience and we stared in wonder at the hundreds of brightly coloured goodies on display. Many of the little shops lining the street had tiny, olde-world style, glass-bottle windowpanes that distorted the things on the other side.

The old country town had been granted a Royal Charter in the long and distant past, allowing it to hold an annual animal market. At the top end of the market stood The Vaults where we had our hair cut. Down near the Bridge Street level crossing was the old, stone-built, Memorial Hall - formerly a corn mill - that had a large wooden floored room where dances were held. There was an old antique shop that had once been a cinema, where a strange box-like structure hung out over the pavement and this odd structure had been part of the projectionist's room. Nearby there was a row of old, stone, railway cottages; a tobacconist's hut and some wooden benches under a low stone wall where we sat and rested for a while.

We were taken to see a Punch and Judy show and although a bit shocked and frightened, we were fascinated and totally absorbed at the same time. The actions of the hook-nosed, long-chinned, hunchbacked Mr Punch were dreadful. He murdered his baby by banging its head on the walls and floor because it cried; he then bludgeoned his wife to death when she disapproved and he hurled their bodies out of the window. The policeman put him in jail and he was sentenced to death by hanging, but he throttled the hangman with his own noose and escaped. The show gave us a glimpse of a cruel and savage time in England's history, but, on reflection, was it any worse than was happening in war-torn Europe? Brutal Nazis were slaughtering weak and vulnerable people on a vast scale, and like Mr Punch they seemed to have thrown all decent human values out of the window.

We were taken for tea in a café near the old Memorial Hall and had pikelets thickly spread with real, deep yellow, farm-produced butter. A year later the cafe was to become one of the many British Restaurants that the Government was setting up all over the country. Churchill had suggested setting up these canteen-like communal feeding centres during the blitz so that nutritious, three-course meals would be available for a under a shilling (5p). They were to be non-profit making and were to be staffed by the WVS who would produce nourishing meals from non-rationed foods. With the pootering tunes of a nearby steam organ still ringing in our ears, we were treated to scrumptious curd tarts and tired out but happy we boarded the train to return to the warm, loving atmosphere of Grove House. The train was crowded with heavily laden country dwellers heading back to Levisham station after a good day out. It gave the local women a chance to do some shopping and to stock up their larders and many of them were met at the station and made the last leg of their journey on horse-drawn carts.

On a warm October day of hazy sunshine an elderly gentleman from The Settlement led us out onto the verandah by the playroom to have our photographs taken. The picture was made into a postcard and sent to all the parents and I still treasure that fading black and white photograph.

Grove House October 1940, George far left, author third from right front row, Eric back right.

Soon afterwards we were gathered together and sat cross-legged around the wooden-cased, wireless set in the dining room. We knew that it must be for something special. We were to hear the fourteen years old Princess Elizabeth make her debut broadcast in which she asked all evacuees to 'try their best to be brave and cheerful, as everyone had to be prepared to make sacrifices in these dreadful wartime days.' The bombing of London went on continuously for fifty-seven days and Buckingham Palace had been bombed twice in the five weeks prior to the broadcast. The first bomb had shattered all the windows but, luckily, the Royal family had been staying at Windsor Castle overnight. The poor people living near to the industrial parts of East London took the brunt of the raid and there were colossal fires with hundreds killed in the crowded dockside areas. The tragic events didn't really register with us at the time as our age and lack of understanding must have protected us. To us the war seemed very exciting.

A few days later, as the days grew cooler and the nights were drawing in, Kitty celebrated her twenty-first birthday; an important 'coming of age' occasion in those days. At twenty-one a person was deemed to be an adult and no longer subject to parental control. As the remains of the day gave way to dusk a small party was held in the cosy warmth and brightness of the dining room. We were already warmly tucked up in our beds and a fire burned brightly in the grate as a nice get together of Kitty's friends took place. Alan Brown, her fiancé, had been brought over on the motorbike of his friend, Lloyd Thorpe, the nephew of the postman. Most of the time his fingers were intertwined with Kitty's or he had his arm around her waist. Tommy Gibson, the jolly farmer from Cropton, was there and it was said that he was keen on the attractive Rosemary Waters. The constantly smiling and cheerful Artleys came over from the station house to join the party.

Plainly wrapped presents (patterned paper was very scarce by then) were brought and given and Mrs Ruonne, as her present, had baked Kitty a nice big, two-layered, sponge cake with damson jam in the middle. She had iced it, put candles on it and decorated it with a '21' and the 'key of the door'. They enjoyed open sandwiches made with crusty farmhouse bread topped with tasty egg, ham, corned beef or cheese that were followed by home-made fairy cakes, cream slices and, as a special treat, a sherry trifle. The room echoed to the sound of laughter and happy voices as they exchanged light-hearted anecdotes and later they gathered round the piano to sing the popular songs of the time. To break the ice a few glasses of port and sherry were drunk while the men had beer. Kitty was young, in love and very happy.

At the end of the month as nature's mighty pulse was slowing, we had cold north easterly winds that made the dry, crinkly, brown leaves that still clung to the beech tree by the gate rattle and fall. The sycamore trees lost the glory of their crimson, russet and golden foliage and there were early morning frosts on the grass. The lawns were covered in damp leaves and had a thin smattering of double-winged sycamore seeds that we called helicopters. It was a time of dampness and decay and writhing wraith-like mists rolled down the hillsides to gather in the dells and hollows making the thick brown layer of leaf mould soggy underfoot. The mists muffled our footfalls as we walked in the depths of the dark, dank, dripping woods. The horses had been taken into the shelter of their dry and cosy straw-littered stables to sleep at night and were relishing their first feedings of nutritious, summer hay, as there was no grazing to be had.

In November the men from the Ministry called to inspect the stock and the Artleys had to hide their second pig in the privy down the yard until they left. The law only allowed people to keep one pig for their personal use; any other pigs were supposed to be sold (cheaply) to the Ministry of Food and the piglets had to be fattened up beforehand. Most of the carcass of the second pig was bought by Miss Thorne and the salted and muslin-covered hams and flitches, which were hung from the hooks in the kitchen, kept us supplied for weeks on end.

As the long sleep of winter began, thick, dank fogs shrouded the big house turning the shrubbery and trees into looming, vaguely threatening spectres. To me they were hazy and amorphous, shape-shifting phantoms of the woods just like the misty wraiths that dwelt at the periphery of my vision, which always - on turning to see them - moved rapidly away. Or was it only the creeping, grey fog playing tricks on my young impressionable mind again? As an extra precaution at bedtime I knelt to pray fervently asking the good Lord to, "Please, protect Mam, Dad, our George and me from ghosts, evil spirits and things that go bump in the night." I then curled up under the covers hiding from the unspeakable terrors that lurked in the vast and frigid darkness of the night.

At night an intense blackness now covered the land, as the blackout here was almost total. The edges of the station platforms had been painted white to make passengers aware of the dangerous drop down to the track. The platform paraffin lamps were lit for short periods of time only whenever a train was due to stop and the glass panes had been painted black, except for a small square in the bottom corner. This allowed just enough faint light to be shed downwards onto the flagstones and they were known as glimmer lights. One dark and cloudy late afternoon in November after the sun had set behind the western ridge, Anne-Marie and her brother were returning from school in York, when the train, for some unknown reason, stopped a little way out from the station. Richard, thinking they had arrived, opened the door in the total darkness and stepped out falling on to the cinders beside the track. He was badly grazed; but thankfully no bones were broken!

On an earlier occasion he managed to catch a small adder, which he had put it into an empty milk bottle to take to school. When they boarded the train the carriage had quickly emptied and they had it all to themselves. It was Richard who showed us how to put halfpennies on the line to be squashed flat by the train wheels and being very young and gullible, we thought that this made them into pennies. We tried to use them in the chocolate vending machine and were disappointed when no chocolate came out.

December came in with icy winds, frosts and snow and with the dark, cold nights now twice as long as the days, the shutters were closed and the blackout curtains were put in place long before teatime. As a special treat we were taken on Mr Brown's coach to a Christmas concert at Cropton village hall. Six months earlier, a Mrs Todd who lived with her two daughters at The Croft, had formed a club for the local youngsters and the evacuees from Middlesbrough and they put on a show, which was a great success. We thoroughly enjoyed it and immediately after the final curtain they were asked if they would put it on at nearby Hutton-le-Hole.

In the days leading up to Christmas, Santa Claus was never far from our minds and our excitement increased, with much of the joy being in the anticipation. We helped to cut and paint strips of paper in red, yellow, green, blue and purple and, linking them together, we made chains which were hung in loops across the playroom and dining room. We had saved up all our silver foil wrappers, from which we made tree decorations and we thought that they looked just as good as the 'bought' ones. Our attempts at painting Father Christmas with his reindeers and sleigh were pinned up on the walls. The gardener brought in sprigs of red-berried holly, along with ivy and mistletoe, which grew as a parasite on the bark of the local oak and apple trees. The Christmas tree, which was set up in the corner, had a fairy on the top of it and it was decorated with lots of our glittering homemade baubles and tinsel. Cotton wool was laid on top of the branches to represent snow and we had hung some of the long, pendulous, light brown, spruce tree cones on them.

We were so excited as we emptied our bulging stocking on to our beds on Christmas morning. People did not have quite the same quantity or quality of food as they had the previous year as the shipping losses were really starting to bite, but the Government had allowed us a few extra rations over the Christmas period. Even so, Dinner Lady still managed to cook us a lovely Christmas dinner of roast chicken with bacon, sausagemeat and herb stuffing; crispy roast potatoes; fresh vegetables and rich steaming gravy. This was followed by steaming plum pudding with lashings of hot custard. Later, after a short nap, games and a tea party, with paste sandwiches, mincepies, cakes, jelly and custard, was held. The Calvert and the Artley children came over and we laughed, giggled, and thoroughly enjoyed the party. We excitedly pulled Christmas crackers but I never did understand the jokes that were printed on the slips of paper inside. Father Christmas came with a sack full of lovely presents and this year it was Kitty's fiancé, Alan, who played the part of Santa Claus. We sniggered shyly behind our hands when we saw him kissing her under the mistletoe.

He and Kitty were married at St. Gregory's Church, Cropton, the following month and Alan's friend, Lloyd Thorpe, was their best man. They lived with Alan's parents in the bungalow in the forest until they moved to nearby Kirby Misperton. Kitty and Alan continued to live at Peep o' Day bungalow for a further three years, by which time he was driving lorry loads of logs from the forest to Pickering station.

Although we were far from home, Christmas still managed to weave its magic spell and many of our presents were the result of a year's hard work by the dedicated ladies of the local W.I. (with Mrs Stancliffe as their Chairwoman). On Boxing Day several parents came to share the festive season with their children and I was flabbergasted when Mrs Robson gave her daughters, Nancy and Sylvia, a lovely, yellow banana each. I soon put it out of my mind when Mam brought me a bus conductor's outfit with a flat, peaked cap and a ticket machine that went ding when the little lever at the side was pressed. In those short, dim days, as the year was fleeing fast, there were shortages of almost everything.

10. 'An Hour-glass on the Run'

The wireless set that sat on a shelf in the Harris's kitchen had a polished walnut veneer and a delicately carved sunrise fretwork through which the cloth-covered speaker could just be seen. They enjoyed listening to Band Wagon with guests such as George Formby and starring Richard 'Stinker' Murdoch and 'Big-hearted' (or big-headed, as some said) Arthur Askey. It had recently been moved to the same time slot as Lord Haw-Haw's broadcasts in the hope that it would stop people listening to his propaganda. The set was seldom turned off, except at night or when it began to spit and crackle as the accumulator ran low. When this happened it was carried to Len Ovenden's cycle repair shop which he had set up in the garage of his house on the corner of York Road and South Lane. Taking it there to be charged up, at tuppence a time, was one of Archie's chores.

On it they heard the new Prime Minister call the Dunkirk rescue operation "A miracle of deliverance", but he also added, "Wars are not won by evacuation". In a grave voice he announced, "We are about to be plunged into what I fear will be total war....but we shall defend our island home and ride out the storm whatever the cost and we shall outlive the menace of tyranny". This country had never been in greater peril and the public now found themselves closer to the front line than they had ever been. With the enemy just across the narrow English Channel, an airborne and sea assault was likely at any time. Mr Harris kept a sharp axe in the shed for chopping sticks and on hearing the news, his wife brought it into the house and locked the front door, grimly saying to Archie, "If any German paratroopers try to get in here they will be in for a very nasty surprise," and she meant it.

At that time Hitler's aggression seemed to be paying dividends. The Germans were well fed and delighted with his easy victories and he was hugely popular. He was seen as an all-powerful leader and the Germans thought the war was all but won. Hitler thought Great Britain would be forced to sue for peace. As the threat of an invasion loomed large, the ringing of the church bells was stopped; they were only to be rung as a warning that the invasion had started. Mr Harris said, "They might send troops from Norway to attack on t'East Coast." Winston Churchill then made one of his most memorable speeches saying, "The whole fury and might of the enemy must very soon be turned on us. Hitler knows that he will have to break us in this island or lose the war....Let us therefore brace ourselves to our duties and so bear ourselves that if the British Commonwealth and its Empire lasts a thousand years men will say, 'This was their finest hour'".

On listening to the news bulletins, Mrs Harris learned that Italy had entered the war on the German side. The next day, which was the twelfth, it was reported that British troops had made a short, sharp raid into Libya driving back the ill-equipped Italian forces, who surrendered in their hundreds. Whitley bombers from Linton-on-Ouse flew out to bomb targets in Italy for the first time, having to refuel in the Channel Islands. The Regia Aeronautica (the Italian Air Force) based in Sicily – who had formerly been their friends - bombed Malta as it posed a serious threat to the Axis supply route to North Africa. Italian businesses that had been here for years were attacked by rampaging mobs and when Gran visited Archie she told him, "Several ice cream salons and cafes in Middlesbrough had their windows smashed. Mobs of angry men roamed the streets looking for 'I-ties' to beat up and many of them were taken in to the Town Hall cells for their own protection. Policemen and soldiers had to stand guard on their shops and business premises overnight."

Within days, Winston Churchill ordered that all adult male Italians were to be interned; the fact that many of them had been born in this country did not prevent them from being rounded up. Many were despatched to Canada or Australia and others ended up in internment camps, most of which were on the Isle of Man, where armed soldiers patrolled the barbed wire fences. It was said that the Italians were noisier and more high-spirited than the Germans and their volatile temperaments often led to fist fights. There were also many arrogant Nazis among the German prisoners who cockily declared that it was only a matter of time before Hitler crushed Great Britain and they refused to help with the harvest as that was looked on as aiding the war effort.

That June there was a long spell of sweltering hot weather and a temperature of 85°F [29.5°C] was recorded in North Yorkshire on the ninth of the month. In York the heat was on in a different way as, unbeknown to the local people, a top secret conference was being held in the magnificence of the *Station Hotel*. Its chairman was Anthony Eden and he and the Army Chiefs of Staff were discussing the morale and general state of the 'demoralised army', as they called it. Britain's future military tactics in the aftermath of the Dunkirk debacle were top of the agenda and some were in favour of a peace settlement with Germany. Even Lord Halifax, a friend of the King, wanted to sign a peace deal with Hitler, but the suggestion outraged the pugnacious and defiant Churchill. Many of the Generals had doubts about the conscripts' loyalty and their will to fight as many men had deserted. Indeed, some of the shell-shocked soldiers brought back from Dunkirk swore that they would never fight again and some were so demoralised that they had thrown away their rifles. These views of the British Tommy, of course, proved to be completely wrong!

On July the first the Channel Islands were bombed and within a few days they were occupied by the Germans; the only part of the British Isles to experience German rule. The Germans called the invasion Operation Green Arrow and looked on it as the first step in the conquest of the whole of the British Isles. Not long afterwards Haxby received its first evacuees from there. The night before the invasion, a Madame de Routon had managed to get a group of children out on a cattle-boat and many of them were very seasick during the rough sea crossing to Southampton. When they arrived at Haxby station they had no means of contacting their parents or homes and had no personal possessions, except for a few underclothes. Miss Curry commented that, "They looked a very sad bunch indeed."

Captain Tom Pulleyn had recently learned that his growing band of LDV men had been renamed - at Winston Churchill's suggestion - the Home Guard. His unit now included the odd veteran of the Great War and one or two seventeen year-old boys and they now had regulation arms; ammunition; hand grenades; thunder flashes and a Bofors light anti-aircraft gun. They were now much more disciplined and were officially recognised as a military force. Tom was a tall, black-haired, well-built man with a pronounced limp, as one leg was slightly shorter than the other, and he looked very smart in the uniform of an army officer. Proudly and prominently displayed on his shoulder tabs were the three pips that denoted his rank. His uniform consisted of brown leather shoes and gloves; a peaked flat cap; a khaki shirt, collar and tie and his Sam Browne belt shone like russet glass. On his right hip he sported a .38 Smith and Wesson pistol in a brown leather holster and as he marched along he kept his swagger stick tucked neatly under his left armpit. When on manoeuvres and exercises he wore the thick and coarse battle dress, known as BD, just like the 'other ranks'.

Among the twenty or so men and four youths was Tom Parrott the horseman and many other local farmhands, railway workers', salesmen and builders. They had khaki packs, webbing belt, straps and anklets and in the canvas bag on their chests they carried a heavy-duty elephants trunk gas mask. They now had a forage cap; a steel helmet and black, heavily studded boots, which had to be kept clean and shiny by the vigorous application of spit and polish. Carrying an old - but still reliable - British .303 army rifle with its canvas sling and heavy wooden stock, a few of the less experienced lads were secretly nursing badly bruised shoulders caused by the savage recoil of the rifles on the ranges at Strensall Camp. The Home Guard had become compulsory by this time with much stricter discipline and Mr Harris read reports in the *Yorkshire Evening Press* of men and youths failing to turn up for duty - after a long, tiring day at their regular job - being fined or spending a month in prison.

To the people of Haxby, Churchill was 'the man with the big cigar and the even bigger heart' and his eloquent speeches stirred the nation. He would never give in to Hitler and his toadies and he convinced the people that we would never be beaten. They now knew that we had to fight Hitler alone and they were exhorted to avoid waste of any kind. Ministry of Information leaflets and posters urged the public to 'Make-do-and-Mend'. The slogans appeared on cinema screens and in all the magazines and newspapers of the time. Everything from waste paper to jam jars, bottles and even bones had to be saved. The glue that held together the plywood framework of the new Mosquito aeroplanes was made from old bones. When buying cigarettes the men left the cardboard packets to be re-used and most kept their fags in slim, metal, cigarette cases. Phrases like 'Kill the Squander Bug' and 'A Clean Plate means a Clear Conscience' were to be seen everywhere. From the twentieth of July, the buying and selling of new cars was banned, as steel was urgently needed for armaments and weapons. Cars were not contributing to the war effort and were classed as luxuries.

Newspaper and wireless appeals exhorted everybody to 'do their bit' and Lord Beaverbrook, the Canadian newspaper magnate, came up with a scheme to raise money and boost morale. He introduced Spitfire Funds, whereby people could adopt and name an aircraft and hundreds of thousands of pounds poured in from people in all walks of life. Archie, Jimmy, Harry and the others handed in half of their pocket money during Spitfire Week. Gran said, "Middlesbrough has adopted a Spitfire and they've called it Erimus after the town's motto and the LNER have raised the money for two Spitfires called The Flying Scotsman and The Cock of the North after their two most famous express trains."

Lady Reading broadcast an appeal to the women of Britain pointing out that it was of vital importance to hand in every bit of aluminium they could lay their hands on. The vast number of weapons lost or left behind in occupied France had to be replaced. Archie and the others combed the two villages collecting things; such as old torches, canisters and aluminium pots and pans. Around five hundred new Spitfires and Hurricanes a month were being turned out at that time and Jimmy said, "Who knows, maybe Mrs Harris' old aluminium saucepan is now part of the wing of a Spitfire." Even the World War One tank and Boer War cannon that the boys had seen earlier were taken away for scrap, as were the vintage Crimean War muzzle-loading rifles that had been on display on the Blue Bridge at the Foss confluence in York. It was said that the young princesses, Elizabeth and Margaret Rose, had handed in their miniature aluminium tea set, but it turned out that most of the aluminium pans were of too low a grade to be of any use. It seems Mrs Harris had sacrificed her much-prized pans for nothing but it had made her feel that she had 'done her bit' for the war effort.

In that summer of shimmering heat, there were the odd wet and monotonous days and Luftwaffe night-time bombing raids took place on London and twenty-one other British towns and cities. Hull and Middlesbrough were raided several times and high explosive bombs hit the I.C.I works and the Transporter Bridge. In the late summer and early autumn the so-called Battle of Britain took place in the skies over southern England as Reichsmarschall Goering had sworn he would smash the RAF. He felt confident that his Luftwaffe could bring Britain to its knees on its own.

The Queen paid a visit to Linton-on-Ouse airfield and was to be taken to Strensall Army Camp afterwards. Mr Fox, being given advance notice of the route, knew that she would come through Wigginton and Haxby. On the day the locals lined the route and even Mrs Harris walked down to the junction of Usher Lane and Station Road to see the royal party pass. There was great excitement among the children at school and the staff took them outside to see the convoy of shiny black cars. Jimmy and the other infants from St.Mary's hall were brought over to the main school playground and Archie lifted him on to his shoulders to get a good look. Queen Elizabeth waved her hand in her usual regal manner as her car, with the royal pennant fluttering in the breeze, passed by.

There was increased activity overhead at this time as Bomber Command had begun to mount more heavy-bombing raids on German cities and ports. Number 4 Group had moved into its new headquarters at Heslington Hall on the south eastern edge of York. On clear moonlit nights the skies above Haxby literally vibrated as the deep throbbing of the new Rolls Royce engines of the Mark III Whitley bombers was heard and felt causing the windows and the crockery on Mrs Harris' shelves to rattle. Most of the airmen billeted in Haxby and Wigginton worked for the maintenance unit at Shipton, but a few were aircraft ground crew members, derisively referred to as penguins. On Wednesday, the seventh of August, the first civilian death occurred in York. In a raid on the Osbaldwick Lane area a twenty years old girl was badly injured and died in hospital the following day. Four days later Spitfires damaged a Junkers 88 reconnaissance plane over Linton-on Ouse airfield, which later belly-landed on Newton Moor, near Whitby, killing one of its crew of four.

By this time Archie had started to have the odd cigarette. Maybe he was emulating the heroes he had so admired on the flickering silver screen in the Wiggie Rec or at The Picture House in York. He, no doubt, held the mistaken belief that smoking made him appear to be more grown up and Mrs Harris, rather than attempting to discourage him, had started to sell him fags which he had to pay for from his hard-earned wages or from the meagre 6d (2½p) postal order that he received from his mother each week as pocket money. If Gran had known she would have hit the roof . In the late summer evenings and at weekends, he often worked in Bob Abel's fields helping to get in the harvest behind the whirling, clacking blades of the self binder. When he was not working Mrs Harris sent him, Albert and Jimmy out 'from under her feet', as she put it. They would call for Harry and go walking for miles and they came to know the country lanes and narrow snickleways (old rights of way) as well as the backs of their hands.

One day Archie borrowed Mr Harris' old sit-up-and-beg bike and he and Harry cycled out under a clear blue sky. They found their way, along lanes that no longer had signposts, to Clifton airfield, which now had three, arrow-straight, concrete runways whereas, at the start of the war it had been grass covered. It was being used by the RAF Army Co-operation Command and they gazed through the wire mesh of the perimeter fence in wonder as Westland 'flying carrots' took off and landed. Damaged aeroplanes of various types were brought here as the Armstrong-Whitworth maintenance unit repaired their Whitley bombers in the blister-type hangars.

The airfield was about two and a half miles from Haxby on the outskirts of York just west of New Earswick. A few weeks back the Home Guard had sighted a German reconnaissance aeroplane clearly silhouetted against the clear blue of the summer sky as it circled around above the airfield. To combat a possible airborne attack glider traps were set up on the flat area beside the river Ouse known as Clifton Ings. It would have been a perfect spot for gliders to land. To prevent this a number of huge metal stakes were driven deep into the earth set at an angle with thick wires stretched between them. The boys cycled round there to have a look.

In mid August the boys were walking up Moor Lane near the sandpit by Beresford's pond, when they were startled by the tall, unkempt, wild-eyed vagrant known locally as 'Dick-Dick'. His real name was Richard Dickinson and he generally slept rough or, whenever possible, in local barns and farm sheds. He had long, lank, greasy and matted hair and sported a long, ragged and disorderly beard. On his head was an old battered and faded trilby hat that had seen better days. Beneath his torn and greasy mackintosh, which was tied round the middle with a piece of coarse twine, he was skinny and round shouldered. He walked with the aid of a stick as he had a wooden leg. It seems that he had lost his leg after falling from a farm cart as a youngster and, whenever it needed renewing, a joiner in Wigginton made him a new one. His lone shoe was filthy and flapped open at the toe. He was odd in his behaviour to say the least, but nevertheless, he was considered to be harmless. On seeing the boys he hobbled towards them shouting, swearing and waving his stick about and they - taken aback - thought he must be going mad and decided it was the better part of valour to leg it in the opposite direction. They were definitely not going to hang around to find out if he was harmless or not.

On September 2nd Mr Harris sat reading his *Yorkshire Evening Press* newspaper, in which was an article headed ' STRUCK BY RAF VAN' and the subtitle read 'Accidental Death of Haxby Man'. It stated that at about half past ten on the twenty-fifth of August, Dick-Dick had been seen on Front Street, Wigginton, hobbling towards Haxby. It was a dark and moonless night and he was in the middle of the road, which was of course unlit. A RAF vehicle, which was travelling at only fifteen m.p.h. due to the blackout, hit him from behind. A local man, Harry Wrigglesworth, was standing by his garden gate and he stated that Dick-Dick had made no attempt to get out of the way before the offside wing of the dimly lit RAF van struck him. An inquest was held at the York Law Courts, under the auspices of the Coroner, Colonel Innes Ware. Aircraftsman Eric Parsloe, the driver, stated that he had two sidelights and his hooded near side headlight on when he suddenly saw a dark object on his offside. He braked and pulled to the near side but his van hit seventy-three years old Mr Dickinson who was admitted to York County Hospital with concussion and a slight cut on the back of his head. He lapsed into unconsciousness, died of a haemorrhage of the brain six days later, and was buried in Wigginton churchyard - the village of his birth. A niece stated that he was an unemployed farm labourer and was known to have been sleeping in a hut on Mr James Pearson's Thornville Farm up on The Moor. She added that he had been getting 'a little mental' of late. Mr Harris was sad to hear of his death. Old Dick had been a local character for many years.

By late August the London blitz had started in earnest and thousands of civilians were killed, injured or rendered homeless by the devastating bombing that took place night after night. On the wireless the calm, unemotional BBC announcers read out the grim details in cultured tones. Whitley bombers from the local airfields were now going out on 'barge-bashing' sorties, i.e. bombing the invasion barges that were assembling in the French channel ports. Bombing and navigational aids were still in the early stages of development and there were heavy losses of men and aircraft. Several simply got lost and many never even reached their targets. Their bombs were often jettisoned into the sea or were dropped on open countryside. The public was not informed that the bomb aimers often missed their targets by as much as three miles.

The exceptionally hot and sunny late summer weather turned into a cold and cloudy autumn and, back at school, the small partitioned-off classrooms were now more crowded than ever. The slightly formidable Miss Curry was living with her mother on Gillygate, York, and she now had fifty-nine children in her group alone. Her calm manner masked a steeliness of purpose and when necessary she could be quite strict and she seemed quite remote and austere to some of the children. Jimmy was now in her crowded group and she had continued the practice of punishment with the table tennis bat or a plimsoll. Her strong character and a powerful sense of vocation were to see her through a lifetime of dedicated teaching. Some of the new evacuees in her group paid scant regard to their personal hygiene and a few of them ponged to high heaven. Nurse Lealman was sent to have a word with them and their foster parents.

She visited her patients in the surrounding area in her Ford 8 motor car, which had cost her £115 brand new just before the war.

Like all the motor cars of that time it had to be hand cranked to start it and this involved the insertion of a long metal handle into a small hole under the radiator grid. It was then given two or three quick turns and as it fired it tended to kick back. The trick was to avoid being hit on the wrist by it. There were no synchromesh gears in those days and to change gear the driver had to perform a tricky double-declutching action using both feet. By this time most cars had been mothballed until the end of the war because of petrol rationing.

For local calls she used her bike or went on shank's pony. Bikes had become precious items and were often a person's sole means of getting around and, in her white starched apron, cap and blue uniform, Nurse Lealman was a common sight. She regularly inspected the heads of the schoolchildren for lice and many of the new arrivals and a few local children were found to be badly infested. Nurse Hart, from the Red Cross unit at Haxby Hall, had recently given a talk to the school on head lice saying, "The louse (Pediculus Capitis) feeds on blood and its bite causes severe persistent itching. Overcrowding and close contact with those infected helps to spread the infestation. The white eggs of the louse, commonly known as nits, become firmly attached to the hair and a DDT solution or Lethane is often used to treat them." Nurse Lealman said, "You must comb your hair over a newspaper using a fine toothed steel comb, then wash it with the solution. You must continue this treatment over several days until all of the tiny white eggs have been dislodged." Several children had also contracted impetigo due to their constant scratching.

One of the recent evacuees, Terry Waddington, a lad from Bridlington who was now in Jimmy's group at St. Mary's hall, was found to have nits. His father had recently been posted to the RAF crash recovery unit, 60MU, at nearby Shipton and his work involved inspecting crashed or shot-down aircraft. The badly damaged aircraft, or any re-usable parts, were taken to Shipton on 60-foot long trailers called Queen Mary's where they were repaired, reassembled or cannibalised for spare parts. It was a gruesome job at times as human bodies or remains had to be removed.

Terry's mother worked as a cook's assistant at Haxby Hall and her son and his four years old sister were billeted in the spacious bungalow of Mrs Evans and her small son on Usher Lane just past the Crooklands Lane turn off. It had an Anderson shelter partly buried in its large back garden, which had lettuces growing on it. Mrs Evans' husband had been killed while serving with the army in Egypt. Initially Terry went to see his mother at the Hall after school but these visits were curtailed in case he passed the problem on to others.

Archie, Harry and Jimmy were fortunate not to get nits, but poor Thelma's hair was covered in them. Mrs Harris was disgusted and called her all sorts of names, and she made poor Dot comb out the white nits and the pale grey scurrying lice on to a broadsheet newspaper. Dot hated it and whined, "Do I have to?" but Mrs Harris was completely unmoved. The lice made a horrible, sickening, cracking sound when she squashed them between her thumbnails and how Dot avoided getting them was a mystery as they slept in the same bed. Mrs Harris treated Dot like a domestic drudge making her carry out all kinds of dirty jobs and household chores. Dot wasn't quite 'the full shilling' but she was good-hearted and Jimmy got angry at the way she was treated. Some of the locals were none too happy about this second arrival of 'dirty vaccies' who brought such problems to the village, whispering, "Yer can catch all sorts off 'em." They were shunned and treated like 'untouchables'.

The local kids gave those with nits a hard time, calling them Scabbyhead and Nitty-nut or worse and the adults were astonished to learn of the atrocious slum conditions that many of them had come from. Eventually, the plight of the thousands living in these deprived conditions was brought to the attention of the Government and the knowledge was to lead to William Beveridge's Report in the immediate post war years. As a result long overdue improvements in living standards were finally brought in following the introduction of the National Health Service in 1948. It promised comprehensive care 'from the cradle to the grave' and was to be paid for by weekly National Insurance contributions taken from the workers' pay packets.

Many of the well-to-do could afford to go abroad to escape the bombing and the papers said that the Government had set up a scheme allowing a number of working class children to be sent abroad for nothing. Churchill did not agree with this as he thought it smacked of defeatism but, on *Friday the thirteenth* of September, the SS *City of Benares* weighed anchor and slipped out of Liverpool bound for Canada. Now painted dark brown, she had a hundred child evacuees with their nine escorts, many adult passengers and a crew of over a hundred on board. She had a convoy of two corvettes and a destroyer. On the seventeenth a violent storm was building just as the children had gone to bed. She was three hundred miles from the West Coast of Ireland when a U-boat spotted the unmarked passenger liner, and thinking she was fair game, it fired a torpedo and she was hit. There was panic and chaos on trying to lower the wooden lifeboats and she sank thirty minutes later. Two of the escorts and fourteen of the children, who had been in the bitterly cold water in their pyjamas for sixteen long hours, were picked up by HMS *Hurricane* the following day but many passengers and crew drowned or died of exposure. A full lifeboat had set sail for Ireland and after eight days they were spotted by a Sunderland flying boat. HMS *Antony* was sent to their rescue picking up forty adults and six boys. Only twenty of the eighty children survived and out of four hundred passengers and crew two hundred and forty eight were lost. The evacuation of children across the Atlantic was brought to an abrupt halt.

Later that month Japan entered the war having signed a pact of non-aggression with Germany and Italy. It was seen as a warning to the Americans not to enter the war and with the Germans just across the channel every town and city in this country was now within range of their bombers. The Luftwaffe now had the use of about four hundred French airfields and consequently the number of air raids increased. As a result more children were evacuated to Haxby.

Churchill, now the voice of the British people, had recently declared, "Hitler knows that he will have to break us in this island or lose the war....but we shall defend our island whatever the cost shall be," before adding, "It is better to die fighting than to be a slave nation."

Civilians in the south saw the clear blue autumn skies criss-crossed by white vapour trails as dogfights took place day after day. The sun glinted off the fighter planes as they looped and weaved in and out with the pilots often hanging upside down in their straps. Side slipping and rolling - never in a straight line for a second - reminiscent of swarms of gnats on warm summer evenings. It only took a few minutes for the raiders to cross the Channel so there was very little warning and the tinny rattle of distant aircraft cannons shattered the peace and quiet of the sleepy English countryside. On September 15th the Luftwaffe attacked in force as they had been led to believe that the RAF only had fifty fighter planes left. They were let down by poor intelligence and, taken by surprise by around 300 fighter planes, their losses were large. Winston Churchill, partly concealed by the haze of smoke emanating from his huge cigar, was present in the plotting room for much of the action. The RAF were sorely stretched but unbeaten as the dogfights went on almost every day until the end of October. The stubbornness of the RAF's defence set the Luftwaffe the greatest problem they had faced so far and Goering was furious when Hitler postponed Operation Sea-lion.

Harry and Jimmy knew of him from reading the comics. In *The Dandy* there was a cartoon strip called 'Addie and Hermie' in which Hitler and Goering were lampooned unmercifully and *The Beano* had 'Musso the Wop'. The British public had seen him on the cinema newsreels arrogantly posing in his ridiculously large, wide-brimmed, white cap with his uniform partly covered by braid, ribbon and medals. The landing barges had been attacked regularly from the air over the last three months and Hitler finally disbanded them and sent them to other stations of war, much to the relief of the people of Haxby and the entire country.

Winston Churchill stayed at his beloved Chartwell whenever he could find the time and he was often seen on the newsreels doing a spot of gardening in his blue siren suit that was a bit stretched at the waist. He loved the view from the house and the lake with its black swans where trout rose from time to time to dimple the surface. He was still inspiring the British to fight on and to ride out the storm and was a much-loved figure. He epitomised the bulldog spirit of the people; a symbol of hope, who inspired the belief that Great Britain could and would achieve the impossible. He created a mood of defiance so that it never entered our heads that we might lose. He paid generous and heartfelt tribute to the brave RAF

Spitfire and Hawker Hurricane pilots, declaring in one of his most memorable speeches, "Never in the field of human conflict was so much owed by so many to so few".

It had been a close run thing with great loss of life on both sides but it proved to be a major factor in keeping the so far, all-conquering Germans out of England. The WAAFs at the aircraft plotting tables were the unsung heroines of the piece. Fighter Command's holding operation had allowed Bomber Command time to build up its power and many of the crews now came from the defeated countries; most of them from Poland, France and Czechoslovakia. Britain's defiance gave hope to the conquered nations. It was a beacon of light in the darkness of oppression.

Archie, by now a tall, strong, handsome, wavy-haired, fifteen years old, was always smart and well dressed. He was one of the few who attended the village school wearing a long-trousered suit with a waistcoat, a white shirt and a tie and he kept his black shoes polished so that you could see your face in them. When working at Abel's farm he wore a denim boiler suit when he helped Tom Parrot to muck out the stables and feed and groom his beloved horses. Since early spring he had given a hand with the ploughing, the horse raking and the seeding of the fields. He enjoyed walking behind the great, sturdy, dependable farm horses and hearing the jingling of the chains and harnesses. As the year progressed he worked late into the long sunlit evenings and he enjoyed bringing in the hay from Bob Abel's small thorn-hedged fields.

In the muggy heat of late summer he often joined the toiling, sweating farmhands in the fields as they followed the flailing, wooden-blades that pushed the heads of corn into the horse-drawn cutter and self-binder. The scene was reminiscent of gulls flocking behind a paddle steamer as the reaper-binder swept through the sea of golden corn leaving a swath of stubble in its wake. As the twine-bound sheaves were thrown out at regular intervals, Archie swooped in to pick them up to prop them against each other to form pyramid-shaped stooks that allowed air to circulate and dry them out.

Abel's farm maintained its long tradition of using horses only (rather than tractors) and Archie helped Tom with the ploughing as the year moved on. Flocks of screaming gulls followed the team of horses, looking from a distance, like tiny scraps of white paper blowing about in the wind. At other times he was kept busy topping and tailing the mangolds and beet (i.e. chopping the leafy tops and roots off with a sickle). It was a slow, backbreaking job as the beet had a long taproot making it difficult to pull up. Haxby was in a major beet growing area, which made it of importance to the war effort. Due to shipping losses cane sugar was not getting through. The beet was collected in lorries and taken to the sugar factory in York where the pulp was dried, pressed, and used to make animal feed in the form of pellets or nuts. The liquid residue, after the sugar crystals had been extracted, was spun off and boiled down to make molasses. Spent lime, a by-product of the sugar extraction, was bagged and sold to the farmers to spread on the fields to improve the soil conditions. In those austere times nothing was wasted.

Archie used to bring to the house bags of reeking cow and horse droppings mixed with straw for Mr Harris to put on the manure heap at his allotment but Mrs Harris drew the line at letting him use the smelly stuff near the house and she was none too pleased when Archie came home ponging as bathing was now strictly controlled in order to save water. Finally the Indian summer came to an end and in early October Haxby suffered howling storms as the ragged rain clouds raced across the sky. Even the Whitley bombers were temporarily grounded by the awful weather. Autumn moved on and it became dank and hazy with morning frosts as Archie volunteered to do some potato picking. The October half-term break was known locally as Tatie Picking Week. It was another backbreaking job but he was happy enough to do it if it meant a bit of extra pocket money.

One group of potato pickers gathered at Tom Bentley's Haxby Lodge Farm that was up a track off Usher Lane while others went to Jock Britton's fields down Landing Lane. Archie chose High Grange, old man Outhwaite's farm, which lay up a frozen and rutted track near the top end of Moor Lane. William (Bill) Outhwaite had been running the old place for the last twelve years and had previously been at Golden Hill Farm, just to the east, where his sixteen years old son, Basil, had been born. A little further south off Moor Lane there was a small cottage on the corner of the track that led to Grange House Farm where the Lazenby's had farmed for the last eight years and it was here that the Home Guard unit was now based. Basil had recently joined them and was now their youngest member.

Archie and the others were picked up and taken by horse and cart to the potato fields early each morning. The farm tracks were rock hard from the overnight frost and the fallen leaves crunched under their feet. On arrival they were given a white enamel pail with thick wire handles around which the wooden handgrips revolved. They could see the vapour from each other's breath hanging like mist on the icy air. The hedges were hung with black clusters of ripe, juicy blackberries and festooned with flimsy gossamer webs on which the frozen dew drops sparkled like diamonds in the low rays of the morning sun.

A great, sure-footed, Shire horse flared its nostrils as it calmly plodded along dragging a wide potato-lifter with whirling wire-tined spinners over the frozen mounds. The spinners broke open the long mounds of earth throwing white, soil-caked potatoes to both sides as the pickers trailed behind it like hungry birds. Their voices carried a long way in the stillness of the cold morning air as, bending double, they picked up and threw the potatoes that clattered noisily into the pails. When full they were emptied into one of the hessian sacks, which had been laid out at intervals beside the freshly turned furrows. These were collected in and hoisted up into a large open sided wooden cart that creaked and groaned as it was drawn along by another huge, steaming, chestnut-coloured Shire horse that was more than seventeen hands tall at its withers. The great beast's muscular haunches rippled and shone as it towered above twenty years old Ernie Lockwood, a local farmhand. He and his younger brother, Shil, who worked at Church Farm with Mr Harris, were also in the Home Guard. At first the spud pickers thought it was all great fun as they laughed and larked about, but as the morning slowly wore on, their backs and muscles began to ache. Their fingers were painfully cold and wet from contact with the slowly thawing soil and the pace of the work slowed dramatically. The shouting red-faced foreman constantly urged them to, "Get a move on or t'spuds will never be got in!"

215

They were glad of the short break at mid morning and again in the afternoon. An attractive, well-endowed, Land Army girl arrived with a huge, steaming can of very welcome tea. Wearing khaki-coloured dungarees and wellies that were clogged up with mud, she was one of two new arrivals who were later seen around the village wearing green jerseys, fawn knee breeches and thick khaki socks. At other times they wore soft brown felt, pork pie hats or a headsquare that was tied under the chin. They had been among the first to respond to the appeal for female labour as it was either that or be called up into the forces or to a job in a factory.

Mr Harris and the older farmhands initially resented them, complaining that, " They're prepared to work for less than us." And they feared that it might lead to their already abysmally low wages being reduced even further. The girls were paid about thirty shillings (£1.50) a week, having to pay half of it out on their board and lodgings. The working hours were long and tiring, especially in the summer months. They were billeted in Billy Best's house alongside Haxby Green and they often had to run the gauntlet of catcalls and wolf whistles from the airman billeted in the village. Or did they secretly enjoy it? They were not too happy at having to pass a crowd of leering, local youths and farmhands as they returned to their lodgings at the end of a hard day's work. The locals took some time to get used to the unusual sight of girls wearing slacks; as trousers were called at that time.

In the damp field the potato pickers took a short rest sitting on the dry sacks that had been laid out on the slowly thawing grass on the sunny side of the hawthorn hedge and some of them had a smoke. Archie cupped the glowing tip of his fag in the palm of his hand, as he had seen the local soldiers do. It helped to warm his fingers a bit and he thought that blowing the bluish-white smoke out in a double stream from his nostrils made him appear manly. A few of the other youths were blowing smoke rings in a vain attempt to impress the landgirl.

The big, busty, knowing girl came under Archie's avid and admiring gaze as she bent over displaying her well-formed bottom. He couldn't take his eyes off her and on noticing his intense interest, she sarcastically asked, "Would you like a photograph darling?" There was a small, gold-coloured badge embroidered on the right breast of her jersey; an area that seemed to attract a great deal of his attention, and he came to the conclusion that the hard graft and tedium of the job had its compensations and he was also getting paid for it. The Land Army girl was just one of the many young women who had chosen to serve on the land, thus enabling more of the younger farm workers to join the armed forces. As there was a scarcity of men, they were being trained in all aspects of farming, including dairy work. Eventually some were able to drive and repair tractors as well as any man. Archie was dressed in Mr Harris' old bib and brace overalls and wellies that were now heavy and thick with mud. Hard-wearing denim was only used for working clothes in those days - not as a fashion item. Although he was worn out at the end of the long, backbreaking day, Archie perked up when he was handed his daily wage of one florin (two shillings or the present equivalent of 10p). It was paid out at the back door of the farm by Mrs Laura Outhwaite, the farmer's wife, and, as an extra perk, the pickers were allowed to take home a few, very welcome, potatoes.

Gran visited again at the end of the month and she said to Archie, " A few days back there was a bombing raid on the West Lane and Grove Hill areas, a landmine was dropped at the Furness shipyard and a lone German plane dropped four high-explosive bombs on the Marsh Road area." Marsh Road was not far from our house and just round the corner from my pal, Eric's family. "I think the target was either the gas tanks, the Britannia Works or the railway marshalling yards," she continued. "Twenty people were killed and the injured were treated at the First Aid Post on Lord Street where Evelyn and Hilda are working as helpers. Ethel Gaunt is in charge there and Evelyn is doing some part-time cleaning at her big house on St. Paul's Road." Archie told Harry that fifteen houses had been totally demolished, thirty-odd would have to be pulled down and four hundred others were badly damaged.

It was a precarious time and the number of U-boat attacks on merchant ships had increased significantly, as the Germans attempted to lay siege to the British Isles. The severe shipping losses led to increased coal and food shortages and tea, that most sacred of British institutions, was now rationed at two ounces (56gms.) per person per week. There would be no more adding of 'a teaspoon for the pot'. The sugar ration was cut to eight ounces (225g.) and to make matters worse there would be no more bananas. No fresh or tinned fruit would be imported, apart from a few oranges, as the shipping space was badly needed for essentials. Nationally marmalade was hard to come by and Archie and the others were lucky that Mr Harris was growing onions and other vegetables on his allotment. Since the occupation of the Channel Isles there were real shortages of items like onions and tomatoes.

Mr Harris now kept a small plot at the bottom of the back garden to grow dandelions, whereas before the war they would have been treated as weeds and dug out. The leaves were used to supplement his evacuee's intake of greens but Jimmy called it rabbit food. Mrs Harris used them for salads and as pot herbs, as she held the old belief that, when boiled, dandelions were good for the blood; opened the breathing tubes; killed worms in children and aided sleep. This belief had recently been reinforced by the avuncular Dr. Charles Hill, MP, when he spoke of 'his friend the dandelion'. Known as The Radio Doctor he gave a five-minute talk on health every morning and Mrs Harris never missed that or *The Kitchen Front* that came on straight after the eight am news. Some of their neighbours were not too happy when the dandelions went to seed and hundreds of the feathery seeds floated into their gardens and took root. We called dandelion flowers *pee-the-beds;* others were not quite so polite.

By this time one of the air raid sirens was down a little lane on the eastern side of York Road, almost opposite Eastfield House. The siren, with its green, cylindrical steel drum and wind-up handle, had been mounted on the flat roof of Maurice Holliday's little bungalow from which he ran his cobbling business. It was manned and operated by two local air raid wardens and it had been activated a number of times in recent months and its reverberant, blood curdling, two-tone rising and falling wail lasted for two minutes, which led to it being called the Moaning Minnie. A constant one-minute wail was given to indicate the all clear.

On the evening of November the tenth Mr Harris said to himself, "The papers are definitely getting much thinner," as he sat in the kitchen quietly reading *The Yorkshire Press*. There was a report on the death of the former Prime Minister Neville

Chamberlain who had died of cancer the previous day just six months after leaving office. On another page the headlines read, 'FIRE DAMAGE AT CASTLE HOWARD: Great Central Hall and Dome Destroyed'. The grand eighteenth century residence lay just ten miles to the north east and was the home of the aristocratic Howard family who belonged to one of the great English dynasties that had been in existence since before the Tudor times.

The Harris's never missed the nine o'clock news and the boys could hear the muffled voices of the announcers in their bedroom, which was directly over the kitchen. They were reporting that Coventry, a centre of light engineering where cars, aeroplane engines and munitions were manufactured, had been raided by more than five hundred Luftwaffe planes and almost flattened. Most of the factories were close to its heart where there were large numbers of historic half-timbered buildings. The magnificent Gothic cathedral of St. Michael was destroyed leaving a burnt out shell and the vast conflagration consumed most of the city. Almost every street was set alight and five hundred and sixty eight civilians were killed. The eleven-hour long raid was one of the most devastating of the war and it set the pattern for all of the air raids that were to follow. Parachute flares and incendiary devices were dropped by the first wave of bombers, lighting up the area, which enabled the second wave to place their high explosive bombs more accurately. The Luftwaffe planes were guided to their target by means of high-frequency radio beams sent out from transmitters in Germany. Their navigational aids were far more advanced than ours at that time. After the news the family liked to listen to the *Postscripts* written and read by the North Country writer, J.B.Priestley. These were very popular and they had started at the time of the Dunkirk evacuation.

There were air raids on the Sefton Lane area of York in which two people were killed and several houses were badly damaged. In late October and into November, the siren was sounded again, as there were three nuisance raids on Clifton and Linton-on-Ouse aerodromes. In cold and foggy weather a soldier died in an air raid on the water works on Landing Lane. One of the Junkers 88 bombers, based at Eindhoven in Holland, had been en route to attack the aerodrome at Linton-on-Ouse when it encountered thick

219

fog over the North Yorkshire Moors and crashed into the steep hillside at Glaisdale Head killing its crew of four. The site of the crash was just up the railway line from us at Grove House.

The night-time bomber activity continued and on a cold and clear moonlit morning in mid November Archie, Ducky and Jimmy were woken by the loud and plangent tones of a low flying bomber. From about 6.30 a.m. onwards they heard planes passing over the fields to the north every few minutes and they kept rushing to the bedroom window to pull aside the black sateen curtains to see the familiar shapes of a number of Whitley bombers heading west. The eerie white light of a gibbous 'Bombers Moon' had turned the lawn and shrubs of the back garden to silver. It was like a floodlit stage with the moon casting deep shadows. As the first fingers of light stroked the eastern horizon the aircraft trailed home with ragged holes in the canvas of their fuselages. By 8 a.m. that Wednesday morning it was broad daylight and they were up and getting ready for school when they heard the sound of yet another aircraft coming in very low over Widd's field. It had been half an hour since the last bomber had passed just as the sky was starting to turn to grey in the east. The boys dashed out into the garden in time to see the badly damaged Whitley lumbering past with a great gash in the port side of its camouflaged fuselage.

They were unaware that they were witnessing history in the making as the young pilot of the Mark V bomber was Leonard Cheshire of 102 squadron, which had moved to Linton three weeks earlier. He was destined to become the legendary Group Captain Cheshire, VC, OM, and Lord Cheshire of Woodhall after the war. It was not until after the war that they learned that this was his third sortie over Germany in the last six days and that his plane was one of several involved in a raid on Cologne during which they flew low over the twin towers of the beautiful cathedral after following the Rhine that looked like a silver ribbon in the brilliant moonlight. Flying through heavy flak - which made a growling roar as it spattered lumps of hot metal through the skin of the fuselage - they had bombed the rail marshalling yards. An anti-aircraft shell passed right through the Perspex of their forward gun turret and out the other side blinding and deafening Cheshire for a while causing him to loose his grip on the control column. The aircraft had plunged downwards out of control and another shell exploded just above the port wing causing the flares in the rack to explode. This tore a huge strip out of the side of the fuselage; blew the door off and set fire to the floor close to the fuel tank.

The stricken aircraft dropped rapidly until Cheshire's fuzzy head cleared and he managed to pull back on the control column. The crew, temporarily blinded, coughed and choked on the smoke and the cordite fumes. Their clothes were burned and their faces were charred by the flames and blackened by the thick, black, oily smoke but they managed to jettison the remaining flares and the live ammunition before putting out the fire. It seems that all of this took place as a freezing wind whistled through the huge hole in the flapping canvas of the fuselage. For the next five hours, Leonard Cheshire struggled to bring the badly damaged aircraft under control, flying, literally, on a wing and a prayer, but he managed to steer the shot-up bomber across the grey North Sea. Navigating from memory, as the maps had been sucked out of the aircraft, he brought her safely home to Linton avoiding the built up areas. Much to the relief of the exhausted crew, he flew the battered plane in low over the perimeter fence making a perfect landing before taxiing slowly to one of the 'frying pan' hard standings. They had made it; but only just!

That afternoon, unable to sleep, he and two of his crew went into York to see a Fred Astaire and Ginger Rogers film. Two days later he was transferred to RAF Topcliffe, twelve miles to the north and, for his courage and presence of mind during that near fatal bombing mission, he was awarded the Distinguished Service Order. His badly damaged bomber was taken to Clifton aerodrome on the back of a Queen Mary where it was repaired and was flown back to Linton-on-Ouse airfield in late December. In heavy rain it stood waiting at the end of the wide, rain-wet, tarmac runway that disappeared into thick, low cloud, as an incoming Whitley flew into it breaking it clean in two. Later that month Mr Harris told the boys that the RAF - with a hundred and twenty seven bombers - had raided Hamburg, in what was, up to then, the largest air raid in a single night.

By this time the public had learned that British and Greek troops had thwarted an attempted invasion of Greece, driving the

Italians back into Albania. In North Africa the Italians had advanced sixty miles across the border into Egypt. General Wavell, in command of the Western Desert Forces, ordered General Sir Richard O'Connor to mount a counter attack and, in a brilliant surprise move, he attacked Marshal Graziani's foothold at Sidi Barani and pushed the Italians out of Egypt. Even though outnumbered ten to one, they managed to capture tens of thousands of Italians some of whom ended up working on farms in the Haxby area. In the New Year O'Connor's troops fought their way west taking Tobruk, Benghazi and El Agheila, forcing the enemy back almost as far as Tripoli. The people of Haxby, in the grip of another severe winter, were finding the rationing, the blackout and the reports of so many lost battles hard to bear. News of this rare success was a much-needed fillip that helped to lift their spirits no end.

Jimmy was woken from his sleep when a local air raid warden, Joe Lockwood, on seeing a chink of light at the front bedroom window, knocked on Mrs Harris' door. The brave man, in his steel helmet and dark blue boilersuit, told her in no uncertain terms to "Put that bloody light out!" She confronted him at her front door with a coat over her nightie and her hair tied up in rag curlers. She must have been a fearsome sight with her doughy jowls wobbling as she told him what she thought of him. "Why don't you go and join the Army like a real man instead of harassing people," she shouted. She knew very well that, as a market gardener, he was exempt but still said, "I couldn't care less if you are medically unfit, exempt or too old. Don't come here bothering law abiding folk." "I'm going to report you to PC Manging," he retorted, to which she replied, "You can tell him what I think of him too, while you're at it!" She was not amused; in fact she was fuming. "Doesn't the man understand that it's a damn nuisance having to go outside in the cold to check that no light is showing!" Mr Harris and others had to suffer the brunt of her ire over the ensuing days.

At school, just before Christmas, some of the evacuees from Hull were upset to learn that on a frosty night the city and the dockside had been set ablaze. Hundreds of incendiary bombs had rained down throwing out fountains of spluttering white fire that ignited everything it touched. It was said to have been so cold that the water from the fire hoses had frozen into sheets of ice, which reflected the leaping flames. Over forty fires destroyed many of the houses and the town centre was a raging inferno. The orange glow in the night sky to the east - emphasised by the total blackout - could be seen from Haxby and it was reported later that they had been seen from as far away as Denmark.

The harsher rationing measures of 1940 were beginning to bite and it was to be a much bleaker Christmas for all this year. Many had grated carrot and swede into their Christmas puddings, as there was now no suet available and currants and sultanas were scarce or impossible to obtain. It was a time for 'making do' and the pulling in of belts. Mrs Harris made mock cream for the Christmas pudding using cornflour, vanilla essence and sugar. The next day Gran and Aunt Hilda visited again after an interminably long, slow, journey with the train stopping at every station. They told the boys that Archie's brother, John, had just gone back to his training camp at Cheddar after four days of embarkation leave and that he was expecting to be posted abroad very soon. They collected Archie and Jimmy and walked down York Road as frozen snow lay under the hedgerows and their breath condensed on the icy air. As the snowflakes floated down, they were made welcome and enjoyed another plentiful Boxing Day meal as the Misses Law and Barker were still relatively unaffected by the food shortages that most of the other locals were experiencing.

Archie was growing up fast and he now enjoyed looking at the daily cartoon strips (again no pun intended) of Jane in the *Daily Mirror*; a WAAF who regularly bared all for the cause. He was becoming more and more restive at having to stay so long, as he was at least a year older than the others at the school. He was frustrated and had only tolerated being here because of his promise to take care of Harry and Jimmy but he now felt that they were capable of looking after themselves. He had had enough of it and yearned to be back in his mucky old town looking for a job. Gran realised that Harry and Jimmy were now well settled, and she agreed that he needn't stay any longer and arrangements were made accordingly. She said to herself, "A little extra money coming in would be very welcome and will make things easier for me." Much to his delight, it was agreed that he would not go back to school after the Christmas break and he would return to the family home early in the coming year.

So the year came to a close with the very cold weather continuing in the same vein. It was an atrocious winter with dense freezing fog and heavy cloud. And, on the first day of the New Year and on many days thereafter, it snowed and lay. Under their thick blanket of snow the ploughed fields were like sheets of corrugated steel and Mr Harris was glad to get home out of the cold when he finished work for the day. A new radio programme called *The Brain's Trust* had just started and he enjoyed that.

On the sixteenth the banshee wail of the siren was heard again as another air raid took place on York and a middle-aged man died from his wounds in hospital. Later that month, one of the airmen billeted in Haxby let it slip that Leonard Cheshire, DSO, had been posted back to RAF Linton having been promoted to the rank of Flying Officer. He was to be part of the newly re-formed 35 Squadron which would be involved in bringing in to service the big, new, four-engined, Handley Page 'Halifaxes, the crews having been carefully selected from the whole of Number 4 Group. The Mark 1 prototype had first flown in October 1939 and the Mark II in August of the following year, their production having been delayed by Lord Beaverbrook's campaign for more fighter planes. The aim had been to build the bombers with two Vulture engines but there were insufficient of these and they were fitted with four Rolls Royce Merlins instead and the move proved to be very successful. The five new Halifax bombers were larger and faster than the Whitleys with a Perspex blister just aft of the bomb bay, and it had a much enlarged bomb carrying capacity. They were more complicated to fly than the old lumbering Whitleys that now had few friends but were still being flown out on bombing missions. Cheshire was to play a major role in the teaching the new techniques.

It was a time of heavy loss of life for bomber aircrews with only one-in-five of them completing a tour of thirty operations. If they did so they were rested for six months. Most of the RAF lads had their hair thickly plastered with Brylcreem and, naturally, they became known as the Brylcreem Boys. They looked very smart in their neatly pressed, pale blue uniforms with the silver wings on the left breast, and it was customary to leave the top button undone and to wear a silk scarf. When they occasionally came over to the *Red Lion* and the *Tiger* for a 'wet' (Forces slang for a beer) they found that the beer - in short supply like everything else - was watered down to make it last out. The drinking hours were from eleven in the morning till two in the afternoon, and from six to ten o'clock at night, but they were often treated to free beers after hours. Harry, Archie and Jimmy hero-worshipped them and when they attended the dances at the Wiggie Rec they were exceedingly popular with the young ladies of the two villages.

The Red Lion, Haxby in 2003.

11. The Land of Lost Content

In January the snow that lay six inches (15cms) deep around Grove House muffled our footfalls and round about us the deep drifts had created a magical and fantastic scene. The snow changed the look of everything and it was now a hushed snow-filled world. It was piled up against the house by the strong, bitterly cold north easterly winds and the hedges and the rhododendron shrubs were transformed into great white mounds and humps. We caught a glimpse of the white rump of a fleeing roe deer near the pond, which hunger had brought down from the forest in search of food. Being very wary animals they try to avoid human contact and if they detect even the slightest scent of a person they cough to warn the rest of the herd who spring into flight and dash for cover. Strange birds and other small, hungry creatures came into the gardens leaving tiny prints on the crisp white sheets of virgin snow. Snow thickly blanketed the lawns and the drive and we competed with each other to see who could leave the most footprints in it.

We helped (or hindered?) the nursery assistants in building a snowman. The snow was brittle - not too wet - and therefore ideal for making snowmen and snowballs and it creaked as we rolled it in to large balls to make the body parts. We patted and moulded him into shape using coal for his eyes and buttons with a carrot for his nose. Sticking a pipe in his mouth, Kitty tied one of the gardener's old mufflers round his neck and put a flat cloth cap on his head. The stillness of the dozing valley was rudely torn apart and the naked woods echoed to our shouts and laughter as snow lay heavy on the leaves and boughs of the spruce trees. We happily raced and jumped about in the thick drifts and had snowball fights. The Stancliffe girls were away from home, so Jack Pickering brought their sledge from the outbuilding where it had been stored all year. Sitting one of us in front of him, he took us on hectic, scary flights with the sledge going pell-mell down the steep snow-covered lane until he dug his heels in and skidded to a halt on the level bit just before the railway crossing. We squealed in delight. Later we sucked on the long icicles that we had snapped off the portico eaves and ran about in our wellies until our legs began to hurt above our socks that had slipped down. The wet tops had chafed the skin making a red ring that was very sore and when we were taken in to the playroom, red-cheeked and blue-nosed, the caring nursery assistants smeared our legs with soothing Vaseline or Snowfire ointment.

Eric and I, along with a few of the other five-year-olds, had been having lessons with Miss Thorne, but she was not a fully certificated teacher; therefore, steps were being taken for us to start our formal education. Jack Pickering's children had been attending the old school up in Newton village for some time and arrangements were made for Eric to be billeted with a Mr Wilson Sleightholme up there. Known locally as Will, he was a farm worker and a part-time tailor (in casual employment with Dowson's in the village) who had lived in the village with his wife, Mary, for a number of years. Their old place was rented at a rate of fifteen shillings (75p) a week and was called Ivy House, but it was really two old brick cottages knocked into one. It was the second house on the left, after Saltburn Cottage, which stood at the top of the steep path up the hillside and it stood beside the narrow hedge-lined back lane that led into the village. Before the war they had supplemented their income by taking in paying guests and were noted for always providing a comfortable bed and a good breakfast.

Like all the other houses in the village, they had no water supply, obtaining it from a natural spring down in the valley by working the cast iron lever on the hand pump in their stone-flagged kitchen. Alternatively, it could be pulled up in a bucket from an underground cistern. They also collected the rain, channelling it into wooden butts and using it to water the plants and for general cleaning. There was no electricity to the village and smoky paraffin lamps and candles were used for lighting. They grew their own vegetables in a dug up area of the paddock and collected fruit from their garden according to the season. Eaters and cooking apples were 'laid down' over the winter.

The house stood next to the tiny school where Eric became a pupil under Mrs Baxter, the strict headmistress whose husband kept bees. The Sleightholmes had previously taken in an evacuee from Hull that came from a very poor family who occasionally sent him coats and trousers that were too small. Mr Sleightholme used his

227

tailoring skills to adapt them to fit. He also altered the thick, heavy, Yorkshire worsted suits of the local farmers as they lost or gained weight. They only wore them for family baptisms, weddings and funerals and for special church services like those at Easter, harvest time and Christmas and they were often handed down to the eldest son when the father died. Clothes were made to last in those days. Mrs Sleightholme was kept busy knitting socks, mitts, balaclavas and jumpers as the young lad had arrived with no undervest and very little else and he was found to be suffering from impetigo. Apparently he didn't like it there and soon went back to Hull.

Initially Eric wasn't too happy either. In the darkness of his strange and lonely bedroom the cold wind from the moors moaned as it crept around the cottage and nagged away at the red pantiles on the roof. Its icy fingers got into the ill-fitting casement window making it rattle as he knelt by his bed to say a little prayer that we used to say together at Grove House. It went something like:

'Lord keep us safe this night, secure from all our fears.
May angels guard us while we sleep till morning light
appears.'

Eventually, he settled in at his new home and was very happy there. He was well looked after and loved and he stayed there until the war ended four and half years later. He enjoyed feeding the goslings and the hens, which provided them with fresh eggs as they ranged freely in the long grassy paddock, where the pony and trap was kept. From the bottom of the paddock there were magnificent views down into Newtondale and across to the high moors to the east. When the time came for him to go home, Mrs Sleightholme wanted to adopt him but his parents were keen to have him back and there were floods of tears. Mr Sleightholme was an honourable man, but he felt that some of the villagers thought that he was dodging his duty by staying at home, so he volunteered for the army and was never seen again. I was not to see Eric again, except for a brief spell soon after the war and it was to be a further fifty-odd years before we came in contact with each other again.

I loved it at Grove House where I was secure and cared for by trustworthy, kind and loving people and it seemed a truly magical place to me. In the smoke and chemical-laden atmosphere of Middlesbrough I was often ill and seemed to get every childhood illness going. Here, in the sylvan beauty and tranquillity of this secluded wooded valley, I was flourishing and growing tall and straight, like the surrounding spruce trees. Fresh air and exercise were honing my appetite and I was filling out. Living a tranquil, simple and wholesome life, I was happy and the world seemed to be a lovely place. Anne-Marie still came into the garden to pick the bashful snowdrops that pushed through the snow but, in my blissful innocence, I was unaware that great changes were being planned and these were soon to change my cosy, cosseted little world forever.

In early February mother came to visit us and she told me that my Uncle Archie was back home and had started work washing and filling milk bottles at Donaldson's Dairy. "It was only eight years ago that milk was sold in bottles for the first time," she told Kitty. A few months later he began his apprenticeship as a steel plater in the Bridge Yard that was part of the sprawling Britannia steelworks that was itself part of Dorman Long Limited. The firm was justifiably proud of having built the Newport (Tees) Bridge as well as the world famous bridge that spanned Sydney Harbour, which was the largest and heaviest arch bridge in the world at that time.

It seems that arrangements had been made for me to replace him at Haxby as I should, by rights, have left the nursery school as soon as I reached the age of five, ten months earlier. I had been allowed to stay on as my younger brother was still here and Mam wanted me to go to the same billet as her sister's son. I was rather apprehensive of what was in store for me and hated the thought of having to leave, as I had loved it so much at Sutherland Lodge and here. However, Mam assured me that it would be nice to have Jimmy to play with and she assured me that he would look after me and I would like it. Mother came through to take me to my new home but George was to stay at the nursery school until he was five.

The day I left Grove House for the last time was a sad, sad day for me. I cried as if my heart was broken (and maybe it was) and there were tears in the eyes of the nursery assistants. My favourite grown-up, apart from Mam and Dad, was Kitty who was now married to Alan, becoming Mrs Catherine Brown. She had given up her job and they were both living happily at Peep-o Day bungalow. My little brother, George, and several of my tiny friends had come to see me off; they were all loved and so precious to me, and most of them were sobbing openly. I tried to speak to them as I sensed that I would never see them again, but my heart was too full and I could not get the words out. I never forgot Kitty who had shared her love and knowledge with us and I will owe her a debt of gratitude until the day I die.

All too soon the train, that had a great steel snowplough fixed to the front of it, pulled in at the snow-covered platform. On that dreary, dismal day under a sullen, leaden sky, which was loaded with yet more snow to come, the final kisses, hugs and best wishes were exchanged before Mam and I mounted the high wooden step of the railway carriage. It was a bitter wrench and such a sorrowful parting! My whole being was suffused with an overwhelming love for that beloved place and its kind and caring people and I grieved for all that I was to leave behind. I still think back to those wonderful times where I had lived and played so happily. It was truly a haven of peace and love. To this day memories of those days well up from the depths of my soul, like milk coming to the boil, and they will live in my heart forever. I am filled with a glow of gratitude and pleasure when I think of those sweet, much-treasured times. It was my Elysium; a place that overflowed with tenderness, love and kindness.

As I set off for pastures new a chapter in my short life closed and a new leaf was about to be turned. The great steam locomotive slowly huffed and puffed its way out of the beloved station and I gazed at the small group that stood huddled together waving until they were out of sight. I snuggled up into the warmth of Mam's body feeling sad but secure enclosed within her loving arms. She held my tiny hand and I lay my head against the softness of her bosom and she hugged and kissed me, holding me ever so close calling me her precious little lost lamb. I looked through tear-blurred eyes on the beauty of my secluded valley for the last time. It had been a safe haven from the storms of life and I had been so happy there. The dark green of the pine and spruce trees and the bare limbs of the deciduous trees stood out starkly against the

230

brilliant whiteness of the snow and involuntary sobs racked my slender frame as I realised that I would never see it again. There was an empty ache in my heart as fond memories of the happy times spent there rose up and I think the following verse expresses perfectly my sentiments at that sad time:-

> *"That is the land of lost content,*
> *I see it shining plain,*
> *The happy highways where I went*
> *And cannot come again."*

> *A.E.Houseman. (1859 - 1936)*

Children are very resilient and soon bounce back and by the time we reached Pickering, I was my usual pestering and attention-seeking self again. My normal ebullience returned and I was forever asking, "Can I (this)?" and "Can I (that)?" As we had to change trains here, we had a mug of strong, stewed tea and a hard rock cake in the refreshment room as a bitterly cold, piercing wind blew along the covered platform. Mam bought some liquorice allsorts, one of my favourite sweets, for the journey and suggested that we should sit for a little while by the warmth of the open fire in the Ladies waiting room.

Eventually, we clambered onto the train for Malton, which steamed through the tiny, quaintly named Marishes Road station as thick flurries of snow blurred the telegraph poles that raced past the carriage windows. After a flat, six-mile journey south the track linked up with the main Scarborough to York line at Rillington where the line turned west through the Derwent valley. In the wan winter sunshine the meandering river, which was seldom out of sight, looked like a silver serpent as we clattered along beside snow-blanketed fields. We pulled in to the station in the small market town of Malton, which Mam said, was called Derventia in Roman times.

The train to York was packed full of soldiers and airmen. Mam had somehow obtained permission for us to leave the train at Haxby station, which was normally closed to passengers but, since it had to stop there to deliver certain items, they could see no problem in us getting off. Several soldiers (sojers, to me) got into our carriage. Their shiny black boots clattered on the floor as they carried in their rifles and bulging kitbags. Removing their forage caps, known as cheesecutters, they shoved them through the shoulder tab of their battle dress blouses. As they lifted their kitbags and webbing packs onto the overhead netting of the luggage rack, the nap of their uniforms, which was wet with snow, was starting to curl up. The soldiers lit up their Woodbines and after a while the carriage reeked of smoke and one of them opened the window a crack to let it out. Animal heat rose from the dampness of their uniforms, as they slowly dried out. As we continued our journey, still following the course of the river, two of the soldiers, their coarse khaki uniforms feeling rough to the touch, made a bit of a fuss of me and gave me a boiled sweet to suck.

The train (and the soldiers) steamed on as we crossed and re-crossed the snaking Derwent, passing through the oddly named Huttons Ambo station and skirting the bare woodlands and the snow-clad parkland of the vast Castle Howard estate. Without stopping we passed through the pretty little, stone station that had been built for the Howard family's private use. It stood, with its solid and chunky chimneys, within a loop of the river about two miles from the magnificent, Baroque style edifice. One of the soldiers said to Mam, "Guests, such as Queen Victoria and her retinue, were met 'ere and were tekken t't'big house along t'country lanes in elegant horse-drawn carriages. The beautiful, glass dome at t'centre o'it were t'first of its kind to crown a private residence in England. Everything about it were on a grand scale and it were built with pale, yeller local stone."

As we passed we caught a glimpse of the domed colonnaded family mausoleum that stood on the top of a snow-covered hill in the distance. The soldier said, "The big 'ouse were built in t'early eighteenth century for Charles Howard, third Earl of Carlisle, who were t'First Lord o't'Treasury. They were great landowners and peers of the realm and 'ad formerly 'ad close connections wi't'monarchy. Lady Ann Boleyn (mother of Queen Elizabeth) and Catherine Howard, were t'second and fifth wives of Henry t'Eighth. They were t'pretty young nieces o't'scheming and ambitious Henry Howard; third Duke of Norfolk. Their marriages were arranged to

232

keep in favour wi't' King but both of 'em were be'eaded for 'avin' love affairs with certain courtiers."

The soldier obviously had a keen interest in history and he went on and on - whether Mam was interested or not - "For more than seven hundred years the family played their part in changing the course of English 'istory and Lord William Howard, known as Belted Will, were said to be 'skilled at marrying heiresses'. 'E 'ad acquired t'estate - the site being occupied by five small villages - through 'is marriage to Elizabeth Dacre. Charles Howard, great grandson o't'fourth Duke of Norfolk, cleared t'villages in order to build t'ouse close t't'owld castle at Helderskelfe, which 'ad been destroyed by a disastrous fire in 1693." Barely pausing for breath, he added, "Three months back much o't'ouse were destroyed by yet another fire."

Vanburgh's magnificent dome was not to be rebuilt for another twenty years after the fire that Mr Harris had read about in his newspaper. It had been discovered at 5 a.m. on Saturday the ninth of November 1940 at a time when none of the family was living in the house. A small number of soldiers were billeted in it as well as a hundred and thirty, teen-aged, girl pupils and the staff of Queen Margaret's School; the same school that Kitty and Mary had worked at as housemaids before the war. The well-bred girls and their teachers had been sent here from their fine school building in Scarborough. Miss Joyce Brown, the music mistress at the high-class private school, had discovered the fire and raised the alarm.

The soldiers had been in the old south east wing of the house and had thrown some papers onto an open fire before going to bed. Unbeknown to them, the fire had taken hold in the unswept chimney and the Malton Fire Brigade was called out. In their efforts to put out the fire, they had attempted to draw water from the lake but the hosepipes and pumps became blocked with leaves, lilies and other vegetation. During the delay the wind fanned the flames and the fire spread rapidly to the Great Hall above which were the Saloon Rooms, then being used as a dormitory. Queen Victoria had slept here when she had visited the great house in 1850. By the time York Fire Brigade got there, twenty rooms and the multi-paned central dome were well alight and the lead of the great cupola had collapsed inwards.

The girls had used bed sheets to take their books and most of their personal belongings outside and had carried out several valuable objects laying them on the snow-covered lawn of the Boar Garden where they stood shivering. Thirteen extremely valuable Canalletto paintings, a few Sheridan mirrors and several other rare art treasures were lost or badly damaged in the blaze. When the snow turned to rain, they carried the family 'treasures' back in to the building, which was still burning and, fortunately, none of them came to any harm. For the next few years much of Castle Howard was left open to the sky with several of its once splendid rooms gutted and certain parts of its beautiful white stonework are pink to this day due to the oxidation caused by the tremendous heat of the fire.

The Hon. Geoffrey Howard, the third son, was an officer in the Green Howards and on his returned wounded at the end of the war, he lovingly restored most of the house, opening it to the public in 1952. He became chairman of the BBC Board of Governors and was influential in the house being used in the filming of the television series 'Brideshead Revisited'. The Castle Howard railway station scenes were actually shot at Levisham Station and the hugely successful series helped raise funds to restore the house to its former glory.

The piercing train whistle sounded as we continued our journey with the swaying of the carriages making us lurch from side to side as we clattered over the points. The smell of the men's warm, damp khaki uniforms pervaded the carriage as we passed through other tiny, quaintly named stations with names such as Crambe and Flaxton, which stood beside the flat snow-covered floodplains of the meandering river. Every mile was taking me away from all that I loved and I resented it but, by then, the snow had stopped and the sky had begun to clear. We stopped at a place called Strensall where the soldiers put on their forage caps, heaved their bulging kitbags on to their shoulders and waved goodbye to us as they got down from the train. We had a last glimpse of them as they clambered over the high wooden tailboard of a camouflaged, dull-green, two-ton, canvas-covered army lorry. Mam said, "They'll be going to the big camp about a mile off."

We crossed the river Foss on a narrow railway bridge that had a wide iron pipe running alongside it and after a further two miles or so, we drew in at the small, neat station on the eastern side of Haxby. Mam put on my mitts and pulled my woollen balaclava helmet over my head before crossing the long, hand-knitted woollen scarf over my chest and tucking it under my armpits. She pulled my coat collar up round my ears and we stepped down onto the frost-rimed slabs of the platform. A smiling, thickset, middle aged man wearing a baggy, flat cloth cap and a thick brown overcoat came forward to meet us. I noticed that he had a pronounced limp and he introduced himself as Harold Mann, explaining that he was a close friend of my new foster parent. "Ah'm sorry," he said, "but Mr Harris couldn't come as 'e's 'ad ter work on t'farm. 'E asked me to come and tek yer t't'ouse."

Mam thanked him for coming and he took hold of my small, scuffed and scratched cardboard case and we followed him along the white edged platform. He led us through a white-paled, wicket gate and over the shining metal of the twin railway lines. The low, sallow afternoon sun was making no impression on the rime of frost that twinkled like stars on the heavy wooden sleepers. As elsewhere, the station name boards had been removed, so as to make it more difficult (in theory) for the enemy (should they arrive) to establish their whereabouts. A wooden rest shelter stood at the back of the up platform and nearby there was a wrought iron bench, a row of white painted wooden palings and a small ticket office.

An old station house with an elegant Georgian entrance porch stood by the gates of the crossing. The countless steam trains that had passed close by for nearly a hundred years had turned its old stones black and behind it there was a long established and well-frequented coal yard. Beyond it there was a large, elevated, metal, water tank that had a wide tubular arm with a canvas sleeve that could be swung out to refill the steam engine boilers. The wide, white-painted, five-barred gates were still shut and Mr Mann's pony and trap stood at the other side. His horse, Monty, was having a nap with one rear hoof, slightly bent at the hock, resting on the other. Mr Mann lifted my case up through the little door at the rear of the small open carriage and helped me and then Mam, up the little iron step. After he had dried them with a cloth, we sat on the shiny, wooden-slatted seats that ran parallel with the panelled sides.

'Lenmuir', Wold View Terrace, Haxby in 2002.

Harold said, "The stretch o't'road from 'ere t'traffic roundabout at top o' York Road is called Station Road." We sat in the little carriage wrapped in thick woollen blankets as the shaggy-coated pony trotted along very gingerly as the road was treacherous with a thin, glass-like layer of ice on top of the compressed, frozen snow. Monty flared his nostrils and snorted from time to time and his warm exhalations hung like clouds of steam on the cold winter air.

On the right, we passed the double bay-windowed frontages of a pair of large and impressive, semi-detached houses and Harold told Mam that the sandstone-built houses were called The Laurels and The Cedars. Both had large stone quoins at their corners and were set back behind low stone walls with wide gateways and gravel drives. Dark evergreens and bare-limbed deciduous trees stood in the front gardens and the names of the big houses were carved on their square, solidly built, stone gateposts. Mr Mann said, "They were built for auld Sam Sutton, a JP, around t'turn o't'century. 'E 'ad a successful financial business in Scarborough, but 'e lived at t'Laurels with 'is wife until 1911. Over t' years 'e invited lots o't'local kids to 'is 'ouse for tea and gave 'em a gift every Christmas," before adding, "Me wife used ter work theer, tha knows."

The pony's long, shaggy mane was blown about by the icy, cutting wind as Harold turned right onto Usher Lane immediately after passing a very large house on the corner. Mr Mann said, "Yer see yon small, white-flecked bricks in t'walls, well they're were made in 'Axby." It had a long garden along one side surrounded by a four feet tall (1.2m.) wall and Harold said to Mam, "Its 'ome of a plump little lady called Mrs Lumley who used ter be an infant teacher at t'village school afore t'war."

We stopped at the gate of a semi-detached house on our left. The house had a small front garden behind a low privet hedge that, like its neighbours, had a thin layer of frozen snow on it. Beneath its square-bayed windows was a small, snow-covered rockery and on the wall to the right of the front door was a wooden plaque that read: 'Lenmuir'.

Mrs Harris came out with a thick coat round her shoulders and carefully picking her way along the ice-covered path that ran beside the house. Harold handed us over without much ado and returned to his job at Abel's Church View Farm with the pony and trap. As she led us slipping and sliding along the path past the coalhouse door, Mrs Harris instructed us that her evacuees were never allowed to use the front door. We went through a wooden gate between the back corner of the house and the shed and turning left, went up three steps and in through the kitchen door. This was to be my sixth address in under six years.

Mrs Harris seemed to carry her own chill in to the house with her along with a blast of icy, wintry air. Inside, on the left, a door led into a large, walk-in larder and a second door opened into the bathroom. Due to the long journey and the effects of the cold, the pressure on my bladder was unbearable and I was 'dicky-dancing' as I desperately needed 'to go'. I couldn't wait and I dashed into the bathroom to go to the lavvie, which was tucked away in an alcove behind the larder. Above it a chain with a wooden handle hung down from a cast iron cistern and opposite there was a large, white enamelled, claw-foot bathtub with two shiny brass taps, which stood beneath the sloping ceiling under the stairs.

From the bathroom I could hear muffled talking and on going back into the kitchen, Mrs Harris seemed remote, forbidding and glacial in the cold wan light of that chilly winter afternoon. She had a pallid complexion and a blotchy face that reminded me of the poisonous foxglove bells in the woods at Grove House and she was wearing a faded, washed out pinny over her ample bosom. Her face and arms were freckled like a bird's egg as she peered down at me through her heavy horn-rimmed glasses and when she shook my hand her limp, flabby fingers, that looked like pork sausages, felt cold and clammy. There was no smile and not a glimmer of warmth in her greeting; the only bit of warmth came from a coal fire that burned in the grate behind a wooden hearth surround.

To the right of the back door there was a cast-iron, gas cooker and next to it a square, vitreous china sink with a wooden draining board stood below the kitchen window. In the centre of the room was a wooden table covered with a cream and blue-checked oilcloth. When the stiff formalities and the minor pleasantries were over, she made tea in a large brown pot placing a hand-knitted tea cosy over it. The tea was poured into white, half-pint (0.28 of a litre) mugs and she invited us to help ourselves to the broken biscuits that lay on a chipped and cracked plate. The square table was slightly wobbly and a piece of cardboard had been stuffed under one if its legs to balance it. The oilcloth was covered in a network of tiny fissures and fine cracks that matched the mugs and the wooden forms that stood along three of it sides.

Mrs Harris seemed old to me and I heard Mam say in a tremulous voice, as she handed over my green ration book and National Registration Identity Card, " I trust that you'll take good care of him." To me, Mrs Harris' congeniality lacked conviction and she seemed formidable and icily polite as she studied the items in her pale podgy hands. That fawn-coloured card is still in my possession some sixty-six years later. Mrs Harris then said, "He will have to sleep in the back bedroom with Donald and Jimmy. Don't worry about him Mrs Wright, he'll get the same treatment as the others." This could have meant anything, as I was not to know how she treated them.

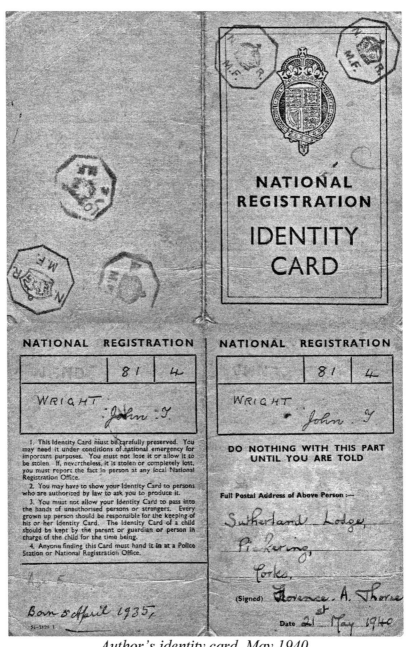

Author's identity card, May 1940.

She then led us up the stairs after going through the front room, which was kept as a 'best room' only to be used for special occasions. It had a wooden picture rail high up on its faded, print-papered walls from which a couple of gloomy-looking pictures hung on long cords. There was a settee and two armchairs beside a small, tiled fireplace and on the chimneybreast a round mirror with bevelled edges hung on a long chain. In the rectangle formed by the bay window was a sturdy wooden table covered with a velvety, maroon cloth with tasselled edges. In the centre of the room lay a threadbare rug with a margin of brown, bare floorboards around it.

A porcelain ornament, about ten inches (25cms) tall, stood on the mantle shelf above the empty fire-grate. It portrayed a young washerwoman holding the rim of a wicker clothesbasket with one hand while the other side rested on her hip. Her fair hair was tied back beneath a tight fitting, pale-coloured bandanna and she had a short, black, sleeveless waistcoat over a light-blue, frilly-necked blouse and her pale-lilac sleeves were rolled up above her elbows. She was wearing a yellow apron that covered the front of a wide, flowing, red skirt that came to just below her knees, while on he legs she wore white, knee-length socks. On her small, dainty feet there were shiny black shoes with square, silver buckles. I liked it as it was the only bright and cheerful thing I had seen in the house so far.

The wooden stairs leading up from the small entrance hall were covered by a threadbare runner held in place by tarnished brass rods and at the top was a small landing. To the left an open door led in to the front bedroom, through which I caught a glimpse of a double bed, a dressing table, a large wardrobe and a bedside cabinet. To the right was the door of the tiny box room and straight ahead a door led into the back bedroom that contained a bed, a chair and a plain wooden wardrobe. The floor, which was covered with lino, had just one small clippy rug by the bedside and a glass-shaded electric light bulb hung on a length of brown flex. Strangely, where the ceilings met the front and back walls of the house - normally at right angles to each other - they curved down about four inches to form a concave juncture. A thin, decorated, paper frieze ran round the top of the distempered and stippled walls. Mrs Harris started to unpack my case, saying coldly, "This is where you will sleep."

We went back down the steep stairs and in what seemed like no time at all there was yet another sad and tearful parting. Mam hugged me to her as if she would never let go and it hurt to see the pain and anguish in her eyes as she smoothed down my hair with a bit of spit, as it tended to stick up at the crown. She wiped the tears from my cheeks with her hankie and gave me a kiss, softly whispering, "I must go now. Be a good boy. Jimmy will look after you and I will see you again very soon. Bye-bye sweetheart." At that she was gone. She had to hurry to catch the bus into York and once there she would have to get the train to Darlington and hope that she did not miss her connecting train to Middlesbrough. Train journeys were slow and tedious at that time with many unscheduled stops and delays. She loved reading but the use of faint blue lights now made this almost impossible.

No sooner had she gone than Mrs Harris' false good cheer disappeared and she became brusque in her manner as she said, "I will not tolerate any rudeness or cheek. I expect you to be quiet at mealtimes and to speak only when spoken to. Children should be seen and not heard and there is to be no swearing, shouting or running in the house. You must abide by all the dos and don'ts listed on the door of the cabinet in the kitchen or there'll be trouble".

My feeling of wellbeing dissipated as quickly as the smoke that drifted up from her seemingly ever-present cigarette. Not long afterwards, Jimmy, Donald, Thelma and Dot came in from school and I was introduced to them. I barely recognised Jimmy, who I had not seen for eighteen months, as he had grown a lot and was now a good-looking, fine-featured, young lad. He had soft light brown hair that was combed back and parted on the left with a soft, wavy quiff topping his high forehead. Eighteen months is a long time at that age. Promising that he would look after me, he took me up to our bedroom to show me his toys and comics to take my mind off Mam's recent departure. I cried for a long time as we sat on the bed huddled together like a couple of street urchins. I felt lost and frightened in this strange, unfriendly and terrifyingly new place.

I was slow to settle in as I was very shy and I always felt ill at ease with the obsequious Donald, whom everyone called Ducky. He had clammy hands and shifty, darting eyes that always seemed to be watching me. Dot was a thin, droopy girl with short dark hair and a fringe cut just above her eyes. She seemed a bit dopey and slow-witted as she told me that she had a brother, Raymond, billeted at another house in the village and that they had been living with their parents in Church Street, Middlesbrough at the time of the evacuation. I liked the congenial, lively and no-nonsense attitude of Thelma straight away and we got on well from the start. She was a bright, clear-skinned, good-looking, level-headed sort of girl with a small heart-shaped face and intelligent brown eyes.

When Mr Harris came home from work, I also took to him. He was smallish, but strong and stocky with muscular arms that had a thin covering of fine fair hairs. A smiling, aquiline-nosed, ruddy-faced, down-to-earth kind of man who smelled of soil and sweat. He said, "Ow do, lad. Welcome to our 'umble abode. Mek yersel at 'ome and don't be frightened ter ask for anything."

Wives always gave the working men the largest portions in those days and they were all hungry and tucked in to a meal of rabbit stew and dumplings with thick slices of crusty bread. I picked and fiddled with my food as I didn't like the tiny bones in it and my shyness and the strangeness of my surroundings had taken the edge off my normally healthy appetite. There was only room for the two adults and the two big girls on the home-made, wooden, side benches, so Ducky, Jimmy and I sat, squashed together, on the bench at the front of the table. This was where I was to eat my meals from that day on.

Mrs Harris was not given to kind words and she always seemed to wear an expression of displeasure and was very strict. She made it crystal clear that the house, and particularly our bedrooms, were to be kept neat and tidy at all times, saying, "I'm not here to run after you lot or to pick up your discarded clothes," before adding, "and Jimmy you had better keep John right or you'll have me to answer to."

"Yes, Mrs Harris," he meekly replied.

To me she said, "Our bedroom, the parlour and the pantry are strictly out of bounds."

Her kitchen sink was brown stained and the gas oven was coated in burnt-on grease and it was obvious from the start that it was going to be a case of do as I say and not as I do. That night it

242

took me a long time to get to sleep as I lay between the two bigger lads snuggling up to Jimmy's warm back, but eventually I must have dozed off.

I was a resilient and amenable young lad and I had no choice but to accept the new regime and get on with it. There was no laughter in Mrs Harris who always seemed to look on us with unforgiving eyes and her cold stare could take the warmth out of the sunniest day. She said and did many unkind and unpleasant things, which I felt deeply and thought very unfair. Her philosophy seemed to be: Give them a good hiding and they won't do it again. Such treatment came as a shock to me so soon after my cocooned life in the nursery school where I had been accustomed to love and tenderness. Mr Harris, on the other hand, was always kind, affable and gentle with us and when his wife was not around, he let us get away with many minor childish mischiefs. He had smiling eyes that crinkled at the corners and he would often secretly slip us a sweet or two from behind the now depleted sheets of his *Daily Express* newspaper when she wasn't looking.

The next day our Jimmy, who had picked up the local dialect and speech mannerisms, said, "I'll show yer t'way t't' shops". He took me into the village centre to show me Torvill's newspaper shop where comics could be bought, which was just over the road from the school that I would be starting at on Monday. I became even more interested when he told me where mouth-watering gobstoppers, aniseed balls, penny chews, lemon barley and stretchy jelly babies could be had. He was referring to Bryant's little shop with its sweet, sugary-smelling interior that was on the other side of Front Street and it was to become a regular port-of-call for us. I found that Haxby was very old with a quaint mixture of farms, ponds, greens, stone walls and wrinkled, red roofs. Along Front Street many of the oldest buildings had undulating roofs of grey slate or terracotta pantiles.

Mr Harris had told Harry that, "Axby's typical of many o't' auld North Yorkshire villages bein' originally just one long street. It were founded by t'invading Danes who were good farmers and traders as well as being mariners. It sits between t'river Foss - from t'Roman word 'fossa' meaning a ditch - t't' east and Wigginton, t't'west. In distant t'past when t'ancient Forest of Galtres were cleared large areas of fertile land became available for farming. This area became t'property of Ealdred, who were Archbishop of York in 1069 and on 'is death it were 'anded down to 'is successors. The boundaries o't'village, 'ave barely changed in t'last three hundred years." "Before 1770, farming o't' land were based on t'open field system," he continued. "Local folk were given long strips of land in t'four main fields and they also 'ad access t't'common grazing land t't' north o't'village, now known as The Moor. The landowners then started to enclose t'fields and farming was still t'main occupation in t'village when t'war started. Only it's now in t'ands of a small number o' rich landowners. They now employ many whose not-too-distant ancestors once owned and worked t'same land. Farming is now even more important cos of t'Axis blockade, which is causing severe food shortages."

Many of the locals, including Mr Harris, were still happy to till the land and raise animals as their ancestors had done for years without number, but it was poorly paid work. The main road through the village followed the boundaries of the ancient fields as it ran through it from east to west. Life here had changed very slowly and very little over the last few decades and cows still ambled down Usher Lane at milking times.

Front Street with its wide grassy verges was the main thoroughfare and it opened out on the south side to form the village green near its western end. Jimmy said, "Our teacher told us that t'big copper beech at t'far end o't'Green was planted thirty years ago to celebrate t'Coronation of George the Fifth. For King George the Sixth's Coronation four years back a commemorative bench was placed near it and there are two more; one on Station Road and one on York Road." He then informed me that, "Those old houses and cottages by The Green are two or three hundred years old and are still lived in." He had been told that a pair of the cottages had, at one time, been a Dames School with the teacher living in one and holding classes in the other. "Miss Curry said it were run by unqualified, elderly women who were not very good at teaching reading and writing and the lessons were quite rudimentary - whatever that means! Working mothers left their children there each day for a small fee."

Front Street was lined by rows of little shops and cottages, interspersed by several larger 18th and 19th century dwellings, farmhouses and smallholdings. The well-frequented *Red Lion* on the north side and the *Tiger Inn* on the south, had been public houses for over a hundred years. The *Tiger Inn* had been formed by the modification and joining together of two of the old cottages and in it, in times past, the local farmers and smallholders had gathered to pay their annual rents. Behind Front Street there were back lanes, also lined with older houses and businesses. Some like Boynton's joiner's yard, had been established for more than 80 years. Front Street started from the grassy roundabout at the top of York Road and ended at the Wyre pond; the western boundary of Haxby where ducks skittered and floundered about on the thick layer of ice that now covered its surface. Just to the west of it there was a short open area, before it became Wigginton Front Street.

Jimmy, who was one year older than me, held tightly on to my hand as took me down York Road to call on my young uncle, Harry. His *grand* billet put ours in the shade and I got a bit of a shock on going through the front door, for looming over us was the head of a large, shaggy Highland cow. It had great long horns that curved outwards and upwards and it had been stuffed and mounted on the wall of the hallway some years back. Apparently it had once belonged to Miss Barker's family, who had been farmers for many years and it seems that, in the not too distant past, it had been a top class beast. Miss Barker said, "It won many prizes at agricultural shows, such as The Haxby Show, which was a very popular annual event before the war."

I was very surprised by the poshness, the space and the superior quality of everything. Compared to our humble and basic, but relatively new, billet it was a palace. At Usher Lane there was barely room to swing a cat, even if we'd had one. Harry introduced me to the Misses Law and Barker and they could not have made me feel more welcome and at ease. The warmth of their reception was in sharp contrast to the one received at the hands of Mrs Harris and I found them very nice and friendly in their genteel old-fashioned way and came to like them very much. A pleasant, outgoing couple, lively of mind and well spoken, they delighted everyone with whom they came in contact. They were noted for their Olde-World hospitality and good manners and they obviously loved Harry a great deal, fussing and doting on him (much to his embarrassment).

Miss Law was a 46 years old spinster lady of average height who was rather thin and wiry and of a slightly nervous disposition. She wrung her hands a lot in a sort of handwashing action and there was always a faint scent of Pond's moisturising cream, sweetly scented soap and smelling salts about her. She had an almost pathological fear of germs and there was not a speck of dust to be seen due to her constant obsessive dusting and polishing. She was of a more reserved and nervous nature than Miss Barker who was a jolly fifty-two years old, easy-going, homely woman who was on the small side with a matronly figure, but she couldn't be called fat. She enjoyed life and exuded kindness and goodwill and when she laughed, which was often, her whole body wobbled and shook. I never heard Miss Law laugh out loud, she only smiled sweetly from time to time. They were cousins and had been very close and loving friends for many years.

Miss Elizabeth Ann Barker was born at her father's farm near Sutton-on-the-Forest three miles to the north west as the crow flies. Her ancestors had lived and farmed there for a hundred and fifty years or more. In 1923 when her mother, Sarah, died of a heart attack, her father, Thomas, worked on at Westfield Farm for a couple of years before retiring and buying the fine town house on York Road. His sepia tinted photograph hung in an ornate, gilded frame above the mantelpiece in the parlour. He left the farm to his son, Arthur - who was still there with his wife, Jane, and their children, Sarah and Thomas - and came to live at Haxby with his daughter. He promised to leave her most of his money on condition that she looked after him and didn't marry. Miss Barker's mother's maiden name was Law and she had a brother called John, whose daughter, Elsie May, was born in 1895. Elsie moved in with her cousin shortly after the death of her father.

They were a friendly and generous couple who had an air of gentility about them and had become accustomed to living the high life. The middle-aged ladies loved to entertain and be entertained and were wholesome company and their friends and family were often invited to their garden parties. They dressed fashionably in clothes of top quality and enjoyed shopping at top stores, like

Marshall and Snelgrove's on Davygate in York. Good clothes were becoming much more difficult to obtain and their pre-war wardrobe had to last much longer these days. After a day of shopping they looked forward to a cup of tea and a couple of mouth-watering, fresh cream cakes in the refined atmosphere of the restaurant in Betty's Café.

The large, imposing three-storey building, on the rounded-off corner in St. Helen's Square, had high, plate-glass windows and square-shaped, white columns flanked its wide entrances. It had enjoyed a reputation as a high-class venue for many years. There was well-padded seating for up to 220 people and it was frequented by celebrities and the local rich and famous. It was a world of uniformed waitresses and white linen tablecloths; a place where fashionable people liked to meet for tea and a tête-à-tête. It seems that the place had recently become a magnet for servicemen based at the camps and airfields in the Vale of York. American, Canadian, Australian, New Zealand, South African, Free French, Czechoslovakian, Polish and RAF officers were now amongst its customers but it was out of bounds to 'other ranks'. Some left their photographs or other mementoes in what they called Betty's Bar or The Dive on the ground floor. Others scratched their signatures on the frame of the large mirror in the oak-panelled bar that the RAF crews nicknamed The Briefing Room. After the war it became a kind of memorial to the many young men who perished.

The middle-aged spinsters had been regular clients prior to and during the early months of the war and their self-indulgence had angered Mrs Harris, who often asked, "Why should the well-to-do eat as much as they want? It's always seems to be the common folk that have to tighten their belts and do without." However, with her buxom bosom and generous behind, she didn't appear to be too undernourished.

The couple often wore trench coats or belted tweed jackets with square-looking, padded shoulders when they visited the place and their pleated skirts reached to just below their knees, as this was the 'in thing' at that time. Under their jackets they usually sported a small ruff of lace or a high-boned, lace collar on white frilly-necked blouses, often with a cameo brooch at the neck and long strings of genuine white pearls. They nearly always wore a small, soft, felt, pork pie or slouch hat tilted over one eye. Their hair was expensively coiffured to curl around the edges and they were accustomed to wearing top quality silk or Lisle stockings. In the chillier months both were shod in strong, sensible, flat, rubber-soled shoes. Heeled shoes had been the style for well-to-do ladies about town in the late 1930s, but in the early part of the war they had been asked to wear shoes with flat heels, and most of the ladies felt that it was their duty to do so. The aim was to save on wood, which was in short supply, and even paper was now being made from straw. It had been recycled so often that it was now coarse in texture and of a yellowish colour.

They got in quite a flutter and blushed like peonies when a dashing Polish officer bowed, clicked his heels and kissed their hands. They thought that the Poles and the Czechs were so colourful and handsome and one even wore a dragoon-like, Ruritanian-style hat that was adorned with large white plumes that reminded the ladies of a recent Hollywood swashbuckler called *The Prisoner of Zenda*. Some wore heavily braided uniforms with the tassels on their golden epaulettes dangling from the shoulders. Many of the Poles, who were sometimes referred to as Polacks by the locals, had large floppy berets. Although embarrassed, the maidenly pair were quite flattered by the gallant behaviour of the flamboyant foreigners who all seemed to have extremely good manners and spoke politely in broken English. They were pleasantly impressed, but found their names, which seemed full of unpronounceable letters such as j, y, z and k. In recent weeks, the formerly well respected, licensed premises had started to lose something of its good name as too many young women were flocking there to consort with the free-spending servicemen.

People had started to suggest that 'nice' girls should not be seen there, so they switched their allegiance to Terry's Restaurant and café whose unlicensed restaurant seated two hundred and stood just across the road. There was a large, springy, dance floor in the room upstairs and the pair would call in for afternoon tea, often in the company of Miss Barker's sister-in-law, Jane. Terry's was, of course, the city's other major chocolate-making firm and their brands were prominently displayed in the large bow windows. Later in the war part of their factory was taken over to produce aircraft propeller blades.

There always seemed to be a lad standing outside selling the *Yorkshire Evening Post* in all weathers and he would bawl out newsworthy items from time to time in his efforts to attract buyers. In the refined and genteel atmosphere of the high-ceilinged establishment there was a low, genial, murmur of refined voices as waitresses in black dresses and frilly white aprons passed in and out taking orders, as quiet, soothing music added to the relaxed ambience. Some cleared the dishes from the brilliantly white tablecloths while others carried food in and out. Despite the clinking of teacups and cutlery and the clatter of food trays the paper lad's tortured, elongated vowels still managed to reach their ears. Miss Law wondered whether they were trained to do this or did it come naturally?

12. And so to school

It was cold and frosty with a leaden sky as Mrs Harris took me to the village school that Monday morning to be enrolled as a new and very apprehensive young pupil. Fortunately I was placed in the tender care of the gentle-natured Miss Francis in the 'baby' class at St. Mary's hall. Not much older than Kitty, she was slim and of medium height with short, wavy, mid-brown hair. Wearing a Tweed two-piece, she tended to push her head forward as she clumped along on flat, sensible, rubber-soled shoes. Of a kind and pleasant disposition, she usually wore a smile and she believed that you could accomplish more by kindness than you could ever achieve by force. She was not as bossy and strict as the slightly aloof and formidable Miss Curry, whose hair was severely tied back and held in place by Kirby grips. Miss Francis's friendly nature, calmness and gentle manner had a great deal to do with my settling in fairly quickly in the infant group. She had been Jimmy's teacher for part of the previous year and he said, "She's nice and I think you'll like her."

Even so, initially, it was not a happy time for me. In my unsettled state, I felt a rather lost and out of things as I gazed at the exposed rafters, purlins and tie beams of the rooftree above me. The schoolroom seemed dark and cheerless and the small windows only let in so much cold winter light. The atmosphere seemed strange and depressing and this was reinforced when I looked out of the window at the church graveyard. I had a morbid mental experience in which I imagined that I could see the skeletons of the village forefathers laying cold and still beneath the snow-covered sods. Even the lichen-splotched headstones, which leaned at all angles, looked mottled and diseased. Mam had told Harry that, "The gravestones face east so that when the souls of the occupants rise they will be facing the Lord. This ancient custom is a throwback to pagan times and is associated with the worship of the sun that rises in the east."

My imagination ran riot and I prayed that I would not be there when the rotting corpses came up. I felt shivers up the back of my neck and I buried my face in my arms. Even though I was among so many children, I felt lonely, sad and apprehensive, as I did not know any of them. To make matters worse it was said that some of the local parents had told their children not to mix with the 'vaccies', as they called us. They were inclined to blame us when things went missing or if their kids got in to arguments or fights.

Following so soon after the coddled and insular life of the nursery school I found this new way of life hard to accept and my heart ached for Mam, Kitty and my friends at Grove House. It had been an enchanted place to me and I longed to be back there being hugged and cosseted and told that I was loved. I resented being so cruelly torn away from the things that were so familiar to me, and felt angry at having my loving and secure world so abruptly taken away for a second time. It seems that we do not appreciate what we have in life until it dawns on us that we may not encounter it again. I kept my head down hoping to go unnoticed, indulging in day dreaming the hours away 'wool-gathering' and clock-watching. For a time I did not seem to fully connect with what was going on around me.

It was slightly reassuring to know that I would be with Jimmy again at playtime, as he was working away happily behind a curtain that separated us from the group of the stern Miss Curry in the other half of the hall. Time seemed to pass slowly and I tried to hide my sadness, shedding my bitter tears once I was alone. We had been told from our earliest days that big boys don't cry and I tried hard to suppress my tears and felt ashamed when they came unbidden. The only time that I was able to be by myself was when I visited the school toilet or in the Harris's bathroom. There was no privacy to be had anywhere else. Gradually I made the necessary adjustments to overcome this new and daunting phase of my life.

The teacher on duty started the school day by blowing a long blast on her whistle. The powers-that-be had stated that bells were only to be rung if an invasion was imminent and a rattle was to be used only if toxic gas was present in the vicinity. On hearing the whistle we stood perfectly still waiting for the command, "Get in lines!" A second whistle was the signal for us to march into the building in military style where we hung our hats and coats on the rows of low wooden pegs in the cloakroom. We took off our outdoor shoes, put them into a basket, put on plimsolls or sandals and lined up to be taken to our class area.

Our teacher called out the names in the register and marked the column with a tick or a cross every morning and afternoon. We were called up to her desk each morning to be given a spoonful of cod liver oil, quickly followed by a spoonful of concentrated orange juice to mask the vile taste of it. This was followed by a spoonful of gooey, sweet-tasting malt, which I loved. The same spoon was used for all three and it was not washed between one child's turn and the next. On Monday mornings the dinner register was filled in - with those who were to stay for school dinners taking their one shilling and eight pence (8.3p) out to the teacher. Some of the local children and many of the evacuees were entitled to free dinners depending on their family's ability to pay. We, always being hungry, envied them and wished that we could stay but that would have meant that Mrs Harris would have to pay for the meals out of her evacuee allowances and it was much cheaper for her as things stood.

We were then put in pairs and marched to the main school 'hall', which was actually two classrooms made into one by pushing back the folding glass and wood partitions, which had hinged, military-style, brass handles that folded down to lay flat within a circular recess. In these morning assemblies we had to endure the boredom of communal hymn singing, starting with a hymn, such as *He who would Valiant be* or *Jerusalem*, led by the vicar, the Reverend. K. Donald. We then chanted the morning-prayer and I recollect him as being a kind, gentle and understanding man who seemed old to us but was probably middle-aged. It was customary when prayers were being said to stand with our eyes closed and our hands held with the ends of our fingers pointing upwards and touching the chin. From his high place on the platform the Vicar looked down on the heads of our now quiet and subdued group. He and the head seemed very posh to us and we held them in awe, as they were figures of authority far removed from our way of life. They inhabited a different world to us and, unlike the kids of today, we would never have dreamed of approaching them to ask anything.

The headmaster reiterated the fact that God had placed us where we were in the social order and that to try to change this preordained scheme of things would be sinful in His eyes. We were instructed that we must order ourselves lowly and reverently to our betters at all times and had to listen to an arid lecture on morals and decent standards of behaviour that, literally, went over our heads. Once we were in a quiet and humble frame of mind the first lesson - Scripture- commenced during which stories and lessons from the Bible were read to us.

At the morning break the children collected a straw and a small, wide-necked, glass bottle of milk, that held a third of a pint (183cc.), from the milk monitor. On pushing in the cardboard seal with our thumb, we sometimes soaked ourselves with a fair portion of the contents, before drinking the remainder. For many of the scruffy evacuees the free milk and dinners were about the only things that interested them in the elementary education system. Unless they were exempt, the children had to pay a ha'penny (half of an old penny or about 0.2p) for the milk and we usually raced each other to see who could finish first. We were told that milk strengthened our bones, thus reducing the incidence of rickets and we had seen too many skinny, bow-legged children hobbling around in callipers in the streets of Middlesbrough before the war. It was no good saying that you did not like milk; you got it anyway and the teacher stood observing us, not allowing us outside until it was all gone. If it was dry we were allowed to play outside, but we did not get out much during that first month, as it was very cold with days of snow and ice interspersed by slightly milder wet ones.

The alphabet was chalked on the blackboard with a picture of an object that started with that letter beside it (e.g. a = apple, n = nib, I = inkbottle). The facts to be learned were relentlessly hammered into us by means of soul-destroying, rhythmic repetition and we chanted it day after day until it was assumed that we had absorbed it and knew it by heart. We learned parrot fashion. Again and yet again we rhythmically chanted saws like: "Twelve inches in a foot", "Sixteen ounces make one pound, fourteen pounds make one stone', etcetera, ad infinitum and the multiplication tables were taught by this same time-honoured use of rote. We repeatedly chanted our 'times tables' ending up, hopefully still together, with ".... and twelve twelve's are one hundred and forty-four." The four fundamentals of sums were taught by using a range of coloured counters for adding, taking away and simple division.

Writing mostly consisted of copying well known maxims from books or words from the blackboard. The younger children were read to; the older ones had to take their turn at standing up to read passages out loud and the-powers-that-be seemed to expect children to progress at the same rate. We now know that this is not the case. Miss Francis tried to enrich our vocabulary and use of words by means of group discussions but she was not able to give us as much individual attention as she would have liked, as there were far too many in the group.

I enjoyed Art, which involved drawing, painting and making things from all kinds of materials and Miss Francis allowed us a certain amount of free play and gave us pictures to copy. Sheets of newspaper, thick with paint as they had been used over and over again, were spread out for us to work on and most seemed to enjoy making a colourful mess with paints and crayons. I discovered, to my surprise, that I was better at pencil drawing than most of the other children but I do not recall my latent talent ever being encouraged or exploited. In those early war years our work often revealed our inner fears and anxieties and most of our drawings and paintings at this time took the form of lurid war scenes portraying soldiers fighting or ships being sunk by enemy U-boats. We often drew pictures of German aeroplanes, with black crosses on them, firing at people adrift in the sea. Following reports of four raids on York in which five people were killed, our pictures showed bombed houses with ambulance men putting dead or injured people on to stretchers. It seems that we were regurgitating things we had seen in the papers or heard on the wireless.

Physical Training, known as PT, was of the 'arms stretch, knees bend' variety, but Harry, Jimmy and I called it Physical Jerks. We were stood in lines in our white vests and baggy, navy blue football shorts that were held up by a length of elastic in the waistband (if you were lucky like Harry) and his group had PT outside in the schoolyard where they shivered from the cold. Our PT lessons were carried out in St. Mary's hall with the benches and desks pushed back to the walls or on the field out the back when the weather was fine. We had to run, jump and stretch to the

254

commands, "One-two, one-two" etc. The girls wore white blouses, and baggy, navy blue, school knickers with elasticated legs that often had a small pocket on the front in which they kept their hankie and other mysterious objects. Both sexes wore plimsolls, known as 'Plimmies' locally, which were usually carried to and from school in a cloth bag with a drawstring, but to us Middlesbrough lads they were always known as sandshoes. The girls sometimes had dance lessons accompanied by a teacher playing the piano and the older boys played football on the sports field behind South Lane. Mr Fox encouraged and was keen on sport and took the older boys for football and cricket.

I soon got to know most of the children and one of the locals I took a liking to was a bonny, little, fair-haired girl called Margaret Bush, who was the youngest in our group. She lived in the first of the last pair of terraced houses on Wold View Terrace with her mother Mrs Lily Bush. She was to become a lovely, curly-haired blonde who was well known for her lovely singing voice and her beautiful rendition of *The Old Rugged Cross* at the annual Sunday school drama shows.

I was paralysingly shy and extremely self-conscious among what seemed confident children and if I became the object of attention for any reason, I tended to turn scarlet with embarrassment. If you wanted a pencil or needed to go to the toilet, you had to raise your hand and I had seen others doing it, but I had an irrational dread of being noticed. I tried to make myself small and kept my head down, putting my arm round my work so as to keep it hidden in the hope of going unnoticed. I hated going to the old brick toilet block in the playground, which reeked of pee and Jeyes fluid, but I would 'pay a call' just before going in to school and then try to last out until playtime. I was often bursting to go but would never ask, "Please Miss, may I leave the room?" if I could help it. I could not get the slits in the thick leather finger-like strips on the end my braces onto the buttons at the back of my trousers and, to my intense mortification and acute embarrassment, the teachers had to help me. I developed a strong aversion to trouser buttons, which exists to this day. People tried to hide their phobias in those days, unlike today, and I still dislike the look and feel of buttons. The introduction of trouser belts and zips was a godsend to me

We vaccies were often looked on as 'non-persons' and were blamed for anything that went wrong and, in the 'big' school, there were sometimes fights in the playground between vaccies and the locals. It is easy to forget the mental pain that we suffered as children. Life, at that time, seemed fragmented and unreal as I tried to find my way in a strange and daunting environment. The longing to be accepted by our peers and to be a member of the pack can be very powerful and we choose to forget the devious, shifty and furtive methods we used to ingratiate ourselves. I tried at all costs to avoid the wrath and the withering scorn of the adults in power over me. Children in those days did not have half of the confidence and assurance of the modern variety. I was a dreamer, like Mam, and was too timid to ask for things to be repeated when I did not understand them. I had a fear of appearing silly in front of my peers and, consequently, I did not learn the basics of most subjects and therefore failed to make much progress. In those days children were expected to be, as Mrs Harris repeatedly pointed out, seen and not heard. Speech was silver, silence was said to be golden; so who was I to challenge these tried and tested, time-honoured saws?

A lad in Jimmy's group that I got on well with was called Bernard Fisher and when we played football in the field on the other side of North Lane, Jimmy and I always wanted to be in the same team as him and another local lad called Duncan Steel. They were very good players and their team always won. Bernard was one of a large family living next door but one to us. He was the eldest son of twenty-eight years old Mrs Mabel Fisher (nee Brooke), a chubby, busty, motherly and loving sort of woman who usually wore her dark straight hair cut quite short. Bernard was destined to become the Hull City and - at a later date - Bradford City goalkeeper. His brother, David, was four years old at that time and he had a cute little two-year-old sister called Maud.

All of the Fisher children were born at home - delivered by Nurse Lealman - as was the normal practice in those days. Being the district nurse-cum-certified midwife, she was a regular visitor at their house over the years. Although a bit bossy at times, she was well liked in the village. Maud became a pretty, wavy-haired, pert and rounded little girl; "a right little moppet," as the local folk said. I would often see her running about in her little cotton frock with white ankle socks and sandals as she played in their front garden, behind the large wooden double gate, or on the pavement by the privet hedge, at the front of their house. I would have liked to play with Bernard, but we were repeatedly told by Mrs Harris not to mix with the other children and *never, ever* to bring them to her house. Maud grew to womanhood in Haxby, marrying there in 1958. She became an auxiliary nurse, firstly at Haxby Hall and later at the District Hospital in York where she nursed for close on forty years.

Bernard's grandfather, Mr Myers Brooke, had moved out of his old stone cottage near the roundabout when his wife died just before the war. By the time I arrived in Haxby he was living with his daughter and her family on Usher Lane. It seems that Mr Robert Foxton Bell, the local market garden proprietor whose brother owned the garage just across the main road from the *Red Lion*, had taken him in as a two years old child. On growing up, he had served his apprenticeship with him. I remember him as a small, thin, serious and gaunt-faced man who always wore a black trilby hat with a muffler, tied tightly at the neck and tucked into his collarless shirt. He enjoyed a bit of gardening and we often saw him going about on his old bike carrying a scythe and sickle. In his later years he worked as a lengthman for the council maintaining a set area of the local roads, keeping it clear of litter and reporting any holes or cracks that appeared. He kept it salted and gritted and cleared away the snow in winter and in spring and summer he cut the grass verges regularly. In the autumn he ensured that the drains were kept free of leaves.

Mrs Fisher's husband, Jim, who was seven years older than her, was based in Palestine with his unit for a large part of the war. He was a regular soldier who had been stationed at Strensall camp with the West Yorkshire Regiment when they first met. A bit of a rum' character who enjoyed a regular drink and a singsong in the pubs, Mr Fisher was a bit of a Jekyll and Hyde character. He was a kind, cheeky, fun-loving man when sober but a blundering drunk when in his cups and he was reputed to be a little too fond of the ladies. Mrs Harris used to say, "This village has more than its fair share of drunks." The Fishers' house and its twin had been built with no fireplace in the kitchen, therefore the family spent most of their time in the front room. The boys told Jimmy that when they had RAF lads billeted with them, they slept with them in the double bed in the back bedroom. Their granddad always slept in the box room and Maud, who had initially slept in a drawer as a baby, now slept in a single bed in her mother's room.

Talking of sleep, we infants still had a half-hour catnap in the early afternoon but we did not lie down as we had at the nursery school; we rested our heads on our forearms on the deeply etched lids of our old wooden desks. It was often difficult to sleep, especially when the great circular saw was whining and screeching, as it sliced through the great balks of timber at Boynton's carpentry and joinery yard further along the lane. On quiet days sound travelled a long way. The teachers were ordered to carry out kit inspections on the evacuees at least once a week and if clothes needed repairing or replacing their parents were contacted. Mrs Harris was forever sending letters to Middlesbrough asking for more clothes for us, but for some reason we didn't always get them even though Mam and Aunt Hilda swore that they had sent them.

A local ARP unit had been set up in Wigginton in 1937, combining with the Haxby ARP a year later. The County Director, Air Commandant Godman, had held a meeting in Wigginton recreation hall to explain what being an ARP man involved and the ARP Officer for the Flaxton area, which included Haxby, was Mr Ralph Butterfield. I was surprised to find that Dr Riddolls, our elderly general practitioner, was a member when men from the unit came to our school to give demonstrations and put up aircraft wall charts showing the silhouettes of British and German aircraft. They told us where we could and could not go and what to do if an air raid took place. They showed Jimmy's group how to use sand, stirrup pumps and buckets of water to put out small incendiary fires, explaining how to deal safely with the strange-looking butterfly bombs that had a metal casing that split open on impact to look like wings. We carried out regular air raid drills when - on the teacher's command - we practised getting down quickly to sit cross-legged underneath our desks but we fervently hoped that we would never have to do it for real.

We had regular visits from the ARP wardens based at Haxby Hall, during which we practiced putting on our heavy gas masks. On duty the wardens wore wide-brimmed 'tin' helmets with a white W painted on them and a navy-blue, one-piece, denim boiler suit with a badge on the breast. Harold Mann was responsible for the York Road area and Mrs Horn, the billeting officer who lived on the Park Estate with her husband, Alf, drove the ambulance. She had been issued with one of the very few telephones in Haxby as she was on call twenty-four hours a day. They had a Morrison shelter under the table and when the siren sounded, her evacuee, Betty Sheridan, had to sleep in it. Betty, the middle one of five children who came from the Cannon Street area of Middlesbrough, was adopted by her foster parents and was to spend the rest of her life in Haxby.

The ARP wardens put up a poster that stated, 'Hitler will send no warning - so always carry your gas mask.' The rubber mask had a large, lozenge-shaped, celluloid eyepiece and at the front was a canister that had small circular perforations, which filtered out any gas but allowed air through. It was 3.5 inches (8.5 cm.) in depth and about the same in diameter. They were uncomfortable to wear and most of the children hated them, feeling that they were being suffocated, while others found the stench of the rubber unbearable. The chin was placed inside and the mask was pulled over the top of the head by placing the thumbs under the three white canvas straps attached to the rubber by metal buckles at the back. They could be adjusted to give a close fit and the mask was removed by pulling the straps forward over the head from the back.

The fitting instructions were printed on the underside of the lid of the box, ending in a warning printed in bold capital letters and underlined, which stated: - 'DO NOT TAKE RESPIRATOR OFF BY PULLING THE CONTAINER UPWARDS OVER THE FACE'. Initially, I experienced an awful choking sensation when the mask was on and I would start to sweat, which caused the eyepiece to steam up, at which point I began to cry and panic before quickly ripping the mask off. Later, Miss Francis was given a supply of green demisting capsules to rub on to the visor and when these ran out we used soap to keep it clear. In time I got used to wearing it, as did thousands of other children. To test that the mask was properly fitted our ARP man, Mr Joe Lockwood, placed the palm of his hand over the perforations on the front of the cylinder for a few seconds, and if you struggled to breathe it was correctly fitted. The rubber sides of the mask would sometimes make a rude fluttering noise like the present day whoopee cushion as we breathed out and we laughed until our sides hurt. Embossed on the lid of the box was the word TOP which enabled people to find the lid in the dark.

In my class group there was a shy, quiet, reserved little girl called Eva Pulleyn who was usually better dressed than the rest, and she lived just along Front Street in a large, stone-built, four-bedroom house called 'Churchside' that was set back from the road. The old house, situated between the church and South View, the large three-storey red brick home of Fred Nottingham, still had cast-iron, black-leaded fire ranges with gas brackets and mantles for internal lighting. Behind it there were a number of old brick outbuildings surrounding a long courtyard.

Fred Nottingham was retired but in his prime he had been a top-class, professional with Yorkshire County Cricket Club that had been County champions several times before the war. Fred had been in those great teams and had played with many established international cricketers as well as many young, up-and-coming, England players. Amongst them had been Norman Yardley, Arthur Wood, Hedley Verity and Len Hutton. You had to be born in Yorkshire to play for the county in those days. Hedley Verity was a brilliant, left-arm, spin bowler who had played for England forty times and had set a world record by taking all ten wickets in an innings on two separate occasions. When the war started he became a Captain in the Green Howards and my Uncle John had trained under him prior to being posted overseas.

Eva Pulleyn came from a large family and her father, sixty-two-years old Francis John, known as Frank, was a bricklayer and a brickmaker by trade. He used the ground floor of the granary as workshops and her elder brother, Foxton Ronald, known as Bill, kept a vintage Lanchester car in the stables. The old car dated from before the Great War and he enjoyed restoring and tinkering with it in his spare time. Building materials, such as cement, bricks,

260

timber, sand, flagstones and the like were piled up around the yard or were stored in the outbuildings.

On eastern side of the yard there was a huge two-storeyed barn half full of rectangular straw bales where Eva kept a lamb. With its winches, wooden steps and trapdoors, it was a paradise to Jimmy and me when we played there with Eva. We would leap about on the straw and jump down from the loft into the area where her three squealing pigs were kept. Next to it was another brick building in which there was a washhouse and copper. On a shelf in one of the outhouses, above the iron mangle and the fluted, aluminium, poss tub, there were bags of Sharp's meal, which was mixed with the potatoes that were too small to sell and boiled-up for pig feed. Rhode Island Reds and scarlet-combed Wyandottes busily clucked, scratched and pecked at the grain scattered on the concrete of the yard and the family kept battery hens in the old brick granary above the stables. Nearby were tins of Jeyes Fluid, that was used to sterilise the hencoops, which always had a slightly sour smell. On other shelves there were packets of Colman's starch with red and black labels; packets of Sunlight soap; red and white boxes of Reckitt's Blue Dolly Bags; white cardboard boxes of Borax; Lux Soap Flakes and other washing products.

At the North Lane end of the yard there was an old wooden shed with open areas of grassland at each side of it. On the roof of the granary was a white-painted, wooden dovecote but all we ever saw going in and out of it were pigeons. Eva had to explain that; "Pigeons with their pink chests and bronze backs are known as turtledoves and their fledglings are called squabs."

In the corner of the field on the other side of North Lane her dad had a brickyard. Next to it was a field owned by George Tindall of Westow Farm, a big, stone, double-bay windowed farmhouse on the south side of Front Street opposite the schoolhouse. When the weather was dry we were allowed to play in it at break times and sometimes lessons were held in it. If it was too wet and muddy we had permission to go in Mr Pulleyn's courtyard on the understanding that we did not move or damage anything. There was no playground at St. Mary's hall and the church graveyard was out of bounds to us.

We made dens in the prickly straw bales stacked in the barn, getting our arms and legs scratched and sore in the process, and we scrambled up the wooden ladder to the loft as nimbly as spiders. Wide-eyed with wonder we gathered round to watch the men as they worked on the black, open topped vintage car that had large, shiny, brass lights, thin white-walled tyres and wire-spoked wheels. They cranked the old engine with the starting handle until it puttered into life but the long metal handle had been known to suddenly whip back. It could break a thumb or crack the wrist if it was not held properly and released at the moment the engine 'fired'. The transverse engine sat beneath a short, flat bonnet between the front mudguards with its radiator set slightly back from the front axle. We giggled excitedly when we were allowed to sit on the wide, shiny leather back seat that was forward of the back axle so that the passengers were not bounced about too much. The highly polished wooden dashboard gleamed in the weak winter sunshine as I sat on the wooden box set into the wide running board and the car was driven around the yard. We took turns at squeezing the rubber bulb that made a deep honking 'parp' come from the shiny brass horn.

The Pulleyns were a respected and long established family in the village and Eva was the youngest. Their family tree had many branches and its roots had been firmly set in the local soil for generations and members of her family had built many of the houses in the village. Her grandfather, John Pulleyn, born into a Wigginton farming family in the middle of the last century, was the first bricklayer in a family that was to produce many more. Some, like her sixty years old Uncle, Robert James Pulleyn, were to play an important part in the civic affairs of the area, becoming Lord Mayor of York from 1939 to 1940. Sadly, his wife, Ethel, had died in his first year in office. Their official residence at that time was the impressive and historic, three-storeyed, two hundred years old Mansion House that stood on busy Coney Street right in the heart of the city. The founder of a successful firm of building contractors, he owned the Grand Picture House on Gillygate and was still an eminent member and alderman of York City Council.

Eva had six stepbrothers and three stepsisters and her thirty-five years old stepbrother, Tom, had built the row of houses near the roundabout on Front Street on what had once been Jefferson's Farm. The end house was Rowland's Bakery and shop and he had also built Wold View Terrace. He, his wife, Gwen, and their two daughters lived in a fine house that he had built on York Road facing Haxby Hall where Gwen was involved with the ARP and the Red Cross. As mentioned earlier, Tom was in command of the now forty-strong local Home Guard unit.

There were also three sisters and a brother from her father's present marriage His first wife, Alice, their eldest daughter, Emma, and Alice's mother had all died in December 1918, victims of the terrible Spanish Flu epidemic that had swept the country claiming the lives of thousands. One of her stepbrothers, born in 1916, was christened Edward *Verdun* Pulleyn in memory of the infamous battle of that year fought in atrocious weather conditions with enormous and tragic loss of life on both sides. As the cold, rain and mud turned the flooded trenches into a living nightmare, a young man called Rommel was fighting valiantly on the German side. He had risen through the ranks to become a first lieutenant while, on the French side was Henri Petain, later called The Hero of Verdun. Verdun Pulleyn was living with his mother-in-law, Mrs Parker, in the first bungalow on the left up Usher Lane and they had a lad from Hull billeted with them.

Frank Pulleyn had partitioned off part of his large house to form a one-bedroom house that he sold to Robert Wray and he rented out part of his yard for him to stable his horse and cart. Mr Wray, whose flat cart was known locally as a rulley, delivered our coal, which was neatly stacked in one hundredweight, hessian sacks next to a pair of heavy metal scales. Humping the sacks on his leather-clad shoulders, he emptied them into the coalbunker. The bottom of the coalhouse door must have scraped across the path for a long time, as it had left an arc-shaped mark on the flagstones.

Lord Woolton, the head of the Ministry of Food, previously called the Food Department, was an experienced pre-war administrator who was looked on as a sensible and fair man. The obtaining of food and other essentials was an ongoing problem and with some women it had become an obsession that controlled their lives. If word got round the village that a shop had something in, a queue formed in no time and Mrs Harris usually sent one of us to stand in it until she could get there. Lord Woolton, on becoming concerned at reports of traders profiteering by selling food at excessive prices, had recently imposed a price freeze on more than twenty items, including coffee, cocoa, rice, spaghetti, and - to our delight - jelly, custard and biscuits.

His department issued leaflets and published items in the newspapers under the title Food Facts and these gave advice on how to make cheap and tasty meals and how to cope with the food shortages. Their aim was to help people make the best of what was available and his best known recipe, using vegetables, no meat and a little fat was the Woolton pie. Although some were helpful, many of the food leaflets became known as bumf (i.e. bum fodder) and ended up hung on a loop of string in the village lavs. Mrs Harris listened regularly to the five minute wireless programme called *The Kitchen Front* that was broadcast at 8.15 am from Tuesday to Friday while Dot was at the sink washing the breakfast dishes. When she finished them we would set off for school.

During the half term holiday Mam, Aunt Hilda and my Uncle John paid a short visit. Jimmy and I enjoyed being seen with our Uncle John as he was now sporting sergeant's stripes on his Army uniform that had knife-edged creases. Being in the forces gave a man standing and Gran felt proud to sew the stripes on for him. He was on embarkation leave again and his battalion had been in training near Dorchester and in the Cheddar Gorge area. On seeing the long list of Dos and Don'ts pinned up on the Harris's kitchen cabinet he said, "It's worse than being in a prisoner of war camp." The belts and cane that usually hung there had disappeared and his words were to prove to be prophetic. He said that during the recent snowstorms, "Our platoon got cut off at the notorious Porlock Hill and we had to dig our way out to get back to camp."

Each time Mam had to go it became more and more heart-rending for both of us and just before leaving she held me close and cuddled me into the warmth of her well-rounded bosom. Tears welled up in her eyes and in my mind's eye I can still see the red double-decker bus, with its advertisement for Tower Ales distorted by my tears, as it left for York. That night and every night, I knelt by the side of the bed and prayed to God asking him to keep

Mammy and Daddy safe until the war was over so that I could go home with them again.

Pointing out where Libya was on the large world map, Miss Curry told the assembled school that, "British and Australian troops under the command of General Wavell have carried out a surprise attack capturing the port of Tobruk and during the advance over 25,000 Italians have been taken prisoner. This great success has helped us to secure the eastern Mediterranean."

Being so young and with the fighting so far away we felt safe here and the facts did not really register. We thought that it was all very exciting and Miss Curry kept us up to date on the fluctuating progress of the war. It was one of very few successes up to that time and, as such, the news was gladly received by the people of Haxby

13. Village Life and People

That February there were several keen frosts with deep snow lying on the fields and, on the Monday of our half-term holiday, a bone-invading chill crept under the back door and slid across the floor before climbing up our backs. Being washday, condensation misted the windowpanes distorting the view of the back garden as it streamed down wetting and lifting the edges of the criss-crossed anti-blast tape. The kitchen was the centre of most of the household activity and articles of damp laundry hung everywhere blocking off any warmth from the fire and adding moisture to the choking fug already caused by Mrs Harris' constant cigarette smoking. She coughed and wheezed as the blue smoke curled up to the brown tobacco stained ceiling. The heavy dankness, which hung like a sullen cloud, made us feel listless and lethargic.

Rousing ourselves with an effort, Thelma, Dot, Jimmy, Ducky and I put on our warmest clothes and got the wooden sledge from the garden shed. Mr Harris, who was at work on the farm, had made it in his spare time. We were glad to get out to breathe the clear, sharp, frosty air, which lifted us out of our stupor. Blinking like emerging moles, we came out into the weak sunshine that shone from a cloudless, pale-blue sky and, being low on the horizon at that time of year, it cast long shadows. As we crossed Usher Lane with great care, the icy wind blew the cobwebs from our minds. The surface of the road glittered and sparkled like diamonds as the sun glinted off it and every roof and hedge was white with hoarfrost.

We made our way beside thorn hedges to the frozen Windmill pond that lay at the far side of a snow-covered turnip field and there was a hard glistening layer of ice on top of the deep snowdrifts. By the pond, which we were told was bottomless, stood an old, rusting irrigation pump with its twisted metal vanes creaking and groaning as they turned slowly in the bitterly cold north east wind. The surface of the pond was frozen solid and we skittered about on it in our hobnailed boots, landing on our backsides more often than we stayed on our feet. For a while we took turns, two at a time, on the sledge while the others held the rope and pulled it along. We whizzed up and down trying not to crash in to the crowds of villagers on the ice; most of whom were floundering about and falling down just like us.

After collecting a fair number of bruises on various parts of our anatomy, we decided that we would slide the sledge down a bank of frozen earth that sloped steeply down towards the ice-covered pond. Jimmy, who was a bit of a daredevil, volunteered to go first but, when the sledge hit the thin ice at the edge it creaked and then there was a deep, ominous growl as it split open into several clear, green-edged shards. Jimmy and the sledge shot straight through into the icy water but luckily, he did not go completely under the ice and was able to hang on to the floating sledge. A group of grownups seeing what had happened quickly dragged him out of the bitterly cold water. He was shocked, shivering and soaking wet but we soon got him back to the house where he was put into dry clothes and warmed through by the coal fire with the washing now moved aside.

We thought that he would get a really good hiding from Mrs Harris, but she, surprisingly, felt sorry for him. It seems that she had a bit of a soft spot for him and the canes and belts remained untouched on that occasion. Maybe she feared that the evacuation authorities would blame her for allowing us to go into a dangerous situation unsupervised. She was, apparently, just greatly relieved that he was all right and none the worse for his icy ducking and decided that it was best to say nothing and let it pass. Shortly afterwards she turned on me saying, "Just look at the muck on your bum."
I foolishly replied "I can't see my bum from here." At which, she clouted me round the ear, saying, "And that's enough cheek from you!" Stars danced before my eyes and my ear rang.

Several people had accidents on the icy roads and Harold Mann was often late in delivering the milk as his shaggy pony, Monty, had difficulty keeping its footing on the hard-packed, frozen snow. Snow fell on ten consecutive days piling up in deep drifts by the hedgerows. Mrs Harris and the other women still had their milk ladled into jugs, as glass bottles were hard to come by and it was not until the end of March that winter loosened its icy grip with the snow finally thawing leaving heaps of dirty slush at the roadsides.

HARRY MANN ON MILK ROUND, HAXBY 1934

By this time cooked dinners had become available to the pupils of both schools, which was a real a boon to parents that worked. The meals were served from the counters, hotplates and gas ovens newly installed in the corner of St. Mary's hall and the ovens helped to keep the place warm on cold days. The meals were brought by van from the large cookhouse at Strensall army camp in aluminium containers. The overcrowding meant that the dinners had to be served in two separate sessions and we were pleased to learn that we would have to finish our morning lessons a little earlier to allow time for the hall to be prepared. The dinner ladies included Mrs Brown, Mrs Blows and Mrs Lund who lived close by in the old cottages on North Lane and had children of their own at the two schools.

The milk was delivered in aluminium crates with the one third of a pint bottles in wire compartments. They were stacked outside in the playground by the double doors at the back of the main school and when playtime arrived we often found that they were partly frozen with plugs of solid cream standing about an inch (2.5cms) above their necks. We sucked on them as if they were creamy iced lollies. During the long spell of snow and icy weather the crates were brought into the classroom a little earlier and placed near the green cast iron radiator to thaw out. The bottles had thick, waxed paper seals that had a small, indented, central portion that you pushed in with your thumb. At playtime Harry, Ducky, and their pals had made slides on the icy playground and had great fun adding a few more bruises to the collection that they had already acquired.

Miss Curry, having received the latest war news from the wireless bulletins, informed us that " Hitler has responded to the shambles in North Africa by pouring in large numbers of well-equipped, battle trained, reinforcements. The Italians were widely scattered and in complete disarray when the Germans landed at Tripoli with Erwin Rommel, one of Hitler's favourite generals, in command of the highly trained panzer force. A brave and cunning adversary, he has reorganised the Italians troops that had not been taken prisoner. Unfortunately many Allied troops have been despatched to Greece to honour a pledge given last year. This has left the Allies short of experienced men and the situation has thus become more alarming. Rommel launched his offensive earlier than expected and the tide has turned in Germany's favour again. Caught out by the speed and shock tactics, the advanced British positions have collapsed and the troops are being driven back across the desert. This sudden move took General O'Connor, the conqueror of Libya, by surprise and he, and four other British Generals, are now prisoners-of-war and Rommel's spectacular advance is causing shock waves over here."

Earlier in the year the Army had set up a searchlight in a field on the western side of Moor Lane opposite the Home Guard blockhouse. It was close to Lazenby's farm and was manned by regular soldiers, with the Home Guard also taking their turn on duty. We had seen the army lorries being driven back and forth taking sand from the pit close to Beresford's pond. We went up there to help fill the sandbags and, when we were given a penny for our troubles, we were thrilled to bits but we soon tired of it. It was too much like hard work and there were easier ways of earning a penny to spend on sweets. Harold Mann often gave us a penny for helping him on his milk round.

Sometimes we heard distant explosions from up Moor Lane way where the Home Guard were practising lobbing live hand grenades into Beresford's pond. At first they had no Mills bombs, so they used potatoes or large stones instead and on finding out, Mrs Harris retorted, "It's a waste of good potatoes if you ask me!" Their ammunition was stored in corrugated-tin huts on the grass verges alongside Cross Moor Lane and these were guarded and kept well padlocked at all times. We would have liked to watch the action but they had closed off the road with Home Guard men manning the roadblocks.

At the end of March, Uncle John was home again on yet another embarkation leave. He had been vaccinated again and issued with a khaki drill uniform (KD), so it looked certain that he was going to see active service again; but this time in a hot, desert region. On March 19th - a fine, dry and sunny day - he lined up on parade as part of the 150th Infantry Brigade (Northumbrian Division) as the Corps Commander, General Harold Franklyn, inspected them on a large field at Winscombe in Dorset. There were rumours that they were to join the MEF in Egypt and on returning from their six-day embarkation leave the men were inspected by King George VI himself. With him were Lord Derby, Winston Churchill and other cabinet ministers. All their equipment and stores were packed and they were ready for the off.

In January the amount of meat allowed to each adult per week had been reduced by threepence (1¼p) to one shilling and sixpence worth (7½p) and it was then reduced further to only one and tuppence worth (nearly 6p). In February the off-putting, muddy-looking, wholemeal bread - the so-called National loaf - was introduced and it was not at all popular. It was a heavy blow when jam, syrup, marmalade and treacle were put on ration in March; collectively a total of 8 ounces (227g.) per person per week being allowed. Rationing was at its lowest level so far and it was even officially forbidden to feed crumbs to the birds. From that time onwards Mrs Harris would only let us have margarine or jam on our bread - never the two together! The margarine was thinly scraped on and off again and we seldom tasted jam or syrup which, if I remember rightly, came in a big yellow tin with 'Tate' written inside a red diamond shape. We lived mostly on bread, lumpy potato, heavy suet dumplings or we had rabbit meat made into stews or pies as it was not rationed and was readily available. We were growing kids and were always ravenous so we ate whatever was put in front of us or we stayed hungry. After every meal our plates were always shiny and clean, as we soaked everything up with bread or even licked the plate when Mrs Harris had her back turned.

In late March, Mr Harris read in the paper that Leonard Cheshire had celebrated the award of his DFC at the *Half Moon* public house in York with his crewmembers who were now sergeants not officers. They enjoyed the pleasure of female company in the dim and cosy intimacy of the De Grey Dance Rooms on St.Leonards close to Bootham Bar. He was still volunteering for the most dangerous sorties and often flew with the young and inexperienced pilots, giving them invaluable advice and trying to make them feel more at ease.

Nature Study at school now took the form of walks beside the piebald ploughed fields armed with bags, nets and a wide variety of containers. We skipped along in pairs with the girls hand-in-hand with their best friends and we added our spoils to the cluttered up nature table. By drawing things, which I enjoyed, it helped me to remember details of shape, number of legs, parts of an insect's body and suchlike and I was to find this approach invaluable later in life. In March when the weather turned slightly milder we collected frogspawn and watched the tadpoles hatch out to hang on the stems of the pondweed in their fish tank. Miss Francis explained that, "They do this by means of a sucker under their heads and they breathe through those frilly external gills that look like tiny wings."

Later we fed them on bits of Spam or flaked fish food and I was fascinated on seeing them gradually absorb their tails. Spam was tinned, spiced, luncheon meat sent from the USA and Canada and I loved it. We watched the tadpoles grow and develop back legs and, much to our amusement, for a short time they only had three until the fourth eventually broke out through their skin. The tiny frogs lost their tails and were then obliged to leave the water feeding on aphids by shooting out their very long, sticky tongues, which happened so quickly that it could not be seen by the naked eye. They had, by that stage, to breathe through their newly formed internal lungs. At this point we trooped along to Widd's pond and released them back into the water, which had become churned up and made murky by the dabbling, beady-eyed ducks and the shy and furtive moorhens.

Some of the older boys at the main school were kept busy digging, planting and weeding on the school allotments. This backbreaking activity had assumed much greater significance as many vegetables were now in very short supply. The allotments were situated on the south side of Station Road between Haxby Hall and the old station house. A certain group of older boys who the headmaster classed as thickheads or numbskulls, had to take care of his garden and woe betide them if he saw any of them messing about. He used to give them a crack on the back of the neck with the knob on the end of his RAF swagger stick. He thought that these lads would be more gainfully employed out of the classroom where a close eye could be kept on them. They often carried spades and four pronged forks over their shoulders and occasionally clattered one of the other lads on the head as they turned round and they could easily have poked someone's eye out. They were quite happy to be outside away from the soul-destroying syllabus, averring, "Schools a bloody waste o' time any'ow. It stops us getting' on wi't'real' work on t'farm. Yer can't learn farm jobs from books!"

Mrs Harris always seemed to send us on errands just as we were planning to go out to play and when I came back empty-handed, Mrs Harris shouted in my face, "Are you completely empty-headed or what?" Due to daydreaming, I often forgot what I had been sent for and after getting a clip round the lug, I had to go back with a written order. Chalked drawings had started to appear on walls and doors in the village showing the top half of the face of a bald-headed character with a question mark growing from the top like a single hair. He had big round eyes, a long, blobby nose and part of the fingers of both hands showing over the top of a brick wall. Remarks like, "Wot no jam!" (or any other commodity) were written beneath it. This little character, known as 'Chad', became a symbol for the increasing wartime shortages.

Mr and Mrs Winterburn, a childless couple, were our next door neighbours. Don, born and brought up locally, was a bricklayer and his wife, Bessie, a neat but rather thin lady, was the sister of Mrs Moore at number four. We called her Grandma Moore but she was known as Lily to her neighbours. Her only son, Robert, was in the Royal Navy, and she had a succession of airmen billeted with her. She and Mrs Winterburn had come to Haxby from the Newcastle-upon-Tyne area and her son was to marry one of Eva Pulleyn's sisters and work at Rowntree's chocolate factory after the war. Don was a close friend of Bert Cocker, a slim dark-haired man who worked with him in the local building trade, and they went everywhere together. Mr Harris often had 'a bit of a crack' with them in the Working Men's club. Bert lived at number five with his wife, Annie, and her infant son and seven-year-old daughter, Barbara, who was in our Jimmy's group at school. They had two WAAFs (Women's Auxiliary Air Force), called Audrey and Marge, billeted with them at that time and later in the war, two of the RAF crash recovery lads stayed there.

Poor Dot was made to clear out the fire-grate every morning and reset the fire for the day. She would put loose paper on the grate, place screwed up newspaper and small sticks above it before adding a few lumps of coal and lighting it. When the fire took hold she would prop the shovel up and cover it with an opened out sheet of newspaper to make it to draw. Sometimes the sulky fire went out and at other times the newspaper caught fire sending bits of black, charred paper floating everywhere; either way, Dot, who just stood there looking blank, got an earful and a clip round the ear from the irascible Mrs Harris. She was told to put yesterday's ashes on the flower borders and to spread the cinders on the garden path as Mr Harris said they kept the weeds down and helped kill slugs and snails.

On Saturday mornings Jimmy's chore was to stand in the queue for bread at Mr Eric Rowland's little bakery at the junction of York Road and Front Street. Eva Pulleyn's sixteen-year-old sister, Betty, assisted Mrs Rowland in the shop and, although bread was not on ration, flour and yeast were in short supply, and only regular customers could have bread put aside for them. It seemed that every time Jimmy left the house Mrs Winterburn would stop him and ask him to fetch her bread. He willingly obliged but after a time he got fed up with it as he suspected that she must be hiding behind her net curtain waiting to waylay him and she had never given him a penny for saving her the time and effort of going for the bread herself. So, one Saturday, when he had been waylaid for the umpteenth time, he went to the bakery for our bread and told Mr Rowland that Mrs Winterburn was not happy with the bread and that she did not want any more from him. When the angry Mrs Winterburn told her of this, Mrs Harris was furious and made her husband punish him. Reluctant to do so, but not daring to oppose her, he took Jimmy up to the bedroom where he administered half a dozen whacks with his thick leather belt. One landed on his backside, but five of them 'accidentally' landed on the bed, and he told Jimmy to cry out at each stroke so that Mrs Harris would be none the wiser.

A lease-lend system with the U.S.A. was agreed, as the country was on the verge of bankruptcy and a relieved Winston Churchill made one of his more eloquent and stirring speeches in which he said "Give us the tools and we will finish the job". The loan was needed to provide these tools as well as food and weapons. Rowntrees was one of the factories involved. Single women aged twenty to twenty-one years of age had recently been 'called up' by Ernest Bevin, the Minister for Labour, so that more men could be released for active service. Thousands of women chose to go in to the works and factories but married women with young children were still exempt, although they could work if they wished as several local day and night nurseries were being set up. Men aged over forty-one years of age, who were exempt from military service, were also involved and they were paid a basic wage of £3.0.6d.9 (£3.02p) a week, while the women received only £1.18.0. (£1.90p) for doing the same work.

The outside of the huge chocolate factory was camouflaged in green and brown and the windows were blacked out making the atmosphere inside claustrophobic and the lights had to be kept on all day. The Rowntree family held anti-war convictions like all Quakers, but this did not prevent them from forming a new company under the innocuous sounding name of *County Industries Limited*. Under the umbrella of this company the upper floors of the building, that had formerly produced Rowntrees Fruit Gums, were being used to pack and arm 37mm shells, with only a small part of the factory now making chocolate. The fuses were inserted into the nose of the shells on the top floor behind a protective screen. It was a highly dangerous occupation, but the workers were prepared to do it if they felt they were making a significant contribution to the war effort and the factory was in full production twenty-four hours a day, six days a week.

They worked twelve-hour day shifts for two weeks, then night shifts for the next two, and as a precaution they were obliged to rub a clear, red, jelly-like barrier cream called Rosalex onto their hands to reduce the risk of dermatitis, as some had developed red and itchy skin rashes in the early days. They were entertained, during the long boring work hours, by means of a Tannoy system that blared out popular music and songs recorded by the stars and the big bands of the day. The BBC broadcast *Music While You Work* twice a day, especially for war workers and a new variety show called *Workers Playtime* was relayed at lunchtimes. Big names of the day, like Vera Lynn and Flanagan and Allen, broadcast *from a factory somewhere in England,* - the place never being named for security reasons. These broadcasts were received in households all over the country and were very popular. Mrs Harris always had her wireless on.

The factory had installed a huge reservoir of water on the roof, the contents of which could be released to dowse any fires that broke out. Royal Observer Corps members on the roof worked shifts round-the-clock straining their eyes searching for the tiny specks in the sky. It was not easy to identify them when there was cloud cover and they kept in contact with a linked network of military tracking stations relaying messages informing them of the whereabouts and numbers of enemy aircraft sighted while a small army of girls worked below. They were still producing the famous Rowntrees milk chocolate bars, fruit gums and pastilles and the air was full of the sickly sweet smell of cocoa and chocolate. A great deal of the dark chocolate was used in aircrew rations and it was an important component of their escape kits, along with maps, a compass, a razor and a rubber water bottle, only to be used if they crashed or had to bale out in enemy territory.

At least once a week our Jimmy took me to Bryant's shop to buy sweets with our bit of pocket money. We liked the black liquorice 'bootlaces' and the round, penny-sized Pontefract cakes the best and, for some reason, we always called them Pomfret cakes. Bryant's shop no longer housed the post office, which had been taken over by Mr Eric Rowland and his family and set up in what had been the bakery. Where the post office counter had been there was now a wooden framework with rows of biscuit boxes fitted into it. These had glass lids that were set at an angle so that the contents could be seen and reached easily and broken biscuits could be bought quite cheaply. Above them the shelves were now more thinly stacked while the front window still had mouth-watering sweets displayed in square-shaped, glass jars.

The Halifax bomber had only recently been brought in to service and we heard on the grapevine that a squadron of them had arrived at Linton-on-Ouse airfield. We often saw them over the village and new aircraft were being delivered every few days. The exhaust flames from the cowlings of their Hercules engines could be clearly seen at dusk and their vibration rattled the ornaments and plates on our shelves. It seems that they were to replace the relatively slow and obsolete Whitleys that were by then 'nobody's friend'. In the early months of the year the newspapers reported that Halifaxes of Bomber Command were attacking targets on the French coast.

The air raid warnings had increased in recent weeks and one night in early March the mournful, fluctuating wail of the siren sounded yet again. Just after 9.30 pm we were rushed downstairs to lie under the front room table, which had been pushed against the wall as directed. The girls were with Mrs Harris in the cupboard under the stairs but the long sustained note of the all clear was not sounded until quarter to four in the morning. We trooped wearily back to bed, but at least we didn't have to start school until ten o'clock that morning. In the darkness of those winter mornings we sometimes saw the returning bombers briefly lit up by the beam of the local searchlight, which was flicked on and off to show that the aircraft had been recognised. Our sleep was often disturbed and we turned up at school dull from the lack of it.

On my sixth birthday Mam, with her gentle ways and winsome smile, paid us a short visit and whenever she appeared it felt as though the sun had just emerged from the clouds. Before she left she gave us a few coppers to buy sweets and a comic and Jimmy still had a bit of the money that his mother had given him on his seventh birthday two weeks back. We thought we might try another visit to Torville's little shop, as Bryant's was always busy and crowded. It was set back behind the wide grass verge that bordered the south side of the main road and the front door was a bit difficult to open, as its wooden frame tended to swell after a spell of wet weather. On this occasion, Jimmy gave it a hefty shove with his shoulder and it burst open and we startled the customers as we staggered amongst them accompanied by the loud clanging of the bell above the door.

The wooden counter was almost hidden beneath newspapers, magazines and comics. It was owned and run by a small, busty, spinster lady called Miss Susanna Torville who was going grey, even though she was probably only in her fifties. She seemed like a real old biddy to us and her parents had bought the shop before the turn of the century and it had not changed much in all that time. Miss Torville weighed our sweets in the large gleaming brass pan of the white enamelled Avery scales with extreme care, even to the point of taking off three small sweets and replacing them with two slightly heavier ones to make sure that the weight was absolutely spot on and not a fraction of an ounce over. There was a step towards the rear of the old shop, which led to her private living quarters and in the gloom of the interior customers, including us, had a habit of stumbling down it. The Bullivant family, who were related, often helped in the shop and their daughter, Sybil, was in Jimmy's group at school. After that we went to Bryant's for our sweets. Mrs Bryant, a big upright sort of woman, was not so fussy if the sweets weighed a little more than our few coppers justified and she always put them into a conical-shaped paper bag twisted at the top to close it.

Comics were very popular with children in those days before there were any television sets but many of them, such as *Tiger Tim's Weekly*, had been forced to close down due to paper shortages. The *Beano*, which cost tuppence (less than 1p), had previously had twenty-eight coloured pages but now it was smaller and only had eight with coloured print only used on the cover pages. The comics were now full of war themes with spy stories and tales of unexploded bombs and every day, while we waited for our tea in the kitchen, Thelma would read to me. Mr Harris was not in from work so she would read out loud the rhyming couplets under the Rupert Bear cartoon strip in his paper. I really looked forward to this as I loved the adventures of the little bear in the red, high-necked jumper, yellow scarf and large-checked trousers who lived in Nutwood along with his best friends Algy Pug, Bertie Badger, Podgy Pig and Tigerlily, the Chinese conjurer's daughter. I also liked Lily Duckling who went around in a cape and bonnet.

In April it was said that Mr Harris' hero, Leonard Cheshire, had completed his tour of thirty operations when he flew out on his first bombing operation in one of the new Halifax bombers to attack the Baltic port of Kiel with its dockyard facilities and U-boats pens. It seems that it suffered little damage, as in the following month German U-boats sank a further fifty-eight ships. Miss Curry told us that the Germans had destroyed Yugoslavia's army in just one week and had driven the Allies out of Greece with another mini-Dunkirk type of retreat to the beaches. Some 50,000 troops, many of them Australians and New Zealanders, were taken aboard waiting naval vessels but most of the artillery, motor transport and heavy equipment had to be left behind again. This was terrible news for the people at home with Crete and Malta now the only British outposts in the Mediterranean Sea. King George II of the Hellenes and his Government had been evacuated to Crete by Sunderland flying boat.

On April 13th, Easter Sunday, we were bathed and put on our Sunday best and I remember wincing as Mrs Harris roughly combed the cotters out of my hair. We were then taken to matins at St. Mary's church with its honey-coloured, buttressed, sandstone walls and long, steeply-sloping blue-tiled roof. At the end of Holy Week, as the large, brown, sticky buds on the horse-chestnut tree by the gate were starting to split open, it was nice to see the greenery and the spring flowers after a long, snow-covered winter. The daffodils growing in profusion on the green and between the graves, were dancing and rocking in the gentle breeze as our group of seven went in through the arched doorway of the old stone porch. As we walked behind the high-backed wooden pews, Mr Harris, looking very smart in his highly polished Sunday shoes and dark pinstriped suit, removed his black trilby hat but the women kept their hats on. Hymnbooks were handed out - except to Jimmy and me – and we

278

walked to a vacant pew near the back of the crowded church. A musty smell mingled with the pungent, earthy odours emanating from the villagers packed in serried ranks on the shiny, wooden pews. "Was it the smell of God?" we wondered as the slanting rays of the sun shone through the lancet windows on the south side of the church illuminating the dancing dust motes. It took some time for our eyes to adjust to the dim interior where stained glass windows depicted saints with links to the North Country such as Bede, Hilda, Oswald and Cuthbert; each one crowned by delicately carved, cinquefoil, stone tracery.

The early spring sunlight alleviated the darkness of the north wall as it shone through a fine, Victorian, stained glass window that depicted Jesus as the Good Shepherd and Mary as the mother of God. This window served as a memorial to the late William Abel Wood, an Alderman and Justice of the Peace, who he had died in 1913 aged eighty-five with the deaths of his son, Jacob, and his wife, Sarah Ann, added underneath. They had owned and resided in Haxby Hall. Next to it was another fine stained glass window depicting the apostle, Saint Matthew, which was dedicated to the memory of Alfred Walker; another earlier resident of Haxby Hall. The other three depicted St. Mark, St. Luke and St. John.

Our Harry - now thirteen years of age – was prinked out in his Sunday best, wearing a smart, short-trousered suit with a white shirt and tie. The Misses Law and Barker, resplendent in white gloves, smart hats and fashionable coats with expensive brooches on the lapels were a picture of sartorial elegance as they listened intently to the resonant voice of the Reverend Donald. I knelt on a padded, finely embroidered, upholstered hassock and asked God to look after Mam and Dad. When we stood up we were always slightly behind everybody else, opening and closing our mouths pretending to sing hymn number 143 that begins "Christ the Lord is risen today, Alleluia!" Our voices were drowned by the loud, heartily singing congregation and the choir that stood behind the intricately carved reredos screen looking clean and smart in their long cassocks and freshly starched white surplices.

The deep, bass voices of the farmers and the farmhands, with their weather-beaten faces and big red hands, rang out as they sang uninhibitedly, with great joy and thanks to the Lord, as their ancestors had always done. Their intense masculinity and simple primitive faith was plain for all to see as they enthusiastically belted out "Sing to the Lord with cheerful voice" and their voices contrasted sharply with the high pitched voices of the young boys in the front row of the choir. There were no choirgirls in those days. We just mouthed the words as we did not know them and we were not able to read too well anyway. Even if we could, the others held the hymnbooks too high for us to see.

The brass cross on the altar shone with the effulgence of burning gold and the brilliant white of the altar cloth matched the pure white of the vicar's chasuble. He had worn a purple one in Lent. There were arrangements of beautiful spring flowers decking the choir stalls and the ends of the pews and the freshly picked primroses and daffodils stood out in the dim light, brightening the more sombre and shadowy areas of the old church. Several of the pews emptied as the vicar began the ritual of Holy Communion and the villagers returned to their places one by one having knelt at the altar rail to take the sacrament. Some still had the consecrated wafer melting in their mouths and a few had a look of smug satisfaction feeling that they might just have opened the door to heaven a chink wider. Our tall, bald-headed, headmaster, Mr Fox, sat there playing the organ, pulling out the stops and pumping the pedals enthusiastically as the music boomed out from the organ pipes and echoed back from the high roof space. The organ was tucked away to the left of the altar and behind it a young lad sat enthusiastically pumping the bellows.

The tall slim figure of Mr John Adrian Nottingham, the parish councillor who lived at South View House with his father, carried out his duties as a sidesman, passing back and forth as he brought the Eucharistic cruets, holding the wine and wafers, from their niche at the side of the altar. The vicar then read the sermon from the wooden lectern above the intricate stone carvings of the old pulpit. In honour of Easter he was wearing a more splendid alb, amice and chasuble than usual with his chasuble symbolic of Christ's seamless coat. During his sermons hell-fire often seemed to crop up as, in his clear, deep-timbred voice, he proclaimed the Easter message and read the collects appropriate to the day, but the

280

words were almost meaningless to us and most of them - figuratively and literally - passed over our young heads.

Before long we grew bored and started to fidget, gazing up at the pine hammer beams and the Douglas fir roof panels that were difficult to make out in the deep shadows. Below them, on long chains, hung the large, wrought iron hoops of the chandeliers and Mr Harris whispered to us, "They once 'ad candles in 'em thar knows." They looked like wagon wheel rims to me and I moved sideways so as not to be directly under one in case it came crashing down on my head. We started whispering to each other until we were 'shushed' by the irascible Mrs Harris so, to pass the time, we tried to read the names on the memorial tablet mounted on the north wall that was dedicated to the men of the village who had lost their lives in the First World War. Mrs Harris had given each of us a shiny penny coin to place on the collection plate that was being passed round. In our boredom we squinted at the words 'D: G: OMN: REX F: D: IND: IMP. that were embossed round the head of King George the Sixth without understanding what any of it meant.

Our foster parents were not especially religious although they believed that we had been put on this earth for a purpose and if there was a purpose in life this presupposed that there must be a God. They believed that Jesus Christ's lessons taught us how we should behave towards each other, although Mrs Harris did not seem to adhere to them herself. She had the good book in her hand but apparently not in her head and could be, as we were to learn, nasty and mean spirited. She seemed to think that going to church was a kind of insurance, just in case there was an afterlife. She might have been better occupied pondering on the wrath of God rather than only on His loving and caring aspects

We were unthinking believers in religion but Mam believed in the Bible in a more profound way and really felt the horror of Christ's crucifixion. She used to say, "If God is with you nothing on earth can harm you." And she thought that Christ's love gave us the strength and patience to tolerate the bad things in life. Religious life had long been all-pervasive to her and she suffered the sadness, the joy and the ecstasy of the various Holy days. At Easter sorrow and joy were closely intermingled, just as they were in her, but there was also a feeling of hope abroad in the spring air. Of a gentle nature, she was a pacifist at heart, but she truly believed that without religion mankind could quickly degenerate into savagery and she believed that that is what had happened in Germany. Her God was a merciful God and she just *knew* that there was a life after death. To her life was only a temporary state, after which all would be re-united with their departed loved ones. She was pleased that we were gong to church services and the Sunday school classes in St. Mary's hall where Miss Curry conducted the singing.

After the parish of Haxby had become independent of its neighbour, Strensall, a fine stone Vicarage had been built on the edge of the village up Moor Lane. The earlier 16th century Norman church, said to be dilapidated and unfit for divine worship at the time, was gutted by fire in 1878 and demolished. The present stone church was built that same year in early Gothic Revival style and was able to seat two hundred worshippers. Its tall belfry had a fine weathercock and housed two external bells. Thirty years back three bays had been added to the nave at the western end and the original bell-cote, which stood where the south door is now sited, was rebuilt further west. The font from the old church, which was 'lost' for many years, was discovered in the garden of Haxby Hall and was resited at the end of the extended nave. In 1921 a new vestry was added and the parishioners had donated wooden pews to act as lasting memorials to their loved ones that had passed on. The base of a very old stone cross still stood in the graveyard close to the porch.

The following Tuesday night we went to bed at the usual time only to be woken in the early hours by the plaintive wailing of the air raid siren. Scurrying downstairs we heard the unsynchronised drone of German aircraft engines and then there were two muffled booms from across the fields to the north west. Soon afterwards the continuous tone of the all clear sounded and we went back to our bedroom but on peeping round the curtain we could see the flames of several fires burning in the distance. There was a red glow in the sky over towards the Plainville area and the next day we learned that a Heinkel 111 had developed engine trouble over Ripon way. The starboard engine had burst into flames, and some said it had been shot down by one of the Bofors guns defending Linton-on-Ouse airfield. The pilot had jettisoned his 1,000-kg bomb and the five-man crew managed to bale out with eyewitnesses stating that, "The great plane somersaulted and looped through the night sky like a giant Catherine wheel with its engines revving out of control." It crashed in a field by Bull Lane Bridge owned by Mr Newby of Low Bohemia Farm, which was about two miles from Haxby and not far from Miss Barker's brother at Westfield Farm.

Several kids failed to turn up at school when we started at ten o'clock the following morning and one of these was the mischievous ten years old Derek Robinson who had gone to the crash site to collect shrapnel. Shrapnel was greatly treasured and highly swoppable in school. "A right cheeky little devil," Mrs Harris called him. Unfortunately for him, our village policeman, PC Bill Manging, who lived with his wife in the bungalow next door but one to Harry, also arrived at the crash site that morning. With his black cape flapping in the wind he chased Derek across the fields holding on to his steel helmet, but the fleet-of-foot little lad was too fast for him this time. However, he knew that he lived on Hilbra Avenue, and catching up with him later, he tore a strip off him as the crash site was dangerous and he should not have been there. By that time Derek's precious 'treasures' were safely stashed away to be proudly displayed to the kids in the schoolyard later.

The engine left a deep crater in the soft earth and the wreckage was scattered over a wide area. Soldiers had rounded up the crew and the Strensall policeman, Paddy Teasdale, put the men under arrest. It was definitely the highlight of the week and it was amazing how quickly the news had spread. Later that day Harry said, "We rushed to the main gate and sat on the low wall getting there just in time to see a party of soldiers and the local Home Guard, escorting a German airman past the school. They had their bayoneted rifles cocked and looked ready to use them. The German had on a wool-lined, one-piece, flying overall with zips on the pockets and wore a leather belt with a brass buckles, a close fitting leather helmet and fur-lined flying boots." I was green with envy at missing out on such a major event and Jimmy and I drew and painted pictures of Luftwaffe pilots for weeks to come.

Soon afterwards under the strictest of security, the crumpled, oil-streaked wreckage was taken away on a Queen Mary covered with a tarpaulin and Terry Waddington's dad had a hand in it. It was taken along Corban Lane to 60 MU at Shipton. We often saw his long, low vehicle parked opposite the school or by the level crossing gates when Mr Waddington was with his family at Mrs Evans' bungalow. Many years later the crash site was excavated and bits of the engine, propellers and other bits were found and a five feet (1.8m.) long propeller blade was kept in a barn for many years by Mr Newby's son.

We were completely unaware that at 4.15am on the twenty-first of April, the 5th Battalion of the Green Howards had marched along roads that were still dark on their way to the railway station near Cheddar Gorge in Somerset. Lots of local people, having risen much earlier than usual, lined the roads to cheer and wave them off even though it was all supposed to be top secret. They had been good to the soldiers and many of them had become close friends. Uncle John was just one of hundreds of soldiers taken by train to Liverpool that day and by noon he had boarded the huge HMT *Empress of Asia* at the Gladstone Dock. They were joined by the men of the 72nd Field Regiment, the Royal Artillery, and the 150th Field Ambulance, while other units of the Brigade, including the 4th Battalion Green Howards, boarded the *Empress of Russia*. Both of these large, three-funnelled ships were pre-1914 CPR. liners that had been built for the Pacific passenger trade and had seen military service in the Great War.

The next day they set sail for Scotland to join a large convoy gathered near Rothesay on the Isle of Bute off the Clyde estuary and two days later Uncle John went up on deck to have a look at their convoy of eleven other large ships. Another sizeable convoy had sailed out ten weeks earlier. It was St. George's Day as around thirty ships carrying thousands of troops set off on their long sea voyage and the naval escort was an imposing one with the cruiser, HMS *Repulse*, fourteen destroyers and an armed merchantman. A lone fighter plane circled overhead as their escort shepherded the great troopships out into the Atlantic Ocean. The seas became rough as they sailed through the Bay of Biscay and many of the men were seasick and white as sheets. Uncle John, with the tang of the open sea in his nostrils, was excited but at the same time a little apprehensive as his first taste of active service was still fresh in his mind. Passing down the north west coast of Africa they zigzagged eastwards through tropical waters. After changing into their tropical kit for the first time, they had a good laugh on seeing their mates wearing the baggy, khaki shorts known as Benghazi Bloomers.

Discipline was the order of the day and they carried out regular lifeboat drills. In the cool of the early mornings, screaming PT instructors kept them busy and fit and these exercise sessions were followed by a compulsory dip in the swimming pool, which they did not object to as the sweltering heat was becoming overpowering. The soldiers participated in deck sports, took part in quizzes and frequented the ship's cinema to see Alice Faye and Abbot and Costello films. When the sun smote them they had to take care not to get badly sunburnt because, if they reported sick, they could be charged with 'sustaining self-inflicted injuries'. Arriving at green, jungle-girt Freetown, Sierra Leone in the early hours of May the ninth, they anchored out in the Bay. Barges brought out goods and coal for the ship's bunkers and black African boys sold nuts and fruit, which were hauled up from their canoes in baskets. Three hot and clammy days later they resumed their voyage and on a beautifully warm and clear night they crossed the equator. Uncle John and the others, who were enjoying a stroll on the deck, could see both the North Star and the constellation called the Southern Cross at the same time. While they were there they heard that Rudolf Hess had parachuted in to Scotland and it was rumoured that he was barmy and they had a good laugh at his expense. John got on well with his company commander, Captain 'Ticker' Whittaker.

At the end of April their convoy was still at sea but in the meantime, Rommel's infantry and panzer divisions had carried out more surprise attacks in Libya, reclaiming the bases that the Italians had lost. The British garrison was surrounded and holed up at Tobruk and the speed of the push by Rommel's well-trained and highly disciplined men led to the British 2nd Armoured Division being annihilated. The Allies were driven back a thousand miles through some of the most arid country on earth as far as the Libyan-Egyptian border and beyond it. The ground gained at such a high cost in terms of human lives was lost again and Hitler was delighted with Rommel who had won the Iron Cross (First Class) for his bravery and leadership in World War One. Under the remorseless rays of the desert sun, hundreds of bloated, putrefying, Allied corpses lay covered in black flies that feasted and grew fat. Tobruk was cut off thus starting what was to become a long and protracted siege and Churchill, who had reluctantly given the order to send out troops to aid Greece, was blamed for the debacle. However, it was Anthony Eden, recently moved from the War Office to the Foreign Office, who had suggested the move feeling that our promise of aid must be honoured.

For many years an ancient May Day custom had been performed in the school playground at Haxby, with the maypole being erected on the tarmac in front of the bike shed. A garland was fixed to the crown and from it long white ribbons were suspended. The prettiest girls, in their green and white dresses, held these as they danced around it accompanied by the band, which was composed of recorders, tambourines and triangles. Thelma and the others had rehearsed for this day for several weeks. Lively and quick-witted, she was as sharp as a knife and she never let the grass grow under her feet. She and Dot were as different as chalk and cheese. The younger children, including Jimmy and me were gathered together in the playground to watch this colourful rite of spring.

"This time-honoured Christian custom is carried out to welcome the coming of summer." Mr Fox explained. "The crown represents the sun and the ribbons represent the sun's life-giving rays." We enjoyed the lively music and the dancing and were happy to escape from the crowded church hall into the warm spring air. The girls danced in and out between the girls coming round the other way causing the ribbons to intertwine around the central pole creating an intricate, colourful and convoluted pattern. Shortly afterwards one of the girls, crowned with a garland of flowers as the May Queen, was paraded round the playground flanked by her two 'royal' attendants.

It was not until many years later that I discovered that this 'innocent' Christian custom had erotic pagan origins. Bound up with the praising of the eternal life-giving force, to the ancients it had been a wild and joyful celebration of fertility and birth. It was closely associated with the Celtic May Day festival of rebirth, known as Beltane, when peasants performed the sacred

286

Bacchanalian 'dance of life' to appease the Gods. It expressed the great joy felt by the people at coming safely through the dark times of the winter and was a time of joyous revelry and great merriment. The blackthorn, symbolic of the end of the winter, comes into white flower before the leaf buds open and its limbs are still bare. Although the hawthorn does not blossom till mid May, the white blossom of the blackthorn is intertwined with it to form the garland. With its potent erotic perfume, it came to symbolise spring and the renewal of life. Each year the sappy May Day garland was ceremonially raised to the tip of the phallic maypole and a similar garland formed the crown of thorns as worn at the crucifixion of Christ. This and other peasant lore was frowned on and suppressed by the established church, but traces of it can still be found in folk customs and various writings.

On May 4th the clocks were put forward one hour giving us two hours of extra evening daylight, known as double summertime as the clocks had not been put back the previous autumn. It meant that it was light well after bedtime and light again before we got up in the morning and we took full advantage of this, playing in Widd's field until long after tea. The farmers and the farmhands, a robust, cheerful lot with shining red faces and large, rough hands, worked later into the evenings.

We were always made to say Grace before meals, but it wasn't the swift hand of God that we feared. If any of us ate anything before grace was said we got a clout from Mrs Harris. Breakfast usually consisted of porridge made from 'Quaker Oats' mixed with milk and water. I tried hard to be good and polite at breakfast as Mam had told us that, "God is a silent listener and a guest at every meal." But it was difficult to be good all day; especially when Jimmy kept pulling faces at me and trying to get me annoyed. It had been light for a good two hours as our little group walked to school on those early summer mornings.

The East Coast was now easily accessible to the Luftwaffe and the evacuees from Hull were anxious about their parents' safety and couldn't wait for them to visit again. The evacuees from there told us that the town had suffered repeated bombing between March and May with hundreds killed and thousands of houses damaged. In early June it suffered its fiftieth air raid and was left without gas when the mains were fractured. At night the raging fires lit up the night sky and the orange glow could be seen from Haxby. On the night of May the eleventh the siren at Haxby sounded for yet another alert and we learned later that RAF Linton had been badly damaged in an attack by three Junkers 88s. When Mam visited us she told us that six bombs had been dropped on the Newport area and one had landed inside the steel casing of one of the huge gasholders not far from our house setting it on fire and providing a spectacularly frightening display.

The Wigginton and Haxby Women's Institute (W.I.), who had recently completed twenty-one years in existence, were doing their bit for the war effort. Their needles busily clicked away, as they knitted scarves, jerseys, woollen hats, balaclava helmets and socks, which were parcelled up and sent to local men serving in the forces. They also made garments for the local children and the RAF men billeted in the two villages. By the early summer they had hired canning equipment, setting it up in the kitchen of Mr Tom Midgeley's Manor Farm in Wigginton. Using fruits preserved and stored from the previous year they were kept busy jam making using an assortment of tins and jars. They sealed the jars with round paper lids tied on with thin string and put them on sale in the village shops. They produced an amazing 263 lbs. (120 kilos) in the first two weeks of the operation and the local housewives snapped them up eagerly. Mrs Harris made sure that she got her fair share, but we were still denied jam and margarine on our bread at the same time.

To help the worsening food situation, Mr Harris went out and caught rabbits using hand-whittled, wooden pegs to which he attached wire snares (locally called 'sniggles'). His big square hands were callused and ingrained with soil and were those of a man accustomed to hard manual work. He knew all the rabbit runs near his allotment and in the local fields and he set snares in the deep grass under the hedgerows in the evenings. He would then go out early in the morning when the dew was still on the grass, picking a few mushrooms on the way. Once the rabbits were removed from the sniggles he spliced the skin of their hind legs and brought them home slung on a long stick taken from the hedgerow that he rested on his shoulder. The open fields, with their covering of fresh, lush grass, were alive with rabbits and field mice and Mr

Harris told us that he often heard the forlorn cry of a rabbit as he approached. Death was always waiting in the wings in the form of slinky stoats with black-tipped tails. Brown on top and white underneath, their kittens would eat anything, including insects.

Mr Harris, who never talked much, said to us, "One mornin' I spotted a large 'are and walked very quietly straight towards 'im until I were quite close an 'e didn't move. Their eyes are set on t'side o' their 'eads thar knows and they can't see owt in a line directly in front of 'em. It 'adn't scented or 'eard me, even though they can rotate their ears through an 'undred and eighty degrees. Wind were be'ind it and when I got close, t'great sandy-coloured beauty made a dash for freedom. 'E weaved and jinked 'is way across t'open fields ter disappear amongst tall clumps of last yeer's sere grasses." I had never heard him talk so long and so animatedly about anything before.

We were often given rabbit stews and I came to like the taste of the white meat that was a bit stronger than chicken. We had also started to have bland tasting, mass-produced, vegetable rissoles that had only recently been introduced and could be bought at the Co-op store for eight pence (3p) per pound (454g.).

14. Stormy Waters

The Wiggy Rec, a wooden building on the main street at Wigginton, was shared with the RAF. Several lorries painted in dull RAF blue were usually to be found parked in its grounds and Sergeant Ellery made it abundantly clear that he was the man in charge there. He was responsible for getting the large numbers of airmen billeted in the area - most of whom worked at the aircraft maintenance unit at Shipton-by-Beningborough about five miles to the west - to and from their places of work every day. The large hut was also used by the RAF every Wednesday to show films. The latest, 'Turned Out Nice Again', starred George Formby as a half-soaked but loveable, ukulele playing, working-class chap who was always being put upon and its title became one of Mr Harris' favourite sayings. Maybe Mr Harris identified with him. The musical 'Broadway Melody' featuring the suave Hollywood song and dance star, Fred Astaire, was also shown around that time but I don't recall ever being taken there.

Regular Saturday night dances were held there as the RAF lads had formed a good dance band and many of the local ladies were to have fond memories of these dances in the years to come. There was no alcohol served in the dancehalls in those days but there was plenty available in the three nearby pubs, which were crammed to the doors in the hour or two before the dance started. Many of the RAF lads used to call in at Walker's fish and chip shop on Front Street, Haxby, for their suppers.

RAF Sergeant Ellery received regular news bulletins on the wireless that the RAF had installed and he passed this on to Miss Curry, who then informed us. The latest news concerned Rudolph Hess; Hitler's former deputy who had been flown across the North Sea in a twin-engined Messerschmitt 110D where he parachuted on to a farm near Glasgow. He had always admired the English and the way in which this small country had managed its vast Empire and he was thought to have with him a proposed peace plan believing that Great Britain couldn't win. Thinking that the people were now hostile towards Churchill, he expected it to be accepted, but the offer was rejected and his arrogance quickly disappeared when he was put in jail. He was said to be unstable and mentally ill.

By this time Greece was in German hands following a huge airborne invasion with heavy losses on both sides. Many Allied troops had been taken prisoner and the remainder were evacuated to Crete, which fell to yet another massive German airborne attack near the end of May. The Italians had attacked in the east of the island and it was all over in just twelve days. 18,000 men had - yet again - to be taken off by the Royal Navy who put themselves in real danger in order to carry out the evacuation. The ships were attacked from the air with grievous losses of troops and seamen and the 13,000 Allied troops left behind were taken prisoner. Lack of fighter air cover had much to do with it and yet another defeat was a bitter disappointment to the British public.

At that time Germany was at the height of its military power and was sweeping all before it. The prospects of victory for the Allies seemed remote. With the people well fed and happy after his easy victories, Hitler was hailed as the greatest field commander of all time. No General dared to question his orders and he demanded the allegiance of the masses. The continent of Europe was under Nazi oppression and they now occupied or controlled most of North Africa. The occupied countries were being used to supply Germany with foodstuffs, industrial goods and slave labour. We learned that German troops were massing on their eastern borders and on the 22nd Hitler, blinded by his own conceit, hurled his mechanised divisions at the vast Soviet Union and his former allies were in retreat. This meant that he now had war on two fronts and the threat of an invasion on this country all but disappeared. It was to be Hitler's greatest mistake!

Derek Robinson's collection was the envy of the other boys and in it he had regimental cap badges, cloth insignia, uniform buttons, spent bullets, small pieces of sharp-edged shrapnel and several bits of Perspex that he claimed came from crashed aeroplanes. His cheeky, grinning face could be seen in the playground with his pals Peter Beresford and our Harry as they swopped what they had for any duplicates that he had. Looking at his 'treasures' often caused us to arrive late for a meal at our billet and, as a result, we received another cuff round the ear and a piece of Mrs Harris' sharp tongue to go with it. She was in an even viler frame of mind than usual around that time as a stray bomb had landed on the gas works at Heworth Green in York causing the gas pressure in the village to be low for a week, which made it difficult for her to provide hot meals.

Times became even harder when it was announced that clothes were to be rationed from 1st of June, not because of shortages, but to make more factories and workers available for the war effort. At first, the scheme did not take into account the fact that young children grow out of their clothes very quickly, but the following month children were allowed ten extra coupons and wool was put on ration. No special ration books for clothing were issued and the locals were obliged to use spare coupons from their food books for some considerable time. Each person was allowed sixty-six coupons a year but a man's suit could use up nearly half of this and a woman's suit or coat took eighteen coupons; if you had the money to afford one. Civil defence workers, the police and Auxiliary firemen (AFS) got extra coupons as their jobs involved heavy wear and tear. The ribs of Mrs Harris' corsets where made of whalebone, which was now hard to come by, but she only wore them when she went somewhere special and most of the time she looked like a sack of potatoes tied in the middle.

We enjoyed fifteen hours of sunshine on one day in June and long, hot sunny days thereafter as the blazingly hot summer seemed to go on forever. When coal was put on ration on July the fourth, it was not really noticed until the weather changed for the worse later in the year. The sugar ration was doubled from eight ounces to one pound, for that month only, as large amounts of summer fruit were readily available. Mrs Harris' excess fruit was stored in her larder in sealed Kilner jars.

We were made to change into our old shabby clothes as soon as we came home from school and we each had a list of household chores and errands that had to be done before teatime and by now the long list of Dos and Don'ts had grown and God help us if we didn't abide by them. We had to clean and polish our school shoes over an old newspaper and the girls had to help Mrs Harris in getting the tea ready and had to do the washing up afterwards. After tea we were sent out to play until near bedtime, unless it was raining, when we were sent up into our bedrooms to play with our meagre toys and games. There were no books in the house, only newspapers and the odd magazine like *Picture Post, Illustrated* or *Woman's Own,* which cost twopence (1p) and came out every Wednesday. Although I was unable to read I enjoyed looking at the pictures.

We often found small white booklets in the house, called *Old Moore's Almanack*, which Mrs Harris bought at Torville's shop. There were prophecies in black print on the front cover and they had black and white hieroglyphics and cabalistic sketches on the inside pages. There were things like the phases of the moon, tide tables and rhyming verses predicting catastrophes and disasters yet to come. It all seemed a bit spooky to us but most people were superstitious in those days. Mrs Harris was *very* superstitious and she told us that we must never pass each other on the stairs, put our shoes on the table, or leave our knives and forks crossed on our plate. If we did so we would always have bad luck and she believed implicitly in the horoscopes printed in the *Daily Express* that cost 1d. (0.4p) at that time. We practised our own magic rituals, one of which involved touching the top of our front gate and walking backward up to the Fisher's gatepost. We then had to touch that before we could turn to face the right way and I repeated this ritual every time I went out. It's amazing how a little magic can lift the spirits as the Harry Potter books have proved.

So many people were being killed that a number of the bereaved turned to Spiritualism with seances being held all over the country. It seems that some people tried to ease their grief in this way in the hope that they might get in touch with their departed loved ones. However, there was grave (no pun intended) concern in government circles that people were being duped and a few unscrupulous people were taken to court and fined or imprisoned. The Royal Navy looked on the Spiritualist Church as an official religion and it was even rumoured that Winston Churchill had leanings that way. Air Chief Marshal Sir Hugh Trenchard, known as The Father of the Royal Air Force, strongly believed in it. After he had been replaced as Commander in Chief of Fighter Command after the Battle of Britain, he had written wrote books on the subject averring that he had met 'dead' RAF pilots in his sleep. Renowned journalists, such as Hannen Swaffer, wrote about such cases in the newspaper.

Living next door to us was a young childless couple called Mr Len and Mrs Sarah Hayes. He was a rat catcher on the local railway and they had evacuees called Albert and Phyllis Davies, a brother and sister from Sheffield, staying with them. Mr Hayes kept long, flat-backed ferrets with tiny, beady, pink eyes in cages at the bottom of his back garden. He had one of them peeping out from inside his shirt as he told us that the males were called 'hobs' and he didn't mind us watching as he fed them on mice and old chicken legs that were unfit for human consumption. As they ran about the slinky creatures had a strange habit of suddenly leaping up into the air. Later the family took in the brothers Laurence and Harry Wright, who went to the village school with us, but Mrs Harris reiterated that we were never to play with them or to bring them to her house.

Mr Maurice Nolan, who lived in the first house in the next pair but one to us, had a son and a daughter from an earlier marriage, and we overheard Mrs Harris say disapprovingly that he was now living tally with his new wife-to-be. She added that there had been a shotgun marriage, but we didn't understand what she meant and that year a new baby arrived at the house. She told us that it had been found in their rhubarb patch and, for a while after that, whenever Mr Harris took us to his allotment, we looked under the rhubarb leaves to see if one had been left there. We were nowhere near as worldly-wise, knowledgeable or confident, as the youngsters of today. Mr Nolan was employed locally as a bookie's runner and one day, passing the couple on Usher Lane, we asked if we could see the baby and when we looked into the pram a horrible 'pong' assailed our nostrils. From our back garden we could see a long row of Terry towelling nappies flapping and fluttering in the breeze.

When the summer holiday arrived we were sent out to play; but not until we had done our chores, eaten our breakfast and completed our errands. We all had to run messages but poor Dot always had more jobs to do than the rest of us. We were given orders not to come back till dinnertime, and God help us if we were late for that. Then we were let loose again until teatime; unless Mrs

Harris heard on the village grapevine that one of the shops was selling some hard-to-get product, in which case, one of us had to go and stand in the queue to save a place for her. After tea we were sent out to play again until near dusk. On Sundays and Wednesday afternoons we were safe as all the shops were shut.

When we came back after playing out, our legs were usually scratched and sore from the hay, the brambles and the grass seed-heads, that we called 'arrows', that got stuck in our woollen socks, that were usually concerntina'd round our ankles and looked like the blacksmith's bellows. In the heat of the afternoon, leg weary after hours of incessant activity, we would flop down on the grass and give way to indolence. We would lay spread-eagled on our backs half-hidden in the Yorkshire Fog in Widd's field. I enjoyed the feeling of somnolence as the heat was reflected upwards from the sun-warmed soil. Lying in a tangle of bodies, we used each other as pillows, and I would watch the fluffy, cotton wool clouds floating serenely by across the azure of the wide summer skies and surrender to the moment. As the sun warmed my face the sunlight that filtered through my closed eyelids turned the insides pink. One moment I lay quiet and relaxed; the next my sleepy, languorous reverie would be brought to an abrupt end as Jimmy or one of the others jumped on me and knocked the stuffing out of me. The quiet, restful moment then turned into scrimmaging and horseplay that usually ended up in a 'roughhouse'.

On those glorious summer days we ran wild and free. We climbed trees and fell over sustaining bruises and cuts that bled, dried and formed scabs. Our knees and elbows were always yellow with iodine. We wandered round the local countryside, getting hotter and sweatier as the day wore on and we came to know every lane, snickleway, house, farm, barn and field in the area. Day after day the sun beat down bleaching our hair and turning our faces, forearms and legs a ruddy bronze in colour. Occasionally the sky darkened and the air cooled and when heavy summer showers fell we sought shelter in a barn taking the opportunity to make dens in the hay and secret passages between the straw bales until it faired up. The parched and dusty earth darkened as it soaked up the life-giving rain and we left the cool shady depths of the barn, blinking like coal miners emerging from the pit. Screwing up our eyes against the dazzling brightness, we enjoyed the warm kiss of the sun on our skin. After the chill of the rain we felt newly invigorated as sweet, freshly released scents emanated from the flowers, the wet leaves and the steaming grass. Sadly, the tassels of corn that had danced in the sun now lay forlornly on the earth after their heavy battering. The smell of the rain-wet soil rose up to mingle with the summer air and we drew its nectar-like freshness deep into our lungs and it was sheer bliss to be young and alive.

Mrs Harris lacked the gift of loving-kindness and didn't seem bothered whether we got lost, injured or drowned as long as we kept well out of her sight. The open countryside was ours and free for the taking and we revelled in it spending most of our time outdoors returning to the house just to eat, sleep and do our chores. 'Seeing' German soldiers hiding behind every hedge and tree, we stealthily crept up on them and 'killed' them. As we played in Widd's field amid scents of rye grass and foxtails; we would sometimes see real soldiers walking along the lane and, one day, we knew it wasn't right when one of them exposed himself and pee'd what we thought was milk and we edged further away from him. From the field we were able to see whether Mrs Harris had come out into the back garden to wave a tea towel above her head to indicate that it was time to go in. While we waited there were always newts and things to be caught below the coruscating, breeze-ruffled surface of the shallow pond.

As we breathed in the sweet odours of that glorious late summer the days were long and hot, and the nights were short and warm and life was seldom dull. After expending so much energy in constant activity we slept soundly in our beds at night and I developed a deep and lasting love of nature. On the tenth of August the clocks were put back again by an hour bringing the double summertime to an end. The evening shadows lengthened, but it was still light until ten o'clock at night. Ecstatic days were followed by humdrum days when nothing much happened and Jimmy and I often argued and fell out, but the bond of blood and friendship was strong and we soon made up and became the best of pals again. We stood together if anyone threatened the other but, more often than not, it was Jimmy who protected me.

Mr Harris often read out items from the newspapers, which were getting thinner and thinner. Leonard Cheshire, the brave and widely liked bomber pilot, was often mentioned and he had become something of a hero to us. The most recent item stated that he, with four other Halifaxes from Linton, had joined seventy Halifax bombers in a bombing raid on Berlin. On his return he had circled round to land with only three of his Merlin engines firing, another cut out on landing and a third stopped as he was taxiing in to the dispersal point. It was said that bomber crew survival rates were now averaging around three weeks and Leonard Cheshire was living on borrowed time. He had either been very lucky, a brilliant pilot or both to survive this long. Mr Harris lionised him and to him he was the bravest pilot that ever lived. We often saw and heard the bombers going out at dusk. On a day of pouring rain in October he was promoted again, this time to the rank of Squadron Leader and he was to become the most decorated pilot in the RAF.

When Mam visited again she told me that she had given up her job as a housemaid in the large house on Newport Road owned by Mrs Ethel Gaunt, who was later to become the Lady Mayoress of Middlesbrough. Mam couldn't bear to be parted from her 'baby boy' for long and she was now back at Grove House with our George. Working as an assistant cook to Mrs Ruonne again, she was sharing a room with a tall, slim nursery assistant called Rita Bird who had replaced my beloved Kitty. Mam said, "Rita, who comes from Middlesbrough, is in her early twenties, has shoulder-length, permed, mousy-coloured hair and is very kind and considerate," before adding, "It makes it much easier for me to visit you now and I missed you both terribly when I was in Middlesbrough. I now go to the little church in the valley with the Artleys every Sunday and they send their best regards."

Dad was now attached to a Durham Coast Light Anti-Aircraft unit and could not get home very often and Mam had temporarily rented our house to a female acquaintance called Mrs Miller who was of the Mormon persuasion. She had felt sorry for her when she told her that her husband had beaten her and kicked her out, as her sister's bad experiences with her estranged husband were still fresh in her mind.

297

Mam could now catch the early train from Levisham Station right outside the door, and, with a couple of changes but many stops, she could get to York to catch the number ten double-decker bus to Haxby. She would write to Mrs Harris about once a month to tell her when she was coming and when Jimmy and I found out what time the bus was due we would run excitedly down the road to meet it as it pulled in by the Co-op store. Mam, not being invited to stay for a meal, often took Jimmy and me to our Harry's billet, which for some reason had now become number twelve York Road. Here the homely Miss Barker and the friendly Miss Law always made us to feel very welcome and we sometimes played clock golf on their lawn. Afterwards we stayed for a nice tea with lots of cakes and sandwiches sat at the wooden table in the back garden but I keenly sensed Mam's pain each time she had to leave.

In late May, during what was said to be the worst storm for sixty years, Uncle John's ship damaged its rudder and had to stay at Cape Town, overlooked by the long, level line of Table Mountain. Later he told Gran, "We were there for five days while repairs were carried out, and from out in the bay the twinkling lights were beautiful to see. There were no blackout restrictions and the town looked like a fairyland with the shimmering lights reflecting on the waters of the bay. When a few of us went ashore two ladies wearing pinafores approached us and invited us to a large hall. Lots of food was spread out on white tablecloths and they told us to eat as much as we could. We thoroughly enjoyed the generous banquet but I felt guilty at eating so well when the folks at home were enduring strict rationing. The sight and scents of hibiscus, frangipani, gardenia and bougainvillaea were overpowering and beautiful to see. The local Boers were hostile but the native British were warm and hospitable and the following day we were invited to visit a cigarette factory behind Kloof Street where we were given five hundred Sweet Caporals, which we shared amongst the lads when we got back to the ship."

After sailing into the calmer waters of the Indian Ocean, they called in at Durban on the east coast of Africa, where they found that they had a reduced escort as several naval vessels had been ordered to leave to take part in a long sea chase. It seems that they had been ordered to engage Germany's newest, biggest and fastest battle ship, the *Bismarck* that had been sighted near Greenland on its maiden voyage. Britain's largest battle ship, HMS *Hood,* trailed her and fired on her and the *Bismarck* returned the fire hitting her three times. Her ammunition magazines ignited and she broke in two and sank with only three of her 1400 crew surviving to tell the tale. Three days later the mighty *Bismark* was sunk by our combined air and sea forces and the nation rejoiced.

The hurried signing on of too many unsatisfactory stokers in Liverpool led to delays as many of them deserted when the ship called in at Freetown, Cape Town and Durban, which meant that Lieutenant Alec Black (in command of the group), Uncle John and others had take their place in the sweltering heat of the stokehold, causing them to fall two weeks behind the rest of the convoy. As they rounded the Horn of Africa and sailed through the Gulf of Aden on their way to the Red Sea the troops caught their first glimpse of the vast desert stretching away on both sides. Sailing into the Gulf of Suez, they arrived at Port Tewfik (now Taufiq) in Egypt, but their ship was to meet an unhappy fate being sunk off Singapore the following year. Due to strict military censorship they were forbidden to send cables home to parents or wives in case information on troop movements reached the enemy. The voyage of about fourteen thousand miles had taken just over two months. The shorter route through the 'Med' was only three thousand miles but the longer route had been necessary to avoid U-boats, air attacks and magnetic mines.

On disembarking in late June, twenty men at a time were taken to El Quassassin, just north of Ismailia, in army trucks where they stayed in a huge tented camp for a couple of weeks of training and acclimatisation. Here the young and inexperienced soldiers 'got their knees brown' but the heat was a great shock to those who had not been east before. Uncle John and his battalion were then moved the two hundred and thirty miles to El Daba, about sixty miles west of the small rail station at El Alamein, which was to become well known to the western world the following year. Out in the desert, about a hundred and twenty miles west of Alexandria, their job was to protect the lines of communication and to defend the aerodromes.

The climate was harsh and the inhospitable and they had to endure vicious dust storms called *khamsins*, caused by the hot winds that blew up from the Sahara Desert bringing great clouds of reddish dust that obscured visibility, clogged up the mechanism of the vehicles and weapons, and brought all training to a halt. The dust storms sometimes lasted for twelve hours or more and the stinging, swirling sand, that almost blinded them, meant they had to wear handkerchiefs over their faces, but it still found its way into their food and drink. There were no accurate maps, and while out on patrols, Uncle John had to navigate using the sun and a compass. When the sun went down they leaguered for the night gathered together in a group with their vehicles and trucks, which always had a brew can suspended at the rear.

The big, black, flies constantly tormented them, landing on the rim of their chipped enamel mugs and their food as they put it to their mouths, and they had to be spat out. Who knows what diseases they carried as they fed on excreta and the dead. They developed the unconscious habit of flapping their hands in front of their faces. The ever-present sand fleas were the cause of suppurating sores that occurred mostly on their knees, and when they removed the bandages the festering open wounds were often crawling with maggots. They were not nice to see but by eating the pus they helped to keep the sores clean. The only redeeming feature was that they were near to the pure white sandy beaches to the north of the Quattara Depression and the sea bathing was greatly appreciated. It did much to counteract the mid-day heat and the torment of the flies that bit like horseflies. The sand away from the coast was a dirty yellowish colour as it was composed mainly of dust and they dug holes in which they had to live, covering them with camouflaged bivouacs.

In early August a large part of 150th Brigade was sent to Cyprus on Royal Navy destroyers. Uncle John's battalion sailed from Port Said on HMAS *Hobart* at 2300 hours on the 15th. arriving at Famagusta at 2 a.m. the following morning. They were given a mug of strong tea and a beef sandwich and their job was to defend Larnaca aerodrome. They relieved the 7th Battalion Green Howards who sailed for Haifa in Palestine two days later and were briefly reunited with a few of their old mates. The intensive training continued with Uncle John's platoon carrying out manoeuvres in Bren gun carriers.

When the new school year started at St. Mary's hall that September it was as crowded as ever but the warm and gentle Miss Francis was still my teacher. She had a quiet, clear voice, which she seldom raised, and she encouraged us to be more sensitive to each other's feelings, in the hope of making us better children. Jimmy had moved up to the main school and, much to his delight, he was now in Miss Rutter's group in the high-ceilinged classroom adjoining the headmaster's house. She was his acting, unpaid deputy. Slim, voluptuous and athletic with slim graceful wrists and ankles, she was sometimes to be seen hurdling over the low wall at the front of the school giving the sniggering lads a brief glimpse of white underwear. Jimmy had developed a bit of a crush on his pretty, dark skinned teacher with the Italian looks.

She had an oval face, high cheekbones and dark, soft, luxuriantly wavy hair and Jimmy loved the way it swayed as she moved. Her eyebrows were dark and she had big brown eyes with long lashes and to Jimmy she was so beautiful. Her vivacity and poise were her greatest assets and he thought she looked like a film star and she could do no wrong in his eyes. The lips of her well-shaped mouth were soft and full and often broke into a glorious smile. I often saw him following her around like a puppy dog being as helpful and polite as could be and making calf's eyes at her. When I exaggeratedly mocked him he gave me a swift punch in the ribs. Harry was now in the 'big boys' form at the western end of the school that was partitioned off from Miss Rutter's classroom and presided over by Mr Fox.

In mid September the Ministry of Food compelled the subsidised grocers to sell hard-to-get potatoes at one-penny (0.4p.) each as they felt that people needed more complex carbohydrates in their diet to correct the imbalance caused by rationing and shortages. Even off-ration foods, like fish and sausages, were hard to get and Mr Harris said, "It's a darn mystery what's in them sausages any'ow." When they became available long queues formed. We were seldom given real potatoes except when Mr Harris brought a few from his allotment at certain times of the year.

More often than not we were given tinned corned beef or Spam with a tasteless dollop of unappetising 'Pom' made from potato powder to which hot water had been addded. We started our day with a splodge of hot porridge made with water, not milk. "That'll put a lining on your bellies and keep you warm," contended Mrs Harris.

Overall our diet was pretty bland and we were always hungry. We ran, walked and skipped wherever we went and went everywhere on shanks' pony, which kept us lean and fit. We seldom saw any fat kids. For our main midday meal we still had lots of rabbit stews with dandelion leaves, nettles and greasy suet dumplings floating in them. We had to say Grace before and after every meal, which never altered from, "For what we are about to receive, may the Lord make us truly thankful, Amen." and "For what we have just received...."

Quite often we were given a plateful of heavy suet pudding with salt on it, which Mrs Harris had steamed in a muslin bag over a big pan of boiling water. It was about the size of a football and it filled us up but it lay like lead in our bellies. We ate what was put in front of us or we went hungry. One day, for a change, she made a Spotted Dick (suet pudding with raisins in it) and I remember getting a clout round the lug for saying something rude about it.

On our nature walks Miss Francis encouraged us to collect the rose hips that bulged red and shiny on the briars at this time of year, and she told us that they would be made into rose hip syrup, which was rich in vitamin C. In the past, we had used their hairy, close-packed, white seeds to put down each other's shirt collars and we called them 'itchy-backs'. In our spare time, we scoured the hedgerows until barely one was left on the bushes for the poor birds to feed on in the winter, and for our efforts we received four pence per pound (under 2p for 450g.). I think I made about tuppence (less than 1p.) profit, but Mrs Harris - to my dismay - made me put a penny of it into the collection plate at church that Sunday.

So the swallows departed for warmer climes and our days in the village passed uneventfully. We popped the white snowberries that clung to the spindly twigs in the hedgerows. The rosy-cheeked apples reached full ripeness and the sweet smell of cider filled the air beneath the trees as the fallers fermented. We ate many of those that were still in reasonable condition, but it was customary to leave the last apple on each tree for the fairies. Locals called the long, curved, brownish-green, sweet and succulent Conference pears, 'banana' pears. As their weight bent down the boughs in the orchards, it made it easier for us to do a bit of illicit scrumping. We did not see it as wrong when fresh fruit was so scarce and we were so hungry. When some of the kids were seen and recognised, they were reported to the school and Mr Fox caned them, and they spit on their hands and held them under their oxsters (armpits) as that seemed to ease the stinging pain a little. Mr Harris said, "We used ter rub a raw onion on our 'ands to deaden t'pain but they're 'ard to come by these days."

The blackberries in the hedgerows grew fat, turning from red to juicy black and they stained our lips, tongues and fingers. As autumn moved on, the leaves of the horse chestnut and beech trees were tinged with brown making them engaging to the eye. We had watched the green, spiky, tri-lobed fruits of the horse chestnut trees slowly growing to full size all through the spring and summer. 'Conkers' became the in-thing again, and as we took the large, bright, shiny, mahogany-brown seeds from their startlingly white, spongy cocoons they had a slight smell of iodine. Mr Harris told us, "In t'First World War we were encouraged ter collect 'em an all. They were used in t'manufacture of cordite that were urgently needed as a propellant fer firing artillery shells."

Using an old skewer from Mr Harris' cluttered shed, we bored a hole through them, and suspended the best ones on thick string. We had dried them slowly in the airing cupboard and soaked them in vinegar to harden them and Jimmy had a few from the previous year that were now dry and really hard. Thinking we were in with a chance, we set forth to conquer the rest but someone always seemed to produce a better one. After many hits and a few wins, the first fatal cracks began to appear in our would-be-champions.

The seven-fingered leaflets on the horse chestnut trees were just starting to turn brown, but they became a sorry sight after the lads had bombarded them with large sticks in their clumsy attempts at knocking down the spiky seedcases. The ground inside the graveyard gate was thickly littered with fallen twigs and leaves and some of the boys received 'six of the best' on their backsides from the headmaster. A number of irate women had complained to him, saying, "Some of the heavy sticks that the boys threw up just missed us when they were blown down by the strong winds. We could have been badly injured"

Jimmy sometimes walked up to Mrs Evans' bungalow to see the various aeroplane models that Terry Waddington's dad had carved for him, but he would not be getting anymore. While working at Linton-on-Ouse airfield, he had been asked to swing the propeller of a Tiger Moth to start the engine. His foot slipped and as he staggered forward, the spinning propeller almost severed his right hand and he had to undergo major surgery and receive treatment for a long time.

At potato picking time, the farmers were starting to get extra help. We saw groups of prisoners-of-war from the camp that had been set up at Strensall, working in the fields for the first time. The Italians wore dark brown battle dresses with a large red circle sewn on the back but the Germans had yellow, diamond-shaped patches on their grey uniforms. They were brought over every morning in army lorries and groups of four or five were dropped off guarded by a soldier armed with a loaded rifle and fixed bayonet and were picked up and returned in the evening. In July, thousands of them had been brought to Liverpool by ship and were put in barbed wire-encircled enclosures all over the country. The farmers were delighted with their new workers and Miss Curry told us that they found the Germans to be the hardest workers. She had said to the whole school, "Don't worry, they are not Nazis. Those have been taken out and put into other special, well-guarded camps". Even so, we were very wary of them and never went near them, as we had heard too many horror stories about them.

Living four doors up from us was Mr Cliff Hartshorn and his wife, Mary. They had no children and he was a harness maker, cobbler and shoe repairer by trade. Partially deaf, he worked in the large wooden shed in his back garden mending shoes for a small fee and he didn't seem to mind us standing there watching him. We would stand there for ages - especially if the day was wet - looking on and marvelling at his speed and dexterity. At last, after many long weeks of waiting, he was repairing our leather case ball and we were eager to get the precious 'casie' back to play with it in Widd's field. I measured my success by how many kicks I got rather than how many goals I scored, which was usually nil. Widd's field was the centre of our little world when we were out of the house.

On Saturday mornings we would sometimes go to watch the village football team playing on the pitch next to the narrow track that ran behind Harold Mann's house and the allotments off South Lane. Here, 'Cobbler' Johnson, the 'Mr Football' of Haxby, was the organiser and man in charge. He worked from his home in Pear Tree Cottage, next to the *Tiger*, mending boots and shoes. The footballers used to change in the old Memorial Hall that reeked to high heaven of Elliman's and Algipan embrocations (sometimes called Fiery Jack), dubbin (to soften the leather), sweaty feet and cigarette smoke. The tops of the player's heavy, leather boots, tied round and round with long leather bootlaces, came above their ankles and had leather studs nailed on to the soles. When it rained the hundreds of round holes that they left all over the pitch filled up with water and we watched from the doorway of one of the two breeze block air raid shelters at the end of the field. I never understood how the players managed to head and boot the large, heavy casie so far. When it was wet and muddy it became as heavy as lead and whenever it came near us we could barely shift it.

There were sporadic bombing raids by enemy aircraft and we knew by the sound of the engines if they were German or British. On clear moonlit nights they seemed to follow the railway lines towards York, but no fatalities occurred and the local Home Guard got in some much needed target practice. Working with the regular soldiers from Strensall Camp, they often had firing practice in the field across the road from St. Mary's hall and as we sat in our classroom, we could heard the shouting of orders and the loud 'pom-pom' sounds of the Bofors light anti-aircraft gun. When the wailing air raid siren woke us during the night we were not too dismayed as it was usually a false alarm and it meant that we could go to school later the following morning without being punished for it. If the all clear sounded after one o'clock in the morning we were allowed to start school at ten and if it was after three we didn't go until after dinner. Even in our little village the war was never far away and Harry said, "You should think yourselves lucky to be living here in safety and stop chuntering about everything." It was all right for him; he was living in luxury while we were always hungry and getting belted for next to nothing.

Over in Cyprus, Uncle John had been sent on a course for infantry officers and NCOs that involved field-firing exercises with men of the heavy artillery units. They had to learn communication methods and be able to work together in the desert. He told Gran later that, from time to time, bombs were dropped on the airfield by Italian aircraft and one day, just as local workmen and an engineer had completed the construction of a new runway, three bombs made huge craters in it. The Company Sergeant Major's tent was blown down by the blast and he was not amused, but Uncle John and his mates were.

At Larnaca there was a salt lake with a large Mosque on the far side and in their spare time Uncle John and some of the men paid it a visit. It was a magnificent place and they were shown round by a Muslim Cleric who gave them very strong, dark, thick, sweet coffee. The walls were hung with fine tapestries and exotic carpets and prayer mats covered the floor. Occasionally they went to the local cinema but most of the films were old ones that they had seen at home. They could walk a long way out on the gradually sloping beach and they 'skinny-dipped' at every opportunity in the clear, warm water. Rain fell on only one day in the three months they were there. They were paraded and inspected by General Sir Claude Auchinleck; a tough and tenacious Ulsterman, who was most impressed by the Brigade's progress and their general state of preparedness. He had been appointed Commander-in-Chief, Middle East, replacing General Wavell whom Churchill had relieved of his post following Rommel's astounding successes. In the first week of November they sailed, with their weapons and equipment, to Haifa in Palestine and in a coded letter to his mother, he said, "The place is full of lemons, grapefruit and big, juicy, Jaffa oranges that are very cheap to buy." They were almost unobtainable in this country.

At home, V for Victory signs began to appear on walls and doors, in windows, on the buses, in newspapers and magazines - in fact everywhere. The determined and pugnacious Winston Churchill, affectionately known to the people as Winnie, gave his famous palm-forward, two-fingered V sign whenever he appeared in public. It was all carefully designed to raise the morale of the people and to keep up their fighting bulldog spirit and, because of him, the British public never doubted that we would win in the end. The dark chilly nights started to draw in with more dull and rainy days and, if we were 'good,' we were allowed to stay up late to listen to the wireless on Thursday evening at 8.30 p.m. We had to promise to be quiet or else we would be sent 'up the wooden hill to bedfordshire'. The extremely popular fast paced comedy show 'I.T.M.A.' (It's That Man Again) was on for half an hour on the Forces Programme, having switched from the Home Service early in the war. The title had originally referred to Hitler but people thought it meant Tommy Handley and we soon came to know the signature tune played by the BBC Variety Orchestra and picked up all the catchphrases. Everyone in Haxby seemed to love the larger-than-life characters and their sayings. One of the much-loved characters was Fusspot, which was what Mrs Harris called me.

Sam Costa (as Flying Officer Kite) had a huge handlebar moustache and the airmen in the village said that it wasn't a proper moustache unless it could be seen from behind on the port and starboard sides. The character that sticks in my mind most was that mysterious and scary character called Funf, who was supposed to be a German spy. It was actually Jack Train speaking into an echoing empty tumbler and Mr Harris used to frighten us if we were talking or making too much noise in the bedroom, by shouting up the stairs " Watch out, Funf's coming!" Whenever we heard that and slow heavy footsteps on the stairs, we scurried into bed and hid our heads under the covers too scared to utter another word.

The call up age for men had been lowered to eighteen and a half years and at the other end of the age scale men up to fifty years of age were now eligible for military service. There was a drive for salvage, including jam jars, paper, scrap metal and the like and the people were told that it was to be recycled and used to make military vehicles, weapons and aeroplanes. The vast quantity of weapons and vehicles lost at Dunkirk had to be replaced and even old rags were pulped and used to make paper. Collection points were set up and we got a farthing for a jam jar and a ha'penny for a bottle, but they were not easy to come by.

The news was delivered in the comforting, authoritative, cultured tones of Alvar Liddell and Robert Dougall. They had recently announced that the Wehrmacht troops (the regular German Army) in spite of the Russians scorched earth policy, were at the gates of Moscow and thousands of Jews were being shot or sent to the camps as slave labourers. When the rains started the German vehicles got stuck in the mud and when the snows came they had to endure temperatures of minus 27 ° Fahrenheit (−15 ° C). Without winter clothing thousands of them froze to death. It was a war of attrition and the German offensive was grinding to a halt. They also announced that a German U-boat had sunk an American destroyer on convoy duty near Iceland with seventy sailors perishing

In North Africa the British and Commonwealth Forces had been reinforced and the Western Desert Force was now known as the Eighth Army. Operation 'Crusader was launched in late November (the Germans called it The Winter Battle) with a massive array of Allied tanks and men attacking the combined German and Italian forces. They were ably aided by the Desert Air Force which now controlled the skies but it was heavy going as the rains had turned parts of the desert into a quagmire and the guns got bogged down. The Allies had advanced forcing Rommel's army back to the Tobruk area, as the British air and naval forces operating out of Egypt and the island fortress of Malta had deprived him of the necessary supplies. His troops were short of food, fuel and ammunition but, although outnumbered three to one, Rommel had still managed to check the piecemeal and uncoordinated Allied thrusts. A cunning adversary, he had knocked out large numbers of Allied tanks and vehicles, but lost a third of his own force in the process.

Tobruk was relieved after being under siege for thirty-three long weeks and the top brass, wrongly, believed that they had won the war in North Africa and that one more push would give them Tripoli. In truth, it had been a close-run thing with confusion, lack of communication and out-dated tactics. Rommel knew how to deploy his tanks and he backed them up with infantry; on the other hand, the British were inclined to make headlong charges as though they were cavalry units fighting the Crimean War. The top brass still tended to treat tanks as if they were steel-plated horses and kept

308

charging headlong into the full force of the enemy. The Germans had 88mm anti-aircraft guns but they were using them as anti-tank weapons and they could knock out a tank at well over a mile. The Allies were losing too many men and battles from a position of strength and, after fighting bravely, Uncle John was to say later that the men were baffled at being thwarted so often. On that occasion most of Rommel's armoured units were destroyed but he lived to fight another day.

It was reported that the Luftwaffe had moved a whole Corps from the Russian front under the command of Field Marshal Kesselring and ferocious air attacks were now being made on Malta. The Germans knew that when Malta was strong the Axis forces in North Africa suffered. The island was the key to a sound strategic position for both sides, so the enemy sent more U and E-boats into the Mediterranean to cut off their supplies. A British battleship and a cruiser were sunk and an Italian U-boat torpedoed and sank the great British aircraft carrier HMS *Ark Royal*. Such grievous losses made it easier for the Axis war machine to deliver food, fuel, arms and men to Libya. The British lost command of both the air and the sea and Malta came under prolonged siege. The Allied land forces in North Africa were now scattered and stretched over long distances making supply that much more difficult.

On the 7th of December the US Pacific Fleet laying at anchor in Pearl Harbour, Hawaii was devastated in a surprise attack by over three hundred Japanese' warplanes that flew in at speed, sinking many ships, and killing 3,000 servicemen. The USA and the British Commonwealth responded by declaring war on Japan and Germany and Italy declared war on the USA. It was now a worldwide conflict. Three days later the Japs sank two British ships off the coast of Malaya; one of them being the cruiser HMS *Repulse* which had been part of the convoy that had escorted Uncle John on his long voyage to Egypt.

While the desert battles were taking place, Uncle John's battalion of some seven to eight hundred men had been camped at Jalama, in British-controlled Palestine. They were based inland from Haifa in a lovely jasmine-scented setting close to the foot of Mount Carmel but there were malarial mosquitoes everywhere and they had to use mepacrine everyday. At night the bed legs had to be stood in pots of paraffin to protect the men from the stings of the akrebah (giant centipedes that were up to six inches long). On November 16th the Padre, Captain Burns Jamieson hired a bus to take them on a tour of the Holy places mentioned in the Bible. Uncle John told Gran that they visited Cana - the hill on which Jesus had fed the five thousand - and Nazareth, Mary's Well, and the Sea of Galilee (Lake Tiberius). Climbing up from Tiberius the fan belt of the bus broke and the driver had to reverse down before using a silk stocking in its place and the men were relieved to get back to camp. It was a wonderful day out that he was to remember for the rest of his life.

As not much transport was available, marching and climbing formed a large part of their training, and as Uncle John and the others prepared for battle they became superbly fit and hard. The sun bleached his hair and turned his skin nut-brown and one night they were marched to Nazareth, rested and marched back the following morning, and he had to hook his thumbs through the straps of his heavy backpack to take the strain off his aching shoulders. They finished off with an extremely strenuous exercise on the slopes of the 1800 feet (546m.) high Mount Carmel that really toughened them up. They were now at the stage of refitting with guns, vehicles, mortars, Bren guns, wirelesses, signalling equipment and the like as a German drive through the Balkans was in full swing. They were expecting to be sent to the Caucasus Mountain region of Iraq and Persia (now Iran). Other units of the 50th Northumbrian Division had gone to Iraq taking the best of the weapons with them, which meant that the 4th and 5th Battalions of the Green Howards were left with the inferior stuff.

This was the state of things at the end of November when they were ordered to leave Palestine and move to the Western Desert. Boarding an old steam train, they left at 04.30 hours and arrived at Kantara twelve hours later, but the heat of the day and the hard wooden seats did not make for a comfortable journey. After a wash, a meal of bully beef and potatoes and a smoke they set off again, arriving at the huge base camp of Amryha (just outside Alexandria) at 08.30 hours where they spent a week before setting out on yet another uncomfortable and wearisome journey to join the Eighth Army. There were rumours of an advance to Benghazi, and possibly beyond and in the bivouac area at Bagguish they dug holes in the stony sand and laid camouflaged sheeting over them. The weather was appallingly cold as they lay huddled up in their woollen balaclavas and greatcoats while torrential rain flooded their holes. The blackness of the desert sky was lit up for several seconds at a stretch by sheet lightning and Uncle John said had never seen such spectacular electric storms.

Three days before Christmas they moved west again on the military railway line that ran through Mersa Matruh. They pitched camp at Bir Thalata, a desolate spot in the desert some fifty miles east of the Egyptian-Libyan frontier and, as Uncle John sat in his hole in the ground, he could see the smoke from the locomotives bringing up more and more supplies beyond the ridge. Here they spent Christmas with the padre and the cooks making a special effort to give them a pleasant time and even though real Christmas fare was not available, they did their best. The squally weather, the sandstorms and the high winds didn't help matters but they were now ready for active service and their spirits were raised on hearing that Benghazi had been retaken.

From mid December onwards snow fell at Haxby and the ground was covered in an unbroken white sheet. We brushed the snow from our clothes, which were becoming threadbare, patched and shabby by this time, and watched as it scattered on the icy wind. Single women and childless widows between the ages of twenty and thirty were now being called up into the armed forces or they could choose to work in the factories. As another Christmas approached we were kept busy at school drawing greetings cards and hanging decorations that we had made from strips of coloured card and paper. We enjoyed the school Nativity play, the carol singing and the school Christmas party, where we played games and made right pigs of ourselves.

Just before we broke up for the festive season we were gathered together and a hush fell as Mr Fox entered the room as we were in awe of him and felt constrained in his presence. The assembled children were told of great changes that were soon to take place and we were given a letter in a sealed envelope. As I hopped and skipped up Usher Lane the glittering, frozen snow that crackled under my feet, sounded as if I was treading on cornflakes. There was a spring in my step and by the time I reached 'Lenmuir' it was snowing heavily again with the fat swirling flakes bringing the promise of a white Christmas. It was my first at Haxby and, to my delight, that promise was fulfilled.

The Government tried to make things a little easier over the Christmas and New Year period by relaxing the strict rationing of certain foods. The details were printed in the Food Facts section of the newspapers, food flashes were shown on the silver screen at the Wiggy Rec and leaflets explaining the changes were sent to every household. In December a 'points' system for foods that were scarce but not rationed was introduced to prevent food being bought up in huge quantities by the well off. A set number of points per month were allocated but it still had to be paid for.

Ever-smiling Mam, whose love was boundless and unconditional, came to see me on Christmas Eve, which was on a Wednesday that year and she blushed like a peony when Mr Harris gave her a kiss under the mistletoe that hung over the kitchen door. She must have left a present for me with Mrs Harris when I wasn't looking. She was sorry to go but she had to be with George on Christmas Day. The next morning I ripped the brown wrapping paper from my present in great anticipation, not thinking about the difficulty Mam had probably experienced in getting it, and we had a nice Christmas dinner as Harold Mann had killed one of his chickens for us. As a special treat at teatime, Mr Harris roasted the chestnuts that he had collected earlier. Putting them on a shovel, we watched them jumping and splitting as he held it over the fire and we thoroughly enjoyed their hot, sweet taste.

Over the past year a fine new school, called the Joseph Rowntree Secondary Modern, had been built. All those over twelve, or who were to become twelve in the present school year, were to go there and it meant that our Harry, Harold Mann's son, Brian, and thirty-five other children from Haxby and Wigginton would be amongst its first intake of a hundred and fifty pupils. Their departure meant there would be room for the older infants of the two villages, including me, to move up to the 'big' school.

15. Early 1942

The new school was on the eastern side of York Road about a mile and a half from the village centre south of the Hilbra railway crossing and it became known locally as the 'Joe Row' (pronounced Joe-Roe) school. The school managers present at the simple opening ceremony included Stephen Rowntree, the highly respected third son of Joseph Rowntree, the founder of the famous chocolate firm. The family had been generous benefactors in the area for close on a century. The ceremony took place at 9.30 a.m. on the twelfth of January which marked the start of the new spring term as the holiday had been extended to save on fuel and the smart up-to-date canteen served hot meals for the first time.

Harry, Peter and Brian Mann were surprised at the size of the school that was made up of large, red brick, two-storey, flat-roofed buildings. They felt a bit lost in the long corridors that were lined with modern classrooms that had one side made up of glass and wood that reached to the ceiling. There was row upon row of new wooden, lidded-desks and they had had a different teacher for each subject, whereas at Haxby they had had the same teacher for every lesson. The school had a well-stocked library, a separate assembly hall and a dining room. The emphasis was on practical skills and there were large rooms and laboratories for science subjects. There were facilities for woodwork and metalwork and they even had their own forge. The girls, who all wore black gymslips, had practical cookery classes using modern ovens and the older girls even cooked the joints for the school dinners. In those days it was accepted that a woman's place was in the kitchen and they had needlework rooms stocked with the latest Singer sewing machines.

There is no one to equal children in the speed with which they make friends and Harry made pals easily. His best pal, Peter Beresford, was nearly two years younger than him. He lived in one of the large semi-detached houses on Hilbra Avenue and his maternal uncle, Bill Clark, was a close friend of Harry's next door neighbour, Max Danby. Bill's oldest son, Alan, was in the class below me at the church hall and his dad, who had joined the Royal Engineers in early 1940, was posted to Gibraltar and then India where he drove convoy lorries. Harry was a close friend of Max's son, Geoff, and they were always round at each other's houses. When the Misses Law and Barker had to go away for a few days Harry stayed with the Danbys.

The pair of gentle spinster ladies had bought Harry a good second-hand, three-speed bicycle with a Sturmey Archer hub gear that ticked over quietly when he freewheeled. It was his pride and joy and he oiled it and cleaned it till it gleamed. I would often see him with the bike nonchalantly propped up against his thighs, as he stood with a crowd of girls around him. The bike boasted an enclosed chain guard and had a small leather saddlebag with a puncture repair kit in it and every morning he called for Peter and they rode down York Road in all weathers. During the first few weeks in the new school the cold was so intense that it hurt to breathe and Harry's gloves sometimes froze on to the handle grips. Snow fell and lay, often to a depth of several inches and on the way home the boys had to avert their faces and squint their eyes to avoid the needles of snow blown on by the strong, vindictive, north easterly winds.

As the sharp frosts and snowy weather persisted, I was delighted at the prospect of starting life in the 'big' school with the others. As we trooped along the snow-covered roads, the bushes and the gossamer-like spiders' webs were white with hoarfrost. By the time we got there our fingers were blue and our noses were red but even in the classroom it was bitterly cold with ice on the inside of the windowpanes. Our fingers hurt as the blood gradually flowed back into them and it took a long time for the coke-fired boilers to feed hot water through the pipes to the green, cast iron radiators. I was pleased to learn that I would still be in Miss Francis's class; a teacher whose smiling demeanour and friendly tone of voice brought a touch of warmth and sunshine to those wintry days. Several teachers had stayed for only short spells and being with her for another year ensured some continuity.

The very tall windows of the high-roofed, Victorian classroom looked out onto the snow-covered playground and the crumbling bricks of the bike shed. The wooden sills, which were about four feet (1.25 m.) from the ground, had been designed to prevent schoolchildren, like us, from seeing out and thus being distracted. The small glass windowpanes were, of course, criss-crossed with the ubiquitous brown anti-blast tape and their upper parts were opened by means of the long white cords that hung from them. We sat on the bench part of the old wooden desks that had been made shiny by generations of shuffling bottoms. The lids were covered with scratches, graffiti and ink blotches left by countless village children; many of them now parents and grandparents themselves.

There had been an influx of several 'new' children into our class as the formidable Miss Curry told us that Singapore had fallen to the 'Japs' on Christmas Day. Most of them had been attending the tiny school in Wigginton, but due to increasing numbers of evacuees, a few had been having their lessons in the Minister's vestry or in the corners of the old Wesleyan Methodist Chapel. This elegant, sixty years old, Byzantine-style, stone building was on an open area known as the 'The Butt Stees' and it stood between the two villages on land bought from Henry Driffield, the brick and tile manufacturer. One of the new lads was John Wade, who was a month older than me. He had lived with his parents on Cannon Street, Middlesbrough, prior to the war and his relatives lived next door but one to Great Grandma Knights. He had been among the first evacuees sent here.

He was a cheerful lad with a round, red, moon-like face and he now sat next to me and we became good pals. I showed him how to do pencil sketches of spitfires and soldiers in uniform, as drawing was one of the few things that I was good at; apart from chattering and laughing, which tended to land us in trouble. As we crouched over our ink splotched, penknife-etched desks, John said, "I were billeted with t'Allinson family at seventeen Front Street, Wigginton when ah first came 'ere yer know. Their owld, three-bedroomed, terraced 'ouse had a firtree in t'corner of its small front garden that were right easy ter climb. We walked t't'house from t'railway station when we came 'ere at start o't'war. The people 'ad t'choice of billeting RAF lads or us evacuees and Mr and Mrs Allinson kindly took me in. They were a 'appy and 'ard working family with two kids. That were eight year old, Bernard, and baby, Pauline, who were only about ten months old."

I was green with envy when he had told me, "Bernard had a real Meccano set and an electric, model-train set an all. It 'ad two engines, carriages, goods wagons, stations, tunnels and tracks. One o' t' engines were a glossy green 'Flying Scotsman' and it were all laid out on t'floor of his big bedroom." 'How lucky could you get?' I thought. "Mr Allinson worked at gas works on t'outskirts of York an 'e pedalled to work every day on an old 'push-bike'. When he were not at work, 'e spent a lot of 'is spare time working in 'is two gardens. One of 'em were directly be'ind t'house and t'other were on t'lane that led down t't' church. 'E were allus busy so I didn't see him all that much."

"Through a gate at t'bottom o' their back garden, after passing t'outside toilet, was a big field that 'ad a pond and a small brick building in it," he continued. "Next door, in t'first house, were t'Fletchers and they 'ad a fair amount o' land an all. Mr Fletcher, were just a little fella. 'E were a butcher and a farmer and 'is parents 'ave lived and farmed there since before t'turn o't'century. They 'ad a butcher's shop and a barn that were full of straw and hay bales. Me and t'lads from next door used ter make dens in it. They 'ad a cow byre where they milked t'cows by 'and we played in t'fields for 'ours an 'ours." He was a right chatterbox and I couldn't get a word in edgeways. He told me that the Fletcher's two sons, who were young men at the time, worked on the farm. John said he enjoyed helping them out by putting the beet and turnips into the opening at the top of the shredder while one of them turned the handle. The Fletchers had two young evacuees from Middlesbrough who had a brother in lodgings in Haxby. At a later date one of them was taken seriously ill and was taken into York County Hospital but when his mother was informed she refused to come, stating that she 'did not wish to know'. John told me that during the snowy days of early 1940, he and Bernard had built a real igloo in the corner of the yard and had sat snugly inside in the glow of a lighted candle.

Robbie Smith, who repaired church organs, lived next door to him and in the white cottage at the end of the terrace lived the Howards who had yet another six years old Middlesbrough girl called Lily McManus billeted with them. John had been pleased when his sister, Sheila, who was three years older than him, was billeted just three doors away. Across the road was the *Black Horse* public house and at the end of the block was Tom Midgeley's Manor Farm. Their son, Brian, was now attending the 'Joe Row' school with our Harry and the others.

John was moved another three times before he came to Haxby School and was now living with Mr and Mrs Charlie Dixon and their daughter, Enid, at Holme Farm. This was a smallholding just west of the Co-op store and his sister and six other evacuees, one of whom was Dot Sirman's brother, Ray, were billeted there. He said that Mrs Dixon was really nice and was very kind to him and he often helped Mr Dixon, to 'muck out t' osses'. Charlie was fat and strict and did not have a regular job. The Shaws, who lived on North Lane behind the *Red Lion*, kept their horse and cart in the rented yard behind the Dixon's house and used it to collect the domestic waste. John said, "Mrs Dixon treats me really well. A nicer person yer couldn't wish ter meet. She works five days a week as a domestic servant and cleaner for Mr Butterfield. One of my regular chores is ter collect three copies o't'evening newspaper from Torville's shop and tek 'em t't' Butterfield's, Dixon's and their friend Mrs Lee. Ah do odd jobs for Mrs Butterfield from time ter time, such as sorting out logs for t'fire."

At the end of the month I was delighted when Mam and Dad came to see me. She told me that she had replaced Dinner Lady who had given up her post as cook. Dad had managed to get a forty-eight hour leave pass and they wrapped Jimmy and me in newly knitted, warm, woollen scarves and balaclavas and holding our woollen-mitted hands, they took us through the snow-covered village. They spoiled us rotten, buying us cakes, small toys, sweets and comics from Torville's, Thompson's and Jefferson's shops. Dad was wearing his khaki gloves and had his thick greatcoat on and I felt so proud to be his eldest son and to be seen out in the village with him. I was tender and very sensitive around the ribs and Dad, knowing this, tickled me until I almost wet myself with laughter. He repeatedly threw me up into the air and caught me in his strong arms after Jimmy and I had bombarded him with snowballs. When he laughed his whole face lit up.

He was proud of his regiment and its badge - a side view of a large-wheeled cannon - was tattooed on the bulging biceps of his right arm. He told us tales of the tigers, the elephants, the monkeys and the panthers he had seen in India and said that they had employed local 'boys' (called 'dhobiwallers') to do their washing and cleaning. I thought that Mam, although her cheeks were lightly rouged, looked rather tense and pale but the strain of the war left many people feeling run-down and anxious and children are quick to pick up on those things.

Whenever they came to see us - even when Mrs Harris knew in advance - they were never offered a meal and were unable to stay overnight. We had so much to say, and the time fled, and all too soon it was time for them to leave, as they had to catch the red, number ten, double-decker bus back to York Station. I turned away with my heart breaking after yet another sad and touching farewell. My lip started to tremble and the tears rose unbidden and I tried to take my mind off them by taking my newly bought *Beano* comic up to our cold bedroom. I tried to immerse myself in the adventures of Big Eggo the ostrich, Pansy Potter the strong man's daughter, Lord Snooty, Tommy the tin can boy, and Herman the German. The latter, of course, was a caricature of Goering, but it didn't work! As someone once said, 'happiness unalloyed is not for sentient beings' and I could not get the thoughts of Mam and Dad out of my head. I huddled under the bedclothes with my knees up to my chin shaking and crying my eyes out. I felt so alone and homesick and the snow falling from a leaden sky reflected my feelings.

After my tears were spent I looked out of the window to see that the back garden was thickly blanketed in pure virgin snow and large, fluffy flakes were coming straight down before twisting and swirling around close to the ground. The falling snow, that looked like smoke being blowing about on eddies of cold air, fascinated me. It settled softly on the skeletal twigs and branches of every tree and shrub and heaped itself up on top of the trelliswork and the garden fences. It piled up on the clothesline making it look like a thick white rope or a ship's hawser. It formed large white pompons on the skeletal remains of the hydrangea flowerheads so that they looked like white lollipops or white woollen balls on long sticks. Composing myself, I dried my eyes and rushed downstairs eager to play in it. Such is the resilience of childhood! Great clods of soft fresh snow clung to the soles of my shoes making them seem like deep-sea divers' boots. The sky was the colour of slate and we played out in it till teatime and it was dark before six o'clock.

In early February the cold was so intense that, much to our delight, the school was closed for two weeks. The antiquated heating and water pipes had frozen solid and when a thaw came they burst causing floods. On those bitterly cold and frosty days the thickly lying snow became ice-encrusted and in some places the wind had formed it into weird shapes. The top layer froze and overhung looking like waves about to break and the dormant stems of the cow parsley were snow-capped. The ploughed fields were like corrugated iron under their blanket of snow and there was a thick layer of ice on Mr Harris' rain butt. We spent a good deal of our time enjoying the unexpected extra holiday up on the icy slopes by the windmill pond, where the rusty, metal vanes of the old irrigation pump groaned and creaked forlornly as they swung to and fro in the icy wind. We sat on old tin trays and slid down the steep inclines keeping our feet raised off the ground. As our giggles and screams of pleasure were carried through the thin icy air we were completely lost to everything. Nothing else mattered and we wished that it would never end.

In that silent frosted world the little birds suffered; but they weren't the only ones. Our cold noses, nipping fingers and frozen mittens eventually drove us back indoors and, once inside, we got a clout round the lugs for getting our clothes wet. At other times we got lashed on the legs with the thin cane that Mrs Harris selected from her growing collection of implements of punishment, which she appeared to enjoy wielding. The canes and belts that hung on the wooden strut supporting the kitchen cabinet were a constant visual threat. If we did not settle down quickly at bedtime she would shout up the stairs, "Get to sleep or you'll feel the belt around your backsides!" There seemed to be no warmth or affection in her and we were being thrashed more and more often.

On going back to school our sleep was often disturbed by the deep throbbing sounds of low flying British bombers, while at other times it was the mournful wailing of the banshee-like air raid siren that shattered our rest. It often startled us into full wakefulness in the middle of the night but, fortunately, most of the warnings turned out to be false alarms or the enemy planes were nowhere near us.

The small bedroom fires were never lit and on bitterly cold mornings we often got dressed under the bedclothes with our teeth chattering. We had learned from bitter experience not to put our bare feet on the cold brown lino. The lack of sleep left us sleepy and lethargic in school, which did not make for much progress. With the teachers overstrained, harassed and numbed by anxiety, it was not exactly an ideal situation but, after being up half the night, we tended to be quieter and less boisterous. Even so, the village school with its rigid and stultifying syllabus appeared to Jimmy and me to be the most stable part of our tottering world. We felt safe there surrounded by the other children and our teachers.

The newspapers reported that things were not going well for the Allied Forces in North Africa and 'the Med'. Malta was under constant attack by enemy aircraft based in Sicily. As a result, the British air bases were not able to mount attacks on Axis shipping and men, food, fuel, ammunition, weapons and tanks were now getting through to reinforce the Germans in Tripoli. The conflict had died down and for a time there was only sporadic fighting as both sides built up their supplies and prepared for the next offensive. However, earlier lessons had not been learned and the mistakes were being repeated with disastrous consequences.

Uncle John's unit was ordered to rejoin the rest of the division presently in Iraq and they were put on five hours notice to move there, but, just as they were ready to do so, the order was reversed and they were given four hours notice to move west into Libya. The situation around Benghazi was causing the Allied troops to fall back. His unit made an exhausting one hundred and twenty-mile drive through a severe sandstorm and heavy rain to Bir Harmat, which was about thirty miles south west of Tobruk, and twenty-four hours later they received their first anti-tank guns. During the daylight hours Uncle John went out on Bren gun carriers to reconnoitre and at night he led patrols out to view the situation and harass the enemy. He found it difficult to tell which were Allied troops and which were Germans, as many of the enemy were driving around in British vehicles captured in the recent fighting. Rommel himself - having taken them from a dead soldier - wore British desert goggles that he preferred to the German ones. Water was carried in two-gallon (nine litre) petrol cans painted white with each man allowed one gallon a day. A German Warrant Officer, lost in the desert, became the Brigade's first prisoner.

Rommel went on the offensive again, and the Allies were again taken by surprise. In a three-day running battle his troops routed the British 1st Armoured Division and the Allied troops retreated after suffering heavy losses of men, tanks and vehicles. At the end of the month, Rommel retook the port of Benghazi. His tactics were superior to those of the Allies and it was one of 'The Desert Fox's' most brilliant campaigns. Hitler was so pleased that he promoted him to the rank of Colonel General, the second highest rank in the German Army. Things had gone wrong yet again and the Allies, dispirited after going through so much with little to show for it, withdrew to the Gazala area. The people at home - wanting to hear that the war was being won - found yet another humiliating reversal hard to bear.

It was nice to have a new friend at school and John Wade told me that in the autumn of 1940 he had contracted impetigo and had been put in an isolation 'unit' in a bungalow near the Hilbra railway crossing. "It all started when I got blisters round me mouth and behind me ears," he said. "They 'ad 'orrible, yeller scabs on 'em. I 'ad ter 'ave loads of 'ot baths and they put green and violet stuff on me. They dabbed me blisters with mercury ointment until t'ard crusts went. When I got better I went ter live with Mrs Longhurst in North Lane." Her bungalow was behind the Haxby 'Co-op', which had a wooden post high up on its rear wall from which a rope and pulley system hung. It was used to lift the traditional ten stone sacks of flour and sugar up to a door on the upper floor. John said, "Mrs Longhurst's husband were away in t'forces and she 'ad a daughter, Sylvia, and twin girls at 'ome. I were well treated but I weren't there long. I were taken in by t'Smith family who 'ad come 'ere from Croft Street in Middlesbrough."

Gran told me that Croft Street was only two streets from Laws Street where Mam and Dad were now living having exchanged houses a year back. Mrs Smith, who was a widow with a glamorous twenty-year-old, daughter, Alma, had rented the large brick, house called 'Rose Cottage', which had a red pantiled roof and stood in the corner of Haxby Green. It looked out on the 'Coronation' bench and the tall, copper beech tree, which had been planted at the time of the Coronation of George V in 1911.

Haxby Green in 2002.

Next door to it, but facing east, was another large brick building called Prospect House that belonged to a quiet and very private middle-aged couple called Wilson. Behind it there were barns, outbuildings and extensive fields and John told me that Mr Fred Wilson, the owner, had befriended him. He often took him into York on the high front seat of his old horse-drawn stagecoach, which made him the envy of every child in Haxby. We often saw him perched on the driver's bench and my imaginations ran riot as I pictured it being chased across the Nevada Desert by Red Indians led by Cochise, the chief of the tribe, who wore a magnificent, feathered head-dress and rode bareback as he fired arrows into it. The coach had curtains at the windows, gracefully curving shafts and tall, wooden-spoked wheels, with the front ones smaller than the back. Sometimes we played at being masked and caped highwaymen with pistols like Dick Turpin who Miss Francis said had been kept in a cell at York Prison while waiting to be hanged.

Mr Wilson, a man of very few words, used the coach to deliver goods to York and to collect tubs of pigswill on the way back.

It may well have been the coach once driven by Tom Holtby, an enterprising and colourful character of old Haxby, whose house still stood. He had been a driver on the York to Doncaster leg of the London to Edinburgh stagecoach but the coming of the railways put the coaches out of business and he became a horse-breaker in York. On coming to Haxby, he bought a large house and the land behind it on the eastern side of York Road where he set up a brick and tile-making venture that failed. It was taken over by the Driffield family and in their hands it thrived for many years. Tom now lies at rest in St Mary's graveyard.

John said, "In the autumn I 'elped Mr Wilson to pick and bag spuds. He'd turn out a few rows with 'is fork on t'land at back of his 'ouse or in t'field 'e owned at back o't'owld chapel. He gave me a thrupenny bit (1¼p) or a silver tanner (2½p) each time." It seems Mr Wilson had taken a liking to him and he enjoyed doing jobs like helping to pick and store his apples and pears on sacking in the loft of his barn. By a strange coincidence, Nancy and Sylvia Robson, the two little girls who had been at The Settlement', Sutherland Lodge and Grove House with George and me, were billeted with the Smiths when John was there.

I loved to hear Vera Lynn singing and when her programme, 'Sincerely Yours', was on the BBC Forces Service we were allowed to listen as long as we stayed quiet. Between her poignant songs she read out messages of love and affection from the wives, husbands, sweethearts and boyfriends of people in the forces. When war broke out she had been a vocalist with the Ambrose Orchestra and her lovely voice and sincerity of delivery helped to link those far away with their loved ones at home. Her moving rendition of *Yours* was the signature tune of the show that had first come on the air in November 1941 and it became an instant hit. She was affectionately known as 'The Forces Sweetheart' and, later in the war, she was to entertain the troops here and in Burma as part of the Forces ENSA organisation. Entertaining the troops counted as war service but with so many to entertain the talent was stretched pretty thin. Some wags said it stood for 'Every Night Something Awful'.

Between early February and late May there was a lull in the ground fighting in Libya but the aerial skirmishes and the observation of troop movements from the air continued. The Allied troops disguised their trucks, weapons and ammunition dumps under netting with brown, yellow and grey patches - the colours of the desert. Behind their lines both sides were busily building up supplies and making repairs. After two or three days the 150th Brigade withdrew to Bir Hacheim (meaning 'The Well of Dogs') on the southern end of the defensive line that ran north to El Gazala on the coast forty miles to the west of Tobruk. The Axis forces had been well supplied and reinforced and air superiority changed hands yet again.

Uncle John was still leading patrols, mostly comprised of young, inexperienced men, in to the austere and arid desert where there were no landmarks. He was not yet twenty-three, but compared to them, he was a seasoned campaigner. The patrols usually lasted four days and there was the constant fear of getting lost with only sand-filled barrels with numbers painted on them as aids to navigation. In the shimmering heat haze, he experienced mirages with close objects becoming reduced in size and seemingly dancing, quivering and floating above shimmering lakes. At night it turned bitterly cold and there was utter silence, but they could not light a fire in case the enemy spotted it. The sand particles carried by the keen winds cut like a knife as they dozed fitfully under a black sky thronged with bright glittering stars. As they slept on the ground by 'sangars' (low mounds of rock) or beside a lorry under a bivouac sheet, the only consolation was the temporary relief from the flies and scorpions. They wore their great coats and scarves on top of their salt-coated, sun-bleached KD, that consisted of shorts, a shirt, woollen socks and low cut suede, rubber soled, desert boots that they called 'brothel creepers'. They stood-to at first light and as the sun rose, the mica particles of the sand shone and glittered. Their hair was matted and they were covered in a film of fine sand, dust and grit that got into the corners of their eyes and their mouths and caught in their throats. Shortage of water meant they became accustomed to being dirty and plagued by sand fleas.

After the war Uncle John told us that, "The sun was a huge red orb as it rose above the flat featureless horizon and the sky was turned crimson by the irradiation of the thousands of floating sand and dust particles. The people back home had no conception of the hardships we had to endure. The chemical-tasting, chlorinated water, used for making a 'brew' or getting washed, was strictly rationed and the staple diet was bully beef and 'hard tack'. These were about four inches square by one inch thick and looked and tasted like large dog biscuits. During the day the heat was unbearable but, if we were lucky enough to get an egg, we fried it on the scorching metal plating of a tank. We were sick to death of 'bully beef' but we heard that 'The Desert Fox' and his men loved it. We were homesick and longed for the rain and the clean cool air of home. We dreamed of hot water, a change of clothes and beds with cool, clean white sheets, and the mail from home was eagerly looked forward to. Many messages of endearment and words of love and affection arrived in those small, blue, airmail letters."

"In mid February Free French troops, with units of the Foreign Legion amongst them, took over the Bir Hacheim position," he continued. "They were armed with machine guns, which were not much use against tanks. Brigadier Haydon's 150th Brigade was moved further north between the Trigh Capuzzo and the Trigh El Abd desert tracks formed by thousands of camel trains. They were four miles apart and ran from east to west. Our 4th and 5th Battalions formed defensive strongpoints, called 'boxes', which measured about two miles in diameter and had barbed wire entanglements, bunkers, listening posts and a few tanks. On the day we arrived, we were shelled by the enemy. There was a Polish Brigade to our right and the 4th Indian Brigade on our left. The Poles were brave fighters and most of them had escaped when their country was invaded. Many of them had been weak and starving when they were released from camps in Siberia after Germany attacked Russia, but they had made there own way down the Volga to join General Anders army. Divisions of the 50th Northumbrian Brigade that had been hurriedly brought back from Iraq soon replaced them and I supervised the men as they dug trenches, infantry posts and gun pits with picks and shovels. Where it was too rocky, the sappers (Royal Engineers) came in with hydraulic drills and explosives. The enemy often bombarded us as we constructed our immense minefields and when we went out on infantry and artillery patrols to cover the gaps between the 'mine marshes', as they were called."

The Gazala line was one of the technical marvels of the war with wide minefields that extended southwards for forty miles from the 'Med' to Bir Hacheim on a scale never seen before. More than a million mines were laid but the problem was - they did not encircle the defensive 'boxes'. It was considered not to be necessary. Uncle John and his mates celebrated his twenty-third birthday in a hole in the ground by acquiring some sausages which they fried on a 'Benghazi Burner' made by pouring a cup full of petrol into a can that had been cut in half and filled with sand before lighting it. The other half was used as a frying pan.

Back in Haxby, Jimmy and I were quite pleased to hear that the Government was urging people to bathe less often. People were not to use more than five inches (12cms.) of warm water and to share. This suited us, as, like most kids, we would not get washed if we could get away with it. It annoyed us when Mrs Harris roughly rubbed our faces and knees with a wet flannel before we went to bed, calling our efforts 'cat-licks'. She used to line us up and say "Hold your hands out," before inspecting the backs and the palms. We never had toothpaste, we used powdered stuff that came in a small round tin but most of the time, we just rubbed salt or soot on our teeth and gums with our fingers.

Every Saturday after tea we were put in the bath in pairs for a 'soap-all-over job', using a block of green carbolic soap and the same water as the two before us, thus ensuring that we were clean for church the next day. As I stripped off Jimmy often got me mad by calling me 'tin ribs' or 'skinny-banana-legs'. More hot water was added when the next pair climbed in and the water became blacker and blacker. Soap was now rationed to a three-ounce (85g.) bar a month and soap powder was in short supply. Before bed on school days we were given a rub - including our legs - and in the morning a wash - excluding legs. More often than not, during the daytime, we were given a quick rub here and there with a bit of spit on the corner of Mrs Harris' faded pinny, the pattern of which had almost disappeared due to the number of times it had been washed.

Quite often we deliberately avoided a wash by getting sent to bed early for squabbling or being cheeky.

The news of the Allies efforts in the war continued to be disappointing and people were tired of hearing reports of defeats and failures. It was to be many years later that I learned that many of the bombing raids over Germany were unsuccessful unless it was a clear moonlit night, as our aircraft navigation systems were inferior to those of the Luftwaffe. In adverse weather conditions, when the targets were obscured by cloud, the bombs often landed nowhere near the targets. The fast German battle cruisers, *Scharnhorst* and *Gneisenau* were a threat to our shipping convoys. Miss Curry told us that, on February 12th in appalling weather conditions they had managed to break out of Brest harbour. Even though it was daylight there was mist, sleet and rain and they had slipped up the English Channel and through the narrow straits of Dover into the North Sea right under the noses of the shore batteries. Fortunately, they were slightly damaged by floating mines, which the Navy called 'vegetables'. Many of them had been dropped over the last year or so, and around this time the United States 8th Bomber Command arrived in this country but they were not ready to carry out bombing missions until August.

At the half term break I was over the moon when Mam visited me again and I was so excited when she came towards me along the ice-covered garden path. Picking her way carefully past the dead, blackened stalks and the frosted seed heads of last summer's flowers, her shy smile on seeing me warmed me through, reaffirming that special bond that exists between a mother and son. Whenever I set eyes on her my heart sang and my unhappiness was forgotten for a while. Mam was reserved and shy in nature and inclined to blush easily and it appears that she had no suspicions concerning Mrs Harris' sly and nasty ways. She was so trusting of people and, believing in the nobility of the human spirit, she believed that there was goodness in everyone. She said, "We must learn to take the rough with the smooth. Life is full of ups and downs and you must know the bitter to appreciate the sweet."

We had been told never to say that anything was wrong and we were too frightened to tell the truth as Mrs Harris always seemed to be hovering close by when relatives visited. I didn't get the chance to tell Mam about the beltings or of the way she treated us. I wanted to tell her of how we often lay in bed covering our ears to shut out her angry raised voice as she shouted at and belittled her long-suffering husband.

By mid March, when a thaw set in, the snow turned to slush and the tyres of Harry, Brian and Peter's bikes swish-swished through the puddles on the wet roads on their way to school. There were very few motor cars for them to worry about as most people went about on bikes at that time. Cycling to and from school the boys often saw Italian prisoners-of- war at work in the now piebald fields.

On a chilly, blustery Saturday afternoon, Harry met up with his young pal, Peter, and with him was his lively eleven years old pal, Derek Robinson, who lived only three doors from him. They cycled up to Wigginton and along Corban Lane into a strong headwind. After a couple of miles they then turned left onto the A19 trunk road by the old, sandstone-built, parish church at Shipton and then right onto a minor road that led to the large airfield on the western edge of Linton-on-Ouse. They had come about eight miles in the hope of seeing one of the mighty Halifax bombers at close range. They caught a whiff of high-octane aviation fuel as a petrol bowser chugged past on the concrete of the perimeter track heading towards one of the Whitley bombers that had served so valiantly since the start of the war.

As slate-grey clouds scurried by above the control tower and the five, large, C-type hangars, the station windsock was fully extended. Nearby they could see the camouflaged, square shaped, flat-roofed, brick buildings and they got quite excited on seeing a long, fat, cigar-shaped bomb on a long trolley being pulled along by a tractor. It was heading towards a huge Halifax bomber that stood on its dispersal pad not far from where they stood peering through the wire of the perimeter fence. An RAF truck pulled up with a squeal of its brakes and a sergeant pilot and his crew of six climbed down. They were all wearing fur-lined boots, thermally heated Irwin jackets, leather helmets from which oxygen masks hung, and inflatable life jackets called Mae Wests, named after a popular, large-busted US film actress of the time.

The airmen clambered up a metal ladder into the fuselage of the waiting bomber. From the cockpit, the pilot gave a 'thumbs up' signal to the aircraft electricians who plugged in a 'starter trolley-acc' (a set of electric accumulators on a wheeled, wooden cart) just as heavy drops of rain began to plop onto the ground. The four mighty engines seemed to hesitate before spluttering, then bursting into life one after the other. The spinning airscrews looked like huge, shimmering, silver discs as the deep-throated roar was torn away on the slipstream. Great puffs of smoke and blue flashes of flame from the exhaust cowlings showed up clear and bright in the gathering gloom. As the pilot opened the throttle a little the great aircraft seemed to tremble. Rainwater streamed from the trailing edge of the wings and the expanse of deep lush grass behind it was blown flat. The ground crew then dragged away the wooden wheel chocks by heaving on the long ropes attached to them.

The mighty Bristol Hercules engines settled and ran more smoothly as they warmed up and the great bomber moved out onto the shiny, rain-wet perimeter track. An RAF fire tender stood by with its headlights hooded as the plane taxied to the end of the long, arrow-straight runway that disappeared into the mist. As the pilot opened the throttle the engines juddered and gave out loud throaty growls as the power burst forth in a series of great surges. They waited for the green flash of light from the chequered caravan, which showed up brightly in the fading light. The ground trembled and the air reverberated as the harnessed energy was released and the mighty Halifax rumbled along the wet, rubber-streaked tarmac sending spray up from its tyres as it picked up speed. The three boys stood open mouthed in awe as the thundering plane lifted off and slowly banked to port. The undercarriage was raised just before the black and sinister-looking clouds swallowed her up.

On their return journey the boys were glad to have the strong cold wind behind them as the rain lashed down on their inadequately clad bodies. They pedalled past the *College Arms*, a watering hole' for the local airmen, as fast and as urgently as they could. The snow that had only recently melted had saturated the fields, and the lads pushed on through a dank, misty, rain-sodden landscape. The sky was alive with movement as low, ragged, slate-grey clouds chased each other across it. They were glad to get home out of the rain that came down in stair rods and Harry's flaxen hair, now darkened and soaking wet, lay flat to his scalp as the excess rain water dribbled down his neck. They were chilled to the bone, utterly miserable and looked like drowned rats, but - eventually - they agreed that the trip had been well worth while and they talked excitedly about what they had seen for weeks.

Most of the women (out of necessity) now went about bare legged but some used gravy browning in place of the hard-to-get stockings. Mrs Fisher got a friend to pencil in the seams; which was fine until it rained. They used the still readily obtainable 'Ladder Stop' as nail varnish, as by that time the real thing had vanished from the shops. Increasing shortages of cosmetics led them to use beetroot juice in place of lipstick and rouge and soot was used as eye make-up. There were more unshaven and bearded men around as razor blades were in very short supply and Mr Harris resharpened his old blades by rubbing them round the inside of a glass tumbler. Some of the older men resorted to the old cutthroat razors still around from their parents' time, sharpening them on a leather strop. Rose hip syrup went on sale nationwide - under fives were to get it free - and two million more children became eligible for free cod liver oil.

Mr Harris read in his *Daily Express* that Winston Churchill had appointed his namesake, Air Marshall Arthur Harris, as the new Chief of Bomber Command. Brusque and bluff, Harris was of a similar nature to Churchill; the man whose determination and doggedness had united and galvanised the nation. He was outspoken almost to the point of rudeness; a broad set man of medium height, who was very confident, ardent and tenacious, but inclined to be abrupt and inflexible.

Vigorous and determined, the new AOC (Air Officer Commanding) aimed to carry the war, by day and night, deep into the heart of Germany. They had been relatively untroubled up to that point, but things were about to change as he planned to send large numbers of bombers into 'the Fatherland' and the occupied territories. Many, including Churchill, thought that this appointment could herald a turning point in the war.

For two and a half years we had battled alone against the might and aggression of Nazi Germany and the morale of the nation was low. Far better armed, the enemy were now in control of the entire western coastline of Europe and, with Britain's fortunes looking dismal, the only real hope of survival lay in a successful switch from defence to offence. German bombing had killed thirty thousand British citizens and many towns lay in ruins with Yorkshire towns such as Leeds, Bradford and the port of Hull set ablaze and badly damaged. It seems that at the time of Harris' appointment there were only seventy heavy and about four hundred medium bombers in full service. However, things were starting to look up as some of the bombers had been fitted with cathode ray tubes that enabled them to pick up signals from transmitting stations (including the masts we had seen at Danby). The new radio-pulse system, codenamed 'Gee', would enable the pilots to 'see' through the clouds instead of blindly blundering on and the navigator would be able to 'fix' his position leading to more bombing accuracy. It meant that they could now accurately navigate there and back, but only up to about 450 miles. With the 'Gee' system they were not yet able to reach as far as Berlin but by the autumn they would have an even more advanced device. Harris believed that a bomber offensive was the answer and it also meant that German arms and men would have to be switched to a defensive role.

By March the news bulletins stated that RAF Bomber Command had begun to mount mass, round-the-clock, bombing raids on Baltic ports and shipbuilding centres, such as Lubeck and the raids, which involved many local bombers, were now being carried out in three successive waves. The first wave dropped flares to light the targets, the second wave dropped incendiaries to start fires and the final wave of bombers dropped high explosive bombs to devastate towns that were already well alight. The fires were so hot and wide in extent that no fire brigade could control them and the port of Lubeck, with its many old wooden buildings, was almost wiped off the map. The RAF had learned from the eleven hour long immolation of Coventry but the new policy of saturation 'area' bombing was to cause some controversy. It led to the AOC being given the sobriquets 'Bomber' or 'Butcher' Harris but, to our delight, Germany was now getting back some of the treatment that it had dished out.

The sight of the great bombers going out night after night was awe-inspiring and it raised the morale of the people no end and gave them fresh hope. The loud drone of the planes disturbed the ragged-trousered rooks in the smooth-barked beech trees making them take to the air just as they were starting to roost for the night. The raucous cawing of the large black scavengers assaulted our ears, and Mr Harris said, "It's worse than t'Women's Institute in their tea break; and that's saying summat!" The cruciform shapes could be seen as black silhouettes against the fading light of the evening sky. To us the mass of bomb-laden aircraft looked like migratory flocks of birds; only they were made of steel, aluminium, wood, Perspex and canvas. They headed out towards the steely grey waters of the North Sea, and once over their target they would lay their huge, cigar-shaped, 1,000-lb. (454 kgs.), high-explosive 'eggs'. The hearts of the brave Halifax crews were no doubt beating in time with the throbbing of their Hercules and Merlin engines. It was not until many years later that I learned that others had flown south from Linton to carry out raids on industrial towns and ports in occupied France. The Krupp armaments and ordnance works at Essen in the Ruhr region of Germany was attacked with a much higher success rate than of late but we had seen the old lumbering Whitley Mark Vs for the last time.

Mr Harris read reports of the bombing raids in his newspaper. Over the Ruhr area, that the aircrews called 'Flak Alley' or 'the Grim Reaper's Happy Hunting Ground', the mighty bombers were lit up by the floating flares that left behind long smoky trails. As they ploughed on through heavy and withering anti-aircraft fire, they prayed they would not be 'coned' in the deadly blue beams of the searchlights. Graceful, speedy and highly manoeuvrable Spitfires and Hurricanes, that were considered to be the finest fighters in the world, escorted them and their role was to draw off the enemy fighters. A few of the new Avro Lancasters were involved for the first time. The earlier Manchester with its two Vulture engines had been dogged by trouble since its introduction and was soon withdrawn but, by lengthening its wings and fitting four Rolls-Royce Merlin engines, the Lancaster had come into being. This reliable and much-loved heavy bomber was one of the great success stories of the war and it became known as 'the Pilots' Bomber'.

The bomb-laden aircraft went out at dusk night after night, juddering our sash windows in their wooden frames and, sadly, some never returned. It seems that Number 35 squadron, still based at Linton-on-Ouse with its Halifax Mark IIs, had been involved in attacks on the *Scharnhorst* and at the end of March they made a night raid on that other mighty German battleship, the *Tirpitz*, which was anchored off Trondheim in Norway. These sorties cost the local squadron three of its Halifaxes and the lives of twenty-one aircrew and a further four were lost - with seven more crew killed - during attacks on the great ship in early April. It proved to be a tough nut to crack!

A number of the airmen in the village were very upset, as they knew many of the Linton aircrew lads and they attempted to drown their sorrows in the smoke-filled, noisy, atmosphere of the *Red Lion* and the *Tiger*. In the madness of war food and clothes were often in short supply but tears were always plentiful. The pubs often echoed to the sounds of drunken airmen and locals singing songs like *Whispering Grass* and *Java, Java* made popular by 'The Ink Spots', round the upright piano. Incidentally, the only black man we ever saw was an American Airforce sergeant who was billeted in New Earswick. Even though the beer was watered down to make the limited supplies last out, the publicans often topped up the airmen's beer-laced glasses on the house. They usually got on well with the locals but occasionally arguments would spill over into fistfights.

On my seventh birthday, which fell on Easter Sunday that year, Mam paid a short surprise visit. I vaguely remember her wearing her best thick Lisle stockings with low-heeled shoes with a strap that buttoned across the insoles. It was a soft, warm, spring morning with a haze of fresh green on the hedgerows and on seeing her, my sadness was lifted by the unconcealed love and happiness that emanated from her. The bond between us didn't need to be put into words. She said that Dad could not get leave but he sent his love and he had recently told her, "We are soon to get women working on the gun battery. At least we'll be able to hear their high pitched voices over the din of the gunfire and they say they will be taught to operate the searchlights. With their nimble fingers they should be good at adjusting the height finders and the predictor mechanisms."

Mam was no beauty in the conventional sense of the word but beauty is in the eye of the beholder - so to Dad and me she was. Neither plain nor beautiful but pleasing to look at, her presence could turn the darkness into light. There was an inner beauty and her lovely pale blue eyes and warm gaze radiated love and serenity. She had a soft and sensuous oval face and her soft, fine light brown hair was parted on the left and combed across the top of her forehead. Unfortunately she, and her younger sister, Hilda, had a muscular defect (medically known as strabismus) that prevented parallel focusing causing a slight squint in their left eye. It was what Gran called 'a lazy eye'. She also had her mother's rather heavy facial features with high cheekbones and a certain 'puffiness' around the nose and eyebrows.

She was a stargazer with an almost child-like innocence about her and she was never far from either laughter or tears. There was a vibrant, passionate, tactile impulsiveness in her and she liked to hug, kiss and touch me as often and whenever possible. She had visions and great hopes for the future when we would all be together again after the war. Fatalistic in her outlook, she believed that those who were good and generous of spirit would be rewarded with everlasting peace and rest in the 'afterlife'. She truly believed that some mysterious force shaped our destiny. When the time came for her to leave she said, "Keep your chin up, darling. The next time I see you I'll have George with me. He'll be coming to stay here quite soon"

Her eyes were misty, her lower lip trembled and a tear hovered on the verge of falling as she hugged me close and kissed me, before - ever so reluctantly - dragging herself away. It was George's birthday the next day and she had to be with him, so, after giving me one last tremulous haunting smile that pierced my soul, she quickly turned away. She waved as she hurried round the corner to catch the number ten into York. I was not to know that my memories of her and Dad would have to last me for a long, long time to come.

That day it was light until nearly 9 pm as double summertime was in operation again and the clocks had been put forward an hour early that morning. This meant that it was just getting light as Mr Harris left the house to go to work at Church Farm. We were not even up for our breakfast of lumpy porridge and the sun was well up by the time we set off on our walk to school.

General Rommel's headquarters was twenty-five miles west of the Gazala line and his men were well trained and had boundless confidence in themselves and their leader. The Eighth Army was situated on a slight rise on the uninhabited coastal plain with the Germans and Italians holding the port and airfield of Derna at the apex of their defensive position. From there they were able to attack the Allies with dive-bombers and fighter planes knocking out several weapons and vehicles but the human casualties were relatively light. Uncle John's platoon was still going out on patrols into 'No Man's Land', which entailed crossing through a narrow gap in the minefield carrying Bren guns and tripods. He had been on a course, put on by the 93rd Tank Regiment, where he learned to use the newly issued two-pounder anti-tank guns. The sand and gravel dunes had crests that were reminiscent of waves on the sea and he was surprised to see that the desert flats (that were wadi-fed) had sprung into flowery glory overnight.

German tanks could be seen moving about like grey beetles and, although they were only two miles away, it was hard to judge distances as the shimmering heat haze distorted everything. Both sides held a deep admiration for General Rommel and thought he was the most brilliant soldier in the Middle East but the Allied troops had, apparently, little confidence in their own 'top brass'. Uncle John and men of 'C' company of the 5th Battalion of the Green Howards made a night raid on a German position and half of the feature was captured in hand-to-hand fighting using fixed bayonets but they were forced to withdraw when it became evident that the rest of the position had been heavily reinforced. The patrol commander, Captain Rhodes, who Uncle John liked and respected, was wounded and taken prisoner and twenty 'other ranks' were killed or captured.

Shortly afterwards regrouping of the forces on the Gazala line took place. The 150th Brigade handed over their position to part of the 1st South African Brigade and took over the Ualeb position from the 200th Guards Brigade who moved east to the 'box' known as 'Knightsbridge'. Field artillery gun pits were dug using bulldozers but there was a shortage of anti-tank guns and the 5th Battalion Green Howards were now in a central position with their 4th Battalion slightly to the north. Both were isolated from their nearest neighbours and were therefore unable to support each other and had been ordered to act independently. Uncle John was to say later, "Our battery had only two hundred and sixty rounds per gun and only seven days food and ten days water had been issued. We had no idea when the attack was going to come."

On a night in mid April, young Alan Clark, Peter Pallier's young cousin at Hilbra Avenue, was woken by the mournful wailing of the nearby siren. On peeping around the blackout curtain he noticed a red glow in the night sky above the distant hills to the north and the Misses Law and Barker saw the same eerie glow from their front bedroom window. A couple of days later Alan's mam said to Harry, "I've been told there's been a heavy air raid on Middlesbrough and the East Cleveland coast. They say a lot of people have been killed and hundreds have been made homeless. In Middlesbrough itself a twenty-four inch (62 cms.) gas main was fractured and caught fire lighting up the sky and it was that and the glow from burning houses that we saw the other night."

Our bedroom window faced west and though woken by the air raid siren we couldn't see the lurid light in the night sky. We were up and swaddled in blankets under the table with Mr Harris and the girls were in the gas cupboard with his wife. Dot said afterwards, "I couldn't get comfortable because the gas meter (that was fed with pennies) was sticking in me back."

We went back to bed when the all clear sounded and in the darkness and chill of that time just before dawn, when the human spirit is at its lowest ebb, I dreamt that I 'saw' Mam in the bedroom. She seemed so real and looked as though she hadn't had time to comb her hair or put on any lipstick. She put her arms round me and quietly sang a soothing lullaby and her soft, radiant smile held the promise of infinite love and compassion. Then she faded away and I seemed to hear her tremulous voice, as if from a great distance, saying " Be strong, my son. Be strong!". I woke with a start to find that my face and pillow were wet with tears and Jimmy said, "You were crying in your sleep, John." I was engulfed by an overwhelming sadness and at that point Mr Harris came into the room. Sitting me on his knee he lay my head on his shoulder and put his arms round me as deep sobs wracked my slender frame. "There, there," he said soothingly. "It were only a bad dream. Go back to sleep now, son." He was an exceptionally kind, sensitive and caring man.

Later that day, April the sixteenth, the Harrises listened to the nine o'clock news after we had gone to bed. The talk and rattling of cups stopped and there was an expectant hush as the soft, hesitant voice of King George VI announced that Malta had been awarded the George Cross, the civilian equivalent of the military VC. The King was a gentle, sincere and dutiful man and it was just three weeks since he and the Queen had visited RAF Linton. Malta sat in the middle of the Mediterranean Sea only sixty miles from Sicily and its position made it of great strategic importance in the defence of Egypt and the oilfields of Persia and Iraq. Such awards were not handed out lightly but the gallant, beleaguered island, smaller than the Isle of Wight, had been under siege for nearly two years and it seemed that it could not hold out much longer. It was thought that the Germans were planning an invasion by sea and air and when it fell, Hitler vowed that he would take Egypt and conquer the Middle East.

The news bulletins said that the tiny island had endured thousands of air sorties and that the once beautiful Grand Harbour at Valetta was full of wrecked ships with the dockyards and naval base rendered unusable. Spitfires had been flown in but had been destroyed on the ground and although a medal could not save them from the Germans it boosted their morale and gave them the will to endure a little longer. A close bond had developed between the islanders and Great Britain that was to last for many more years. Who would have guessed that events in this remote island would have such far-reaching consequences for my Uncle John? Still, who knows what fate has in store for any of us?

16. Blitzed

The nights of the 23rd, 24th, 25th and 26th of April where cloudless with the waxing moon near to the full. From the wireless broadcasts, which always started with 'Last night Bomber Command...', the Harrises knew that there had been bombing raids on the Baltic Coast port of Rostock and that the Heinkel aircraft factory had been severely damaged. The centre of the old town, which was like a tinderbox, had been set ablaze and 100,000 people had fled the flames in panic but the cost to Bomber Command was high as twelve bombers had been lost. Hitler was said to have been livid about the RAF raids that went on for four nights, as it was only four weeks since Lubeck had been devastated. The U-boat nests at the island city were heavily bombed and large numbers of incendiary bombs had set the town, with its highly flammable, half-timbered, medieval buildings, ablaze from end to end. Individual fires had joined up to produce one huge conflagration and Hitler vowed that he would lay waste the cities of Britain in return. The story goes that he had picked up a pre-war Baedeker guidebook to historic British towns and cities and ordered that all the places with three star ratings were to be razed. The cathedral cities of Norwich and Exeter, along with Bath were bombed soon afterwards.

On the evening of Tuesday, the 28th of April, our Harry sat in his room reading the *Yorkshire Evening Post*, which had been reduced to only four pages with fewer and smaller advertisements. One of these showed that the Walt Disney film 'Dumbo' was on at the St. George's Cinema in Castlegate, in York, close to the grassy mound of Clifford's Tower where late daffodils were still in bloom. At the Theatre Royal 'A Bird in the Hand' was being shown, a zany comedy called 'Hellsapoppin' was on at The Electric and there were Hollywood war films on at The Rialto and The Grand. At the Cinema in Clifton a film called 'So Ends the Night' might have been viewed - in retrospect - as a forewarning. The editorial was headed 'REPRISALS', which referred to the recent raid on Norwich, and it commented on York's run of good luck thus far.

That evening as Mr Harris had tuned in to the short wave channels there was much whistling and crackling as he turned the dial. He often searched the overseas channels eager for uncensored war news and that night, during Lord Haw Haw's English-speaking propaganda broadcast, his nasal voice had kept fading in and out, but he thought he heard him warn of bombers coming to York. He took no particular notice as he was always ranting on in that way and many people now looked on him as a bit of a joke. They settled down to listen to 'Sandy's Half Hour' of organ music on the Forces Service. We had been sent to bed just before eight o'clock and all was quiet as the adults went up to their bedroom at half past ten. Mrs Harris had her glass soda water syphon with her as usual and Mr Harris had to be up to start his long working day at the farm by 7.30am. In York soldiers and airmen from the local camps and airfields caught their buses in Exhibition Square after a good night out and all was quiet and still.

It was a beautiful, clear night with a 'bombers moon' and it was about half past two in the morning when we were woken by the loud, unsynchronised drone peculiar to German aeroplanes. They sounded very close and seemed to be almost on top the house as Jimmy, Ducky and I shot out of bed and peered round the edges of the blackout curtain. With our bare feet on the cold lino, we saw that the sky in the direction of Clifton was lit by the eerie flickering lights of Chandelier parachute flares that looked like strange, floating, white Christmas trees. In the bright, eerie, silver light we could clearly see the dark grey shapes of twin-engined Heinkels - the largest of the German bombers. As they roared past at around 200 miles per hour, we could see the black crosses on their wings and the swastikas on their tail fins. We heard explosions and felt the floor vibrating under our bare feet as clusters of incendiary bombs whooshed and crumped into the ground. At that point, Mr Harris rushed into the room and hurried us down the stairs into our allotted places and Mrs Harris already had the girls in the gas cupboard with their blankets round them. The siren, which was supposed to warn of raiders approaching was not heard and the chilling, pulsing wail was not sounded until after the first bombs had dropped. Something had gone wrong!

On hearing the roar of more German planes outside, being too young (or too stupid) to realise the danger, we rushed to the front window and were shocked to see in the baleful white light, several green and light grey planes with long thin fuselages. Jimmy, being an expert, said they were Dorniers and they seemed to be following the railway lines at the far side of the fields. Mr Harris angrily bawled out, "You silly little buggers. Get away from that window!" and grabbing hold of us, he roughly shoved us under the table where we crouched crying and shaking with fear. We were scared, but also shocked by his anger and unaccustomed shouting. Angry shouting and physical punishment by Mrs Harris was the norm but it was most unusual for the generally quiet and placid Mr Harris to act that way. The terrible crumping sounds and the earth-shaking vibrations went on for nearly an hour and a half, during which Mr Harris apologised for his angry outburst. He said, "Ah'm sorry to 'ave been so rough lads, but yer could've been killed by flying glass if a bomb 'ad dropped nearby." He tried to make amends by hugging and comforting us and by giving us a toffee to chew on. As bombs landed the lights flickered and dimmed.

We learned later that waves of Dornier 17s, Heinkel 111s and Junkers 88's had flown up the East Coast with some dropping mines into the sea from Spurn Head to the Scarborough area. They had crossed the coast through a gap in the radar defences somewhere south of Middlesbrough and had flown inland following the moonlight reflecting from the river Foss as it flowed south to join the Ouse at York. The first wave, arriving undetected, had dropped flares to light up the target areas around the railway station, the marshalling yards and other parts of the city. Another wave had done the same at Clifton airfield, the waterworks and the chocolate factory. The incendiary bombs threw out magnesium which flared white, turning to yellow flames as the fires took hold.

Flashes from the high explosive (HE) bombs bleached the night sky filling it with a hellish glare as flames, brick dust and smoke leapt into the air. Miss Curry was to tell us later that as bombs were exploding, dispatch riders careered through the streets and the jangling of the fire engine bells added to the pandemonium. Several people were killed by clattering aircraft cannon fire as they ran out onto the street and one man was identified by the signet ring on his finger - the only part of him to be found. Some of the incendiaries that clattered on to the roofs were very difficult to reach and the bravery of the firewatchers prevented the Post Office and several other buildings being burnt to the ground.

It was reported over the next few days that two of the early targets had been the Rowntree's chocolate factory, and the nearby gasworks. A Junkers 88, a 'flying pencil' (as we called them), dropped bombs on both sides of the footbridge over Rowntree's private railway track. Other swept in on Clifton airfield where aircraft were in the process of being repaired and returned to service. The guardroom and the officers mess received direct hits and fifteen airmen were killed. There were huge craters where the HEs had exploded on the soft ground but the Halifax bombers were safe in the hangars on the other side of Water Lane and were not damaged. A team of civilian defence workers took several hours to dig out a mother and her baby buried under the wreckage of their house behind the Clifton Cinema.

Another wave of bombers had followed the moonlight reflecting from the railway lines leading to the railway station and the carriage works. It seems they were intent on halting or restricting the movement of troops and armaments from here to Hull from where German Intelligence sources knew that armaments were being shipped to the eastern front via the port of Murmansk. The leaping flames of the burning station and the buildings nearby turned the walls of the Minster blood red but, by some miracle, it remained undamaged. The loco running shed was hit and two huge Pacific railway engines were flipped over on their sides as if they were children's toys when a HE bomb exploded between them. The roundhouse at the carriage works was struck along with many of the locos that stood around the turntable.

A blacked-out express train from London to Edinburgh had just pulled in to platform nine packed with servicemen. Railway policemen ran alongside the carriages shouting warnings and a message in a 'cut glass' voice was relayed over the loudspeakers, urging the men to leave the train and take cover. Initially they were reluctant to relinquish their hard won seats and their belongings but they responded in double quick time when a couple of 250 lb (114kg.) HE bombs exploded close by. A stick of incendiaries set the station roof ablaze and burning debris clattered down onto the carriages. A few brave men saved many lives by uncoupling fourteen carriages, leaving half a dozen burning. With the aid of shunters, these were dragged out of the station. The arched roof girders fell in and the iron footbridge over the track collapsed to lay in a tangled and twisted mess among heaps of fallen masonry.

Women porters in baggy blue overalls used sand and stirrup pumps to put out firebombs while others kicked the sputtering devices off the platforms onto the tracks. Twisted girders, broken glass and heaps of rubble lay everywhere and amidst the acrid smell of cordite policemen and ARP men scrabbled in search of the injured or buried. A signalman climbed into the cab of a shunter and pushed a parcel van and twenty coaches to safety. Platforms one, two and three suffered extensive damage and the concrete roof of a crowded, brick, street shelter fell in when a bomb exploded nearby.

Planes peeled away with some jettisoning their bombs on the outskirts of the city. The magnificent, old Guildhall, near Lendal Bridge, was well alight and its great nail-studded door of Galtres Forest oak was blasted and shattered into bits. The leaping flames turned the sky red and so many incendiaries dropped that it was impossible to reach them all and small fires combined to form one larger ones. On the other side of the river in North Street, Rowntree's five-storey warehouse, which had been packed with sugar, was set ablaze and the sweet smell of caramel pervaded the area.

All that was left of the Leopard shopping arcade was heaps of rubble and burning timber with St. Martin-le-Grand Church a burnt out wreck. The heat of the fires melted the lead in the stained glass windows that had depicted the life of the saints and the molten lead ran down in a stream across the pavement. The badly damaged clock still protruded from the wall supported by its ornate wrought ironwork but it had stopped at 3.45 a.m. denoting the exact time of the bombing. The Jersey dairy shop next door to it was totally wrecked and every shop window in Coney Street was shattered. In the Victorian department store of Kirby and Nicholson, shards of glass lay amongst new clothes and expensive fur coats and broken furniture littered the street.

The Bar Convent on Blossom Street, just a hundred yards from the station, and said to be the oldest active convent community in England, was hit and five nuns were killed. The Civil Defence workers, firemen, ARP, and firewatchers were supplied with steaming hot mugs of tea throughout the long hours of the night. Virtually every street suffered some damage and as the city went up in flames many feats of gallantry took place with the unsung heroes showing complete disregard for their own safety. The British Restaurant staff in Aldwark worked a round-the-clock shift system over the following week to keep the rescue workers and the many homeless people supplied with nourishing hot meals.

At Clifton airfield two 250kg. HE bombs, that had buried themselves in the clayey subsoil, failed to explode. The next morning a bomb recovery crew from RAF Church Fenton, fifteen miles to the south, had just examined the entry holes when both bombs exploded. A rescue squad arrived to find a Flight Officer with severe injuries to both legs and he died on the way to the York County Hospital on Monkgate. His sergeant was lying dazed on the edge of the huge crater and, amazingly, on arrival at hospital he was found to be badly shaken but with no bones broken and not a scratch on him. Two corporals had broken legs and were in hospital for the next three months. Patients from the local area, including one or two from Haxby, were sent home to clear the wards to make room for the many injured.

At about four o'clock in the morning we were still cowering under the table wrapped in blankets listening to the not-so-distant bombing that seemed to go on and on. We then heard and felt two very loud explosions that seemed very near and the house jumped on its foundations. They were too close for comfort, making us realise that even our little village was vulnerable. The windows rattled violently, soot was dislodged from the chimney and, as it billowed out in choking black clouds from the empty fireplace onto the hearthrug right next to us, we were petrified with fear. We found out later that a high explosive bomb had landed in a field between Towthorpe and Old Earswick village at the other side of the Foss killing several cows and badly damaging some farm buildings. Mr Harris said, "Mebbe t'plane 'ad bin aiming for t'Army camp at Strensall, or mebbe it'd jettisoned its bombs before fleeing t't coast and 'ome."

After a while we were pleased to hear the sound of British fighter planes attacking the fleeing German bombers. The short bursts of tinny sounding cannon fire seemed to be right above our heads. After that it went quiet except for the muffled voice of Mrs Harris telling poor Dot off for shuffling in the gas cupboard. We stayed where we were for a further half-hour until we heard the all clear siren wail at 4.36 a.m., when we went back to bed, but it was hard to sleep after the fear and excitement. Terry Waddington's father used to give him aircraft recognition leaflets so he was an 'expert' on enemy planes. At school the next day he outlined to Jimmy what he had seen during the night. He said, "I was stood at the door of the Anderson shelter in the back garden when I saw a British Beaufighter firing at a black Heinkel 111. They were both flying very low above the fields across the road. At that Mrs Evans grabbed me and pulled me into the shelter." The following morning he had searched the fields and found many spent links and cartridge cases that we greatly treasured.

Harry, whose billet was a good half-mile closer to Clifton airfield than ours, said later, " I saw a couple of small, single-engine Lysanders in the air just as the raids started. They were practising night landing and taking off. " After the war it was learned that the bombers had followed radio beams transmitted from France. The first wave of about twenty odd aircraft had attacked completely unopposed dropping eighty-five terrifying high explosive bombs that went 'whump, whump' as they hit into the ground.

For some reason it was well after the first bombs had dropped that nightfighters from the nearby airfields were scrambled and we were told later that four enemy bombers had been shot down. One, a Heinkel 111, was shot down by a Free French pilot flying a Hurricane with the crew of five baling out and spending the rest of the war in a prison camp. A Dornier pilot wrote many years later of being shot down after he had dropped four 500lb bombs on the defenceless city. His aircraft had exploded in flames as it skidded along the ground and he and two of the crew of four survived but the radio operator died from his horrific burns.

The new day dawned windy but dry and clear at Haxby. We could see the pall of grey smoke that hung over York where people setting off for work could taste the brick dust in the air. It was reported that they were amazed to see that the River Ouse, which had been silvered by the moonlight, was silvered again by fish floating on the surface after being killed by the bomb blasts. The towers of the Minster and the walls of Bootham Bar stood proud and undamaged as the normal hustle and bustle resumed. Some of the streets - where the rubble was still smouldering – were roped off and plucky shopkeepers could be seen sweeping the broken glass into piles on the pavement. There were several deep bomb craters; some of them filled with water from broken mains. The tail fins of a bomb protruded from someone's back lawn behind a broken fence and people were busily putting sheets of cardboard - provided free of charge by the Rowntree and Terry's chocolate factories - over their broken windows. Tankers brought fresh water to those without piped supplies.

At the railway station a huge clump of coins was found fused together by the intense heat and people walking to work were amazed to see great gaps where houses had stood and half of a piano and a bike hung in the telegraph wires. Nevertheless, three quarters of the normal rail services were restored that day and many years later a round memorial plaque was placed on the wall beside platform 8A in remembrance of forty-two years old station foreman, William Milner. At the height of the raid he had ushered people to safety before going back into the blazing building in an attempt to bring out urgently needed medical supplies when the building collapsed. His body was so badly burned that he was identified by means of his watch chain.

That day we did not have to go to school until the afternoon when Miss Curry addressed the assembled children. She looked tired and her eyes were sore as she said, "I'm sure you are all aware of the dreadful air raid on York. I was on standby in my capacity as a part-time ARP warden and I was in bed at my parents' home on Gillygate when the first bombs exploded. I got my mother and our dog to the shelter as another five bombs exploded nearby. The noise was deafening and the poor dog was terrified. Putting on my steel helmet, warm slacks and a thick jersey, I went out to care for the homeless and the injured. It was a tough few hours for the resolute volunteers, the policemen and the emergency services who were hard at it all night regardless of the risk of personal injury. The steep pitch of the roofs and the narrowness of the ancient streets made the job even more hazardous for the firemen who had to deal with flying glass; escaping gas, flames and suchlike. Several were injured or affected in some way and the local people willingly opened their homes to offer kindness and comfort to those in distress. The Civil Defence workers performed heroically and the firewatchers put out many of the incendiary devices that rattled down on the rooftops before they could cause too much damage. Several people who had given up smoking started again. As the all clear was not sounded until turned half past four, it meant that we could snatch a little sleep before coming here this afternoon." At which point Mr Fox said, "I'm sure we all very much admire Miss Curry's courage, compassion and dedication to duty. She has been through a gruelling and hazardous experience and I hope that you will all respond by being on your best behaviour today. Finally, let's put out hands together to show our appreciation of her sterling efforts on behalf of others. She is a shining example to us all and has done the school proud!"

The Harrises learned the details of the raid from a rushed out edition of the *Evening Press,* who had managed to get the paper out even though their offices in Lendal were badly bombed. The headlines declared 'York dive-bombed and gunned in Reprisal Raid', before adding, 'Coolness and courage under fire characterised the citizens of York last night, when the city underwent the ordeal of what was described by the Germans as a reprisal for the attacks on Cologne, Lubeck and Rostock'. It stated that more than seventy enemy bombers dropped around two hundred bombs causing widespread devastation. Out of a total of 28,000 houses 9,500 were destroyed or damaged. The WVS posted grim lists of the ninety-two people killed, the injured, and those left homeless.

The following day was Harry's fourteenth birthday but Gran was not able to come due to the damage at York station. That night we were woken again by the wailing of the local siren and we quickly took up our air raid positions. But it was not long before we were back in bed as no enemy planes arrived and the all clear was sounded. It was reported the following day that another small raid had been attempted but the coastal defences had kept them at bay.

A day or so later Mr Harris sat at home reading the *Evening Press* editorial that was headed 'The Hun came to York the other Night'. In it there was a picture of a German bomb casing now being used as a charity collecting box. In the *Picture Post* magazine we saw dramatic coloured photographs of the Guildhall in flames; the ruins of the Bar Convent and the badly damaged offices of the 'Yorkshire Press' in Coney Street. It was sad to see striking pictures of the wrecked railway station that made us realise how lucky the village had been to escape unscathed. The raid brought the terror of war that much closer. Until now York, with its narrow, winding medieval streets, had been a sleepy backwater for close on three hundred years. It had been relatively undisturbed by war or violence since Cromwell's Roundheads had set siege to the city in 1644.

Soon afterwards the Princess Royal toured the area and four days later three thousand people packed York Minster for a service of commemoration. In a broadcast by Lord Haw Haw just after the air raid he claimed that the Minster had been left deliberately untouched as Hitler wanted to save it for the day when he would enter York in triumph after the invasion that was soon to come. It took many months to get back to normal and at least one of the deep bomb craters was not filled in until 1945.

Sunday was still looked on as a day of rest and was known as 'The Lord's Day'. Early every Sunday morning it was one of my jobs to walk down to Torville's shop. It was lovely to see the masses of purple aubretia hanging over the garden walls but some of the early daffodils were becoming wrinkled and brown. It felt strange to 'hear' the utter silence as I passed the empty school playground. On Saturdays the Home Guard unit used it for rifle drill. Once at the newsagent's I got the '*Sunday Express*' newspaper for Mr Harris and cigarettes for his wife, as nobody bothered about selling cigarettes to kids in those days. Unfortunately for her, her favourite brand, Craven 'A', had become unobtainable by this time and she would have to make do with Player's Weights or full-strength Capstan's. She could not abide the Turkish cigarettes that were now on sale in the shops. I quite enjoyed this job, as Mr Harris often slipped me a penny that I spent in Bryant's shop where the sweets were scooped up from a square jar and poured into a paper bag. The quiet calm that lay over the slumbering village suited my mood. With very few people about and no noise or hurry I had time to think and I enjoyed what Wordsworth called 'the bliss of solitude'. I could reflect on my confused feelings and the sense of unease and deep disquiet that I felt.

Gran came to see Harry, Jimmy and me that afternoon and I thought she looked unusually pale, old and drawn Trying to maintain a semblance of normality, she said, "My word! How you have grown since I saw you last." Standing Jimmy and then me against her, she measured our height against the buttons on her coat. This became a ritual that was repeated every time she visited and to this day I remember those large, round buttons that were domed and covered in leather that was segmented like the horny plates on the shell of our tortoise.

She then explained why Hilda could not come to see Jimmy. "Your Mam has joined the ATS and has been posted away." She went on to say, "A couple of weeks back we had a really bad air raid and the house was badly damaged along with a lot more round our way. We didn't have time to get to the shelters before a lone aircraft dropped its bombs. There was a roar and a whoosh and we heard a sound like hailstones as rubble and debris landed on the roof. Archie was slightly concussed and cut on the chest by flying glass, but don't worry, he's OK! He had just gone to bed when the window was blown in by the blast and Renee ran upstairs just in time to stop him from stepping out of the big hole where the window had been thinking it was the doorway. The air was full of dust particles and soot and there was blood on the jacket of his pyjamas where the flying glass had cut his chest. The skylight window - which I'd painted black because of the blackout - crashed in on the stairs right in front of me and there was wood and broken glass everywhere and Archie cut his foot on a jagged piece. He has been off work for a few days and has not been able to go to his Air Training Corps sessions, which he loves."

"Next door was badly damaged an all," she added, "and because their front door wouldn't open, Mrs Irvine, passed her little girl, Shirley, out to us through the shattered front window. She is only four and she was really good and never cried at all, but mebbe that was because she was in a state of shock. Renee, who is now working shifts as a trainee overhead crane driver at the Cargo Fleet steelworks, was having her supper after working a two till ten shift when the raid started and they were late sounding the siren. We've had to move into rented accommodation while the house is being repaired and our curtains, carpets, bedding and clothes will have to be replaced as they are impregnated with glass particles. We're now living in rooms in a big Victorian house on Linthorpe Road next to our family doctor. We've got the downstairs rooms and Granny Knights, and your Great Aunt Maud and her three kids have the upstairs rooms. They were bombed out like us and we share the kitchen and we have electricity now but I don't trust that new fangled stuff. There's even an inside toilet and a bathroom, and we're not used to such luxuries. Our houses are all boarded up now and quite a few of the houses on Laws Street were completely wrecked." I thought to myself ' I'm glad Mam's at Grove House with our George'.

By late spring most of the trees had put forth fresh green foliage, but the ash buds were still clenched black and tight. Vigorous green shoots of young wheat had sprung up to hide the brown ridges and Mr Harris was working long hours at the farm. Bob Britton had said to them; "I must have the barley sown and the swedes and mangolds drilled by early May."

The clover and hayseed had been broadcast soon after the harrowing was done and it gave them a feeling of satisfaction to accomplish these annual tasks. Scents of wild flowers and fruit blossom assailed their nostrils and Mr Harris always experienced a deep feeling of contentment when his fellow farmhands were around him. He found their slow, deep-toned and broad-vowelled banter comforting as they worked in the fields talking happily of simple things like pigmeal, mash rollers and fertiliser. The unhurried farming year had scarcely altered over the years but things were starting to change more rapidly now. Nearby Italian prisoners jabbered away in their excitable fashion while an armed soldier stood guard and there were increasing numbers of Land Army girls in khaki jodhpurs these days.

It felt good to be out in the warm, fresh air away from the constrained atmosphere of home. Here he could escape from his wife's incessant nagging. 'She seems to be permanently bad-tempered these days' he thought and he suspected that she was

349

taking it out on the kids when he wasn't there. She certainly took it out on the locals, playing hell with the nurse, the policeman, the postman and anyone else that crossed her path. Most people tried to keep out of her way. 'The war affects different people in different ways,' he thought, "and me and 'er seem ter 'ave little in common these days." He comforted himself with the thought of how relaxing it would be to plod on with the tilling and planting and he found that grinding up the mangolds for the steers helped him to unwind. He tried to put his wife and the bloody war that seemed to be dragging on forever, out of his mind. At the end of each day he knew that pleasant feeling that often follows a spell of hard physical labour but she always spoiled it for him when he got home.

Harry, Peter and Brian had settled in and were now enjoying their days at the 'Joe-Row' school but Harry only had a few more weeks before he left for good. He liked making trowels, spades, chisels and the like in metalwork and Brian, who later became a joiner, enjoyed making the handles and other things in the woodwork room. They all enjoyed working outdoors cultivating fruit and vegetables in the extensive gardens. The school had acres of land on which they planted fruit trees and there were large greenhouses in which to grow cucumber and tomato plants and soon they would be getting in their first crop of hay. Harry particularly enjoyed looking after the pigs and the geese. Recently, he had started a Saturday morning job at Harold Atkinson's butcher's shop on Front Street delivering the orders on a sit-up-and beg bike that had a large wicker basket on the front. In between times he gave the neat and dapper Mr Atkinson a hand in the shop.

On reflection, the evacuation scheme seems to have been a rather 'hit-and-miss' affair dependent on luck or the lack of it. George and I had been lucky at first, but it seemed to have run out since coming here. I was frightened by Mrs Harris' loud voice and intimidating manner as she seemed to have a stone where her heart should have been. Her eyes were cold and she knew how to hurt us. Public Information Leaflet number three proved to be far from correct in our case as it stated that, '.... clearly the children will be much happier away from the big cities where the danger will be greatest.....They will be well looked after.' It was only Jimmy's friendship and caring presence, along with Mr Harris' kindly nature, that made being here just about tolerable. He was an undemonstrative and exceptionally nice man, but he worked long hours and was not always there to mediate on our behalf. When he was at home he bore the brunt of her anger but he tried his best to protect us from her increasingly angry and volatile behaviour.

Wartime anxieties and separations changed everybody to some degree and emotions tended to be heightened and intensified with nerves often stretched to breaking point. We found out the hard way that the choleric Mrs Harris had a cruel and nasty streak. We were now being punished more and more severely for minor misdemeanours or infringements of *her* rules. For example, I had recently been larruped with the belt for tearing my trousers on some barbed wire with the L-shaped tear being a sure give-away. On another occasion I was clouted round the ear for smirking and looking away while being told off. It was all down to nervousness and fear when she shouted straight into my face. "I will not have it. Do you hear?" (Silence.) "I said do you *hear*?" she screamed. "Yes, Mrs Harris," I whimpered in reply. I hated it when she exploded into action and grabbed hold of me. It was so humiliating to be held by the shoulders and shaken like a rag doll in front of the others and I often felt that my head would fall off.

Where does punishment end and abuse begin? Children should be trained not beaten. We had been separated from our loved ones at an early age and that was traumatic enough. We were old enough to know it was wrong to be naughty or to tell lies; especially to adults. But did we deserve this verbal and physical maltreatment just for being mischievous? We reasoned that she was an adult, therefore she must know best, as we had been taught to respect our 'elders and betters'. We were no angels but we were being whacked on the legs or pounded on the head for what seemed trivial offences. Our shortcomings were many it seems. She was losing her temper and resorting to violence more and more often. When she took down one of the belts hanging on the kitchen cabinet, I would flinch in anticipation of the first blow. As we shielded our heads with our arms or hid under the coats hanging on the kitchen door, she lashed at the bare part of our legs below our baggy short trousers and showed no mercy. We were often left with red, stinging, raised weals.

351

It took a long time to shake off the image of her red, rage-distorted, moon-like face and I shut my eyes as the belt whipped down on me over and over again. I can still picture her wobbling jowls and the gingery hairs that grew out of her flared nostrils as she lashed at me. Tight-lipped and scowling, she seemed to enjoy watching us cringe and whimper as we slunk away like puppies with our tails between our legs. It was not the bruises but the wounds inside that would take the longest to heal. She had created a deep dread and uncertainty in us. I vowed that one day I would write it all down but for the time being I had to put up with it, but I would never forget. To make matters worse, the obsequious 'Ducky' Barrett, who was an out and out creep, hardly ever got hit.

Poor Dot, who was as thin as a rake, was cruelly punished for the slightest transgression. She was clipped round the ear or caned on the palms of her hands causing them to become red, puffed up and sore. I still remember the whooshing sound of the thin cane as it sliced through the air. When she had stopped crying she sat there in shocked silence keeping her eyes averted so as not to anger Mrs Harris again. Maybe it was because she was not 'the full shilling' as they said – that she was picked on the most. When this happened, Jimmy and I looked at each other with our teeth and our fists clenched. We felt bad and tears came to our eyes, as her hurting hurt us. We felt guilty at saying nothing but at the same time we were glad that it was not our turn to get it. Mrs Harris could wield sarcasm with deadly effect and she constantly told Dot that she needed her head looking at but, in my eyes, by trying to degrade her she only degraded herself.

We were told that we were stupid, worthless and useless so often that we came to believe that it must be true. We started to display a lack of confidence and were showing symptoms of insecurity. The repeated beatings and the constant telling off lowered our self-esteem and we withdrew into ourselves more and more. It reduced our trust and faith in the adults around us and we felt that we had nobody to turn to for help and support. Even though school afforded some respite, we were too intimidated to confide in the teachers. Our reserves of resilience were almost used up and we instinctively said and did nothing in order to cope. We longed to be reassured but didn't know how to tell them what was happening as we thought they would think we were making it all up. When Gran visited again we tried to tell her but Mrs Harris was always there. She was all smiles, hugging us and putting on a big act of caring.

The more we were punished the more we came to expect it. We started to believe that we must be bad children and deserved everything we got. It is a strange quirk of human nature to feel guilt on being badly treated. Jimmy and I became introverted and withdrawn and began to lose hope and I longed for Mam to hug and cuddle me and soothe my fears but she hadn't been to see me for some time. It seems that I subconsciously started to employ basic survival mechanisms. I learned to 'switch off' my mind and pretend that I wasn't there when Mrs Harris beat me. I believe that the psychologist's term for such a reaction is 'disassociation'.

School provided a structure to our day and Jimmy and I felt safe among the crowds of children. For a time, Miss Francis, with her striking blue eyes and gentle, smiling presence shamed me in to making an effort. There was something about her that made you want to please her; an implicit trust that led to a certain restraint. After a lesson with her I felt better able to cope; she was like a second mother to me and her influence was more potent and lasting than if she had been a strict disciplinarian. Shouting and threatening are barren means of instruction. She taught me to read for pleasure, which enabled me to escape into another world, and was sympathetic when I desperately needed some kindness and understanding. The formerly mind-numbing class routine became a sanctuary in which I didn't have to expend too much time thinking. I put up a defensive screen, joking and clowning to mask the emotional hurt that was holding me back. I became like the vulnerable, soft-bodied caddis fly larva in the pond; a little creature that protects itself inside an armoured covering composed of bits of hard stone that it glues together. I hid inside my own mind and learned to build barriers so that no one would hurt me again.

Miss Francis had said, "Don't be afraid to ask if you get stuck on anything!" But due to feeling worthless and a failure, I was not prepared to risk appearing silly in front of my peers. I would not ask when I did not fully understand something and never put my hand up to offer answers. I was so unhappy and I felt that I was not as clever as the other children in the class. A feeling of hopelessness was dragging me down and my schoolwork began to suffer. I got into trouble due to my increased lethargy and withdrawn churlish state. My emotions were kept bottled up until they came out in aggressive outbursts and I got into fights. I didn't like hurting people but I found that I was good at fighting. At home in Middlesbrough we had been materially deprived, but here we were being emotionally deprived and the effects were to last a long, long time.

There appeared to be two sides to my nature. I was quiet, subdued and deep thinking and needed solitude from time to time. Solitude is not the same as loneliness. Lingering in the silence of the countryside gave me a warm pleasant feeling and I became a watcher of people and things. Still painfully shy and inhibited in company, I dared not reveal my unspoken dreams. At other times I became a more primitive, rowdy boy who ran wild with Jimmy and the others. Recently we had started to take heart-stopping risks, as traumatised children tend to do. We dared each other to do dangerous things and often ended up in even deeper trouble. Those early Sunday morning walks to Torville's shop were my brief periods of enjoyable peace and quiescence. These traits are apparently the two sides of the same coin: the yin and the yang of Oriental philosophy.

Life had become a fear and a mystery and Jimmy and I were emotionally wounded and left with scars that would take many years to heal and some that never did. I had bad dreams and Mrs Harris, in trying to curb our exuberance and love of life, came very close to breaking our spirit. The human spirit can only take so much before it crumbles to dust. We tried to avoid her, as she would give us a smack round the head for the slightest infringement of her rules. We even got a clout for getting in her way but it was hard not to with so many of us in that small house. I cannot speak for the others, who also had their share of beatings, as I do not know how they turned out in later life, but Jimmy and I were being shaped by circumstances over which we had no control.

I was sad and unhappy and had lost that sense of feeling secure and loved, which is the birthright of every child. Every time I heard Vera Lynn softly singing *Goodnight children everywhere* my lip would tremble and the tears would well up and I had to leave the room and rush up to our bedroom. My small frame often shook as I broke down in floods of uncontrollable tears and I felt so terribly lonely, unloved and homesick. I was trapped in a kind of open prison, and as someone once said; 'A cell is never harder to bear than when the door stands open and sunshine and birdsong flood in'. After a time I wiped the tears away with the back of my hand and went back downstairs. Our collective sorrow gradually turned to anger and we decided that we had had enough misery and upheaval. It was time to do something about it! Jimmy and I started to think of running away. Our world should have been filled with love and that would have made everything OK.

The long suffering and undemonstrative Mr Harris seemed to sense our unhappiness and tried to show us more affection to make up for his wife's increasing carping and cruel ways. We appreciated his many small kindnesses but it was not enough. Children have indelible memories and our minds were made up. We waited for a suitable time to make our escape but, in the meantime, we escaped into the great airy spaces of the countryside as often as possible. Our hearts were heavy and the lightness had disappeared from our step as we trudged to school day after day. We were content if we scraped through the day without further hurt and indoors we moped and said nothing or stayed out of the way in our bedrooms. We had long discussions and we asked the others if they were wanted to come with us. Dot and Thelma willingly agreed and Ducky, who was a wimp and a sucker up, reluctantly agreed but only after much persuading. He said, " It's all right for you lot, but Newcastle is a lot further away than Middlesbrough. Ah'd be on me own from there on." We thought we had better keep a close eye on him in case he gave the game away. We decided to go on the morning of Whit Monday, the first weekday of our half term break.

Jimmy went into Mr Harris' cluttered shed and found an old battered saucepan that he kept rusty nails and screws in and we washed it out in the pond. I stole a bottle of 'Camp' coffee and chicory from the Co-op store that had an Indian prince and a kilted Scottish soldier on the label that reminded me of what Dad had told us about his time in India. Consequently I suffered feelings of guilt and remember thinking what if PC Manging found out. Would I be charged with larceny and put in a cell in York Jail? A picture of

Dick Turpin in his cramped cell in York came into my mind. What would Mam think of me? The song *It's a Sin to tell a Lie* kept going round in my head. Dot pinched some broken biscuits from Bryant's and we hid them in a tin under the railway sleepers that formed the little bridge over the drainage ditch up Usher Lane. Thelma stole a teaspoon and a tin of Libby's evaporated milk and we bought a few ha'penny Oxo cubes from Bryant's shop with our few coppers. The thought of going home lifted our spirits no end and we couldn't wait for the big day to come. We thought that Middlesbrough lay just over the ridge to the north of Strensall and that was the way we planned to go.

Whit Sunday was a day of changing cloud and sunshine as we put on our 'Sunday 'Best' ready for church. Mr Harris had built an arch of rustic trelliswork over the path that ran down the centre of the back garden and had trained climbing roses to twine around it. The young, almond-shaped leaves were reddish-tinted and due to the warm weather they were just coming into flower. The girls were wearing light coloured dresses in honour of Whitsun and Mr Harris snipped off a few of the miniature, partly-open buds and pinned one on each of the girls. He then put the stems of others through the buttonholes of our jackets. In church I usually tried to avoid being next to 'Ducky' who always tried to stand next to Mrs Harris. Creeps and unctuous people like him made my flesh creep and Jimmy whispered, "I 'ope he do'n't say owt." So this time I made a point of standing on the other side of her so that I could hear what he said. I barely remember the service that day as my mind was on more important things.

That day the hands of the kitchen clock seemed to crawl round. On going to bed we were quiet for a change. Usually we argued and tiptoed in and out of each other's bedrooms and Mrs Harris often had to shout up the stairs "Get into bed or you'll feel the belt around you! I won't tell you again". Due to an excess of excitement, I lay awake listening to the sound of the rafters creaking as they cooled and slept only for short spells that night. Ducky was snoring and letting off as usual and the night seemed to drag on interminably, but finally the first faint signs of dawn light began to filter around the blackout curtains. It was only six o'clock and too early to get up but eventually a chorus of birdsong greeted the start of the new day. Mr Harris was out and on his way to work as the rising sun bathed the houses in its warm gold-tinted light. It was a glorious morning and I thought to myself that by the time it set I would be back home with Mam. This was the day we had longed for and we could scarcely believe it was here. The lads put on their old threadbare clothes to give the impression that today was nothing out of the ordinary and I had on my ragged pullover that had holes at the elbows as if I was just going out to play.

How we contained our excitement I'll never know. We ate as much porridge and toast and 'marg' as we could cram into our stomachs and we kept two of our mugs after Dot had done the washing up of the breakfast things. We hid them away in Thelma's canvas knapsack while Mrs Harris was outside in the back garden hanging out items of threadbare underwear that had seen too many washes. Thelma was then sent on an errand to the shops. We were ready and eager to be off and tried to hide our excitement as we waited impatiently for her to come back. At the last minute Ducky chickened out saying; "It's a barmy idea and ah'm not coming with yer." We prayed that the oily creep wouldn't give the game away. "Right," said Thelma when she got back, "Let's be off." As we stepped outside the sun was well up but the air was not too fresh and Jimmy exclaimed, "Phew! What a pong!"

The cattle had been taken in for milking at Abel's dairy and there was cow splatter all the way up Usher Lane. Taking care where we put our feet, we collected our supplies from their hidden cache and set off on our desperate bid for freedom hoping we would never see the horrible Mrs Harris again. We were delighted at the thought of going back to Middlesbrough. It seemed that our dreams were coming true at last.

As we hurried past the house, in case Mrs Harris saw us and called us in to go on another message or something, there was a new spring in our step. On reaching Station Road, we went wild with released excitement before we crossed the wooden sleepers of the railway crossing. How we had managed to hold it in I'll never know. Beyond the Landing Lane entrance there were a number of large Victorian houses with ornately carved wooden porches and long, pendulous bunches of light yellow flowers dripped from the laburnum shrubs in some of their gardens. Hopping and skipping up the twisting road we left the houses on the eastern edge of the village behind. Thelma said, "The lane goes north 'ere before it turns t' t'east and crosses Foss Bridge. Ah've been up 'ere before on me friends' bike."

At this point tall metal pylons towered above us and as we passed under the wires we could hear them humming and buzzing loudly. I was a bit frightened and was glad to get past and away from them, as electricity was a scary mystery to me. We followed the lane that was empty except for the odd military vehicle. A little way up the road a local farmhand rode past on his old sit-up-and-beg bike but he took no notice of us, as he knew that the school was closed for the Whitsun break. To our left was the high, grass-covered slope of the railway embankment, some parts of which had been dug over to grow vegetables, so we had a roll down that for a while. Patches of it had been turned black where the sparks from the fireboxes of the passing trains had set it alight. I selected a nice, long, juicy, grass stem to chew on, at which point a ladybird flared its wings and flew away home. We were doing the same thing but I hoped our house wouldn't be on fire.

It was a glorious day and verdant, sun-drenched pastures stretched away into the hazy distance. When a freak breeze stirred the grass in a field beside the road, Thelma said, "It's only t'fairies passing through. They say that if yer sit under a 'awthorn tree at this time o't'year they can gain power over yer."

We then heard the unmistakable, harsh, croaking call of a secretive corncrake from the long grass at the far side of a field. Its 'crek-crek; crek-crek' call made me think of a creaking farm gate. When we reached the concrete pillbox we ran in and out of it pretending we were soldiers firing our machine guns through its outward sloping slits. Nearby a windhover, with a black band along the edge of its tail, hung perfectly still in the sky before swooping down on some tiny creature in the long grass. After much dallying and playing about we reached the low-walled, stone bridge that crossed the Golland Dyke. The grass verges and some of the fields were covered in golden buttercups. Here we made a drink with our oxo cubes and water from the stream but, with the water being cold, they were only partly dissolved and bits floated about in it. We sat on the parapet of the bridge basking in the hot sunshine and rested for a while.

The road swung sharply to the right just before it reached Towthorpe and Thelma said, "I heard that a local man crashed his motorbike and was killed on this bend a few years back." The day was becoming exceptionally hot for the time of year and we took turns at carrying the knapsack. Thelma, who was brisk and businesslike, had taken charge, as, at the age of nearly eleven, she was the oldest and had her head screwed on properly, whereas Dot tended to stand and gawp. As the sun beat down on the tyre-polished tarmac we were so happy and elated and hadn't a care in the world. Jimmy suggested thumbing a lift but nothing came along and Thelma said; "We'll probably get a lift when we get on t'main road. Don't worry, just think what it'll be like back 'ome with our parents." I tried to picture their surprise on seeing us on the doorstep.

Jimmy and I were busting for a 'Jimmy Riddle', so we went behind a bush, but Dot didn't seem bothered about us being there. She just crouched down for a pee in the long grass like a little partridge. Back on the road, we larked about popping the odd tar bubble that had started to form in the sun-softened asphalt and as we skipped along we could hear tiny squeaks and a soft 'plopping' sound as voles dropping from the banks into the drainage ditches. We stopped to investigate things on the grass verges so often that the time just melted away and it was near noon by the time we arrived at Towthorpe Bridge.

As we stood by the low, stone parapet of the bridge we could hear the distant wasp buzz of a motorbike, which gradually grew louder and we had to get out of the way as an army despatch rider suddenly appeared. He was wearing white gauntlet gloves and his motorbike purred as he coaxed it along the quiet by-road. We dropped sticks into the water and dashed to the other side of the bridge to see them float out. By this time the sun was scorching and there was a heat haze over the countryside. Beyond the small, irregular-shaped fields the trees in the distance looked blurred and quivery, and above them peewits rolled and tumbled in the clear blue sky. Getting hot and sweaty, we flapped our shirts about trying to cool ourselves down a bit as sweat ran into my eyes making them sting.

We slid down the embankment and sat on the grassy banks of the Foss where Jimmy punctured the tin of condensed milk by bashing a nail, which he had taken from Mr Harris' shed, into it with a rock. We made coffee with cold water scooped from the narrow river that ran clear and cool beneath the old stone bridge. We were in heaven enjoying our bread and biscuits and it was so still and peaceful with the river gently slapping against the banks, and purling quietly as it meandered along. The water sparkled and the sun beat down and we were glad to be out of it for a while. As we sat huddled together in the shade, Thelma started to sing the Flanagan and Allen song *Underneath the Arches* and we all joined in. We sipped our mugs of cold, horrible-tasting coffee and tried to convince ourselves that it tasted delicious but who cared anyway? The sweetness of the biscuits disguised the taste and nothing was going to spoil our day. We were still delighted and euphoric at the thought of getting away from the nasty Mrs Harris for good. We were going home at last!

17. The Old Order Changeth

It was well after midday on Monday, the twenty-fifth of May 1942 and there was barely a breath of wind as we sat on the grassy banks of the purling river as it sang its quiet song to the sun. Thelma, who was nearly thirteen years of age and had a great deal of nous, said, "We'll have to be moving and when we get to the main road it goes all the way up to Middlesbrough so we should be able to thumb a lift." Quite happy at that we rinsed the pan and the mugs in the water. "Right then," said Jimmy, shouldering the knapsack, "Lets get on."

Rounding a right-hand bend we came to the collection of old, brick buildings that made up Low Farm and Willow Farm which were set back on the left-hand side of the lane. A little further on to our right stood Manor Farm and a small cottage and there was not a soul to be seen. It was only four weeks since that German plane had dropped a bomb hereabouts injuring one of the horses.

Cattle were grazing languidly on the lush grass and flicking their tails to keep away the clegs that constantly plagued them and, having recently suffered a nasty bite from one, I was wary of them myself. The heat of the afternoon was starting to get to us and the landrail, desperate to attract a mate after his long flight from Africa was still making his raucous croaking calls from his hiding place in the tall grasses. He could have been seen as symbolic as we were also crying out for a little love and attention.

We kept stopping to lark about or to investigate things of interest and getting annoyed Jimmy shouted, "I'll thump yer John if you don't stop chucking them Claggy Jacks on me back." Claggy Jacks (Galium, also known as cleavers or Goose grass) were plants that have tiny hooks on their stems, seed cases and the underside of the leaves allowing them to adhere readily to any hair, fur or cloth that they come in contact with, therefore, we were inadvertently helping to spread their seeds. The roadside hedges were white with may blossom and the afternoon was slipping away by the time we reached the entrance to the outbuildings of Grange Farm on the right. As we turned left onto the main road that ran north through Strensall, we could see the extensive Army firing ranges. Lots of army vehicles were passing to and fro but not one stopped to pick us up even though we thumbed them. There was a ramshackle wooden hut with a verandah by the side of the road that was a kind of cafeteria and it had a sign proclaiming that it was 'Mae West's Place'. Thelma said, "It must've been named after that big busty blonde in the Hollywood fillums."

As we trudged wearily on we saw a number of soldiers coming and going from it and we wished we had the money to buy a nice cold drink and something tasty to eat as our biscuits had all gone by this time. Nearby we could see long regimented rows of wooden huts and bell tents and on the right a little further north we passed the guardroom that stood beside the entrance to the vast Army Barracks.

Strensall Road became Flaxton Road as we reached the wide-open spaces of Strensall Common where thickets of trees almost met above our heads. Near the road there stands of silver birch but a little further back was a small forest of pine trees. The common was a tiny remnant of the vast Forest of Galtres that had once covered this area. Mr Harris had told us that the Haxby Home Guard used to come here to train with the regular soldiers from time to time. We could hear an army sergeant using choice language, not really suitable for the ears of delicate young ladies like Thelma and Dot, as he bawled out and berated his sweating underlings. Fortunately, it did not seem to bother the girls who were enjoying the cool and shade under the luxuriant growth. The foliage was thick and freshly green and the occasional chestnut tree that we passed was covered in a mass of red 'candles'.

The birds were quietly twittering and singing and the grass verges were full of dazzling white cow parsley, Jack-by-the-hedge and other tall wild flowers. Seeing a fallen log, we rested for a while and, as we came back into the open, it took a few seconds for our eyes to adjust to the sun's relentless glare. We plodded on placing one weary foot in front of the other trying to thumb a lift from the odd lorry or car that passed. As time passed and the shadows grew longer and the air began to cool. Jimmy and I were feeling hungry and tired and our lightheartedness had evaporated. We began to get worried and asked Thelma, "How far are we from Middlesbrough now?"

"Don't worry," she replied, "We'll be there soon enough."
Niggling doubts began to enter our minds. "What if we are still out on the road when it gets dark?" I whispered nervously to Jimmy. "Don't be such a cowardy custard." he replied, but I think he was just trying to appear brave in front of the girls.

We had heard stories about various ghosts in the area. A phantom on horseback was said to gallop around the area on moonless nights and it was said that an old clergyman had been seen out in the rain one dark and stormy night but. when a van driver had stopped to pick him up he suddenly vanished. Butt Cottage, which stood between Haxby and Wigginton, and the old vicarage on Moor Lane were also said to be haunted and we began to have second thoughts about this running away lark.

At that point Thelma thumbed a black car, which pulled in to the roadside a little way in front of us. Thelma shouted, "This is it!" and we excitedly ran towards it but, as we reached it, a black uniformed policeman got out and waited for us by the car door. He knew who we were as it seems that Mrs Harris had wheedled the information out of Ducky. The oily creep had split on us after we failed turn up for our dinner. It seems she had hurried round to PC Manging's house to report what he had told her and he had telephoned the police headquarters to inform them of the situation.

The police constable gave us a stern ticking off and said, "Right you lot, get in to the car," before remonstrating with Thelma "You are old enough to have known better." He said before pointing out some of the dangers that we could have put ourselves in. Thelma hung her head in shame; Dot looked bemused and we were just relieved that it was all over. On the way back he asked us " What made you want to run away like that?" and we told him how much we had missed our mams and dads and how unhappy we were at being belted so often for nothing, at which he seemed kindlier towards us. It was the first time I had been in a car but I didn't enjoy it because of the guilt I felt. We were taken back to the house on Usher Lane and in a way I was glad to be back safely despite the likelihood of more beatings to come.

When Mrs Harris came out of the house, she hugged us - a hitherto unheard of occurrence - and thanked the bobby profusely. She then took us inside and we thought we would get a real good belting this time but I think she was too relieved to scold us and instead she was quite nice, saying, "Get yourselves cleaned up and I'll warm up your dinners." And, surprisingly, that was the end of the matter. For a time things improved and we were not hit or belted at all; instead we were sent up to our bedroom and missed a meal whenever we misbehaved. Maybe she was worried that she might end up in trouble with the authorities if it got out that she was belting us again. Possibly she had already had a warning. I don't know what she told Gran about us running away but nothing was ever said about it.

At two p.m. on the following day, Uncle John was still two thousand miles away in the arid heat of the Libyan Desert as the Axis offensive began. The Eighth Army's top brass were convinced that the attack would come at the northern end of the Gazala Line but it seems that General Rommel, the wily 'Desert Fox', had other ideas. Four Italian Divisions, led by a few German tanks, made an attack at the northern end of the defensive line and a sandstorm that had been raging all day, cleared just in time for the evening reconnaissance flight to report on these enemy troop movements. Their vehicles threw up great clouds of dust giving the impression that vast numbers were on the move but the bulk of the Africa Korps was gathered opposite the 150th Brigade around the centre of the line where the Green Howards 4th and 5th Battalions were dug in. After the Allied aircraft had gone, Rommel ordered the main strike force to swing south under cover of darkness and he led from the front, as usual.

My uncle, Acting Sergeant John Bradford, could see the enemy flares and the noise was thunderous as enemy tanks and vehicles moved south along their front but on the other side of the minefield. Travelling without lights they maintained radio silence and, as the night wore on, there seemed to be hundreds of them. The flares dropped by the Luftwaffe guided them and at dawn an enemy aircraft flew low over Uncle John's position and dropped a few bombs making him and his men dive for cover. Around breakfast time the sound of battle could be heard to their east. The enemy was now behind them! They had rounded the stronghold at the southern end of the line and moved north towards Bir Harmat. Rommel had outflanked and outwitted them yet again.

By the following day the enemy had established themselves in the area known as The Cauldron and in the fierce fighting many, on both sides, were killed or taken prisoner. Uncle John and the 150th Brigade now stood between Rommel's troops and his supplies and the skirmishing went on all day. The 5th Battalion were running low on ammunition and water and could not fire as much as they would have liked as they were limited to a certain number of rounds each. Twenty, three-ton lorries were despatched to Tobruk for more ammunition and were expected back that night but they did not appear. At midday on the 29th the enemy tanks and infantry could be seen massing ready for a major attack. Their first attack was successfully repulsed and air activity by both sides increased. At night patrols were still going out into the desert attempting to locate the enemy to find out what they were doing.

Soon after dawn on May 30th the enemy to their east mounted a strong attack with tanks and artillery and the Royal Engineers, who were defending the position, were taken by surprise, and the whole company was taken prisoner. The disputed ridge was now in enemy hands putting the 5th Battalion box in grave danger and there were bloody encounters throughout the day. The enemy were close and in great strength and there was a continual exchange of artillery and machinegun fire. The shortage of ammunition was now being keenly felt and the build up of enemy forces could not be stopped. They were lifting mines to create a passage through which they could pass back and forth with ammunition and supplies. Rommel himself travelled back through the minefield to confer with his superiors before returning to The Cauldron where he resumed his offensive.

Back in Britain, as the green of spring warmed into the gold of early summer, there was a very cloudy spell and it turned wet and thundery. By the late evening of the thirtieth it began to clear up and conditions were ideal as the first of Bomber Harris' one-thousand bomber attack force took to the air. It was said to be the greatest concentration of air power that the world had ever seen with the force largely made up of Wellingtons; Whitleys; Stirlings;

Manchesters; Hampdens; De Havilland Mosquitoes; Halifaxes and the new Lancaster bombers. Many of the Whitleys were Group Four aircraft and it was reported that the target was originally Hamburg but the weather was against it. As the skies were clearer on the western side of Germany, the target was switched to the city of Cologne with its heavy industry and its ancient Rhenish cathedral. In Haxby we became aware of the gradually increasing drone of approaching aircraft, which eventually filled the sky over the village drowning out every other sound. Many of them were from Linton and the other airfields, such as Leeming and Dishforth, just to the north of us. In fact, Harry told us later that four hundred of the total force had taken off from airfields in Yorkshire. The very air and the whole house vibrated as the throaty roar of the massed aircraft reached a crescendo before it slowly faded as they streamed south.

The next day the newspapers declared that the sky was black with them as they crossed the coast at Aldeburgh in Suffolk where the full moon created a silvery path across the cold waters of the North Sea. The newspapers used the term Saturation Bombing for the first time reporting that the massive raid had been an outstanding success describing epic feats of arms. They described it as 'a turning point in the war' and it was said that 1,046 aircraft from fifty-two airfields had taken part forty being lost.

Apparently, one of the air gunners came from nearby Huntington and among the bomber pilots was Leonard Cheshire, our hero. The news bulletins said that Cologne had been set ablaze from end to end with forty factories totally destroyed; seventy badly damaged and, in an area of some 600 acres over 3,000 houses were flattened, but the cathedral was left standing. The area of devastation in the city was six times larger than that at Coventry six months earlier, with nearly five hundred killed, five thousand seriously injured and 50,000 made homeless.

On May 31st Mrs Harris allowed us to stay up to listen to the news, which was now something of a national institution which folk endeavoured not to miss. As the chimes of Big Ben came to an end, John Snagge read out a glowing report on the raid which provided a badly needed boost to the flagging morale of Bomber Command and the people of war-torn Britain. Afterwards Churchill was to say, "This is only a herald of what Germany will receive, city by city, from now on…. We are going to scourge the Third Reich from end to end." Two nights later there was another raid involving almost as many aircraft, but time the target was the Ruhr Valley at Essen. During June more thousand-bomber-raids pounded the German infrastructure and the term terror flyers was coined in Germany for the first time.

On the Gazala Line in Libya, the enemy pressure increased as reinforcements streamed through the gaps in the minefields. The 150th Brigade now had insufficient ammunition to prevent the enemy build up and Rommel's men continued to maul the Allied units one by one. Their 88mm guns took out tank after tank and the 5th Battalion suffered heavy shelling throughout the day with many brave men killed or wounded. Uncle John was to tell us many years later that; "The shells flying overhead sounded like a steam train racing past at close quarters and the dead lay where they fell as there was no time to bury them. In the unrelenting blaze of the sun, with their eyes dimmed in death, they became bloated and covered in flies and as they day wore on they began to stink."

As night fell the situation had become critical and Uncle John's unit was pinned down in its slit trenches. After several days under the blazing sun the men were exhausted and short of water and their only the hope lay in the arrival of the ammunition convoy. The news of the successful thousand bomber raid helped to raise their spirits a little and during the night they buried their dead and moves were made to strengthen their position which was now cut off from their own lines and completely surrounded.

At first light battles erupted on all fronts and the 4th Battalion box was taken with many casualties. A few managed to escape but most were taken prisoner and Brigadier Haydon was killed by a shell blast as he attempted to escape through the minefield. The 5th Bn. held out longer than the rest but it was inevitably overwhelmed with General Rommel leading the final attack in person. The 150th Brigade was no more: it had ceased to exist! Rommel was always in the thick of the action, and therefore able to respond quickly as the situation changed around him. Leading from the front, he showed no fear and the men idolised him, carrying out his orders without demur. After breakfast that morning a convoy of fifty RASC trucks set out from Tobruk with ammunition, fresh water and food, leaguering for the night at El Adam, some thirty miles to the east of Uncle John's position. The next day it set off again but after two hours they found themselves surrounded by German armoured cars and a hundred and fifty men were taken prisoner and marched away. They were handed over to the Italians who took them in trucks to join the thousands of men captured the day before. The Germans made good use of the Allied weapons and supplies and it was the usual story of too little too late. As General Montgomery was to say later 'There are no bad soldiers, only bad leaders.'

One day when we were out in the back garden with Mr Harris, he put a finger to his lips to signal us to be quiet and pointed at the sun-warmed felt of the shed roof. On it we saw several blackbirds crouched breast down with their wings and tail feathers fully splayed out .Why they did it we never did find out. By this time, Crompton Farm and a few others were using large numbers of Italian and German prisoners of war and - as there was an acute shortage of farmhands - they were a godsend to the farmers.

On June the first a red-backed ration book for clothing was issued - not that I remember Mrs Harris ever buying us new clothes. Our clothes had been washed, patched and repaired so many times that they were now threadbare and almost unwearable. We ran around like young ragamuffins - even though Gran swore that she had been sending new clothes quite regularly. What happened to them remains a mystery to this day. Our ragged pullovers were unravelled and Thelma and Dot knitted them up again and, in this way, our old clothes became 'new' jumpers. Due to the increasing shortages single-breasted utility suits with no trouser turn-ups, no buttons on the sleeve or cuffs and fewer or false pockets were introduced to save on the amount of cloth used. There was to be no more fancy embroidery allowed on women's underwear and nighties, and the hemlines of women's skirts were fixed at a higher level at which the local men didn't complain too much.

The bulk of the nation's poultry feed had to be imported leading to fewer poultry and, therefore, a shortage of eggs. Powdered egg was being imported from America, thus saving on shipping space. We were allowed a packet (the equivalent of twelve eggs) each four-weekly rationing period, which cost one shilling and ninepence (9p) at Haxby Co-op. The powder was reconstituted by adding water; but to me it never tasted the same as real eggs and in time we forgot what they tasted like. I must admit that I liked the bacon and egg pies that Mrs Harris baked and we had mashed potatoes made from packets of powdered potato called Pom. Mrs Harris would remark, "Beggars can't be choosers." But Harry was getting real eggs regularly supplied by Miss Barker's brother, Arthur, up at Westfield Farm and they swapped some of their excess farm produce for other items that they needed.

That month a new bomber airfield called RAF East Moor came into service to the south east of Sutton village. It had three concrete runways and three hangars and by the end of June it was fully operational. It was only two miles from us as the crow flies and this meant that the numbers of Halifax bombers flying over Haxby increased.

On a bright Sunday afternoon, I was in the kitchen when there was a knock on the door and Mrs Harris said, "Well, don't stand there like one o'clock half struck, go and answer it lad."

Gran stood on the back step, and she said, "I've got a little surprise for you." At which my five years old brother, George, who I had not seen for almost eighteen months, appeared from behind her. He was going to live here with us and Gran said, "Your Mam won't be able to come for a while as she has left Grove House and is back home being kept very busy working as a cleaner for Ethel Gaunt again." By this time I couldn't picture where most of the places were that she kept talking about, as living in Middlesbrough was by then just a vague half memory. Mrs Gaunt did a lot to help the poorer people of Middlesbrough and was well liked and respected by all. She was a very kind a caring person who the family could depend on in times of trouble. Gran told me that she was the head of the First Aid Centre set up in the old Wesleyan chapel on Lower Lord Street, just off Newport Road and Mam was also working there as a voluntary helper looking after the casualties brought in after bombing raids. I thought Gran seemed sad and eager to be away, and she left as soon as she had handed over my brother's papers, his blue ration book and his belongings. This sudden change of living circumstances meant that our sleeping arrangements would have to be revised and Mrs Harris said, " George will have to sleep in the bed with you, Ducky and Jimmy."

We were arranged with Ducky and Jimmy at the normal end of the bed and George and I had to sleep with our heads on pillows at the foot of it - with the sheet and blanket turned back. We often had the sweaty feet of the bigger boys up near our faces and cold draughts around our feet and Ducky often pulled the blankets off us altogether. We soon got used to it and fortunately it was a warm summer.

Two weeks later, Renee, my auntie - by now eighteen years old, petite and attractive - came to visit us by herself. She took George and me along to Bryant's shop and bought us some stretchy jelly babies before taking us down York Road to Harry's lodgings. She seemed quite pleased on getting a few wolf whistles from the local lads and just before we got there she said to Jimmy; "By the way, you know when you ran away?"

"Yes." he replied.

"Well, you were heading the wrong way. If you had gone through Wigginton and up Corban Lane on to the A19 it would have taken you straight up to Middlesbrough."

On our arrival, the Misses Barker and Law couldn't have made us more welcome and they were delighted on seeing George. They seemed to have a weakness for blond-haired children and they cuddled and fussed him and he loved every minute of it. He had now started school and was in Miss Curry's baby class in St Mary's hall. While we were out in their lovely back garden, I overheard Renee say to Harry, "I'm a bit worried about Mam. She sits at home holding her head in her hands and staring into the fire for ages. There seems to be no life in her and she takes no interest in things around her since she got that telegram. Her mind seems to be a complete blank."

It seems she had received a telegram from the War Office that said, 'I regret to inform you that your son, Acting Sergeant John Bradford, is missing. Believed killed.' and she was devastated. She had lost so many children in her life without this on top of everything else and a deep melancholy had descended on her like a dark cloud. However, on a dark night a few days later, her younger brother, Albert and his wife, Hannah, knocked on her front door. As soon as she opened it Albert, who could not contain his excitement, blurted out, "John's not dead! We've just found out that he's a prisoner-of-war!"

Gran was barely able take in what was being said, and Renee was to say later that her mind went from initial disbelieve, to doubt and finally to acceptance, relief and intense happiness. Tears of joy began to flow and she could not hold them back. Her shoulders shook as she sobbed, but these were tears of joy and utter relief. It seems that Uncle Albert and his wife had been listening to a Lord Haw-Haw broadcast on their wireless. In it he had listed the names of several recently captured prisoners-of-war. One of those mentioned was a certain John Bradford, the son of Mrs A. Knight of 15, Forcass Road, Dormaster, Redcar, Yorkshire. It seems that Uncle John had had on him a crumpled letter from his Aunt Hannah and it was assumed that this was his mother. Albert and Hannah *Knights* actually lived in Dorman<u>stown</u>, which was between Middlesbrough and Redcar.

She had to find out if the news was true or not! When her initial excitement had abated a little she went in search of advice but at least she now had hope to cling on to. The depression that had descended on her was suddenly lifted. Mrs Gaunt, who had sound connections, advised her to write to the Red Cross Society and eventually she received a reply from their London headquarters. It was signed in person by the Dowager Lady Ampthill, the Chairwoman, and it stated, 'As broadcasts from foreign stations are not always reliable we fear that this news cannot be taken as official.' before adding, 'We sincerely hope that you will soon receive an official notification confirming that your son is indeed a prisoner of war.'

It was some time before she learned that John, along with three thousand others, had indeed been taken prisoner. He and the few survivors of his company had been rounded up and marched away with their hands held above their heads. They had lost the battle and their liberty but were undefeated in spirit. Hunkered down on the hot sand in the heat of the blazing desert sun, they asked if they could fill up their water bottles, but a German Officer refused them. They complained and kicked up a bit of a fuss and on hearing the commotion, General Rommel and his aides came across to them. Rommel asked, "What seems to be the problem?" On hearing what had happened, he ordered the officer in charge to give them wasser, before saying in good English, "For you the war is over!" He was a man of honour who was greatly admired and respected by the soldiers of both sides.

Uncle John then set out on the long march towards a makeshift prison camp set up under the blazing desert sun. Already exhausted from the intense fighting, he was on the point of collapse and feared that he would never make it. An old knee injury caused whilst playing football before the war, was giving him a great deal of pain and in order to get onto some form of transport he hit it with a rock causing it to swell up even more and, luckily, the Italian officer took pity on him and he was taken the rest of the way in the back of a lorry. The Italians took him westwards along the coast road and at Derna he had his first bath for some time. He was to say a few years later that, "You felt rotten when you were not clean." They were given meagre portions of bread with a bit of warm watery soup.

It took five days to reach the camp at Tarhunah, which was about forty miles south west of Tripoli. Here the men were registered and filled in Red Cross notification cards and were given one hot meal a day, which consisted of three-quarters of a pint of rice and a little salt. Near Benghazi they had to sleep in the open under the trees of an oasis. He had only a thin vest, a sun-bleached khaki shirt and shorts and, at night when the temperature plummeted, the men lay shivering with cold. In the morning they were given a third of a pint of hot coffee and five cigarettes. At all the camps the sanitation was very primitive and washing facilities were non-existent due to the lack of water. The latrine was a simple slit trench and Uncle John was to say later that, "The filth and the smell was appalling," adding, "Many of the men became undernourished and very weak and the conditions and the ever-present flies led to diarrhoea and dysentery becoming rampant." They finally reached Campo 153 at Suani Ben Adam (meaning The Garden of Eden) twelve miles to the south of Tripoli, which he later described as, "A hell hole with fleas, lice and beetles as big as walnuts. We were deprived of food and rapidly lost weight. The camp was surrounded by eucalyptus trees and we woke to their overpowering smell every morning."

By July there were five thousand in the camp and they had all been captured between the first and the twenty-second of June, which was the date of the broadcast by Lord Haw-Haw that Uncle Albert had heard. They learned that Hitler had promoted Erwin Rommel to the rank of Field Marshal and he was said to have been ecstatic on hearing of the Silver Fox's great victories. At fifty years of age he became the youngest soldier ever to hold the highest rank in the German Army. It was not long before he drove the strung-out Allied Forces back over the Egyptian border and, in the process, retook Tobruk, where another thirty-five thousand men were taken prisoner. It was said that the Allies were disorganised and badly led and even though superior in men, tanks and weapons, they were spread out too thinly and fell back to a place called El Alamein.

When Gran visited in late July, she was back to her cheerful self and she told Harry that she had had a letter from the Borough Council stating that the bomb damage to her house had now been repaired. She was told that she could move back in when she was ready and this and the news concerning her eldest son cheered her up no end. As it was a nice day she took us for a walk up Usher Lane and we showed her Widd's field where we usually played. We dared not tell her about the soldier who had taken out his willy and 'pee'd' milk. Dot and Thelma had been with us at that time and had urged us to move away. We didn't understand what had happened but we sensed that it was wrong and were relieved when the soldier moved on but we didn't know how to tell the grown-ups about it.

Gran took us down to see Harry who had now left school and had been offered the opportunity to train as a butcher at W.H. Atkinson's shop on Front Street. We heard Gran saying to him, "It's lovely to be back in our own house but we've had some really bad bombing raids recently. Archie, Renee and me have had to lay awake half the night in the underground shelters on The Common. Some nights the sky is lit up by searchlights and the roar of the German bombers goes on for ages as they drop their high explosives, oil bombs and incendiaries. Archie hasn't been at the Britannia Works long and it was lucky that he wasn't on the night shift the other day. The railway line not far from us was hit and damaged and it's not long since the petrol tanks at I.C.I were bombed and set on fire. The raids seem to be happening more and more often and we're worn out through worry and lack of sleep. You should think yourself lucky that you're here and well out of it."

One day as we were in the playground on our mid-afternoon playtime we realised that the Home Guard were taking part in a mock battle with the regulars from Strensall Camp. They were practising street fighting and we rushed to the front of the school to get a better view of the proceedings. Jimmy and I managed to find a ringside seat on the wall and all the kids were shouting out remarks such as, "Watch out he's behind you!" One of the Home Guard lads had hidden in a half-empty water barrel that stood in front of the garage across the road just before a group of Army regulars appeared from the direction of Wigginton. As they crept along with their faces blackened they came up to the barrel and we were all excitedly shouting, screaming, and pointing at it. One of the soldiers soon twigged and looked inside and the unfortunate Home Guard youth was 'captured' and escorted away. At that point Mr Fox appeared and he was fuming as he shouted, "You lot! Get back into school this instant!" and one or two of the regular troublemakers got a clout round the ear as they hurried by him.

My pal, John Wade, had had a mild attack of scabies about a month back and had been put into the isolation unit set up in The Laurels on Station Road. It was good to have him back and he said, " I 'ated it there. They gave me 'ot baths and plastered ointment on all the scabby bits and that. When I were getting better I couldn't believe me eyes when I went int't'back garden. There were an 'alf-dead vine with real grapes growing on it. I nicked a few and they were lovely and sweet." Grapes were almost impossible to come by at that time.

He told me that the Shaws were always at the school complaining about something or other and we often saw Mrs Shaw cycling round the village in her pinny. She rode so slowly that we thought that she must surely fall off but she never did. John got on well with her and whenever she saw him around the village she would shout; "Get yersel 'ome! Yer Mam needs yer boots for bread tins."

We had to go to Haxby Hall for health check-ups with the grey-haired Nurse Hart who was quite strict and seemed very old to me. We hated having to go to the school dentist who had thick nicotine-stained fingers and stank of cigarettes when he leaned over us and I've had a dread of going to the dentists ever since. Mr Clayton, the school Attendance Officer, who was tall and bald headed, used to come over from Strensall on his old sit-up-and-beg bike in all weathers. We called him the kid catcher but the truancy man's' job would soon become a little easier as Derek Robinson would be going to the Joe-Row School after the summer holiday.

One morning, just before we broke up, a dark green Civil Defence trailer was parked in the school playground. Mr Fox had told us to bring our gas masks to school that day and he led our class outside and lined us up saying, "You are here to make sure that your masks are still working properly and the civil defence men will tell you what you have to do." The man in the blue overalls gathered us into groups of six and said, "You will test your masks by going into the gas chamber with them on. Once inside you will be told to take them off for a second or two. You must then walk quickly out through the door. Don't worry, if your masks are ok and are properly fitted there should be no problems." We reluctantly entered the trailer as instructed and ripped off our masks when ordered to do so by the ARP man inside. As soon as we got a whiff of tear gas there was a mad panic to get out of the trailer as quickly as possible and we tried to hold our breath as we made a dash for the door. As I staggered out into the playground gasping for air, my eyes stung like mad and tears were streaming down my face. It was not a pleasant experience to say the least.

It seems that the powers-that-be had noticed that our old cardboard gas mask boxes where now in a sorry state or non-existent and we were issued with long, round, lidded tins to keep them in. A large amount of cocoa powder mixed with sugar had been sent to this country from Canada and we were told to bring a container to school. We used our gas mask tins and got them filled up but by the time we got to the house the mixture had gone down a bit. We could not resist wetting our fingers with spittle and dipping them into it before licking them clean. This was a real godsend at a time of real shortages and for a while afterwards we were in Mrs

Harris' good books. Just after we broke up for the summer holiday, sweets - already in short supply - were put on ration and this was a real blow to us. Large chocolate bars became a thing of the past as we were only allowed two ounces of sweets per week and small ration-size bars began to appear in the shops. Shortages of milk meant that milk chocolate was very hard to come by and Rowntrees had recently produced wafer fingers covered in plain chocolate called Kit Kat that came in blue wrappers. In August the ration was raised to three ounces but syrup, treacle and biscuits were put on points. We decided to spend our few coppers on the smallest sweets we could find as Jimmy had said, "If we buy Nips, pear drops or Fishermen's Friends they'll last much longer," and in this way we kidded ourselves that we had a lot. Nips were tiny black sweets with a strong liquorice flavour.

The use of cars for pleasure trips was stopped, which didn't affect us but it affected Harold Atkinson, the butcher. Harry told us that he had to lock his car away for long spells now but he was still able to get out a bit as he was allowed 'pool' petrol for his van. This had been dyed pink to prevent it being used for pleasure trips but he told Jimmy that, "He strains it through a gas mask filter, which takes the colour out of it."

Harry had attended the Joe Row School for only six months before leaving at the end of the summer term. He was now fourteen years old and he couldn't wait to start work full time at the small butcher's shop on Front Street. It was four doors up from Bryant's shop and there was an alleyway next to it that led through to the small pig-sticking area in the big yard at the back. At one time it had loose boxes for the horses that had been used to pull the carts of the previous butcher, Tommy Raines. Harold had bought the business from him just before the war and it was here that Harry learned how to kill pigs and drain their blood off to make black pudding.

When we were in the school playground we could hear the doomed pigs squealing and smell the blood. The girls put their hands over their ears to block out the piercing, high-pitched cries and Eva Pulleyn said, "They sound just like a baby crying." Harold only killed them when there was an R in the month, explaining to Harry that, "It's done in order to prevent the meat from going off in the hot summer months as we haven't got a refrigerator." Nothing was wasted and Harry used to say, "The only part of a pig that you can't eat is the squeal."

Harold, a bespectacled, dapper man of medium height, kept his dark hair parted neatly in the middle and it was well plastered down with hair oil. He was one of the few people in the village that had a telephone. Having social pretensions, he was a member of the Golf Club and enjoyed strolling round the golf course in his checked v-necked jumper, cravat and plus-fours. Both he and his wife played tennis and he played for the village cricket team. Being a part time member of the local Auxiliary Fire Service (AFS) based at Haxby Hall, meant that he often had to don his steel helmet and his black uniform, with its double row of shiny silver buttons and a thick leather belt, to attend call-outs and fire drills. He was as proud as a peacock when his team, led by Mr Lionel Winn who lived on The Avenue, won a trophy in a fire fighting competition held at Scarborough.

The little butcher's shop, that had rows of hams hung up on meat hooks, was kept immaculately clean and smelled of scrubbed wood and sawdust. Harold really looked the part in his blue and white vertically striped apron that reached down to his shins, and he wore his straw boater at a rakish angle. He lived above the shop with his wife and baby son, Bruce, although the name struck Harry as a bit odd for a baby. One of our Harry's jobs was to wash down the white-tiled walls, the chopping block, the counter and the work surfaces. Harold was urbane, courteous and polite when serving customers but was deferential to the point of being obsequious as he said, "And how may one help madam?"

Harry said, "He has the typical shopkeeper's manner. He tends to be a bit smarmy and oily especially with the lady customers and it makes you cringe when he sucks up to them. All the same, most of them seem to like it and, if he likes them, he often slips an extra bit of meat, a bit of dripping or a couple of sausages into their shopping basket." He was good to Harry and he gave the housewives as large a ration as the law would allow. These now included Mrs Harris, as she had switched her meat dealer after Harry started working there. Maybe she thought that as we were part of his family she might get preferential treatment.

18. The Turning Tide

So another long, hot, summer holiday started and the great outdoors beckoned. In the languorous summer heat we played in Widd's field and watched the farmhands bringing in the tassel-headed oats, followed soon after by the bearded barley. We now had our George to think about and Mrs Harris said, "Now, you look after him or you'll have me to answer to. Do you hear?"

"Yes, Mrs Harris," I meekly replied.

As he was only five we had to keep a close eye on him, especially when we were by the pond, which was shallow and quite safe as long as he didn't fall over in it. Fortunately for us, Thelma enjoyed holding his hand and taking him everywhere with her and, anyway, we didn't want a little kid hanging around with us all the time. We had more grown-up things to do. Jimmy and I missed our mothers who had not been to see us for some time now but we just had to accept it when Gran said they were too busy to come.

In August Renee came to visit us again and we were over the moon when she gave us three wooden rifles that Uncle Albert had made for us. We seldom got shop-bought toys. She had brought a friend called Francie who worked with her in the steelworks. We heard her say to Harry, "Middlesbrough station was in a right state when we left as it was bombed by a Dornier 217 on the afternoon of Bank Holiday Monday. The plane flew in below the barrage balloons somehow managing to miss the steel cables. There were two direct 'its and the roof fell in and they 'aven't got everything cleared up yet. You've never seen such a mess! There were great buckled roof girders and glass all over the place. Two other bombs fell nearby killing eight people and injuring lots of others. Luckily there was only slight damage to the railway lines or we wouldn't be 'ere now."

Jimmy and I got very excited when she told us they were going to take us to the pictures as neither of us had been to see a film before. They took us into York on the red bus that picked up outside the Co-op and we got off in Exhibition Square and walked into the centre through the old Roman gateway at Bootham Bar. It was the first time I had been to the city and the narrow crowded

378

streets were a bit scary and overpowering at first. I held tightly on to Renee's hand as she took us along Coney Street where repairs to the bomb damaged buildings were still in progress.

They took us to The Picture House for the afternoon showing of a Hollywood film called 'The Black Swan' starring the handsome, swashbuckling Tyrone Power. Before the lights were lowered we gazed in awe at the grandeur and opulence of the place. We had never experienced anything like it and could hardly believe how plush and comfortable the seats were. The brightly coloured cartoons took our breath away and we had a good laugh at the Tom and Jerry cartoons.

At the start of the Pathé news a big black and white crowing cockerel filled the large silver screen. We had seen pictures of Winston Churchill in the newspaper but here he was walking and talking, larger than life. Carrying his silver-topped walking stick and wearing his famous Homburg hat, he made the Victory-V sign with one hand whilst smoking a fat Havana cigar. As he visited a bomb-damaged area wearing a siren suit that bulged at the waist, the people cheered and shouted, "Good old Winnie!" He was a symbol of hope epitomising the bulldog spirit of our beleaguered nation. Renee said, "Everyone admires him for standing up to Hitler and his rotten cronies." Because of him it never entered people's heads that we would lose the war and he had recently given their hopes a boost by declaring that, "The tide of war is starting to turn!"

We learned from the newsreel that Malta had been relieved when a naval convoy finally got through. We were entranced on seeing the mighty ships ploughing through the waves and being attacked by screaming German Stukas. The announcer said that during the three year long blockade there had been very heavy losses of men and ships. We sat transfixed when the main feature film came on and it made a great impression on our young minds and at the end of the film we stood silently to attention while the National Anthem was played.

The feature film fuelled our imagination for weeks to come and during our games in Widd's field we became dashing pirates attacking treasure ships as we sailed the Seven Seas. We fashioned cutlasses from bits of wood and tied bits of cloth round our heads as bandanas. Jimmy played the baddie who had a hook in place of a hand. In reality it was the hook off a coat hanger but he said he was Captain Hook from the 'Peter Pan' story. I said, "Yer look more like Fred Potter, " as Harry had told me, "He's the signalman at the York- Hull railway crossing and he has a hook where his left hand should be having lost it fighting in the Great War." "I didn't know they 'ad pirates in the last war." I said, and got a swift clip round the ear for my trouble. Inside our heads we sailed the ocean blue and shouted things like, "Avast me 'earties! Stand by to repel boarders!" and suchlike. The war games took a back seat for a little while.

When we started back at school in September there were a number of changes. The lovely Miss Rutter was now my teacher and Jimmy felt badly done to as he was now in Mr Fox's group. Miss Rutter, was the unpaid deputy head, and although she was slender-waisted, sprightly and vivacious, she could be quite strict at times. I remember the faint waft of scent that followed her as she passed by and the touch of her soft wavy hair as she leaned over to check my work. Scent was a luxury by that time so I don't know where it came from. Maybe she got it on the black market. When she smiled her rosebud lips parted slightly to reveal a glimpse of sparkling white teeth and Jimmy got jealous when I talked about her and gave me a thump in the ribs. He was eight and half and was starting to change his mind about girls, deciding that maybe some of them had their good points.

There was growing concern over the increased number of road deaths caused by the blackout regulations. At Haxby there were very few cars but a fair number of military vehicles passed to and fro, and while the weather held, we were taken out onto Front Street to practice the recently introduced kerb drill. It was drummed into us, "Look right, look left and look right again and, if the road is clear, walk briskly across. Do not run! " We repeated this routine ad nauseum until it became a lifetime habit.

During Tatie Picking Week Jimmy and I got a job at Haxby Lodge Farm but the girls had to stay in to help Mrs Harris with her cooking, preserving and pickling. They had been taught domestic skills from an early age. We got picked up outside the house early in the morning and we climbed into a farm cart pulled by a huge,

380

chestnut-coloured, Shire horse. We clip-clopped up Usher Lane, past Crossmoor Lane end and straight on up a farm track that led off the Strensall road. The farmer, Tom Bentley, had taken the farm over earlier that year. The work was back-breaking but we weren't expected to work as hard as the older people and we thought of it as a bit of fun and were glad to earn a bit of extra pocket money. During a tea break one of the farmhands lifted Jimmy up onto the back of the great, round-bellied horse and led it a few yards up the field. Jimmy sat there with his legs sticking out as they were too short to go round the horse's flanks and he was terrified as he hung on to the horses mane for grim death. He shouted, "I don't like! I don't like! Get me down! Get me down!" When asked if I would like a go I said, " Not on your Nelly!" Being too little to work a full day we walked back to the house in time for our frugal dinner each day. Mrs Harris put George to bed at seven and I went at eight and I tried to get to sleep before Jimmy and Ducky got into bed at the other end and let the cold air in.

Soon afterwards a frisson of excitement ran through the two villages when a Halifax Mk II bomber on an air test from RAF East Moor crashed behind *The Black Horse* in Wiggington. It came down near Crow Lane, which was an ancient snickleway that came out by the old Vicarage up on Moor Lane. Derek Robinson was there like a shot of course, determined to add to his collection of military treasures. He had been potato picking for the Midgeleys at nearby Manor Farm when the crash happened. He had to keep a sharp lookout in case his old enemy PC Manging was already there on his bike as he called regularly at the farms to check shotgun permits and the like. He told us later that, "The plane 'ad the letters NP on its fuselage and it were painted black underneath so as not to show up so much if it were 'coned' by t'searchlights over Germany."

He added that, "Number 76 Squadron 'as just come back to Linton. 'Ave yer not seen their 'Alifaxes goin' over t'village? They 'ave t'letters MP on em. They say that Leonard Cheshire is back agen for t'third time. Ah went over theer on me bike and saw t'new four thousand pound (1,800kgs.) bombs being loaded on t't'one' o't'Alifaxes. They were on long trolley things and looked like railway locomotive boilers. Most 'ad a rude message to 'Itler chalked on 'em by t'fitters." We wondered how he came to know which aircraft belonged to which squadron. We saw and heard ever more aircraft flying out at dusk as the gallant crews set off on their hazardous bombing missions and we often heard them coming back in the early hours of the morning.

The nights had started to draw in and the leaves on the chestnut trees were turning brown and curling up at the edges. It was a time for the closing of doors and the pulling down of blinds but there was still a bit of light after tea due to the double summertime. As we went for walks, there was a feeling of wistful melancholy in the air that was congenial to my spirit. The hedgerows along Usher Lane, which had become ragged and overgrown, were silhouetted starkly against the primrose and crimson sky to the west. The evening light tinged the fields and trees a ruddy, rosy hue and as we reached Jubilee Farm the upper windows of the old stone-built farmhouse reflected the orange orb of the setting sun. Birds, their feathers ruffled by the breeze, sat in long rows on the telegraph wires preparing for the long journey south. As we came closer they took flight and the sky was turned black by their rolling and wheeling movements. I could hear the wind soughing softly along the wires and the countryside was peaceful and still. I missed Mam and Dad so much and wished that I could fly north and, if they didn't come soon, I feared that I might start to forget what they looked like.

When Gran came again she said to Mrs Harris; "I'm glad to say that I've had word from the Red Cross that John is definitely a prisoner of war. The Italians 'ave got 'im"

"Well, that's a relief for you." replied Mrs Harris, "They say that they treat them better than the Germans and much better than the cruel Japs."

Gran was not to learn till later that her son had been kept in a transit camp near Tripoli for four and a half months. In it there had been hundreds of closely packed tents with twenty-five men to each and they were given just one blanket. Due to the constant torture of the fleas that lived in the sand, it was difficult to sleep and there were long queues at the stinking, fly-ridden latrines. The roll calls could last up to two hours due to men having to constantly hurry back to them. The Italian Corporal Major in charge of the cookhouse helped himself to the men's rations, giving large amounts to the sentries who sold it. At no time were they given fresh fruit or vegetables and consequently they became malnourished, weak and underweight. At last, on October the eighteenth, they were taken to Tripoli in army trucks and were put in the hold of a coal boat that set sail for Italy. John was suffering from feverish shivering fits when - four days later - the ship arrived at Naples in the middle of an electric storm. They were obliged to spend another night in the ship's hold and the next day they were taken to the prison camp at Capua, which was nineteen miles north of Naples, and was known as Campo 66.

Around that time the tide of war had begun to turn in our favour and Mr Harris learned from his newspaper that Churchill had sacked General Auchinleck and replaced him with General Bernard Montgomery. He felt that the small, sharp-featured, slim man who had total confidence in himself, was the right man for the job and so it proved. Very decisive and thorough in his preparations, the men rallied behind him and by now the Eighth Army had the most powerful armoured force that had ever been seen in the desert. Its strength lay in its American Sherman and Grant tanks and it now outnumbered the Axis troops in men and weapons. Montgomery set about making a stand with the aim of defeating Rommel once and for all. The Luftwaffe had been weakened due to their supplies not getting through and the Allies had regained air superiority.

At a little place called El Alamein the Allies attacked while Rommel was ill at home On Friday evening, October the 23rd, Mr Harris sat listening to the wireless and he shouted up the stairs, "The Germans and Italians are copping it at El Alamein! Come and listen to this, kids!" On coming downstairs, we could heard the tremendous din of the big guns, the whoosh of mortars and exploding mines that was being broadcast. It was said to be the heaviest artillery barrage ever carried out. The Axis forces lost many of their tanks and weapons, but they held on until Rommel hurried back to lead them.

In early November they attacked again with Montgomery's 'Desert Rats' carrying out relentless tank and infantry assaults until they finally broke through. The battleground was littered with dead bodies and burned out tanks and thousands of Germans and Italians were taken prisoner but, somehow, Rommel managed to get away. and for the first time one of Hitler's field marshals was being thoroughly thrashed in battle. Rommel's troops retreated a thousand miles back through Libya to El Agheila and the Allies retook Tobruk on the way. Hitler ordered Rommel to stand and fight but Mussolini gave him permission to retreat to the Tunisian border. By this time British and American forces had landed in Morocco and Algiers to his west and Hitler and Mussolini poured a quarter of a million troops into Tunisia ready to make a final stand.

On November 15th as mouldering leaves littered the gutters, Winston Churchill gave the order for church bells all across the country to be rung in celebration of the great victory in Egypt. The people of Usher Lane poured out into their gardens to hear the joyful sound of the external bells of St. Mary's that had been silent for two and a half years. Churchill spoke to the nation with the now immortal words; "We have a victory, a remarkable and definite victory....Now, this is not the end. It is not even the beginning of the end. But it is, perhaps, the end of the beginning."

In Haxby, Mr Harris learned that his hero - Wing Commander Cheshire the new CO at Linton - had damaged his hand and arm when his car skidded on the narrow, icy roads while driving back from a night out in York in the early hours of the morning. That month the first of the new Canadian squadrons took over at East Moor airfield equipped with well-used Wellington Mk III bombers with the letters AL on their fuselages. This meant that we saw a different type of aeroplane flying over the village and many Canadian airmen came over to Haxby on their blue RAF issue bikes as their airfield was only three miles away.

The Americans had arrived in this country earlier in the year and at first we thought that the Canadians were Yanks and whenever we saw them we would say, "Got any gum chum?" and they gave us packs of small white sugar-coated pieces of chewing gum called Chiclets that were wrapped in shiny red paper. Some of the cheeky lads would ask them for cigarettes and they usually gave them Passing Cloud or Sweet Caporal's. The Canadians seemed to be well liked by both the RAF lads and the locals - especially the ladies, some of whom were now wearing the aluminium rings that they had made for them. Their smart uniforms with the Canada shoulder flashes became a familiar sight as they came and went between the three pubs.

The day before we broke up for Christmas, Anthony Eden stood up in a hushed House of Commons and condemned the Germans for going along with Hitler's intention of exterminating every Jew in Europe. He said, "Those responsible for these crimes shall not escape retribution." This was evil on a gigantic scale and it was anything but a happy Christmas for thousands of people across Europe. The terrible plight of the Jews - men, women and children - was often reported in the newspapers.

At school we got swallowed up in the mounting excitement as we were kept busy preparing for the forthcoming Christmas events and time passed quickly. I had a walk-on part in the nativity play but was far too shy for any speaking parts. We got stuck into the eats and enjoyed the fun and games at the school Christmas party. Women were allowed to attend church without a hat for the first time, as their old ones were becoming too tatty and new ones were hard to come by. Gran came through on Boxing Day and brought a few sweets, nuts, lead soldiers and a wooden fort made by one of her brothers, which I thought was great, and Mrs Harris even let me play with it in the front parlour.

On New Year's Eve she let us come downstairs just before midnight to see the annual first-footing ritual: an ancient custom thought to have been brought to these parts by the Norsemen. There must have been a temporary cease-fire in the long-term bickering, as their relationship seems to have be one long series of storms and calms with more storms than calms. Mr Harris stood outside in the snow like most of the other men of Wold View Terrace, the majority of whom had dark hair as that was considered lucky. They were all shivering from the cold with their hands deep in their pockets and each of them clutched a piece of coal and a silver sixpence ready to herald in the New Year. Inside the house Mrs Harris had a small whisky and a piece of cake ready and as the midnight chimes of Big Ben were heard on the wireless Mr Harris knocked on the front door. His wife let him in and he said, "'Appy New Yeer everyone. I 'ope t'war will soon be over and that this yeer will be t'best un for a long time." He handed over the coal and

385

silver saying, " 'Ere's 'oping we 'ave warmth, wealth and good 'ealth in't yeer ter come." Mrs Harris handed him the whisky and cake along with a perfunctory peck on the cheek and this routine was carried out in all of the houses in the village. Several of the men had already partaken of a few jars at the *Tiger*, the *Red Lion* or the club.

It was to be another long, hard, snow-covered winter. Early in the year we were woken by the unsynchronised sound of a German plane overhead and as we peeped around the edge of the blind, snow was creeping up the windowpanes and we could see the underside of the snow-filled clouds lit up by the searchlight. In the powerful beam, we could clearly see the black crosses on the wings of a low flying Dornier but it flew off and the night passed quietly. For some reason the siren had not been sounded and we were not being woken by it quite as often now. Throughout January there was snow and cloud so there was not so much flying. However, there were sporadic attacks on the area.

On those crisp, wintry days we sat shivering in our classroom with the old, wrought iron radiators working overtime in an attempt to combat the bitter cold but the warmth did not reach far into the large, high-ceilinged rooms. One playtime early in the year, I went to find Jimmy and found him very upset and I could see that he had been crying. "What's the matter, Jim?" I enquired. "Well, there was this sixpenny National Savings stamp on t'corner of a desk. It was just laid there doing nothin, so I picked it up and before I 'ad time to 'and it in I was accused of nicking it. The locals always blame us if anything goes wrong and Miss Curry grabbed 'old of me ear and marched me off to be caned by t'headmaster. I told 'er I'd found it but she didn't believe me. Luckily, Miss Rutter came along and spoke up for me, saying, 'Jimmy is an honest lad and I know that he would not do such a thing.' Luckily, Mr Fox believed 'er and she got me off." There was a school Savings Club and most of the kids usually bought a sixpenny stamp every Monday, which they stuck on a card until they had filled it and then they exchanged it for a fifteen-shilling (75p) certificate. We could not afford sixpence a week but we were given one occasionally as a reward for good attendance. The register was marked in the morning and afternoon, which counted as two attendances.

Just three weeks into the year we had just gone to bed when the siren sounded and Mr Harris dashed into our room shouting, "Come on lads, tek cover, quick as yer can!" We dashed downstairs with our blankets and scrambled under the front room table as the girls got into the gas cupboard. We heard the sound of a low flying Jerry plane screaming by directly over the house and there was heavy fire from the local anti-aircraft gun. The noise was terrific and we were terrified when a second or so later there were two loud explosions nearby that made the floor jump. We learned later that a Dornier had jettisoned two bombs. We clung on to Mr Harris as the glass in the front window caved in, but the blast tape held most of it together. My ears hurt a bit and the front door frame was loosened by the blast making it difficult to close thereafter. On York Road the windows of Harry's billet were cracked.

The next day - being a Saturday - we went up Towthorpe Road to see what damage had been done and nearly the whole village and lots of people from Strensall were there. We had not been up that way since we had tried to run away. One bomb had just missed the railway line, making a huge crater in the railway embankment near the Golland Dyke, and the other had exploded in front of Manor Farm. Derek Robinson was there of course and he told us, "The bomb blast killed a coo outright and t'flying, razor-edged shrapnel injured an 'osses tail so badly that it 'ad to be cut off by t'vet." The regular soldiers and Home Guard men were keeping people away but we still managed to get some bits of shrapnel for our collections.

At school during morning assembly Miss Curry regularly kept us informed on the progress of the war and she told us that the Germans troops at Stalingrad had surrendered, adding, "The German offensive, that started so brilliantly, has come unstuck in the terrible Russian winter and this defeat, on top of the victory at El Alamein, gives the lie to the myth of Germany's invincibility. The British are pushing back the Japs in Burma and you should all be very proud of our brave fighting men. It looks like the tide might be turning at last" We didn't know what a 'myth' was and we didn't think much of them telling lies about being invisible. What the tide had to do with it we weren't too sure but we thought it must be good news.

So the long winter days dragged on and as Thelma held George by the hand and took him to the infant school, she had trouble in keeping his shoes dry as he tried to jump in every puddle with both feet. When we had the money, Jimmy and I called at Bryant's shop before school to buy a ha'penny Oxo cube or a small packet of powdered soup to suck on. We wished we had plenty of money like the people at Harry's end of the village and the posh people who lived on The Avenue. We wondered whether the toffs really deserved all the privileges they had and I remember saying to Jimmy, "When I grow up I'm going to have a house full of monkeys and loads of red double-decker buses to play with."
"I'm going to be either a tramp walking all over the countryside or else a train driver." he replied.

Some days flew and others seemed to crawl by and it made a nice change when Renee came and took Jimmy and me into York on the bus. George, being too young to go to the pictures, stayed in the house with Thelma who loved looking after him. It was February and, as Renee took us round by the Minster with its graceful gothic arches, the snow and frost had relented a little. Words fail to do justice to its awesome splendour and Renee pointed out the ugly stone gargoyles that had melting snow dripping from their twisted, slavering mouths which frightened me. She bought us a lovely red-green toffee apple on a stick that had a nice crunchy flat bit on top where it had been stood upside down to dry.

There was an afternoon matinee with Bing Crosby and Fred Astaire starring in the film 'Holiday Inn' in which the hit song was *White Christmas* and we loved every minute of it. Renee bought us a packet of Smith's crisps and warned us, "Don't rattle the packets when the film's on and don't eat the blue one because it's a small packet of salt." We were warm and comfortable in there but I was a bit worried in case a bomb dropped on it when we were inside. Renee said, " Don't worry. If the siren goes they'll put a message up on the screen to tell us to go to the nearest air raid shelter."

The bus was crowded on the journey back to Haxby but Renee let us have the only seat while she stood hanging on one of the straphangers. We had to walk back to Usher Lane on our own as she had to stay on the bus until after it had turned round by the Co-op in order to be at York station in time to catch her train home.

In March the weather turned treacherously cold again and more snow fell and lay but it turned to sleet and rain later in the month. Some days it teemed down all day and we came in from school sodden and looking like drowned rats. Because of the wet weather we had to stay in at the weekend and had to make our own entertainment. We played cards, ludo, tiddly-winks and draughts up in our bedroom but the fire up there was never lit and the house was always cold. On other days we had thick white blankets of dripping, clinging mist or fog and our skin became chapped and sore. After dark when the fog made landing the planes difficult the searchlights in the area were switched on for a time and their beams would cross directly above the East Moor runway. We could see them clearly from our bedroom window, as the runway was only two miles away. As the Wellington bombers with their Canadian crews returned from bombing or mine-laying sorties the lights guided them in.

Just before Jimmy's ninth birthday Mr Winterburn the postman, who did a bit of boot and shoe repairing part-time, brought him birthday cards, but again there was nothing from his Dad. Mr Winterburn had a wooden right leg which he swung round as he walked and his bike had been specially adapted for him. It had a fixed wheel and he used his left foot to turn the pedal while the other pedal remained still. Aunt Hilda came to see him on his birthday wearing her ATS uniform and she looked slim, petite and attractive in it. One of his presents was a brand new leather belt with a metal buckle. Jimmy really treasured it as very few boys had belts in those days; most wore braces to keep their trousers up. Aunt Hilda told him that she was now a nursing auxiliary at Fenham Barracks in Newcastle and was on leave. She took him into York on the red double-decker bus so that they could spend some time together. After giving the three of us a kiss before she left, she seemed more upset and tearful than usual.

A few days later, Jimmy was with Dot in the kitchen and she asked in her slow dilatory manner, "Can I have a look at your new belt?" He passed it over and the next thing he knew she had the belt in one hand and the buckle in the other. Jimmy flew into a rage, grabbed the buckle and threw it at her as he burst into tears shouting, "Now look what you've done you dozy article!" On

389

catching sight of the white enamelled pail next to the corrugated metal wash tub in the corner that had the wooden poss stick in it, he grabbed hold of it and 'hoyed' (threw) it at her causing a small cut on her hand as she raised it to protect herself.

On hearing the commotion, Mrs Harris rushed in and wrapped her arms tightly round him to prevent him causing any more damage. "Get up them stairs and stay there." she shouted at Dot, before taking Jimmy up to his bedroom to calm him down. She fixed the detachable buckle back on to his belt and he was happy again, but he was also very surprised, as he had expected a good hiding at the very least. Instead she had taken his side and had given him a glass of milk and a biscuit.

Finally spring, with its promise of long, warm, summer days, arrived. The snowdrops and crocuses went over and primroses, daffodils, cowslips and forget-me-nots appeared in their due time. Masses of white blackthorn blossom adorned the hedgerows and flowering bluebells carpeted the ground under the fresh green foliage of the trees in the woods. My eighth and George's sixth birthday arrived but only Gran and Renee came to pamper us and take us out for special treats. Gran said; "I know you miss your Mam and Dad but they send their love and they asked me to give you your present and a big kiss from them. They couldn't come themselves because of their war commitments." At that she gave us big wet kisses on the cheek which I immediately rubbed off with my jumper sleeve. I whispered to Jimmy, "I hate all that sloppy stuff. It's alright on the pictures but that's not for real."

At school Derek Robinson had told Jimmy that Leonard Cheshire had been moved from Linton back to RAF Marston Moor saying, "They 'ad a right boozy party up at t'camp and 'is squadron cheered and clapped him." It was a mystery how Derek knew of such things so quickly but there were lots of RAF lads billeted in Hilbra Avenue and maybe they told him. He was also quite pally with the Bousfield twins who had come from Hull at about the time I arrived in Haxby and their dad worked at the aircraft maintenance unit at Shipton and was the local RAF billeting officer. Mr Harris, who was generally not much of a book reader, went into York and bought himself a copy of Leonard Cheshire's new book *Bomber Pilot* and he read out some of the exciting bits to us.

Ten days later, as we were coming out of school, we heard a terrific explosion over towards Huntington village, which was about a mile away. A cloud of thick black smoke was rising into the air and we learned later that a Wellington bomber from the RCAF (Royal Canadian Air Force) East Moor airfield had lost power in both engines causing it to stall and crash into a pair of semi-detached houses killing the crew of five and two civilians. One of the dead was an old lady who had lived in the village for years. Several people - including Derek Robinson - tried to get to the 'prang' but it was too horrific and the soldiers would not let anyone near.

At school Miss Curry informed us that the Battle of the Ruhr had started and that Bomber Command aircraft were pounding Germany's industrial heartland night after night. There was a noticeable increase in aerial activity over the village and we saw lots of Wellington bombers and the new Lancaster bombers for the first time. The Halifaxes seemed different somehow and we then realised that they now had a Perspex 'blister' on their underside. It seems that Leonard Cheshire had pointed out that, "Far too many bombers have been brought down due to unseen night-fighter attacks from their blind side and an underbelly gun turret would make them less vulnerable." He had recently been promoted to the rank of Group Captain and, at the age of only twenty-five, was the youngest ever to attain such a rank.

One afternoon, after a wet morning, we were playing on the grass verges up Usher Lane when Jimmy, who was a deviser of dares, said; "I dare yer to jump over t'ditch." It was deep and the sides were muddy and wet and I refused to do it. " Cowardy, cowardy custard!" he retorted, "Look, I'll show yer 'ow it's done." At that he took a running jump but his take-off foot slipped on the muddy bank and he landed with a splash in the dirty water at the bottom. We were creased with laughing until our stomachs hurt. His clothes were clarted in mud and we suddenly thought, 'What will Mrs Harris say when she finds out?' In all probability he would be in for another belting. Thelma said, " We'd better try and get 'im cleaned up and quick."

The girl's sandals and our boots were in a bit of a mess as well, so we climbed the gate into the field and took them off and it was nice to feel the cool, soft grass under our bare feet. By then the weather had cleared up and the sun was shining as we headed for Widd's pond so that Jimmy could wash his socks in it. We always wore woollen socks that had bands of blue and red at the top that always seemed to end up round our ankles. He rubbed the mud off his trousers and his jumper with a wet rag and whirled his jumper round and round to throw off the excess pond water. He then lay his socks and jumper on the top of the hedge to dry. Luckily it was now warm and sunny and they dried enough for him to put on. The rest of us washed the mud from our footwear.

On going back to the house at teatime we thought we had got away with it as Mrs Harris didn't seem to notice anything wrong and we sat and had our tea as usual. We had a thick 'doorsteps' of bread spread with beef dripping sprinkled with salt and I loved it. Our Harry saw to it that we were kept well supplied with it. We then filled up with plum jam sandwiches without margarine and all seemed well until Mrs Harris suddenly came storming into the room in one of her rages. Grabbing Jimmy by the scruff of the neck, she hauled him off the bench shouting, "Let me see your boots you sly little devil."

He took them off and she closely examined the lace holes and found traces of mud in them. That creep Ducky had split on us yet again. Out came the belt and Jimmy was marched up the stairs and given another good thrashing on his backside as he lay face down on the bed. He wouldn't give her the satisfaction of seeing him cry; although he cried later when she had gone. She was red in the face with anger and the exertion when she came downstairs. "Thought you could fool me did you? Now get up to your rooms and don't come down. There'll be no cocoa and biscuit for you lot tonight." Ducky was allowed to stay up, as he had been a 'good' boy.

In school the days seemed to drag. The gardens were aglow with spring blooms, the lush green fields beckoned and we couldn't wait to get out to play soldiers in Widd's field. We used to put mud on our faces and crawl along in the long grass on our elbows holding a thick stick in our hands pretending it was a rifle as we had seen the soldiers doing. We spent hours like this playing at being Desert Rats like our Uncle John and it never entered our heads that there was no long grass in the desert. Our imaginations ran riot and

392

our 'battlefield' was stained red with the blood of fallen Germans. In our imaginations we heard the crackle of small arms fire as shells whistled past and machine guns rattled. As we charged at the enemy, one of us would fall down with a sharp cry and writhe around in agony. I suppose this was our way of coping with the horrors of the war. When Mrs Harris saw the grass stains on our clothes we got yet another belting. She didn't seem to understand that we were wounded war heroes.

Later that month as we came out of school we couldn't believe our eyes. "Tek a look at that! It's a real spitty. What a beaut!" shouted Jimmy in great excitement. On the grass at the top end of The Green there was a Vickers Supermarine Spitfire with the RAF roundels on its fuselage standing out clear and bright in the spring sunshine. Flaxton District Council had acquired it as the centrepiece of their Wings for Victory fund-raising week. The war effort was costing Britain millions of pounds every day and funds were desperately needed so they charged a few pence for people to go and sit in it. The six RAF officers and ten 'erks' were lined up in front of it to have their photograph taken by the local pressman and among them was the twin's father, Trevor Bousefield. "What's the difference between a Spitfire and a 'Urricane?" we asked Mr Harris. "Well, a Spitfire's only got three propeller blades, its a bit smaller than an 'Urricane, but its faster and more manoeuvrable in t'air." We were thrilled to bits when he gave us a few coppers saying, "Go and 'ave a sit in it for thissen."

As we walked up Front Street I took in its beautiful proportions and its flowing lines. The thin legs supporting it looked so delicate that we thought the wind might blow it over and when we got close up it looked huge to us. We had only seen them up in the sky before now but to me it was a thing of grace and beauty. It seemed to be all curves with not a straight line anywhere. A wooden platform with steps and handrails had been placed alongside it so that people could get up to the cockpit and as I climbed the steps I was trembling with excitement and anticipation. An airman helped me onto the walkway of the wing where it joined the fuselage and handed me a helmet saying, "Here, put this on son." The little door below the Perspex canopy had been dropped down and I stepped through it into the cramped cockpit. The airman on duty pulled the canopy forward to close it and once I was closed in my imagination took flight.

In my head I am now a Battle of Britain fighter ace going into action. I am wearing my Mae West inflatable life jacket in case I end up in 'the drink'. I sit down on my parachute, test the joystick and strap myself in. I adjust my silk polka dot scarf; pull on my leather gloves with the pure silk inners and adjust my close-fitting leather helmet. Then, after adjusting the facemask, I plug in the radio transmitter lead and check the flow from the oxygen tube. I have it all off pat. Then it is just a matter of checking the fuel gauge and the brake pressure and putting the magneto switch to 'on'. I press the starter button and booster coils at the same time and the engine engages with a metallic clung; the three-bladed, Merlin airscrew turns slowly then the engine fires and runs evenly. I check that the door is closed and signal 'Chocks away' to my ground crew.

In my imagination, my spitty waddles across the grass picking up speed and away we go sailing smoothly up into the wide blue yonder and I bank to port. I'm up to four hundred miles an hour in no time and as I float over the countryside, I glance to my right to see the others in vic formation alongside me. My headphones crackle and a voice says; "Come in blue leader. Dorniers at two o'clock high! Out."

"Understood: am engaging: Roger, wilco (will comply) and out," I reply.

I look through my gun sight; press the button and there is a terrific clattering noise and all hell breaks loose. Tracer bullets stream out and the 'glass' nose of the Dornier shatters as bullets rip into it. Thick black smoke, glycol and high octane fuel streams out of her port engine and she goes into a spiralling dive. I stop firing and pull the stick hard over. My machine judders and stalls then fires again and I swing clear. I see the Dornier's wing break off as she plunges earthwards. "Got her!" I shout, "That's one less Jerry bomber to worry about." My Spitfire soars and wheels until I come back down to earth with a bump (literally and figuratively). Sliding back the canopy I lever myself up and out of the cockpit. "That was great!" I shout to Jimmy, " Come on, it's your turn now."

One night after we had gone to bed we were running in and out of the girls bedroom and having pillow fights when Mrs Harris shouted up the stairs, "If you don't get into bed and settle down this minute there will be serious trouble." For a time we kept quiet but then we started messing about again. "I won't tell you again. If there's another peep out of you I'll send Mr Harris up!" she shouted from the foot of the stairs. However, as we were in a silly mood, the running about and giggling soon resumed and the next minute there was the sound of heavy footsteps on the stairs. We shot into our own rooms and Jimmy was just shutting the door when the belt clattered round the edge of it. The brass buckle caught him above the eye and cut his eyebrow, which started to bleed profusely. Mr Harris became really upset. He said "Ah'm so sorry, lad. Ah don't like belting yer but Ellen meks me do it. Ah only meant it as a warning and didn't expect anyone to be be'ind t' door." He dressed Jimmy's eyebrow and gave us all a sweet to suck on but Mrs Harris said, "It serves him right. They had plenty of warnings!" The next day Jimmy had a black eye but he told Mr Fox that he had walked into a door without looking. He liked Mr Harris and didn't want to get him into any trouble.

Not long afterwards the good hidings and belittling comments started again. Mrs Harris, a real martinet, was forever finding fault with us and she was becoming more touchy and irritable as the days went by. She would fly into terrifying rages and lay into us. We were not her children and our noise and high-spirited behaviour seemed to get on her nerves. Maybe that was the reason that she would not let us bring our school pals to the house. I don't think she disliked them but if they were in the house she wouldn't be able to hit us.

Later that month Ducky went home to Newcastle and we never saw him again but we were not sorry to see him go. I had never liked him or he me as he was slimy and lazy (but crafty with it) and the dislike was mutual. He had an oily, sly nature and he sucked up to Mrs Harris no end and we had learned not to trust him or to let him in on our little secrets as he was forever splitting on us and telling tales. Tommy Robson, a scruffy, ten years old lad with a rat-like face who came from Gateshead, took his place. He became known as Geordie Robson at school and I don't remember much about him except that he was a rough, tough lad with a good pair of fists and he knew how to use them. He had no problem in dealing with the school bullies and it didn't take him long to sort out a lad called Harris who was always in trouble for fighting. He had sweaty feet and wore strange-looking boots, which he said were fancy American boots that his Mam had got from a charity shop. After being belted by Mrs Harris he didn't stay long.

On Easter Sunday the bells of St. Mary's pealed out joyfully on the warm spring air as white blackthorn blossom adorned the hedgerows. The same day the twelve great bells of York Minster rang out and were broadcast to the nation. It was the twenty-fifth of April and only that week Winston Churchill had proclaimed to the House of Commons that, "The church bells can now be rung on Sundays and on other special days in order to summon worshippers to church."

Harry, and several other local boys and girls of about the same age - who had all been baptised - gathered at the parish church where the petals of the daffodils in the graveyard were now brown and papery. Over the past few weeks they had been attending the Confirmation classes conducted by the vicar. Amongst them were Brian Mann, members of the Pulleyn family and the headmaster's daughters. Having 'come to years of discretion', the Reverend Donald now considered them fit to be brought before the Bishop. Before they entered little knots of mothers and guardians straightened ties, combed hair and fussed with the girl's dresses. Harry, who was to celebrate his fifteenth birthday four days later, felt a little self-conscious in his smart new suit.

The group was expected to have learnt the Creed, the Ten Commandments and great chunks of the Book of Common Prayer by heart. They had rehearsed the arid theological questions and answers of the Catechism and studied many obscure parts of the sacrament over and over for weeks. Today was the big day. Dr.Knyvett, the Bishop of Selby, laid his hand upon Harry's head of pale golden waves and recited the Lord's Prayer and the Collect before blessing and confirming him. Harry gave his responses in a cracked voice that revealed the onset of puberty, promising, "To honour and obey the King and all that are put in authority under him: to submit myself to all my governors, teachers, spiritual pastors and masters: to order myself lowly and reverently to all my betters." The words served to reinforce and endorse the earlier dictums espoused by Mr Fox, Miss Curry and the vicar. Our little gang went along to see Harry confirmed and we watched him as he knelt at the altar rail to take the bread and the wine at his first Holy Communion. Mam had once said that it was, "The outward sign in continual remembrance of the death of Christ."

On hearing the vicar state, "This is the inward sign of 'the body and blood of Christ' being taken and received by the faithful." I thought all that God-eating stuff seemed a bit vampirish and weird. The Misses Law and Barker, inordinately proud of their saintly looking boy with the golden-halo, were beaming from ear to ear. Gran and Renee had come down from Middlesbrough, but they seemed to be rather quiet and sad. Neither my Mam or Aunt Hilda had come and Gran said; "Your mam is still working at the Red Cross Centre down Cannon Street and Aunt Hilda is still in the ATS where she is a medical orderly and can't get leave very often."

The year before, Aunt Hilda had responded to the many wireless appeals and posters appearing in magazines and newspapers stating that, 'The ATS wants more Women like You'. The recruitment drive released more men for front line service but she must have told them that she had no children. The Auxiliary Territorial Service (ATS) had been formed in 1938 and had been a voluntary organisation but it now had full military status and was to become the Women's Royal Army Corps (WRAC) after the war. From December 1941 women without children could be conscripted but the work usually involved desk jobs or nursing.

19. Comings and Goings

In May, Mrs Harris complained to the parish council - mind you, she complained about everything from the postman to the state of the roads -. stating that she could not tolerate poor Dot's slow wits and dilatory ways any longer, adding, "I want her removed from the house. She is neither use nor ornament and is the instigator of much of the trouble with the others."

When Renee visited again I overheard her saying to Harry, "What children need is stability, not punishment and rejection. Sometimes the problem is not the child but the family that they are put with. They should not be made to feel unloved and unwanted. Not that I can find fault with Mr Harris; he is a really nice man but he should stand up to his wife more. She gets her own way far too much and I think her nasty, spiteful ways really upset him." So, Mrs Horn made arrangements for Dot to be billeted with Mrs Brown, the school dinner lady, who lived on North Lane. She was a very reserved and quiet 'Grandma' type of lady who wore her hair flat to her head and tied in a bun at the back and she always seemed to be wearing a crossover pinny whenever we saw her. Dot was delighted on learning that she was getting away from Mrs Harris at last and she gladly made the move into her new billet.

We were becoming more adventurous and roaming further afield by this time and had started to venture over the railway crossing and down Landings Lane on to the banks of the River Foss to play. At that time of the year the white curds of the elderflowers were just starting to form and tall white candles of blossom stood on the horse chestnut trees. Down by the river the weeping willows dipped their green fronds in the water and the cloying smell of wild garlic was overpowering. The white flowered plants were growing in profusion under the alder trees as I slashed at the stinging nettles with a stick making sure that we always had some dock leaves handy to neutralise any stings. We searched for the little green bugs that made the frothy cuckoo spit on the plants. Apparently it had a foul taste, so the birds left them alone. We squashed the crawling grubs between the thumb and forefinger and called the large green, adult bugs froghoppers. The Home Guard had fastened a rope round a thick overhanging branch of a willow tree to enable them to swing across to the far bank during their exercises and we made good use of it. We played down there for hours on end occasionally seeing a flash of red and blue as a kingfisher skimmed along above the surface of the water.

In school assembly Miss Curry informed us that in North Africa the last of the Axis forces had surrendered and that the Dambusters' Raid had taken place. We had already heard of it from Mr Harris, as it had been the main headline in all the newspapers recently. Nineteen Lancaster bombers of 617 Pathfinder Squadron under the leadership of Wing Commander Guy Gibson had set out to smash the huge Mohne and Eder dams that supplied the power for the industries situated in the Ruhr valley. To do so they used a new type of mine shaped like a wide tractor wheel that was about three feet (1m.) in diameter. These were designed to bounce along the surface of the reservoir, strike the dam wall and sink with the delayed detonation cracking open the wall causing water to flood out into the valley below. The raid was a great success but only nine planes came back and fifty-one brave men died. Their bravery and stirring deeds captured the public's imagination and their story was told in a major film.

In June, when Jimmy's Mam came to visit him, there was a right to-do. Maybe, if Mrs Harris had had a telephone, things could have been arranged beforehand and the ructions might have been prevented. It seems that Aunt Hilda had saved up her leave entitlement from the army so that she could spend some time with her son and, knowing that she could not be put up at the Harris household, she said, "I would like to take Jimmy back to Middlesbrough with me for a few days holiday. It will be a nice change for him." But the words were scarcely out of her mouth before Mrs Harris flew into a rage showing her true colours to her for the first time. She shouted, "Yes you can take him, but if you do, don't bother to bring him back!"

Hilda, determined to have Jimmy with her, stuck to her guns and, going upstairs she packed his case and brought it down to the kitchen. Mrs Harris did not want him to go as Jimmy had been with her from the start and the argument became violent. She threw his case out onto the lawn by the back door and bundled Jimmy and his

Mam down the steps and slammed the door shut in their faces. We were in tears as we peered through the kitchen window watching the furore. Poor Jimmy was scrabbling around on his hands and knees gathering up his things and putting them back into the small case and, luckily, the weather was good and the lawn was dry. Hilda, taken aback at first, became very angry; unable to believe that 'the old dragon' had been so intransigent. We ran out onto Usher Lane and watched them until they reached the end of the road where Jimmy had a last look back and waved goodbye before they caught the bus into York and the train home. I was very upset and cried as Jimmy and I were very close and had not been apart for over two years. We went everywhere together.

Jimmy with his mother (in ATS uniform) in 1943.

Mr Worthington, our lugubrious next door-but-one neighbour and his wife had been in their garden when Jimmy and his mother were thrown out and had heard the shouting. They came to the house soon afterwards to console Mrs Harris who was still upset and tearful as it seems she had had a bit of a soft spot for Jimmy after all. They were the only people in the village that she got on with, even though Mr Worthington was an arrogant, strutting, little man with a sharp, crisp manner who thought he was a cut above the other people on Usher Lane. He jumped at every opportunity to give himself fine airs but he was obsequious and deferential to the headmaster when he went to the school to show some of the older children how to play chess. He was self-righteous but was reputed to be 'a bad little devil' and I once overheard Mr Harris say to Mr Mann, "They reckon 'e knocks 'is wife about at times."

In the days that followed it felt strange going to school without Jimmy and Dot and shortly afterwards two of the little girls that had been with us at Sutherland Lodge and Grove House came to stay in their stead. Sylvia and Nancy Robson were sisters and they had been at The Settlement in 1939 and had recently been billeted with my pal John Wade when he was with Mrs Smith at Rose Cottage on The Green. Sylvia was my age and was in Miss Rutter's group with me, but Nancy was only six and was in the same group as George at the infant school.

The gangly Mr Fox wore grey slacks and a tweed jacket with leather patches on the elbows when he took us for cricket practice in the summer months. Seeing scratches on a boy's hands he accused him of robbing bird's nests and, when he admitted it, he gave him a good thrashing with the cane. The cricket pavilion was an old converted railway carriage off South Lane and we got there from school by crossing the road and cutting down Tiger Lane alongside Cobbler Johnson's little place on Front Street. Anybody who larked about got a crack on the neck from Mr Fox's swagger stick and the persistent troublemakers and bullies were made to clean out the pavilion. The pretty, slender-waisted and nubile Miss Rutter took the girls on to another part of the field to play rounders and as she ran around in her short, pleated skirt several of the older lads seemed to suddenly lose concentration and got themselves bowled out.

As the green of spring became the gold of high summer, cow parsley grew tall on the verges and we saw ever more Lancaster bombers flying low over the village after taking off from East Moor where the Canadians were being trained in their use. The huge four-engined planes had twin-finned tail wings with guns protruding from their snub noses and their dorsal and tail turrets. We learned that the Canadians had now taken over Linton-on-Ouse airfield as part of the newly formed Number 6 Group and they were using RCAF East Moor as a satellite airfield.

Gran came through again saying, "I have had another letter from your Uncle John. He is now in Campo 73 at Carpi, which is a small town in northern Italy not far from Modena. It seems there is a hierarchy and a strict code of conduct in the camp. At first he deeply resented the loss of his freedom and the injustice of being imprisoned when he hadn't committed a crime but he seems to be making the best of a bad job. He says that the men exchange food items from their Red Cross parcels for cigarettes by tacking bits of paper or card on to the telegraph poles with their hut and bed number on them. A packet of coffee can be exchanged for fifteen fags and a tin of Bully Beef can bring twenty. They are in large wooden huts that hold fifty double-tier bunks and, to pass the time, they mess the Italian guards about. At roll calls two of the guards make separate counts and the prisoners keep moving about in order to confuse them. They play Lotto (now called Bingo) for cigarettes and they put on concert parties with some of the men dressing up as women, at which they have a good laugh. He says he gets on well with the Italian interpreter, who speaks English with a Geordie accent, as he used to be an ice cream vendor at South Shields. The first hundred men who line up at the gate looking clean and tidy are taken into town where they can buy tomatoes and watermelons for two liras. Uncle John said they see the women working in the fields but are not allowed to speak to them."

" I'm glad to hear the Red Cross parcels are getting through to the boys. Don't you have something to do with raising money for them?" Mrs Harris enquired.

"Yes, I go round the houses collecting the contributions to the Red Cross Penny-a-Week Fund in all weathers. They are doing a grand job for the boys in the prison camps who really look forward to receiving them."

In the heat of summer big, fat bluebottles buzzed around in the school or lay dead on the window ledges with their legs in the air and the outside lavatories stank of pee and Jeyes fluid. The copper pipes were green with verdigris and there were pee stains on the seats and the floor where the boys' aim had not been too accurate. Sometimes there were brown streaks on the walls were little fingers had been rubbed after the thin San Izal toilet paper ran out. I didn't like going in there as the sharp acrid smell of urine and the stench of shit made me gag. Just before we broke up for the summer holidays Miss Curry updated us on the war situation by announcing that, "The Allied forces have invaded Sicily. One hundred and fifty thousand men landed on the tenth of July and they are moving steadily forward. General Montgomery is leading the Eighth Army, known as 'The Desert Rats' after the long-legged rodent called the Jerboa, and the American, General Patton is in command of the US 7th Army."

I missed Jimmy very much and when Gran came again I cried and pleaded with her to take me home. When Mrs Harris left the room I said to her, "I hate it here and Mrs Harris is always hitting us. Can't I come home with you?"

"Don't be silly now. I'm sure it's not that bad" she replied just as Mrs Harris came back into the room and we were sent upstairs to play while they talked. When we came down nothing more was said. Mrs Harris must have convinced Gran that she did not hit us and we noticed that the belts and cane were missing from their usual prominent place.

I heard Gran say to her, "Hilda has applied for a discharge from the services to take care of Jimmy and last week she had to take Jimmy through to Fenham Barracks at Newcastle, where they were quizzed by her Commanding Officer. Jimmy was made to stand in front of this posh, manly sort of woman who sat behind a large, highly polished desk with her Adjutant. The Adjutant was tall and skinny, with a pronounced jaw-line and Hilda said she reminded her of Joyce Grenfell, the gormless film actress. She spoke in the same curt, clipped, upper-crust manner and Jimmy thought she sounded as though she had a plum in her gob."

The whole thing brought to mind that famous painting by Whistler. Jimmy was separated from his Mam and made to stand in front of the CO's desk and they asked, 'When did you last see your mother?' to which he replied, 'A couple of seconds ago in't room next door.' They thought Hilda had been telling lies to get herself out of the ATS." She then turned to me and said, "Jimmy is staying with Aunt Ruby in Croft Street while his Mam sorts out her discharge. He sends you his love as do your Mam and Dad. Keep your chin up and be a good boys." She did not stay long as she had to catch the Darlington train and on arrival she would have to hope that she was not too late to catch the connecting train to Middlesbrough. It would be a long tedious journey for her with the windows painted over and the blinds down and she would not arrive home until well after midnight. Luckily she enjoyed knitting, which helped to pass the time. She told us that, "Sometimes the trains are so packed with servicemen that they lay on the luggage racks."

During the summer break we heard on the news that Mussolini had fallen out of favour and had been dismissed from office by the King of Italy bringing an end to Fascism. We knew it was good news but it did not really affect us and, as it was another lovely summer, we roamed far and wide in the local countryside. Pink-flowered spikes of Rosebay Willowherb grew tall on the grass verges as large white trumpets of bindweed were fully open in the hedgerows. The days were hot and golden sunlight danced on the surface of Widd's pond as we tried to catch the newts, the silvery-looking diving beetles, the pondskaters and the waterboatmen that skittered across the surface. On leaving the field we always jumped the drainage ditch and Nancy Robson, who had bobbed, mousy hair, and wore wire-rimmed glasses, thought she could do the same and fell in. She was covered in mud and when we got back Mrs Harris unceremoniously dumped her in a bath of cold water with all her clothes on. She got a good slap on the legs and was sent to bed for the rest of the day and we got an earful for letting her do it.

The summers seemed to last forever in those days and one morning, as we walked up Usher Lane, we found that the gypsies had set up camp on the grass verges. Thin blue wood smoke rose from the chimneys of their brightly coloured caravans that were covered in deftly painted curlicues and traditional Romany motifs.

Buckets and pails hung from their axles and inside we caught a glimpse of the silver plates and fine pottery reflected in the mirrors that they seemed to like so much.

Mr Harris said, "They'll 'ave come down from t'Appleby 'oss Fair, which were on last month. They say that t'menfolk deceive people in ter buying clapped-out 'osses. It's said that they make 'em swallow a small eel that wriggles inside 'em and meks 'em appear brisk and lively. 'Sell t'buggers and scram' seems to be their motto and, by t'time t'osses shortcomings are found out they're miles away down t'maze of lanes and byeways. They say they leave special signs so that their mates can follow 'em. They put marks on't tree trunks; break branches and twigs in a certain way; tie bunches of grass in a knot or scatter it on t'ighway." "Make sure you lock the doors to the house and your shed for a bit then." said Mrs Harris, but as an afterthought, she added, "On second thoughts don't bother, it's just a lot of old junk in there and there's nowt worth pinching."

The dark-skinned women went from door to door selling packets of needles, pegs and baskets that they'd woven from stripped willow wands. Others told fortunes and Mrs Harris really believed that they had the sixth sense. We used to see the old women sitting by their campfires puffing on their white-clay pipes while the men were out working on the farms or going round sharpening garden tools on a revolving foot-driven grindstone. We were very wary of them as we thought there was an air of mystery and menace about them and it was said that they stole children and indulged in witchcraft. The mangy dogs chained to their caravans growled and snarled if anyone went near the ragged, filthy children that played on the grass. Their piebald horses were tethered to trees at intervals along the grass verges and the scent of crushed grass, wood smoke and horse droppings filled the air. We were relieved when we went up the lane one morning to find that they had struck camp and moved on leaving burned patches on the grass where their campfires had been. We searched through the rubbish that they had left in the hedge-backs thinking that they might have left something of value but we never found a brass farthing.

When Gran came to visit us again, she told us that, "Aunt Hilda is out of the Army and has got herself a job in the steelworks.

She is living in the front part of a house in Athol Street with her best friend, Dot Burns, and is paying rent to an old lady who hates children. Jimmy is not allowed in when she is in the house and can only go to visit his Mam when the old lady isn't there." George and I hadn't the slightest idea where Athol Street was. "Renee is still driving the overhead crane at Cargo Fleet Steel Rolling Mill," Gran continued, "and Archie is still serving his apprenticeship as a steel plater in the Britannia Bridgeyard. The steelworks are now involved in the manufacture of landing craft and amphibious vessels for the planned invasion of Europe but the workers have been sworn to secrecy."

She had heard from Uncle John again, and she said to Mrs Harris, "He was very upset on hearing of the death of his former training officer, Captain Hedley Verity. He really admired and respected him. It seems he was leading a company of the Green Howards against the Germans who were dug in on high ground close to Catania in Sicily. They could see Mount Etna in the background. Anyway, German machine gun fire set the ripe corn alight and they were clearly silhouetted against it when Captain Verity got shot in the chest. As the Germans attacked he was taken prisoner, dying shortly afterwards. John, who greatly admired his skill as a spin bowler, had keenly followed his brilliant performances against the Australians just before the war and knew him to be a fair, brave and courageous man."

"I read about that in t'*Yorkshire Post*," said Mr Harris, who loved his sport. "Wasn't Wilfie Mannion, the Middlesbrough and England footballer, 'is company runner at the time?"

Sometimes I would see the little curly-haired figure of Maud Fisher, who was usually with her friend, Joan Worthington, tottering around in her mother's high-heeled shoes and wearing her jewellery and strings of beads. She was only four years old and I felt that she should not be out on the road on her own. Taking her tiny hand in mine made me feel more grown up as I took her back to her front garden and told her to play in there. Luckily very few cars came along Usher Lane in those days. One day I noticed Nurse Lealman's bike propped up by the Fisher's front door and I found out later that Maud had pushed a clay marble up her nose and her mother, being unable to get it out, had sent her older brother to fetch her.

As day succeeded day, I found the blazing sun tedious and irksome and I missed Jimmy who had always come up with good ideas for things to do. Flies and biting insects plagued us and dust settled on the leaves of the hedgerows turning them a greyish green in colour. After finding that Nancy had warts on the back of her hand, we thought we would try out an old country cure. Mr Harris had told us that rubbing a black slug on them before impaling it on a hawthorn spike usually did the trick. So we did this and waited as it was said that when the slug died the warts would be charmed away. We examined her hand every day and, to our astonishment, the warts became smaller and gradually disappeared. It was pure magic! On the verges of the lane beside the tall, straggly hedges, goldfinches fluttered and pecked at the thistledown causing the tufted seed heads to float away on the wind. Mr Harris often worked until ten at night getting in the harvest before our summer holiday came to an end, and we went back to school.

I was pleased to learn that my group teacher was to be Miss Francis again and I always felt secure in her comforting and smiling presence. Miss Curry - in comparison - was rather prim and proper as she informed us that the Allies had taken Sicily in August. This meant that Allied shipping was now able to sail to Egypt through the Mediterranean Sea virtually free from enemy attack and things were starting to look up on the war front. She pointed out to us where these places were on the large world map before proudly announcing that, "The invasion of Italy is now underway. General Bernard Montgomery's 8th. Army is steadily advancing northwards from the toe of Italy."

John Wade, my pal with the round beaming face, had been moved yet again, and this time he had been taken in by a Mrs Lee who was a little, dark-haired, pretty lady with a teenaged daughter called Hilda. They lived at Holly House, a large, brick-built house on Front Street between the *Red Lion* and the Co-op corner. They kept hens in coops in their backyard; therefore he got real eggs with lovely yellow yolks. John seemed very happy there and he said, "She's a lovely lady and she looks after me as if I was one of her own and Hilda often takes me into York to help her with the shopping," before adding, "They always have two, three or sometimes four airmen from the maintenance unit at Shipton lodging with them." I was envious when he told me that the lodgers sometimes took him with them when they went to the dance or the pictures in the Wiggy Rec We were never taken anywhere, except when members of our family paid a visit.

At playtimes, Billy Pyecroft, whose dad was a member of the local AFS, could usually be found standing on a box peering over the school wall. He was a scruffy kid who always seemed to have a snotty nose and when it ran down onto the upper lip of his loose, floppy mouth he would lick it off. He was a bit simple and too young for school, but we didn't mind him being there as he was a likeable lad. The family tended to keep themselves to themselves. Young Billy would have loved to play football with us but he was too awkward and uncoordinated in his movements. His older brother, who was a good pal of Bernard Fisher, had been born with two thumbs on one hand. I heard Mrs Harris say that these birth defects were the result of years of inbreeding, which was quite a common thing in the old days. The wireless was helping to break down the isolation of these small rural communities and, as travel became easier, fresh blood was coming in, but there still seemed to be at least one idiot in every village.

I was glad I was not in the headmaster's group at school. It was bad enough having Miss Curry for singing lessons in which we sang mostly traditional songs like *D'ye Ken John Peel, Lavender Green* and *Greensleeves,* which I have hated ever since. The older lads said Mr Fox could be quite sarcastic and he sometimes humiliated the quieter, shy children in front of his 'chosen few'. He also forced children who were left-handed to write with their right hands saying it was an unnatural practice and against God's will. We called left-handed people cuddy-wifters. By this time the lanes were lined with fallen leaves and it was starting to get chilly in the big, high-ceilinged classrooms. Cold draughts crept in and wrapped themselves round our bare legs like a cat and we stood with our behinds pressed to the big, green, cast-iron radiators at every opportunity.

When our nineteen-year-old aunt, Renee, came to see us, I could smell the cheap perfume on her neck. Harry was with her and she was saying to him, "Think yourself lucky that you're with Miss Law and Miss Barker who only give you the best. They seem able to get anything they want. Money definitely talks round here." The cracked timbre of Harry's voice had disappeared now and he spoke in deep manly tones as they took us down to see his foster parents in their comfortable home. A dish of dried lavender scented the air and the homely couple seemed like a throw back to a more mannered age. Harry had nicknamed my little brother Podge as he still had a fair amount of baby fat on him. We were offered a choice of delicious cakes from a gold-rimmed, bone china, cake stand and drank our pop from real crystal glasses.

Renee told Harry that their elder brother, John, had sent Gran a letter and, much to her surprise, it had come from Stalag VIIA (Moosburg) thirty-five miles to the north east of Munich in Germany. While he was in the camp in northern Italy the news of the Allied invasion had reached them and he told Gran (later) that as soon as Italy surrendered the Italian guards disappeared. The prisoners took down the Italian flag and put up the Union flag, which fluttered proudly in the evening breeze. Believing themselves to be free, they celebrated by putting on a concert and some of the prisoners left and made their own way towards the advancing British line. Unfortunately the rest, who had been ordered to stay put by their superiors, paid dearly for their obedience as, during the night, the Germans surrounded and took control of the camp. The swastika flag was now flying on the flagpole and, on September the twelfth, three men attempted to escape. Two of them were shot dead with the other one badly wounded and a curfew was enforced forbidding them to leave their hut after 21.00 hours.

A few days later they were given one Red Cross parcel between six and on the 22nd they were each given two loaves of bread and an apple. They were then taken the forty-five miles to the rail station at Mantova near Verona in lorries with forty prisoners being put into each of a long line of cramped cattle trucks. The train journey north took them alongside Lake Garda but they were not in the frame of mind for admiring the grandeur of the scenery through the chinks in the wooden slats. They only had a couple of buckets to serve as lavatories but, as some of them were weak and ill with diarrhoea, these soon filled up. The stench in the wagons was unbearable and it was a long hundred and thirty five miles to Bolzano with many delays on the way. Sometimes the train was stationary for hours with the majestic Dolomites soaring up dramatically on both sides of the track. The next phase took them eighty miles to Innsbruck through the Swiss Alps via the Brenner Pass and they continued for a further hundred miles to Munich in Bavaria. Here they were given a bowl of soup with a loaf of bread between four men. A further journey of thirty miles brought them to the prison camp at Moosburg near Landshut in the foothills of the Bavarian Alps, which had high wooden watchtowers, each containing searchlights and a guard with a machine gun. Two barbed-wire fences surrounded a compound containing long lines of wooden huts. The journey of around three hundred miles had taken eight long days.

In Haxby, violent October winds hurled the boughs of the tall elms around threatening to throw down the large nests of the ragged and ungainly rooks. It was at this time that the Butterfields received the tragic news that they had prayed would never come. Their son had been killed! Twenty-year old Derek William, known locally as Billy, had been a pilot officer in the RAFVR. Gran visited again and she told us that, "Renee was out with her friend up by the Tees estuary when they saw two huge, concrete caissons being towed up the river by tugboats. During the Allied landings these would be lowered to the seabed where the sea water would be pumped out and replaced by air, thus allowing Mulberry Harbours to be constructed."

She told us that Jimmy was living with his mam and dad again in a small rented house in Pelham Street, near Linthorpe Road, that they were sharing with her friend, Dorothy Burns. They had got back together after he had turned up in uniform saying he was on leave from the Duke of Wellington's Regiment. Later I heard Renee say to Harry, "The swine was wearing a small Sacred Heart lapel badge to make Hilda think he had turned over a new leaf and she fell for his smooth talk and blarney all over again. He is an out-and-out rogue and will steal anything, but he swore that he was now a good Catholic and had seen the error of his ways. He promised her that things would be different this time round, and she believed him. Aunt Ruby had talked her into going back with him after seven years apart."

Later that month Mr Harris informed us that his hero, Group Captain Leonard Cheshire, had become the new Commanding Officer of 617 Squadron, the elite Pathfinder squadron now widely known as the Dambusters squadron. He said to us, "By t'way, did yer know that when 'e were at Marston Moor in June, 'e 'ad a railway carriage brought up from York Station? 'E did it up and 'e and 'is wife lived in it."

The ice formed early in the gutters that winter as tragedy struck the Bradford family yet again! We were told that Jimmy's mother was dead. It seems that prior to her death the violent rows had started again as 'the demon drink' had taken over driving out the man and letting in the devil. Renee said that Hilda had been at Gran's house for her tea the day before. Following her tragic and unexpected death, Jimmy would have nothing to do with his father and he went to live with Aunt Ruby again in Croft Street. Apparently, at the inquest, John Nolan was very vague and offhand about the details of her death and soon afterwards his brother, Pat, beat him up shouting, "You had a bloody good lass there and you drove her to the grave!" He was invalided out of the Army with consumption (TB) soon afterwards, after just three months of military service.

The days in school dragged and I spent much of my time in a trance thinking about poor Jimmy as I gazed out at the dim November light filtering through the tall sash windows. As if the family hadn't suffered enough already. Poor Gran had now lost six of her eleven children with another one a prisoner of war in Germany and she was worried to death about his safety. In December we had squalls of pelting rain and thick fog and we heard that two Canadian Thunderbirds had crashed on their return to Linton airfield from raids on Berlin.

That year it was clear and frosty at Christmas and the celebrations were somewhat muted and toned down but we made the best of it. Gran and Renee brought us the odd homemade toys and a few sweets and Sylvia and Nancy's parents came to see them, which made me feel sad, as mine didn't. Nancy got a doll with a pot head and a cloth body that she loved and took everywhere with her and Sylvia got a doll's house made of thick cardboard. We didn't get so much to eat but we enjoyed what we had and Mr Harris had acquired a few chestnuts, which he roasted for us. He put them on a shovel, and held it over the fire, and we laughed when they split open and jumped about. They were steaming hot and had a lovely sweet taste. We had collected lots of hazelnuts from the hedgerows in the autumn and we cracked and ate them, as nuts were very hard to come by in the shops at that time. We wore paper hats and pulled the crackers that we had made at school from crepe paper and in each of them we found a boiled sweet.

So another year turned and we had snow and frost and had to endure one of the coldest winters on record. Miss Curry told us that the German Navy had suffered a major blow on Boxing Day when the *Scharnhorst* was sunk by HMS *Belfast* and the *Duke of York*. There was thick, low cloud for most of January which made flying conditions difficult and there was less aircraft noise as a result. The ice on Mr Harris' rain butt was four inches thick at times and the driving snow froze on the windward side of the trees and stayed there for days on end. The air raid siren was seldom heard in Haxby these days so we slept well but in school the days dragged.

Our history lessons seemed to involve long boring lists of English Kings and Queens who always seemed to have been good or bad, i.e., 'Good Queen Bees' and 'Bad King John'. The dates when they reigned and died had to be memorised and it all seemed to be a confused hotchpotch of things that had no connection with each other. History seemed to have nothing to do with the present day and us and I tended to fidget or 'switch off' and daydream. I enjoyed learning about the Roman Empire, the Viking raids and the Norman Conquest, which fed my imagination that ran away with me at times. I also loved the Robin Hood legends, the siege of Norman castles and the stories of Richard the Lionheart and his crusades against the infidels.

Geography lessons seemed to be used as a means of infusing us with patriotic fervour. We were told that we were the children and heirs of a proud and mighty Empire and a large, shiny, brightly coloured, world map accompanied each lesson. It was printed on the outer waxy coating of a rolled up oilcloth, which was slung over the top of the blackboard. Large parts of it were pink in colour and it was proudly pointed out that these represented the British Dominions. Our great British Empire spanned most of the globe and we were told that belonging to it gave us many advantages in life. It provided us with true and lasting values and we should be proud at being British, as we were a great race. The conquerors, rulers, guides and protectors of the English-speaking colonies were shining examples of the Imperial spirit and it was implied that those countries were privileged to be fighting alongside us against the Japs and the Nazi tyrants. We were, of course, completely unaware that the balance of world power was rapidly changing. Great Britain was no longer the power it had once been and this early brain-washing took many years to be unlearned.

Mnemonics were often used as aids to memory, one such being the order of the major rivers of North Yorkshire, i.e. SUNWACD, with the initials standing for the Swale, Ure, Nidd, Wharfe, Aire, Calder and Don. We learned the order of the colours in the rainbow in a similar way. The initial letters of the saying *Richard of York gave battle in vain* gave us R, O, Y, G, B, I and V, so I never to forgot the sequence of red, orange, yellow, green, blue, indigo and violet. These tried and tested methods were to stand us in good stead for the rest of our lives. We didn't have electronic calculators; we had to work things out for ourselves.

Soon afterwards I devised a scheme for making a bit of extra pocket money. John Wade and I would utilise our drawing talents to produce comic strips. We started to draw lots of little pictures in boxes similar to those in *The Dandy* and *The Beano*, which seemed like a good idea at the time but it took too long and we could not make enough of them and our profit-making enterprise soon foundered. When we saw Canadian airmen in the village we knew which were aircrew by the wings or other brevets on their breasts and by the white lanyard round their left shoulder that was attached to a whistle in their breast pocket.

On a snowy day in February I was sent home from school feeling unwell with a very sore throat and a high temperature. Mrs Harris was unsympathetic, as usual, saying, "There's no need to make such a song and dance about it. Stop snivelling every time I speak to you, it's probably just a bit of a cold." I developed a blinding headache and she put me on the settee in the front room

413

and drew the curtains to shut out the weak winter sunlight. When I started to vomit, she put a white-enamelled pail on the floor beside me and I was sick in it several times. She thought it best that I should not sleep in the bed with the others and I spent a restless night on the settee where I slept fitfully and had nightmares. As I seemed worse the next day, she sent for Nurse Lealman and I was somewhat apprehensive, as the last time she came I had a painful septic spot on my thumb and, without warning, she had jabbed her scissors into it making the pus spurt out. However, it worked and the spot soon healed up, but it left a scar to remember her by.

When she arrived she said to Mrs Harris, "His face is very flushed, except round his mouth, and his pulse is rather fast. I think you should let the doctor have look at him." She then cycled to the surgery at Wortley House to ask him to call and, in the meantime, Mrs Harris rushed about like a maniac dusting, tidying up the house and putting her best soap and clean towels out in the bathroom.

Dr. Riddolls had been the local GP for the last sixteen years but Mrs Harris had not put her name on his 'panel' when she moved into the house on Usher Lane. Like most general practitioners of that time, he performed small surgical operations in the patient's home and he often worked late into the night. The old, bald-headed doctor with the grey beard and moustache, eventually turned up at the house on his little autocycle, as his large black car had been put in storage to save on precious petrol. "And what seems to be the problem, tuppence?" he said, without waiting for an answer. He always called the local children tuppence and after placing a glass thermometer under my tongue, he examined me. He placed the ivory end bits of his stethoscope in his ears but, unfortunately for me, he hadn't bothered to warm the membrane at the other end before putting it on my chest and as my skin was really hot and feeling as rough as sandpaper, I jumped.

Turning to Mrs Harris he said, "The lad has a very red throat, a 'strawberry' tongue and a rash everywhere - except on his face. The swollen glands in his neck; the redness of his skin and the pale area around his lips are typical of scarlet fever, which is highly infectious and we must get him to the Fever Hospital at Malton straight away. Nurse Lealman will make arrangements for the ambulance to come and she will see that your doors and windows are sealed with tape before the house is fully fumigated. She will have to burn the clothes he was wearing for school and, by the way, my fee for a home visit is five shillings."

Mrs Harris was none too pleased at having to pay up on the spot but she could claim it back from the parish council. When the cream-coloured ambulance came the men knocked on the front door and I was granted the singular honour of being carried out of the house through it. I think that was the only time I ever used it. The canvas stretcher had a wooden pole through each side of the canvas and I remember that the ambulance had small oval windows in its back doors. The house was fumigated before the others came in from school and Thelma told me later that Podge and Nancy were quite upset asking, "Do you think he'll die, Mrs Harris?" Someone must have told them that the disease was still a killer.

On the fourteen-mile journey to Malton, I was 'burning up' but I felt chilly and shivery at the same time and don't remember much about it except for the loud clanging of the bell. I was isolated and barrier nursed behind screens; treated with penicillin and I stayed in the hospital for two weeks. My bedding, crockery and cutlery were kept separate from those of the other patients and the nurses in their white-starched caps and aprons had to wear white gowns and face masks when dealing with me. I was given bed baths and was not allowed visitors. The nurses were gentle and caring, which was something I had not experienced since leaving Grove House three years earlier. My tongue was sore and I found it hard to eat, so I was given lots of milky drinks and soft foods like porridge, soup and scrambled eggs. I particularly liked the jellies, custard and the macaroni, which I called 'pipes' and I loved it when I was given honey, syrup and chocolate; things which we never saw at Haxby. The rash turned scaly then peeled off and as I got better I enjoyed being mollycoddled by the nurses. I liked the quiet atmosphere and felt warm and cared for, except when Matron, who ruled the wards with a rod of iron and reminded me of Mrs Harris, did her rounds. On seeing a man sat on the edge of his bed, she blew up, shouting, "Get off that bed this instant! You are either in bed or out of it, never *on* it. Do you understand?"

I thought the nurses looked really nice as they prepared to go off duty. The staff nurses proudly wore a large, ornate, silver filigree buckle on their belts and the red bands of their navy-blue cloaks were crossed over the white bibs that protected their royal-blue dresses. The colours seemed so bright and very patriotic and I felt happy and secure in their tender care and didn't want to leave.

After being discharged I was still weak and had to stay off school for some time to recuperate. During the day Mrs Harris allowed me to lie on the settee in the parlour and, as the snow lay deep on the ground outside, I felt snug and warm under a couple of blankets. She kept the curtains drawn as the light still hurt my eyes and I quite enjoyed being the centre of attention for a change. Gran came to see me and brought me sweets, comics and chocolate but I was disappointed that Mam was not with her. I thought she might have come to see how I was getting on. In fact I was starting to forget what Mam and Dad looked like and their images were becoming as fleeting and as insubstantial as ghosts. When I started to wallow in self-pity, Gran shamed me by telling me what Uncle John was going through at that time. She said, "He is prisoner, number 220615 and he and the others were taken four hundred miles further east in cattle trucks at the end of October. So don't you go feeling so sorry for yourself. You don't know when you're well off."

It seems that he was now in an immense camp called Stalag VIII B on a barren plain close to the German-Polish border. Built to house British prisoners during the Great War, it was close to a village called Lamsdorf and held over 20,000 prisoners. One day after the war, Uncle John told us that, "When the snows came the vast white plain stretched away into the distance with a huge forest of densely packed conifers to one side. At night the searchlights in the stilt-legged watchtowers lit up the swirling snowflakes, as icy winds whistled across the snowfield creating deep drifts at the base of the barbed wire fences. These stretched for about a mile round our compound and the long, low, wooden, barrack blocks held about a hundred and sixty of us sleeping on three tier bunks. The uncomfortable palliasses were stuffed with wood shavings and each hut had two tiled ovens that were seldom lit, as we could not get enough fuel. We had a few tables and some forms but most got broken up to provide firewood during the intensely bitter winter."

Uncle John (2ⁿᵈ right, front row) as a POW in Stalag 344 in 1944.

"We saved up some of the best food from our Red Cross parcels to have at Christmas and were really grateful to that marvellous organisation." he continued. "They made life that little bit more bearable and were an important link with home. We made paper chains from the labels round the food tins. The Germans put many of the men into working groups chipping bark from the sawn logs before they were used as pit props. Some were sent out to work in factories, on farms or in the Polish coal mines. Officers and NCOs did not have to do manual labour as we were protected by the terms of the Geneva Convention."

He found it hard to talk about it but one day he told Gran that, "The Russian compound was nearby and they were pitiful to see. Most of them were half-starved and stood shivering in the cold in filthy rags as 'Uncle Joe' Stalin had refused to sign the Geneva

Convention. Their fleas had been the cause of a typhus epidemic that had hit the camp before we arrived. Hundreds had died and had been thrown into huge communal burial pits and the rats in the latrines were as big as cats. At the end of the year the camp changed its number to Stalag 344."

After a pause he added, " We were kept within the confines of the camp and boredom was the worst thing. To alleviate it we played 'international' football matches as there were so many different nationalities in the camp. At the early muster, known as Appel, some indulged in goon-baiting to exasperate the guards but the punishment, if caught, was loss of privileges like not being allowed to keep the Red Cross food tins, which were used for many purposes. The guards had been nicknamed Goons as they reminded the men of the great, clumping, malicious creatures (like Scandinavian trolls) in the Popeye comic strip in the *Daily Mirror* before the war. In the deep snow we had to be careful to avoid the inner trip wires, as some of the guards were trigger-happy. The time crawled by and I felt a strong sense of guilt at still being alive while others were fighting and being killed. I experienced overpowering feelings of terrible futility and despair at times."

At Haxby, March continued in the same vein and as I braved the icy roads on my return to school the wind passed through my clothes like a 'flu shiver and I longed for the spring to come. Even so, the crocuses still managed to penetrate the soil's icy heart to burst into flower but due to the long cold winter, they were late this year. It didn't take long for the undeserved slaps and the beltings to start up again but when it came to my turn I tried a different tactic. I had learned the hard way and as soon as Mrs Harris took down the leather belt, I would run full pelt into the bathroom and crouch down in the small space between the lavatory pan and the wall. At other times I would squeeze into the space between the end of the bath and the wall. Either way, when she lashed at me she hit the wall, the pan, the bath top or herself more often than she hit me. She would finally give up and go away fuming and mumbling. "I'll see to you later, you crafty little devil!" she called over her shoulder. I would stay there until I heard her go upstairs then, I would dash outside and make myself scarce. When I came back she had usually cooled down a bit.

As the austere whiteness of winter gave way to the fresh leafy greenness of spring the days grew longer and lighter and we played out again after tea. We had the freedom to roam as long as we returned at the times set for our unappetising, frugal meals. By this time I had started to put a bit of everything on my fork in order to disguise the taste of the things I didn't like - a habit, which persists to this day. The grass in Widd's field was lush and green again but we made a point of avoiding the 'fairy rings'. The grass on their outer edges was darker than the grass inside the circles and Sylvia said; "I read a book that told of children stepping inside these rings and not bein' seen agen. It seems that the fairies 'ad tekken 'em away". It was to be many years before I learned that the rings are caused by masses of tiny fungal threads called *hyphae,* which radiate outwards in the soil like the ripples on a pond when a stone is thrown into it.

In April I was nine and Harry would soon be sixteen when his apprenticeship would begin. He would then go to the abattoir in York once a week to learn the skills of the slaughterman and be taught how to kill and dress animals. Harold Atkinson was good to him in that way and he was to have a thorough grounding, which would stand him in good stead for the future. Harold had big plans for him on the completion of his apprenticeship if he stayed on after the war. Later on, he even attempted to have him exempted from the call up in the hope of setting him up with a van and his own business. Harry's young pal, Peter Beresford, was to take over his bike and his job as the delivery boy. Harold used his little box-shaped van with its small oval back windows to take orders to the more out-lying villages. Harry once said to Renee, "I don't think he ever took a driving test. They just sent a licence to him when it became compulsory."

I clearly remember the loud crunching of the gravel as the steamroller rumbled and hissed forward and back as it resurfaced Usher Lane. We all rushed outside to watch, taking care to avoid the flying chippings, as a man walked in front of it spreading the gravel with a rake. The roller had a big, whirring drive wheel and belt and Mr Harris said afterwards, "It's owned by 'Donkey' Pulleyn - who lives in a caravan next t't auld smithy in Wigginton." The driver in his greasy flat cap had to turn the knob on the top of the tiny steering wheel many times to make the great roller alter direction by just one inch. I loved the smell of the hot tar fumes as the fire flamed and roared beneath the boiler. Unfortunately, I got a taste of a different kind of belt when Mrs Harris found spots of tar on my clothes afterwards.

One day we got a surprise when Renee ran up the side path and started hammering on the back door. When Mrs Harris opened it she was red in the face and trembling and almost fell into the house.

"What on earth's the matter?" Mrs Harris enquired.

"There's hundreds of cows charging down the lane," she gasped.

"Is that all? You townies have no idea about life in the countryside, have you? A few cows can't hurt you. It happens every day. Have you not noticed the cow pats all down the road?"

"Well, I can't abide the big smelly things," she replied, still shaking a bit.

When she had settled down she gave us the latest news from home. On leaving the house to visit Harry she looked up and down the lane to make sure the cows had gone before venturing out. She told him that her elder brother had volunteered to look after the prison camp graveyard. John says he has a mate called Jock Walker, and they are just glad to have something useful to do to ease the boredom of their humdrum existence. Jock is a big, Scottish lad who hails from Edinburgh and John is also very friendly with an Australian called Harry Bader. He is related to Douglas Bader, the Battle of Britain fighter ace with the tin legs who was one of the few RAF prisoners in the camp when John arrived. It seems he was sent there as a punishment following several escape attempts at his previous camp and he spent much of his time in solitary confinement in what they call the 'cooler'. Some years later a notable film called 'Reach for the Sky' was made about Bader's many daring exploits.

Mrs Rust's two little girls had been billeted with Mrs Oliver in the big house on the corner of Usher Lane and Station Road for some time when their mother decided that it was safe enough to take them back home to London. There was a family wedding coming up and she wanted them to be there. Sally and Nancy were lovely, well-liked little girls who were never a ha'porth of trouble

420

in school or out of it and it wasn't long since they had stood beside us watching the house martins collecting mud to construct their nests under the eaves of the houses. They, like us, had been fascinated on seeing the graceful birds repeatedly swooping and gliding down to gather beakfuls of mud from the edges of a puddle. A few weeks later we heard that their house had been destroyed by one of the first German V1 flying bombs. Sally was killed and Nancy, the youngest, had to have both legs amputated.

At school we were kept busy rehearsing and helping to make scenery for a forthcoming pantomime. Miss Curry, who was in charge of the singing practices, had told us that it looked as if a 'Second Front' was going to begin quite soon. She said, "It is vitally important that we in Haxby support the war effort by raising as much money as possible, hence the pantomime" Mr Fox decided that the school should put on 'Dick Whittington' as their contribution to the Salute the Soldier week.

Two weeks earlier the *Yorkshire Evening Press* had printed an editorial encouraging fundraising to support our 'brave fighting men' and Lieutenant-Colonel Sullivan of Moorlands as chairman of the local committee had set a target for Haxby and Wigginton of £5,000. A huge board was erected under the school clock to show how much was being raised. We didn't know what a second front was but we got quite excited when Mr Harris told us, "It means an Allied Army is goin' ter go over to sort out t'Jerries in Europe."

On Saturday the 29th of April, which was Harry's sixteenth birthday, the fundraising began with a concert in the Wigginton recreation hall. On the Sunday we were thrilled to see and hear the East Yorkshire Regiment's band at the head of a colourful parade of men and women from the various services marching to a drumhead service. Members of the ARP, the AFS and the Home Guard marched proudly behind it with the late spring sunlight glinting off their boots and their uniform badges, buckles and buttons. That Monday we experienced a day of blazing heat and Mr Harris said, "It said on't wireless it's been't 'ottest Mayday in livin' memory and we were swelterin' at work." In the evening, when it had cooled a little, Mr Harris took us to see the '25 pounders' - the main British field guns at that time - on The Green. We were also allowed to stay up late to watch a PT demonstration by baton-twirling men in white vests and navy-blue shorts on the football field. It was the most excitement the village had experienced for some time.

On the Friday it was our turn. It was the day of the pantomime at the Wiggy Rec, which was well received, and Sylvia, Thelma and I were in the chorus. The hall was crammed to the doors and Mr Fox was as proud as Punch as he appealed to the people to contribute generously to the campaign. As a result £7,400 was raised that week easily beating the target and the people of the two villages felt proud at having done their bit. There was an air of expectancy as we waited impatiently for the day of the big invasion and the country seemed full of soldiers on the move. It was all very hush-hush and there was deliberately no mention of the increased activity in the newspapers. There were rumours that the east and south coast areas had been closed to the public and all leave was cancelled.

The Misses Law and Barker put up the money for Harry to buy a 1936 Norton motorcycle with a leather seat and springy suspension. Petrol was becoming a little more obtainable and Harold Atkinson had let him have some of his, and he thought he was the 'bee's knees' as he cruised around the village on it. He had filled out and was a handsome, golden-haired youth by this time and several of the local girls had taken a fancy to him. He must have seemed very attractive to them as he sat astride his throbbing motor bike as it purred along like a big cat. He used it to get to the abattoir in York.

When Renee visited again, Harry said to her, "I appreciate their kindness and generosity but I get very annoyed at Miss Law's obsessive behaviour with regard to so-called 'germs'. She even puts sticking plasters on her fingertips and on the door handles. Miss Barker's brother, Arthur, and his nine years old daughter, Sarah, came to see them recently in their pony and trap. He got really angry at the way she wraps her knife, fork and spoon in tissue paper and he told her what he thought of it but it had no effect at all; she was as bad as ever after they'd gone. One day, when the washing was out on the line in the back lane, an old tramp came round to the back door begging. She flew outside in a panic and brought the washing into the house terrified that he might have touched it and put germs on it and she washed it all over again. I think she's a bit loopy and needs to see a 'trick cyclist'. (a psychiatrist)."

After the war she was to have electric shock treatment for her worsening obsessive-compulsive disorder. This was known as ECT - an acronym for electro-convulsive therapy - and she was to spend some time as a voluntary patient in The Retreat, a Victorian lunatic asylum in York. At the end of Renee's visit Harry offered to take her back to York Station on his motor bike but she retorted, "What? Are you kidding? No! Thank you very much indeed."

When the well-spoken elderly spinsters, with their delicate mannerisms and maidenly demeanour, went away for a few days Harry stayed with the Danbys next door. He was a good pal of their son, Geoff, whose dad, Max, drove a lorry round to collect the filled milk churns left on the wooden platforms at the end of the farm entrances every day. He had them at the station in time for the early morning 'milk' train. It seems that Harry used to sleepwalk and Geoff once woke to find him wandering round the bedroom at two o'clock in the morning rounding up sheep for the slaughter. He was fast asleep and could not remember a thing about it the next morning. As time passed Geoff's sister, Marjorie, and Harry became quite close and she was to write to him regularly when he was in Australia with the Royal Navy.

At Whitsuntide, which was hot and sunny, the hues of the freshly burgeoning leaves ranged from light brown to bright green. The tiny new leaves of the oaks and sycamores were tawny brown and tiny lime-green leaflets were forming on the ash trees. The waxy leaves of the ivy, which clung to the tree trunks, were a shiny, pale green that contrasted sharply with the dark green of the previous year's growth. The seemingly infinite variety was a delight to the eye but later in the summer the shades would take on a darker, more uniform look. There were masses of pinkish apple blossom on the trees in the orchards and lilac and laburnum trees were in full flower. The hawthorns dripped with sweet, snowy blossom as birdsong filled the air. Unfortunately, the herd of Friesian cattle at Crompton farm was decimated by an outbreak of foot and mouth disease and the brown-clad Italian prisoners-of-war were brought in to assist with the culling and burying. Fresh soil lay in great heaps as they dug deep pits into which the diseased cattle were dumped and covered with lime before the soil was shovelled over them.

On the 4th of June high winds and heavy rain swept across the countryside bending the green wheat and blowing the crab apple blossom from the trees along the lane. Several Lancasters and Halifaxes flew over the village in the next day or two on their way to bomb the German defences on the French coast and the lines of communication that led to them. Then on the 6th the long awaited news came and we heard John Snagge report that the biggest invasion ever known had begun just before dawn. 'Workers Playtime' was interrupted just after ten o'clock in the morning with further reports on the troop landings and the people cheered and wept with joy. Nearly 200,000 men and six thousand ships were taking part in the vast amphibious operation called Overlord that stretched for sixty miles along the Normandy coast. Some five thousand planes supported the vast armada, but sadly several aircraft from the local airfields were shot down. There was a mood of euphoria throughout the village and we began to believe that we were winning the war at last and that we might soon be back home with our loved ones. In the days that followed the papers were full of reports and maps showing the progress of the Allied invasion and we followed every move forward from the beaches with great interest. The names of lots of little places in far away Europe became familiar to us.

On a hot day in early summer the hazy light gave way to a glowering greyness and the air became humid and heavy. Black and purple clouds gathered and heaved up and before long we heard the deep rumble of thunder as the bruised looking clouds roiled overhead. Violent flashes of lightning crept ever nearer briefly lighting up the darkness of our classroom before Miss Francis turned on the lights. The clouds burst and the rain came down in stair rods and raced along the flooded gutters; it really pelted down. Apparently Mrs Fox was busy ironing clothes in her kitchen when she was violently flung across the room. A thunderbolt had struck the chimney blowing all the fuses in the electric box in the corridor. There was pandemonium and panic amongst the children while in the classroom next to us, Margaret Mann - Harold's eight-year-old daughter - became hysterical. The normally stern Miss Curry, showing a great deal of compassion on this occasion, did well to calm everyone down. We were delighted when we were sent home for the rest of the day. Then, like a great lumbering beast, the storm moved on and the air felt clean, fresh and exhilarating.

Although it was cloudy on most days, summer was awakening and as the pea pods filled out in Mr Harris' allotment, he brought a bag of them back to the house. Mrs Harris gave me the job of hulling and putting them into a bowl. Nancy had just been given a clout round the ear for wetting her finger and dipping it in the sugar bowl and to stop me eating any of the peas she told me to whistle as I worked so that she could hear me all the time. When she left the kitchen I got Sylvia to whistle for me while I ate a few of the lovely sweet-tasting peas. Unfortunately, Mrs Harris soon realised it wasn't me whistling and I got another smack round the head that made me see stars and I was sent to bed and missed out on my tea - all for the sake of a couple of peas. She had said earlier, "If you find a pod with nine peas in it, keep it separate from the rest. It is considered to be very lucky." I didn't find one and it certainly wasn't lucky for me.

At school Miss Curry told us that, "The worst storm for forty years has halted all Allied troop movement from the beaches into France. It wrecked one of the huge Mulberry harbours being anchored offshore for landing troops, vehicles and weapons, and the Germans are putting up stiff resistance and many of our brave men are having to pay the ultimate price." Later, Mr Harris told us that, "Field Marshal Rommel 'ad been away on leave when t'attack started. E'd thought that due to t't bad weather there were no danger. 'Ed bin at 'ome for 'is wife's birthday but 'e quickly hurried back only to find 'e were too late. The Allies were already ashore, but 'e soon deployed 'is tanks and got 'is troops reorganised." It seems that Hitler was interfering by giving orders for Panzer divisions to be moved to the wrong places and Rommel was in despair as he was blocking his freedom to conduct the battle his way.

In the middle of June Hitler sent over his new 'secret weapons' believing that they would win the war for him. The first of the V-1 rockets fell on London causing terror and thousands of casualties. The jet-propelled, cigar-shaped, pilotless planes, which carried a ton of explosives, sputtered and fell silently to earth as they ran out of fuel. They were soon nicknamed 'doodlebugs' but the RAF fighter pilots quickly learned how to shoot them down before they could cause more havoc. It was said that they were now destroying 80% of them in the air but six thousand people - mostly in London - had already been killed by them. Bombers with Canadian crews were flying out from the Linton and East Moor airfields to bomb the launch sites in France and Belgium.

In the first month of the invasion progress was slow, and it took the British and Canadian troops a month to capture the town of Caen. Elite SS troops had moved in and they fought hard and well and were a vastly different proposition to the old or very young German soldiers defending the coastlines but, eventually, the town was levelled to the ground. There were setbacks and many casualties but the Allied bombers destroyed the bridges over the Seine one by one preventing the German troops from crossing. On the 17th of July we heard that Rommel had been badly injured when Allied aircraft attacked his car and he was sent home to convalesce. Three days later a plot to kill Hitler went badly wrong and Rommel was found to have supported the attempted assassination and he was arrested.

For us in Haxby there was now a sense of time hanging in the balance; an air of treading water; a feeling of waiting for something big to happen. Day succeeded day each much the same as the last and we were still getting belted and clouted round the earhole. I had just endured a good hiding when Mrs Harris 'went off the deep end' on finding that I had put my big toenail through one of the threadbare bed sheets and Sylvia was made to sew yet another patch over it. As the summer holidays drew near, school felt more like a holding pen than a place of education. When we were sent to do some hoeing on the school allotment, a stubby, wind-ruffled robin redbreast had sat close by on the handle of a fork cocking his head to one side and trilling away to his heart's content. A child's senses are wide open and I was filled with wonder and pleasure by the sweet song of the bright-eyed, little bird. On another occasion, as we were out on one of our nature walks, we came across a German prisoner-of-war working in one of Outhwaite's fields. The fair-haired man greeted Miss Francis with the words 'Guten Morgen' before he asked her, "How old are ze kinder?"

"Most of them are nine years old," she replied, at which point he took out a small, dog-eared, black and white snapshot of a young blonde woman and a small boy. He became quite emotional as he caressed the faces on the photograph with his fingertips. There was a catch in his voice as he said, "Zese are mein frau und kinder in Deutschland." before turning away to conceal the tears that were welling up in his eyes. Basil Outhwaite reckoned the Germans, who were brought over each morning, were harder workers than the excitable Italians. Some of them had started to carve wooden toys for the children of the village.

We were taken to the field to play rounders and cricket and Mr Fox bawled at me, "Wake up, lad!" as I stood daydreaming in the outfield while the ball sped past me to the boundary. I was too busy watching the swallows, with their swept back wings, wheeling, gliding and fluttering as they caught insects on the wing. My mind would often slip away when I wasn't looking and I would go into a kind of trance. The ants were now much more active and they got everywhere, even though we stamped on them they kept coming. When they swarmed and grew wings, Mr Harris poured boiling water on them. If a bee stung anyone, Miss Francis applied bicarbonate of soda and if a wasp stung as we drank our orange juice she dabbed vinegar on it to deaden the pain.

Gran started to visit more often and I sensed that something was afoot. Unbeknown to us plans were being made for George and myself to go back to Middlesbrough. I was excited and apprehensive at the same time at the thought of going home and seeing Mam, Dad and Jimmy again. Even though Mrs Harris, with her floppy body that spilled at random from her ill-fitting clothes, had made our lives a misery, it had not been all bad. We had been beaten, sent to bed early and regularly derided and any praise had been very rare with the criticism oft repeated. However, we loved the countryside and I had shared many happy times with Jimmy and the others in spite of her.

20. The Return

George and I were so excited when Mrs Harris told us that Gran was coming to take us home but when she arrived I sensed that something was troubling her. The RAF was bombing Germany day after day but I had no inkling of the devastating bombshell that was about to be dropped on us. Gran, normally so steadfast and controlled, took us into the front room and as she sat us down on the settee there were tears in her eyes and a catch in her voice as she said, "I'm very sorry to have to tell you that your Mam and Dad were killed in the bombing of Newport in 1942, so you will be coming to live with me!"

It was the hardest thing she had ever had to do. How do you tell young children such a devastating, life-changing thing as that? At first the words, which fell like hammer blows, failed to register and I sat there with trembling hands unable to speak until grief overwhelmed me and the tears came. I don't know how long I cried for but it set George off and Gran, with her shoulders stooped, put her arms around us and held us to her capacious bosom. Nothing had prepared me for this bolt from the blue and the finality of death was just too hard to grasp! Mam and Dad had gone forever! In the space of just a few seconds my life had been irreversibly changed.

Mrs Harris had packed our cases beforehand, not that we had much to put in them, and, as far as I can remember, Mr Harris was out at work. The farewells were brief and perfunctory with no tears and no promise of any reunions. I can't honestly remember much of the bus ride into York and the train journey home except for a brief glimpse of the towers of the Minster soaring up above the rooftops. I must have been in a state of shock the whole way but I clearly remember us walking down King George Street to Gran's house in the hazy August sunshine. The long terraces of old, two up-two down, street houses were brick-built and it all seemed drab, grimy and grey and there was a 'closed in' feel about everything after nearly five years of life in the wide, open spaces of the countryside. Gran had Archie and Renee at home, so the sleeping arrangements had to be changed to accommodate us. Archie would now sleep in the single camp bed in the tiny box room; Gran and Renee would each have a bed in the front bedroom and we were to sleep in the three-quarter bed in the back bedroom. If Gran hadn't taken us in we would have been put into the grim Victorian orphanage at Nazareth House on Park Road North.

There was still no electricity in the house, which was lit by two swan-necked gaslights on the chimneybreast in the kitchen. On going to bed we had a candle in a holder, which was placed on a chair next to the bed, the only other furniture being a wardrobe and a small dressing table under the window. The coalhouse and toilet were at the bottom of the yard, so there were chamber pots under the bed for peeing in during the night and there was no bathroom. The table took up most of the space in the tiny kitchen. Gran's wooden rocking chair stood by the side of the black-leaded fire range and an old, leather-covered, chaise-longue stood beneath the casement window. There was a cupboard under the stairs and a step led down into a small pantry with a rectangular, white-glazed sink. The back door led into a small area under a closed in lean-to, in the corner of which was a gas cooker.

As I climbed the steep stairs with their strip of threadbare carpet, I noticed that there was a quarter of an inch gap between them and the wall and it dawned on me that it had been caused by the blast from the bomb that had killed Mam and Dad. It was as if a big black cloud had descended on me and I suddenly felt utterly bereft and alone and I sat on the stairs and sobbed my heart out for my dead parents and what might have been. Gran left me to get on with it and, when I had cried myself out, I crawled up the stairs on all fours and got into bed and snuggled up to George, who was sound asleep, and I must have eventually dropped off. The next day my emotions were in turmoil, life seemed wearisome and I did not want to go out or to meet anyone. I found refuge in the small space between the front door and the inner glass-paned door where I sat brooding for a long time - a sad, listless, little boy striving hard to remember what my parents looked like. George couldn't remember them at all as he had been only three when they died, but I had fleeting and poignant memories of their deep and tender love. In my mind Mam and Dad would remain forever young and fair but I began to cry at the thought that I would never again see their beloved faces. As another wave of grief hit me, I curled up with my arms around my bent knees and rocked back and forth.

In our society death is usually hidden from us as we grow up, which makes it all the more shocking when we have to confront it. The only other place in which I could grieve undisturbed was in the brick 'lavvie' down the yard where I would sit feeling sorry for myself. Never again would Mam wake me in the morning with a kiss or take me on her knee and explain things to me. Never again would Dad dandle me on his knee; tickle me; throw me in the air to catch me in his strong arms or gallop and prance around with me on his back. At these thoughts an unspeakable sadness welled up and my small frame was wracked by sobs that hurt inside and out. When the tears, that coursed down my cheeks one after the other, had dried up, I went back into the house with my eyes red-rimmed and sore. I could see the pain and anguish reflected in poor Gran's eyes, for after all my Mam was her eldest daughter and who can ever know a mother's pain when their own flesh and blood is taken from them.

I seemed to see the world differently now and there was a void; a big black hole; a nothingness where there should have been a mother's love and the emptiness was unbearable. I had never felt more alone in my life and when Renee took me out to show me the bombed area, I became jealous of other kids when I saw them doing things with their parents. The roads had been cleared and the great heaps of rubble at the bottom of Booth Street and on Laws Street had been made safe but the scene brought home to me the horror and the reality of the bombing. Powerful emotions kept bubbling up and in my utter distress I cried so much that Renee was obliged to take me back to the house. I was like a sleepwalker and I found it hard to carry out even simple tasks. On the Sunday I went to St. Cuthbert's church with Gran and Renee but it seemed as if it wasn't me walking around, the real me was locked inside. When the vicar spoke of Jesus Christ crying out 'God, why hast thou forsaken me?' at his crucifixion, I knew the feeling and I started to feel anger and bitterness towards Him for having dropped such a devastating bombshell on me when He was meant to protect us. How could He have let such a thing happen? What had I done to deserve this?

Later I sat behind the front door shouting at Him and the Germans, who I hated with a passion for taking Mam and Dad away from me. As I wallowed in self-pity, Gran must have heard me, for she took me into the front room and, sitting me down on the settee, she cuddled and tried to console me. But I got angry with her as well, as Renee had told me that everybody knew, except me and George, and they had said nothing. All the teachers and the nurses when I was in hospital must have known and they had kept quiet about it. Even Jimmy knew! I shouted out, "Why did this have to happen to me? Why didn't you tell me? You lied to us and I'll never forgive you for it!"

The terrible hurt that Gran had endured at the time of the bombing and in telling us never entered my self-centred mind, but I felt guilty about the way I had treated her as I got older. "I was only trying to protect you. I thought that telling you when you seemed so happy would only upset you. I thought it best to wait until you were a bit older. I didn't want to hurt you when you were so young and far away from home," she said in a soothing tone. Feeling that God had let me down, I longed for someone to reassure me; to take away my dark forebodings and to answer the thousand and one questions that filled my head. I became surly and diffident and suffered spells of deep depression with long silences as the 'whys of it all' gnawed away at me. Gran said, "Still waters run deep." which I didn't understand. At other times I whinged and chuntered on and on, until Gran said in exasperation, "Whisht now, you've got my head splitting. You'd better get that chip off your shoulder young man or nobody will want anything to do with you." A deep enduring anger was to simmer inside me for many years and I told myself that I did not need anybody. I became reticent and found it difficult to show affection and just wanted to be left on my own.

Gradually the debilitating grief gave way to a grudging acceptance and I locked the pain away in my heart where it could not be reached. My personal tragedy had eclipsed everything and the emotional pain lay there like a long, dull ache that never went away. Eventually there were no more tears. I had reached that stage of grieving when a strange sense of relief descends as the first wave of grief passes and I slowly emerged from my self-made cocoon. I needed some of that spirit that Mr Churchill had shown when he had said, "We must fight or go under!" I had to buck up and get on with life. I decided that it was fate; you had no choice in the matter: what will be will be!

Shortly afterwards Jimmy called at the house and knocked on the front door as I was sat behind it. Many years later he told me that he had heard a squeaky voice call out, "Who is it?" It was great to see him again after fourteen long months apart, but luckily grief does not linger too long in the very young and by that time the blackness had lifted sufficiently for me to start taking an interest in the things around me again. Jimmy had known the same bitter taste of grief as I had and had got over it but it affected our outlook on things for the rest of our lives. We picked up where we had left off, as if we had never been apart, and he came round to play with me and the local lads nearly every day but, after our tragic loss and the cruel treatment at the hands of Mrs Harris, our self esteem was low and we lacked confidence.

It took some time to get used to the miasma created by the steel and chemical works and the incessant noise from the nearby rail sidings. We played in the drab dusty streets and back alleys and got into all kinds of scrapes but Jimmy's presence helped to lift me out my sullen, withdrawn frame of mind. The resilience of childhood came to my aid again and we climbed all over the mountains of rubble and the charred beams that were being colonised by the weeds, and we made dens in it so that I didn't have time to brood on things too much. It felt strange seeing the broken toilet pans, the empty fireplaces, the pictures and the wallpaper in bedrooms that were open to the sky. They looked like the insides of damaged dolls houses and I felt a bit guilty, as though I was prying into people's private lives (or deaths).

Gran thought that we were out playing games in the street, which we were most of the time, but at other times we were clambering about on the rubble or in the bomb-damaged house on the corner of the block opposite. It had been boarded up but we forced the back gate and the door and climbed the rickety, creaking stairs, edging our way round the huge gaps in the bedroom floorboards and risking a drop of sixteen feet (5m) or so into the cellar below. It was scary but exciting and anyway Jimmy had dared me and I couldn't refuse a dare.

It was quite a while before Gran told me the details of that awful night. It seems that Dad had arranged to take some leave that weekend and Mam had come home to meet him, as they were going down to Grove House to collect George before bringing him to live with us in Haxby. They had packed a case with clothes, shoes and toys and had left it in the front room ready for first thing in the morning. They had just got into bed when the siren sounded at 10.37 pm, as enemy aircraft were in the area. The warning was late and not many people had managed to make it to the underground shelters, which were about a hundred yards away on The Common. They could hear the loud droning of a Dornier overhead as they stepped out of the front door. A bomb dropped on the house and they were crushed under the falling masonry and never heard the continuous note of the 'Raiders Passed' siren at 1.27 am. Renee had been eating her supper after a two till ten shift at the steelworks when the first of four bombs landed nearby with four more falling into the river. She had dashed down Booth Street heading towards our house and was horrified on seeing the devastation. The wrecked and badly damaged houses were illuminated by a great column of flame from a gas main that had been fractured by the explosion. As searchlights and the flashes from the anti-aircraft guns lit the sky, the steel-helmeted policemen would not let anyone near and Renee feared the worst as the area was quickly cordoned off. In her desperation to find Mam and Dad, who she loved so much, she dodged under the tape and an ARP warden shouted 'Looter!' and she was grabbed and told to go home. It was Middlesbrough's worst night for fatalities with twenty-eight killed, including Mam and Dad and eleven children and, as Gran said afterwards, "If you hadn't been evacuated, you'd have been among 'em."

It took the heavy rescue squads three days to dig the mangled bodies out of the rubble and Mam's light brown hair had turned completely white, so that, when Renee went with Gran to the cold white-tiled mortuary at the General Hospital, she did not recognise her at first. She told me many years later that, "Your Mam's skirt was blown off by the blast and your Dad was identified by his tattoos, which included the badge of the Royal Artillery on his right arm, and by certain items in his pockets." Gran said, "Before the funeral service at St. Cuthbert's church and the burial at Acklam

Cemetery, Mrs Ethel Gaunt was really kind to us. She and your Mam had been very close and she loaned us clean white sheets to cover the mirrors and to put up at the windows." It seems that in Suffolk, from where Gran's ancestors originated, they held the belief that the reflection of a person in a mirror held that person's soul and it was customary to cover them to stop the devil gaining access to it. Gran then said, "Mrs Gaunt had kindly paid for the bodies to be laid out in the front room of the Linthorpe Road house."

At least I had not been there when the stillness of death had pervaded the house and had been spared from hearing the hollow thud as soil was thrown down onto the coffins, which lay one above the other. I think my anger would have flared up if I had been present when the Vicar had proclaimed, "Forasmuch as it hath *pleased* Almighty God to take to Himself Evelyn and Alf..." The Imperial War Graves Commission paid for a rose bush and headstone with their names and the badge of the Royal Artillery engraved upon it. In Haxby I had carried on blithely completely unaware of these catastrophic, life-changing events but I wouldn't say that my ignorance had been bliss.

As soon as she was able to get to the wreckage of our house, Renee had searched through the rubble for any trace of Mam and Dad's prized possessions but all she ever found was a bent spoon. She swore that Mam had a hundred pounds in a tin in the cupboard under the stairs but there was no trace of it. The rubble remained there until after the war ended when it was used to fill in the underground air raid shelters on The Common.

In early September I started at the Newport Junior School, the same school that Mam and all her brothers and sisters had attended over the years, and at which Jimmy had been a pupil for just over a year. The Victorian, brick-built school (founded in 1884) was tucked away behind a beetle-ridden pie factory (we called the shiny hard-backed bugs blacklocks), the flea-ridden 'Pavilion' cinema and *The Acklam* public house on Newport Road. Half of the school buildings were being used by St. Paul's, the school just up the road, which had been destroyed in a bombing raid in 1941. Miss Leng was the headmistress of the girl's school, the boys' head was Mr Hague and my teacher was Miss Trewitt, who was man-like and had a thin black moustache. It took some time to adjust to the smelly old classroom, that was crowded with so many strange people and things, but Jimmy was in the year above me and he protected me from the rough, uncouth lads in the playground. Being orphans George and I were now entitled to free dinners that were served by Mrs Heritage who had been a dinner nanny there for the last twenty years. Jimmy again showed me where the best sweets and lovely, creamy 'Dainty Dinah Toffees' and cinder toffee could be bought at 'Toffee' Turner's little shop on the corner of Newport Road and Derwent Street.

At home we had a bath in front of the fire in the zinc-coated tub that usually hung on a nail in the back yard and we had to go to the outside 'lavvie' in all weathers. Its brick walls were whitewashed and a supply of bum fodder (made by tearing the pages of the Radio Times into four small squares) hung on a nail beside the high cistern. To get to it we had to hurry past Gran's 'chickens'- that were meant to provide us with fresh eggs but had turned out to be cockerels - that pecked at our bare legs. Archie, now twenty years old, went down Cannon Street to the slipper baths where he paid sixpence (2.5p) for a good bath every week.

Every day I carried the hurt of my loss and the memories kept crowding in on me. I had morbid nightmares in which I saw my parents mangled in the rubble with their life-blood draining into the dust from the hideous wounds in their bodies, which had the waxy whiteness of alabaster. As the light - which had once shone with joy and love – left their eyes, they slipped away into the long, deep, darkness of death and I would wake with a start to find that I had been crying. In my sleep-fuddled state it would slowly dawn on me once again that they were no more. They say that those whom the Gods love die young, so may they sleep long and well in that silence beyond all suffering. In other dreams I would picture Mam coming through the door smiling with love shining in her eyes and I knew that their spirits had gone to heaven and were watching over me and one day I would be with them again. I sensed their presence in the air that I breathed and in the wind that ruffled my hair. How sad to die in your thirties but, as they say, 'Time like an everlasting stream bears all its sons away'.

Gran was very friendly with the Reynolds family who lived next door but one to her. She had befriended the Nichol family when they first came to live in Middlesbrough from Tudor Colliery in County Durham in the 1920s and Lily Reynolds was Mrs Nichol's sister. The Nichol's had bought a little grocery shop with the front on Cannon Street and the back of it on Laws Street and Mam used to shop there. We called Lily Reynolds 'The News of the World' as she was always gossiping and she knew everybody's business and Gran used to say, "If you want anything spreading around, just tell her". One day, when I was in the back alley, her ten-year-old son, Terry, made some disparaging remark about my Mam - something about her being a do-gooder - and I saw red and laid into him. I beat the hell out of him and had to be dragged away as blood was pouring from his nose. After that, instead of looking on me as a soft country bumpkin, the local lads showed me much more respect and Terry and I became good pals.

The Reynolds family and author (on right), King George Street, Middlesbrough, 1945.

I also became friendly with two local lads. Billy Glasper lived on Booth Street, and Malcolm Barber lived with his divorced mother on Fancoat Street, which had a pickle factory on the corner of it at the Newport Bridge end. Both streets ran off King George Street. Day-to-day life took over and we played the usual street games of tee-ack, leapfrog, tip-tap and marbles (we called the glass ones 'alleys' and the big, much-sought-after, metal ones, 'bongies'). We tied ropes to the crosspieces at the top of the lampposts and swung round on them like Tarzan and we played football and cricket in the street with a wicket or goal chalked on the wall of the gable end of the house opposite us. Most Saturday mornings we went to the matinee at 'The Pav', which we called 'the penny push', to see The Adventures of Flash Gordon or The Perils of Pauline, which always ended in 'a cliff-hanger' with the hero or heroine in grave danger of death but always managing to escape unharmed in time for the next episode. On many occasions the film broke down and the rowdy kids shouted remarks like, "Put a penny in the gas meter!" and stamped their feet until the film resumed. I even remember being taken by Renee to see Charlie Chaplin in the silent film 'The Gold Rush' in which he was so hungry that he boiled his boots and ate them putting the nails on the side of his plate as if they were small bones. A pianist played quickly or slowly to correspond with the action; the dialogue was printed out on the screen and the films were changed twice a week. Food rationing was still very rigorous and on returning to Gran's house we were often sent out again to stand for an hour or more in the long queue outside Meredith's bakery shop on nearby Union Street. After standing all that time, we got just one rice cake to share between the five of us, which was all that each customer was allowed.

In mid September the blackout was lifted after six long years and the gas lamps in the street were lit each evening by a man carrying a long pole affair. We heard on Gran's accumulator-operated wireless, that stood on a shelf in the alcove next to the black-leaded fire range, that our hero, Group Captain Cheshire, had been awarded the Victoria Cross; Paris had been liberated; the Allied soldiers were sweeping through Belgium having broken through the Siegfried line and that the Germans were on the run. Meanwhile Hitler's new secret weapons, the terrifying long range V-2 rockets, had started to rain down on London. In October we heard that Rommel had been forced to take poison (an undeserved and sad end for a very brave and highly respected soldier and human being) and the first German city, Aachen, had fallen to the Allies. British troops retook Greece and landed on Crete again after an absence of three and a half years.

As the icy winter drew on, Gran sent us to Silkburn's Coal depot on Newport Road to buy a stone of coal whenever word got round that they had some in and we brought it home on a rickety, bogie made from bits of wood and old pram wheels. If we had a couple of coppers we walked down to the front room of Annie Storey's house on Cannon Street to buy a bag of winkles in a paper bag and walked home eating them - pulling out the curled up, snail-like molluscs with a pin. Still inclined to be moody and sullen I would sit moping for hours on the padded leather lid of one of the boxes on the end of the fender in which sticks for the fire were kept dry.

Gran would sit in her rocking chair in her pinny combing her long, greying hair that reached to below her waist repeatedly singing, "Come in to the garden Maud for the black bat night has flown." It seemed to be the only bit of the song she knew. Before bed each day she had a bottle of stout that she swore 'kept her regular' and helped her to sleep. She was a good cook (maybe that's where Mam's cooking ability came from) and she kept our bellies filled with good wholesome food, on a meagre income. We loved her home baked fadgies that had a flavour all of their own, the like of which I haven't come across since, and her meat and potato pies that were very tasty and filling. We got jam (and margarine!) on thick, crusty, freshly baked bread and, if we were still hungry, we could always fill up with salted beef dripping on bread. Such a diet would be frowned on these days but at that time we loved it and we had a lot of catching up to do, and were still quite skinny.

Gran went through to Haxby to visit Harry about once a month and Renee, now a pretty and petite twenty-one year old, looked after us while she was away. At school my drawing ability was finally recognised and put to use as the staff prepared to put on the pantomime 'Aladdin' at Christmastime. I was asked to draw and paint a long frieze portraying the Genie of the lamp on three long sheets of paper that were then stuck together and put up high on the wall around the school hall and I was thrilled to bits. The

438

recognition helped to boost my self-belief no end but I was still near the bottom end of the class when we were tested.

Granny Bradford, outside her house in the 1940s.

In December the Home Guard was stood down but it was not officially disbanded just yet. Gran told George and me that as we were officially war orphans we had been invited to a Christmas party at the Assembly Rooms on Linthorpe Road. There was ham and fish paste sandwiches, meat pies, jelly and custard and the like laid out on long trestle tables and I thoroughly enjoyed the eats but I hated the silly paper hats and party games when children raced around giggling, squealing and dodging the adults. I got embarrassed and annoyed when the Mayoress and the other ladies in their fur coats and posh dresses fussed and petted us and ruffled our hair.

It was nice to see the shop windows lit up and decorated on our first Christmas back home, not that we had much but we enjoyed its never-failing magic just the same. We didn't get many toys or clothes and by now our shoes had holes in the thin soles and we put cardboard in them to try to keep out the wet. Gran made us tasty meals with Archie - who was looked on as the man of the house - always getting the largest portion. He 'let the first foot in' at New Year when the house was open to any of our neighbours who cared to pop in for a 'wee tot' and a piece of cake. Christmas was for the children and Hogmanay was for the adults and as the year turned, the noise from the local works and the ships' hooters on the river was ear-splitting. The excitement was contagious and people's spirits were higher than ever this year following the good news from the Continent.

Enemy aircraft still appeared overhead from time to time (probably from Norway, which was still occupied) and when the siren sounded Gran hurried us down to the underground shelters on The Common but no more bombs fell on the area. We huddled in blankets while the adults made tea on methylated spirit stoves and had singsongs. Granny Knights sometimes had something stronger than tea and when she sang and danced and showed her knee-length, elasticated, pink bloomers. Gran would say to her, "Sit down yer silly old bugger and stop showing yerself up!" We kids thought it hilarious.

Gran was dismayed to learn that the Germans, who were putting up stiff resistance, had made a surprise breakthrough in mid December. The Americans had neglected to defend the Ardennes region of Belgium strongly enough, as had the French four years earlier, and the Germans were sweeping forward again in the mist and snow. When the weather cleared the Allied bombers took a heavy toll of the enemy tanks but it took till the end of January for Germany's crack troops to be overwhelmed by sheer force of numbers and the six-week offensive came to be known as The Battle of the Bulge. Meanwhile the Allied Forces were driving back the Japanese, who were a cruel enemy, and the Soviet troops were advancing into Eastern Poland and Gran's hopes of an early release for Uncle John rose.

In late January she visited Harry, who was still at Haxby, where she learned that there had been an earthquake at 1.37 am on the thirtieth of December. Harry said that it had shaken the house waking him up and it had slightly moved the railway lines, which had to be readjusted. It seems that he was quite happy living with the Misses Law and Barker and serving his apprenticeship at Harold Atkinson's shop and he had recently taken up boxing lessons in a club in York. Eventually he was to reach quite a high standard and turn semi-professional.

So the long, bitterly cold winter passed and Jimmy and I played out in the streets and back alleys and on the Newport Bridge where there was a steel sentry box in the shape of a policeman's helmet. We climbed all over the flat roof of the electric powerhouse that stood beneath the iron steps that led up to the top of the approach road of the bridge. Sometimes we swam in the filthy river with raw sewage floating past our noses but we never came to any harm. At other times we went over the river bridge to a railway bridge on the far side where Jimmy dared me to wriggle and weave in out of the steel girders supporting the roadway until I emerged at the other side. Needless to say I did it pretending that I was not scared of becoming stuck halfway along it or of falling off the narrow concrete ledge onto the railway lines twenty feet below. On another occasion we were playing football in the back alley when the ball got kicked onto the lean-to roof at the back of someone's house and Jimmy dared me to go and get it. So, of course, I climbed up and worked my way across the blackened top of what I thought was a solid roof to find out - by falling through it - that it was made of glass that had become thickly coated with grime over the years.

How I survived to adulthood is a mystery, especially when Jimmy was around. George, who was now Gran's new 'baby-boy', was too young to play with us and he stayed at home being spoiled and pampered.

On a clear night in mid February Bomber Command, with more than a thousand aircraft, laid waste the defenceless city of Dresden with the aim of destroying the German transport infrastructure. It had been reported that troops were massing there ready to oppose the advancing Russians who were only seventy miles to the east of the historic Saxon capital. The raid, and those of the following day, caused a gigantic firestorm that swept through the narrow cobbled streets killing around 30,000 civilians. Even though it undoubtedly brought the end of the war closer, Bomber Harris was vilified in the press although, under pressure from USA and the Russians, it was Winston Churchill who had ordered it.

Over the next few weeks the Allied ground troops advanced and spread out along the west bank of the river Rhine in preparation for a massed crossing into the heartland of Germany. Field Marshal Montgomery, to the north, led the British and Canadian ground and airborne troops across on the 24th of March and it was now only a matter of time before Germany would admit defeat. In April Gran was shocked to learn that the advancing troops had found further proof of the rumoured Nazi death camps and crematoria. Thousands of bodies had been burned, after being stripped of their clothes, hair and valuables, with the ashes being bagged up and used as fertiliser on the land. She was worried about the safety of Uncle John, who was, as far as she knew, still a prisoner of war in Poland into which the Russians were rapidly advancing. We stared at the horrific scenes of the skeleton-like survivors at Belsen on the cinema newsreels in disbelief and never forgot. The shocking evidence of these Nazi atrocities only served to deepen my already bitter and intense hatred of the Germans.

Meanwhile, as spring crept on, we played cricket and football a little further afield by crossing Newport road and walking down Laycock Street to the area of tarmac known as the Linthorpe Recreation Ground; or The Rec. Occasionally we walked down Parliament Road, passing by the white marble cenotaph and the Dorman Museum, on our way to the Albert Park where there were wide paths and grassy areas to play on. Beside its ornate wrought iron gates were long lists of names of the World War I dead inscribed on brass panels on the white Portland stone walls. Inside the gates there was a wide path - with, beside it, a drinking fountain, a tall clock tower on a column and a stone-backed sun dial - that led to a bandstand. Nearby there was a Crimean War cannon that we climbed all over. This stood on the banks of the Cannon Lake, close to an arch said to have been built with stones from the original Middlesbrough Priory. It was an exciting place to be as well a haven of peace and tranquillity when we were in a quieter frame of mind, which wasn't often. On going to the larger lake at the far end of the park, we were envious of those who could afford to hire a rowing boat. We played hide and seek in a wooded, hilly area known as Bell Hill - on top of which was the base of the old wooden post that had supported the bell. It was spooky and Jimmy scared us even more by telling us the tale of young Mary Cooper who had been murdered here. I didn't like it up there on my own, even though it had happened many years back.

On the way to the park, opposite the large, impressive buildings of Forbes' Bakery, lay Linthorpe Old Cemetery. When you looked through the keyhole of the spooky old stone building in the centre all you could see was blackness but Jimmy put the wind up us by saying, "If you look hard enough you can see daggers floating about in the air." Close to the road there was a very old grave with a broken stone slab and Jimmy said, "If you walk round it three times and bend down and put your ear to it you can hear the spirits talking." On doing so I received a swift boot up the backside.

The last of the deadly V-2 rockets, which had killed and injured thousands, fell to earth in late March before the Allied troops overran the launch sites. When Gran visited Harry again she learned that Haxby village had not quite seen the last of the war as an enemy plane had recently machine-gunned Walker's fish and chip shop on the High Street. It seems that the pilot had seen the lights of the bus from York at about 10 pm as it reached the end of its journey and was about to turn round by the Co-op shop. Mrs Walker and her two sons were on the premises and as she looked out of the back window she saw the enemy plane heading straight towards her firing its guns. They had a lucky escape as the next day a cannon shell was found lodged in the wall beside the window with further shells found in the cricket field behind the shop. Fortunately, that was the last enemy activity in the area and the intruder plane was said to have followed the RAF bombers home from a raid. It was thought to have been shot down a few miles away, killing the crew of four.

In late April Gran was relieved and excited when she received a telegram from Uncle John (Prisoner number 220615 in Stalag 383 at Hohenfels at the foot of the Bavarian Alps near Munich). It stated that he had been liberated by the Americans and would be home on leave in mid May. In it he wrote, 'I wish you could have seen the boys when the American tanks arrived here. We heard them firing over the hill, and about half an hour later one of the boys rushed into the barracks shouting "They're here!" The poor bloke nearly got killed in the rush to get outside and see them.'

She was to learn later that because he and his mate, Jock, had problems with their knees - which were swollen making them unable to walk far - they had been taken across Germany in cattle trucks. Thereby, they avoided the Death Marches of up to 900 miles that many of their unfortunate colleagues had to endure, including his pal, Joe. It seems that the Germans had forced hundreds of the prisoners out into the snow-covered countryside in one of the coldest winters on record to prevent them being liberated by the Russians. Without adequate food (many survived on grass and stolen potatoes), shelter or clothing they suffered appallingly and many died of sickness and starvation or were shot on their way west. Most felt guilty about being captured and imprisoned and did not want to talk about it when they got home (including Uncle John). Their suffering was overshadowed by the horrors of Auschwitz, Belsen, Dachau and the other concentration camps with their obscene gas chambers and ovens, so their plight was overlooked. In May, Uncle John and the others were brought home in converted Lancasters and Anson aircraft and, on landing, he knelt down and kissed the ground. Later he was to tell Renee that, while he was a prisoner at Lamsdorf, there was often a sickly sweet smell carried on the air whenever the wind was from the north west. It was not until later that he realised what had caused it. Auschwitz concentration camp was only sixty miles away in that direction.

By this time, Renee had let me have the old sit-up-and-beg bike that she had been given by Miss Morton six years earlier. I did it up and Archie taught me how to ride it in the street, which enabled me to travel further afield thus opening up new avenues of enjoyment and exploration. Hitler committed suicide in his bunker in Berlin and the Germans fought on for another seven days before the war in Europe finally came to an end on May 8th with Germany being split into Russian, American and British sectors. In the divided city of Berlin the Russians built a huge wall to stop people from coming out or in. John Wade, Eric Ward and the rest of the evacuees came home from Haxby and returned to Newport Junior School, and we excitedly celebrated the victory with a street party at which there was enough food and drink to last well into the night.

Before long Gran had what was left of her family around her again, except for Harry who remained in Haxby until he was eighteen years old, when he was called up to do his two years of national service in the Navy. John was demobbed from the army, coming home to a hero's welcome with tears, hugs, fluttering bunting and Union flags after three years in captivity. He returned to his old job in the Britannia Bridgeyard. Archie did his national service in the RAF and Renee, having given up her job in the steelworks when the men came out of the services, started work as a 'clippie' (conductress) on the hot and crowded local buses. Jimmy came to live with us at Granny Bradford's where we slept three to a bed and grew up as brothers before going our different ways - but that's another story.

GOVERNMENT HOUSE   CANBERRA

The appeal made in my name has produced over Fifty Million Pounds thus enabling the War Organisation of the Red Cross and St. John to carry out its task of alleviating the sufferings of our sick, wounded and prisoners of war to the fullest possible extent.

It gives me great pleasure to record my grateful thanks to you for your help through the Red Cross Penny-a-Week Fund in bringing about this magnificent result.

Henry

PRESIDENT
RED CROSS & ST. JOHN FUND

June 1945

Mrs Bradford.

The certificate awarded to Gran.

Appendix

Below is a poem that I was inspired to write following a visit to my parents' grave:

The Family Tree

The elder stood above the grave
her roots deep in the earth:
believed to aid, in days of yore,
fertility and birth.
A sudden blast of wind sprang up
from out a leaden sky
to set the branches thrashing
and cavorting up on high.
A pair of hearty leaves
came spiralling to the ground,
to settle very gently on
the grass clad burial mound.

As I gazed on the earthen plot
that stormy autumn day,
I thought of my loving parents
violently torn away.
On a moonlit night, as sirens wailed
in nineteen forty two,
they'd left their bed and quickly dressed,
planning to scurry to
the blacked-out street and the safety
of the shelters nearby;
as a single bomber (sounding close)
droned loudly in the sky.

Long, blanched beams of searchlights probed
the gleaming barrage wire.
There was bedlam from demented guns
and anti-aircraft fire.
Father, home on army leave, planned
to visit us next day.
Mother had the cases packed all
set for going away.
My brother, two, and me, aged four,
had long since gone to stay,
far away from the dangers
of such a fateful day.

They'd reached the door and turned the key
and quickly stepped outside.
A bomb came down; the walls collapsed:
in each others arms they died!
The loving pair – still in their prime –
were buried in the rubble,
as rescue workers scrabbled near
with urgent pick and shovel.
Now they lie in their deep dark bed,
as in days gone by,
in cold embrace, with souls entwined,
eternally to lie.

Ashes to ashes: dust to dust…
We shall remember them.
Age will not weary them;
nor the passing years condemn…

The essence of their mortal lives
exuded through the ground;
taken up by the elder roots
and in its leaves is found.
Tears welled up unbidden, as I
pictured the awful sight;
the flames; the screams; the horrors
of that dread-filled April night.
So many were left homeless -
bereft, forlorn, and sad.
Twenty six others lost their lives
as well as Mam and Dad.

I recalled the sobbing boy as he
sat upon the stair
and his shouts of accusation
at a God who didn't care.
As I stooped to kiss the headstone -
grey, lichened, cold and bare -
the aching void within my heart
was, oh, so hard to bear.
The icy rain was channelled down
the names etched in the stone,
salty tears streamed down my cheeks
as I stood there - so alone.

At that time of pain and anguish,
the loss within me burned,
for in my heart I knew my love
could never be returned.
I picked up the leaves and turned
and slowly walked away:
heart sad at living far from there
and travelling home that day.
Now many years have passed
and time has eased the pain.
Love of a wife and children have
restored my soul again.

The leaves were placed in the Holy book
on the shelf above -
a source of poignant memories
of lost parental love:
treasured mementoes till I die
and return to welcoming arms,
problems finally at an end,
and rid of all my qualms.
Our essences then will mingle;
our spirits shall be free,
borne upwards, incorruptible,
within the family tree.

The author's parents grave, Acklam Cemetery, Middlesbrough.